DARK BLOOD ™

LATOYA MORGAN

WALT BARNA

MOISÉS HIDALGO

A.H.G.

ALLISON HU

BOOM!
STUDIOS

This series depicts scenes of racially-based violence as well as racially-based slurs and language which some readers may find explicit, unsettling, or disturbing. Reader discretion is advised.

Series Designer
GRACE PARK

Assistant Editor
GWEN WALLER

Collection Designers
**VERONICA GUTIERREZ
& MICHELLE ANKLEY**

Editor
DAFNA PLEBAN

BOOM!
STUDIOS
WWW.BOOM-STUDIOS.COM

DARK BLOOD Volume One, June 2022. Published by BOOM! Studios, a division of Boom Entertainment, Inc. Dark Blood is ™ & © 2022 LaToya Morgan. Originally published in single issue magazine form as DARK BLOOD No.1-6 ™ & © 2021, LaToya Morgan. All rights reserved. BOOM! Studios™ and the BOOM! Studios logo are trademarks of Boom Entertainment, Inc., registered in various countries and categories. All characters, events, and institutions depicted herein are fictional. Any similarity between any of the names, characters, persons, events, and/or institutions in this publication to actual names, characters, and persons, whether living or dead, events, and/or institutions is unintended and purely coincidental. BOOM! Studios does not read or accept unsolicited submissions of ideas, stories, or artwork.

BOOM! Studios, 5670 Wilshire Boulevard, Suite 400, Los Angeles, CA, 90036-5679. Printed in Canada. First Printing.

ISBN: 978-1-68415-711-2, eISBN: 978-1-64668-615-5

BOOM! Studios Exclusive ISBN: 978-1-68415-867-6

DARK BLOOD ™

CREATED BY **LATOYA MORGAN**

Written by
LATOYA MORGAN

Illustrated by
WALT BARNA *(Chapters 1-2)*
& MOISÉS HIDALGO *(Chapters 2-6)*

Colored by
A.H.G.
& ALLISON HU *(Chapters 5-6)*

Lettered by
ANDWORLD DESIGN

Cover by
VALENTINE DE LANDRO

BOOM! Studios Exclusive Variant Cover by
MARCUS WILLIAMS

CHAPTER ONE

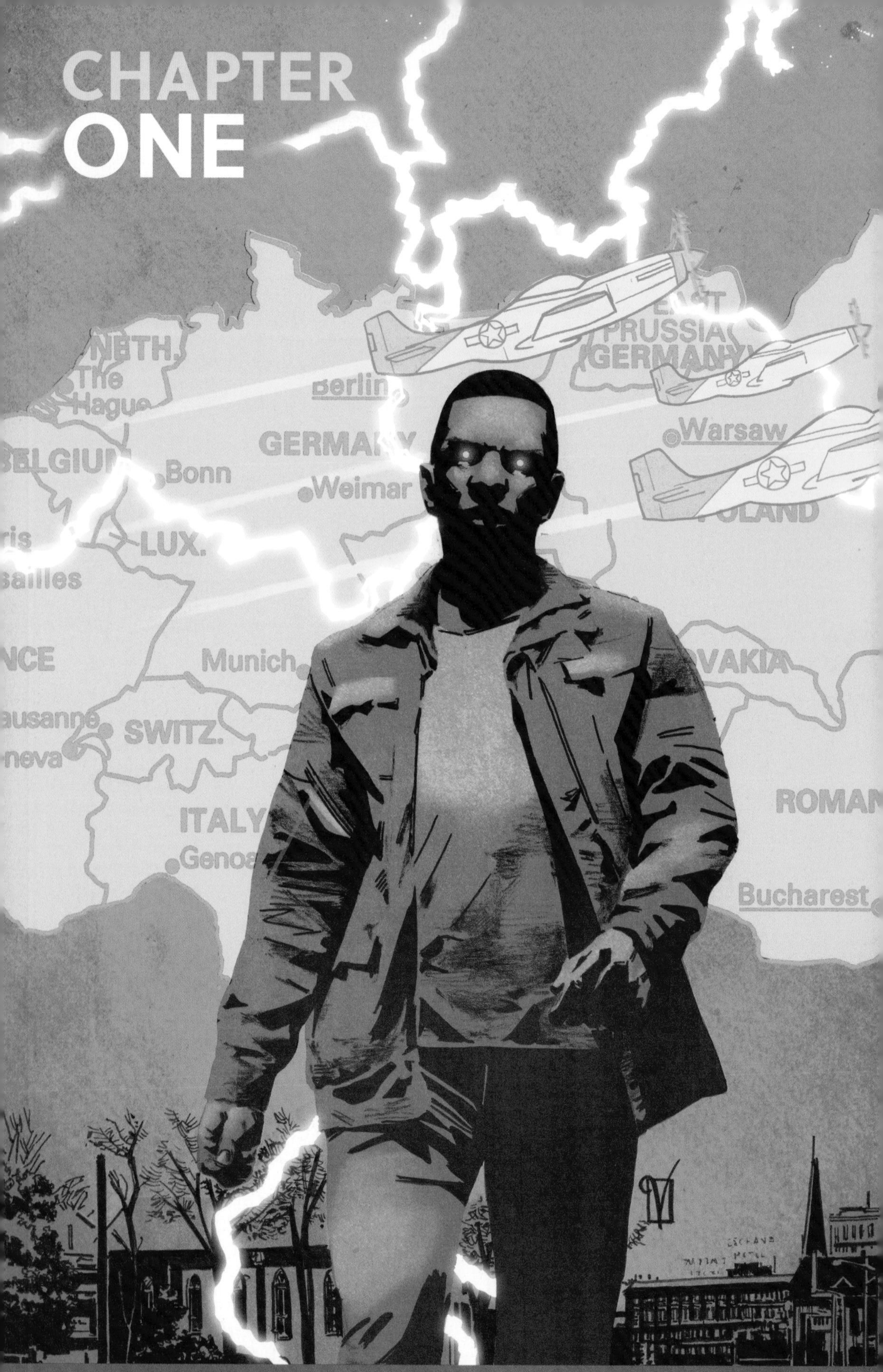

NETH.
Berlin
EAST
PRUSSIA
GERMANY
Warsaw
Bonn
Weimar
LUX.
Munich
SWITZ.
ITALY
Bucharest

Issue #1 Cover
VALENTINE DE LANDRO

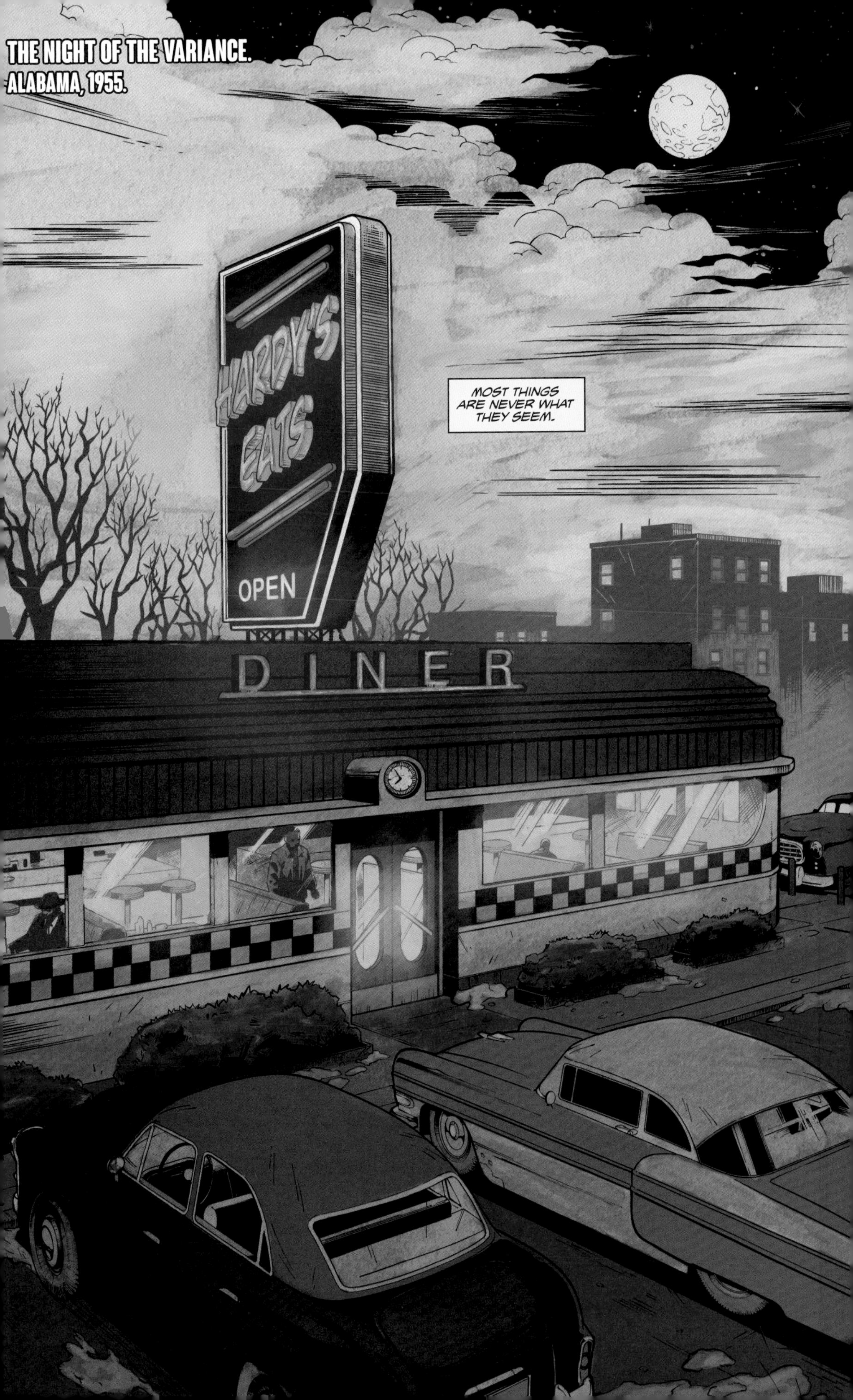
THE NIGHT OF THE VARIANCE.
ALABAMA, 1955.
HARDY'S EATS
OPEN
DINER
MOST THINGS ARE NEVER WHAT THEY SEEM.

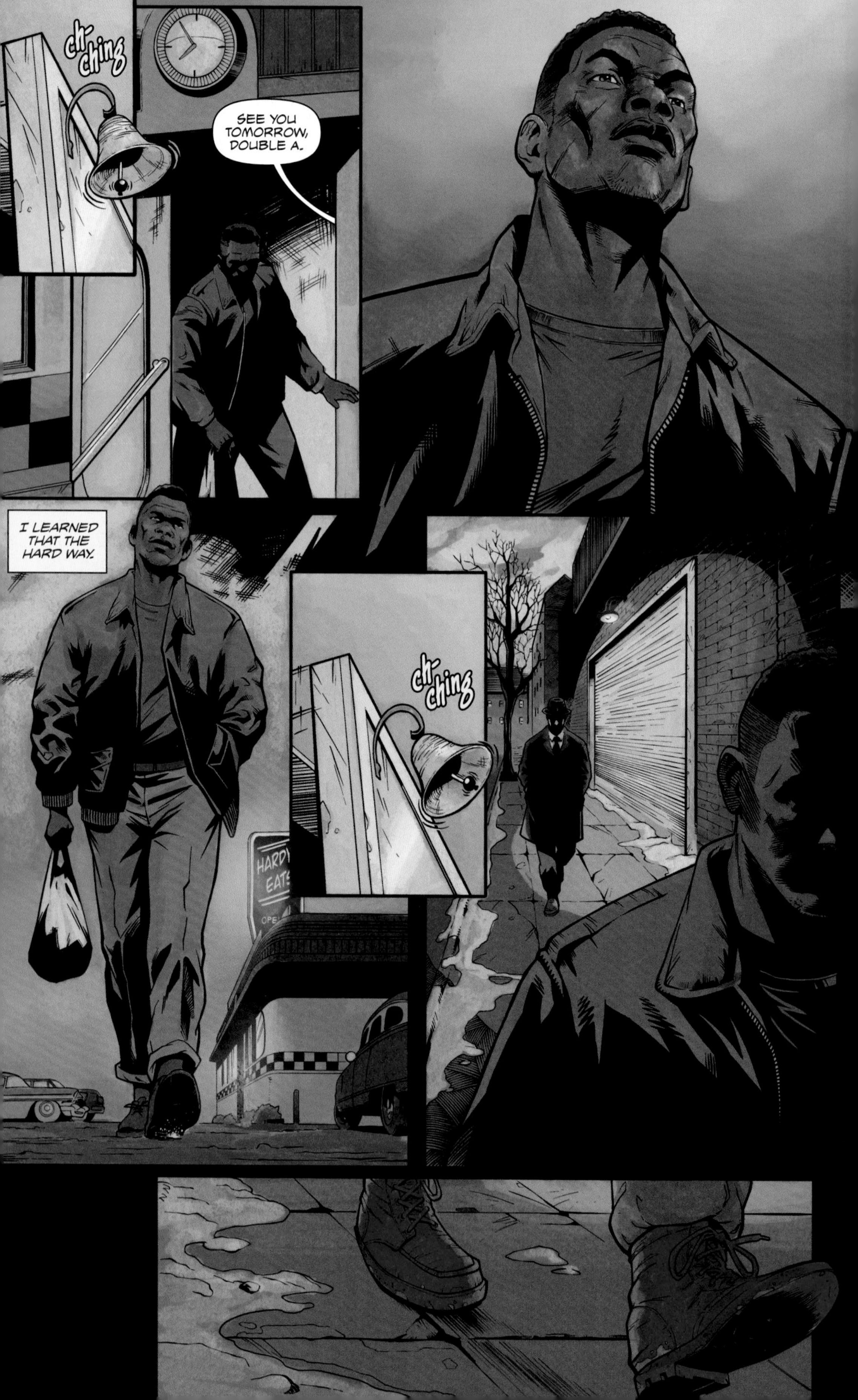

ch-ching
SEE YOU TOMORROW, DOUBLE A.
I LEARNED THAT THE HARD WAY.
ch-ching

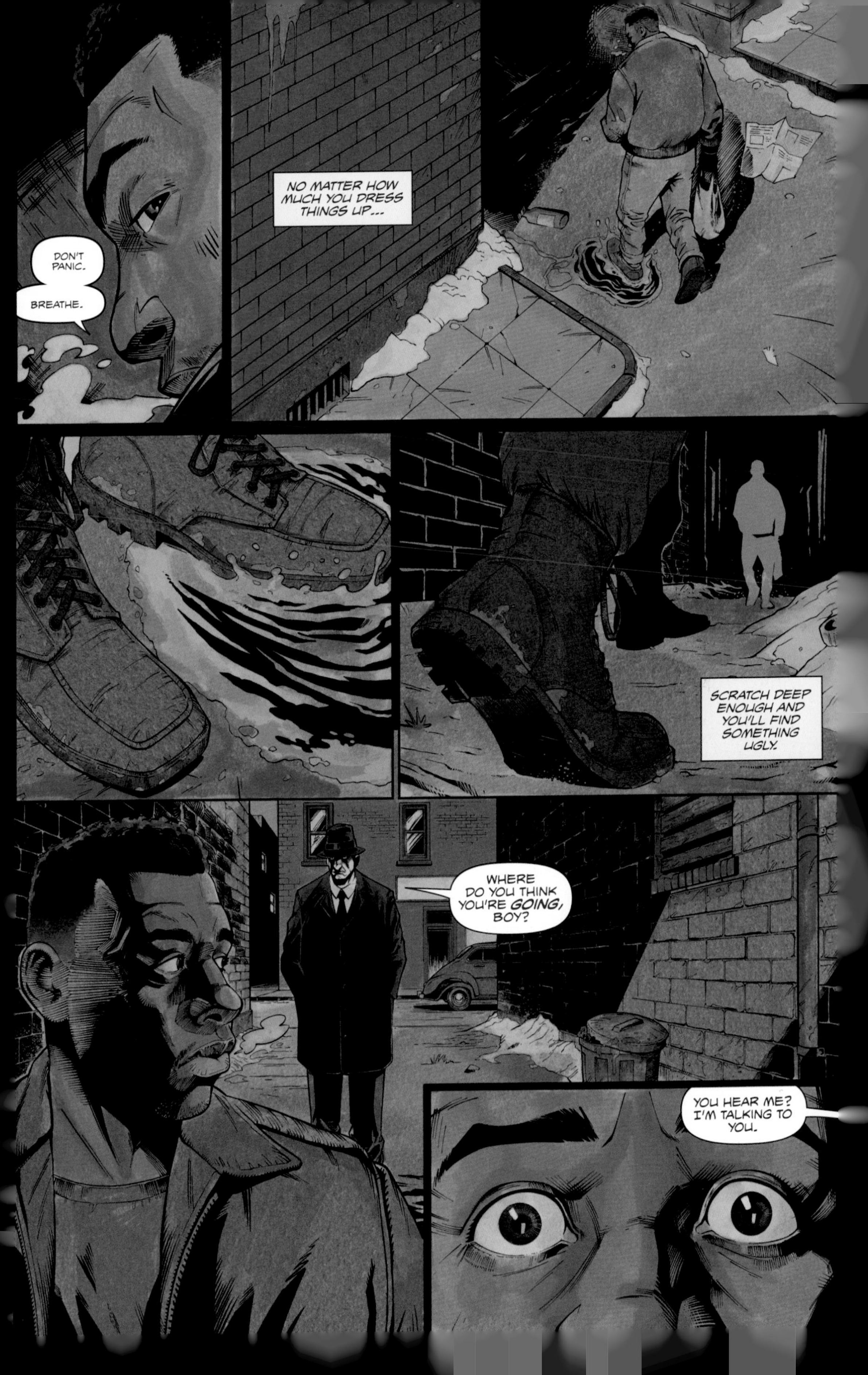
DON'T PANIC.
BREATHE.
NO MATTER HOW MUCH YOU DRESS THINGS UP...
SCRATCH DEEP ENOUGH AND YOU'LL FIND SOMETHING UGLY.
WHERE DO YOU THINK YOU'RE *GOING*, BOY?
YOU HEAR ME? I'M TALKING TO YOU.

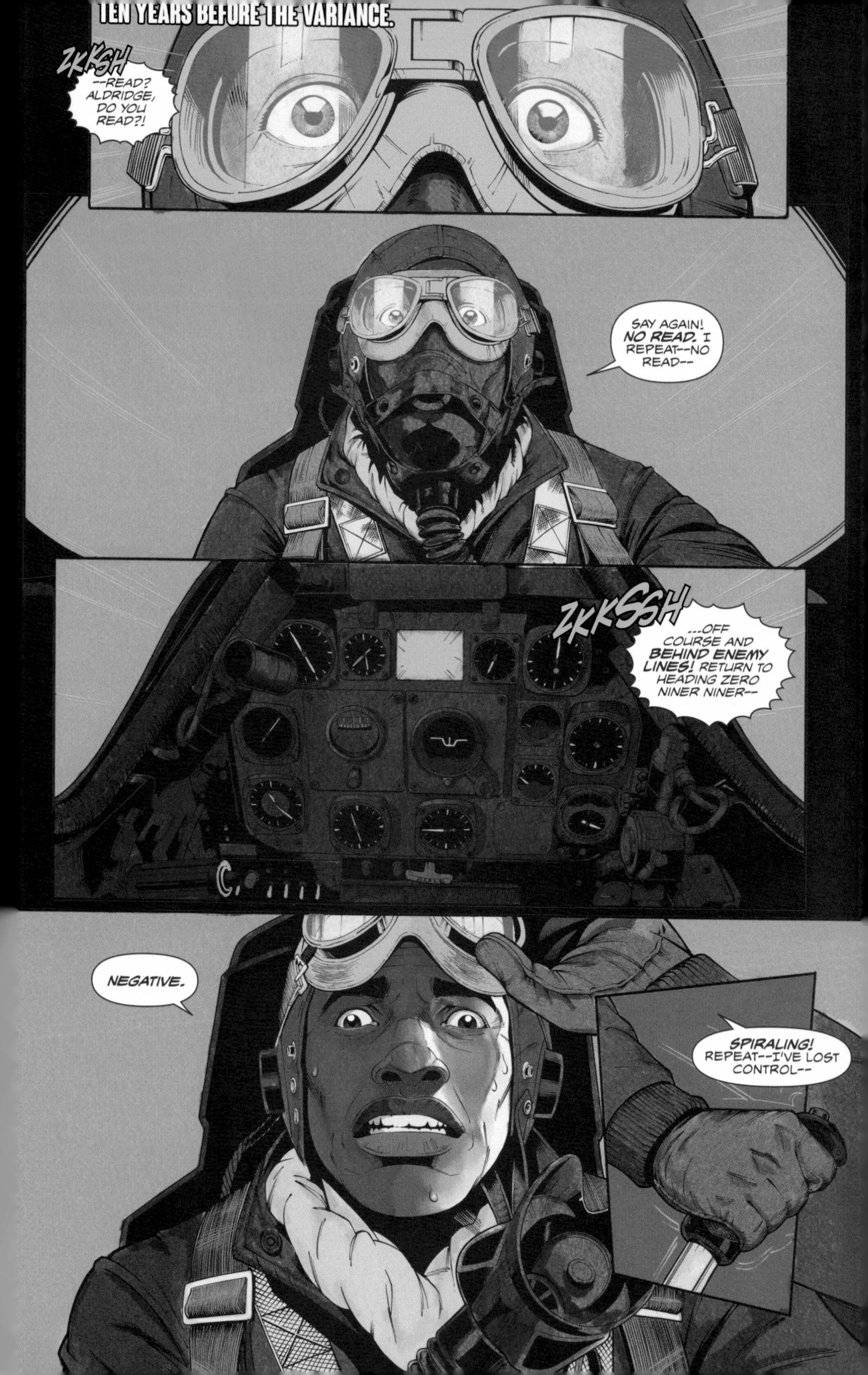
TEN YEARS BEFORE THE VARIANCE.
ZKKSH
--READ? ALDRIDGE, DO YOU READ?!
SAY AGAIN! NO READ. I REPEAT--NO READ--
ZKKSSH
...OFF COURSE AND BEHIND ENEMY LINES! RETURN TO HEADING ZERO NINER NINER--
NEGATIVE.
SPIRALING! REPEAT--I'VE LOST CONTROL--

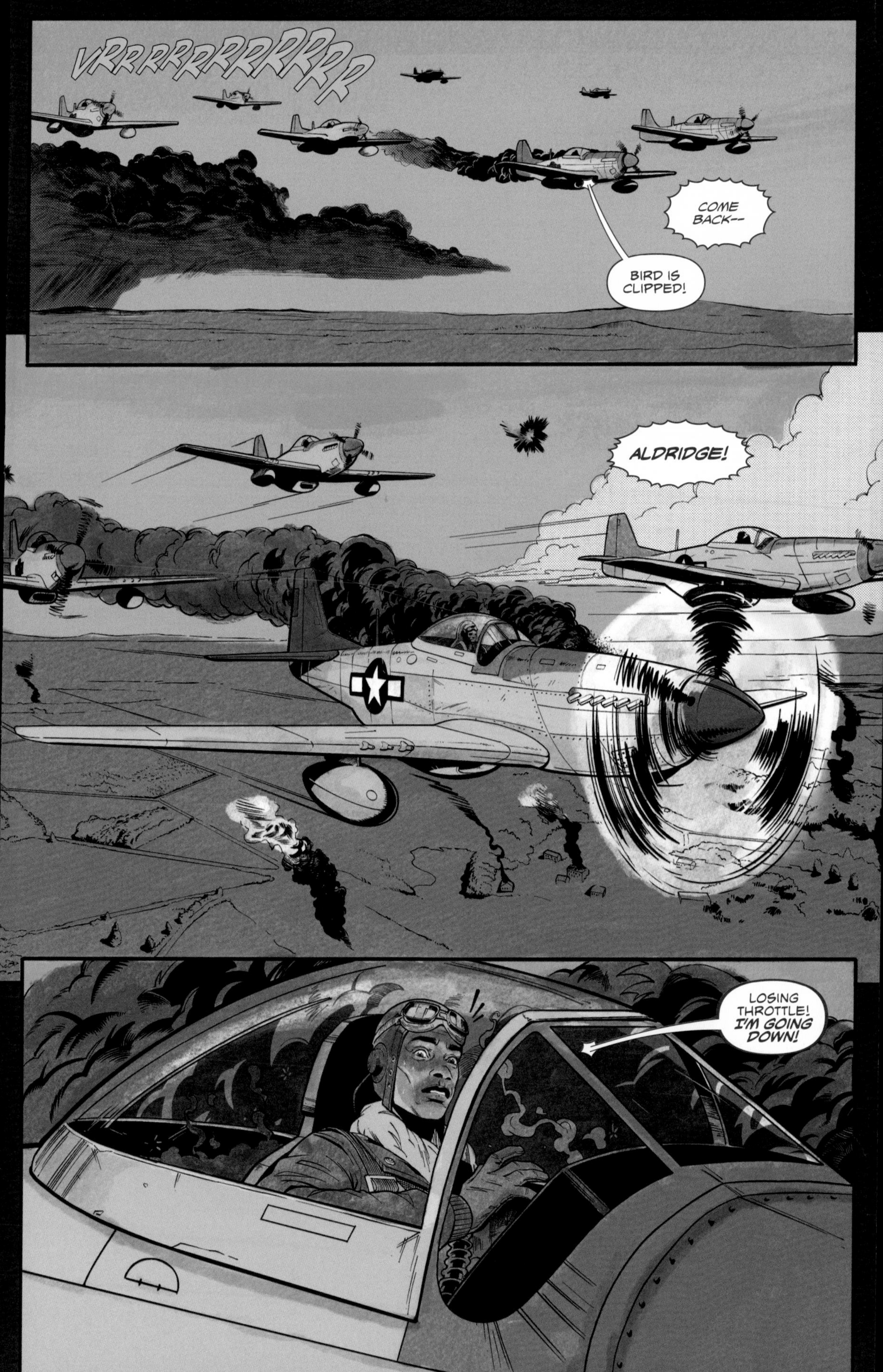
VRRRRRRRRRRRR
COME BACK--
BIRD IS CLIPPED!
ALDRIDGE!
LOSING THROTTLE! I'M GOING DOWN!

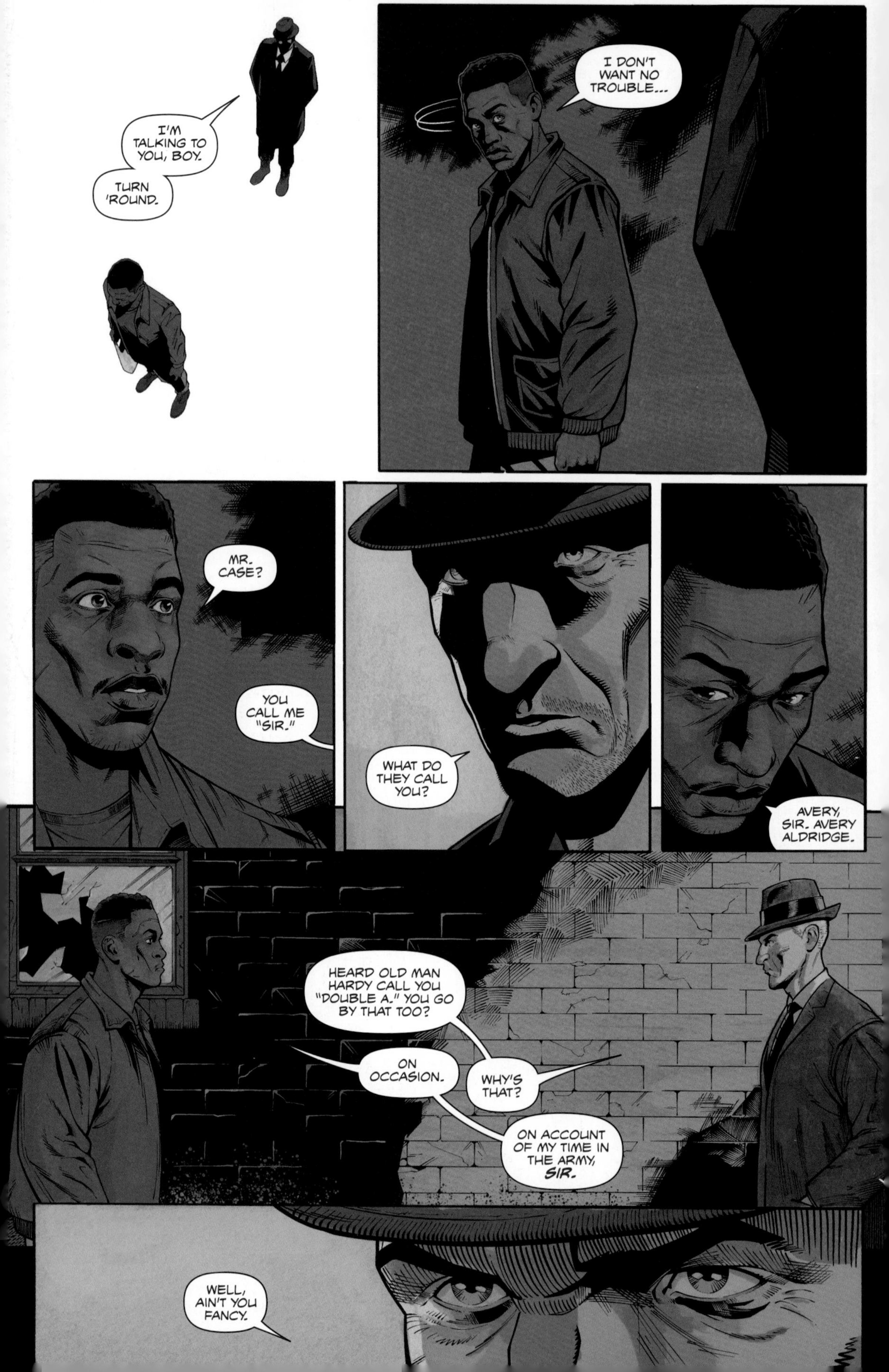
I'M TALKING TO YOU, BOY.
TURN 'ROUND.
I DON'T WANT NO TROUBLE...
MR. CASE?
YOU CALL ME "SIR."
WHAT DO THEY CALL YOU?
AVERY, SIR. AVERY ALDRIDGE.
HEARD OLD MAN HARDY CALL YOU "DOUBLE A." YOU GO BY THAT TOO?
ON OCCASION.
WHY'S THAT?
ON ACCOUNT OF MY TIME IN THE ARMY, SIR.
WELL, AIN'T YOU FANCY.

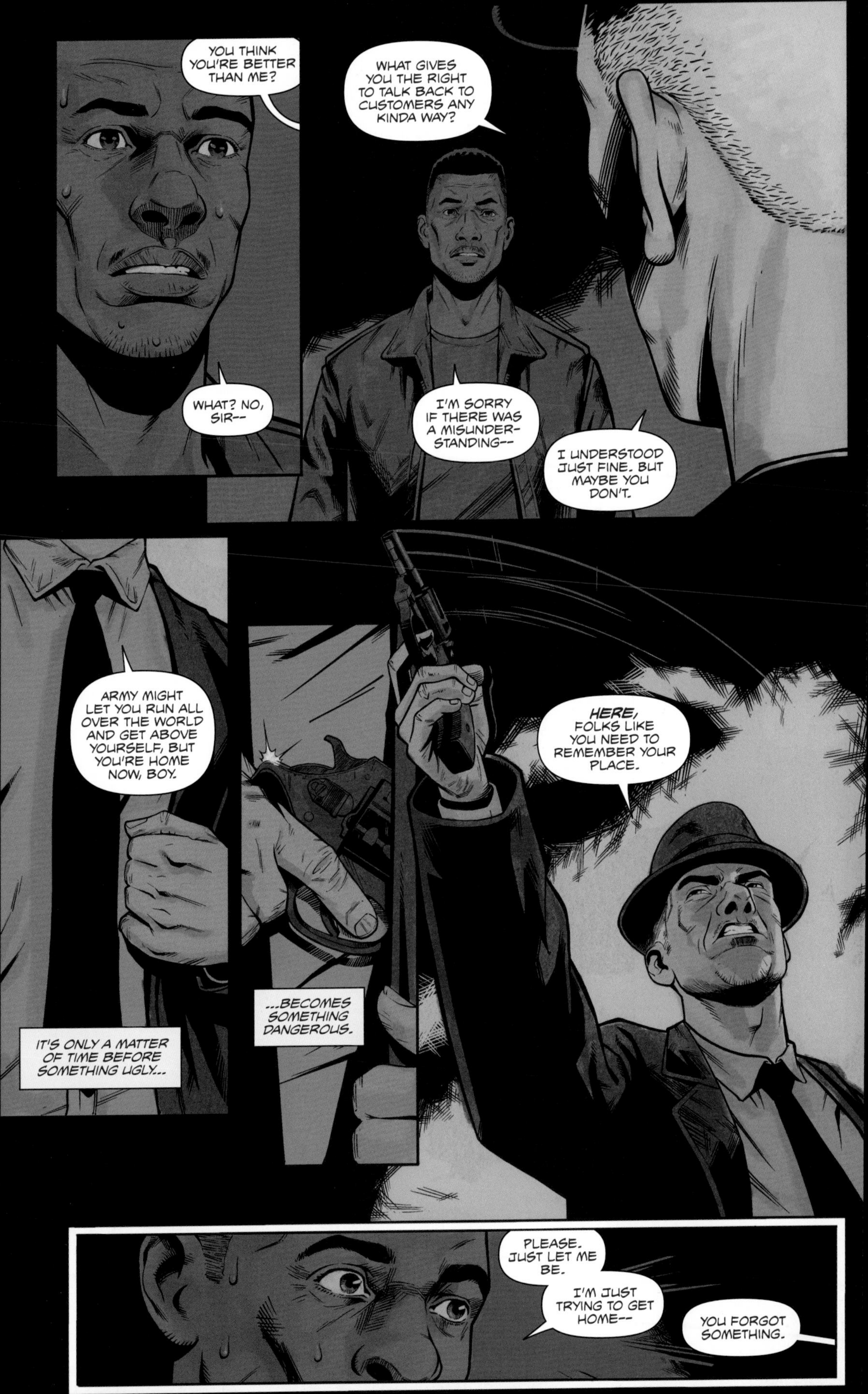
YOU THINK YOU'RE BETTER THAN ME?
WHAT GIVES YOU THE RIGHT TO TALK BACK TO CUSTOMERS ANY KINDA WAY?
WHAT? NO, SIR--
I'M SORRY IF THERE WAS A MISUNDER-STANDING--
I UNDERSTOOD JUST FINE. BUT MAYBE YOU DON'T.
ARMY MIGHT LET YOU RUN ALL OVER THE WORLD AND GET ABOVE YOURSELF, BUT YOU'RE HOME NOW, BOY.
IT'S ONLY A MATTER OF TIME BEFORE SOMETHING UGLY...
...BECOMES SOMETHING DANGEROUS.
HERE, FOLKS LIKE YOU NEED TO REMEMBER YOUR PLACE.
PLEASE. JUST LET ME BE.
I'M JUST TRYING TO GET HOME--
YOU FORGOT SOMETHING.

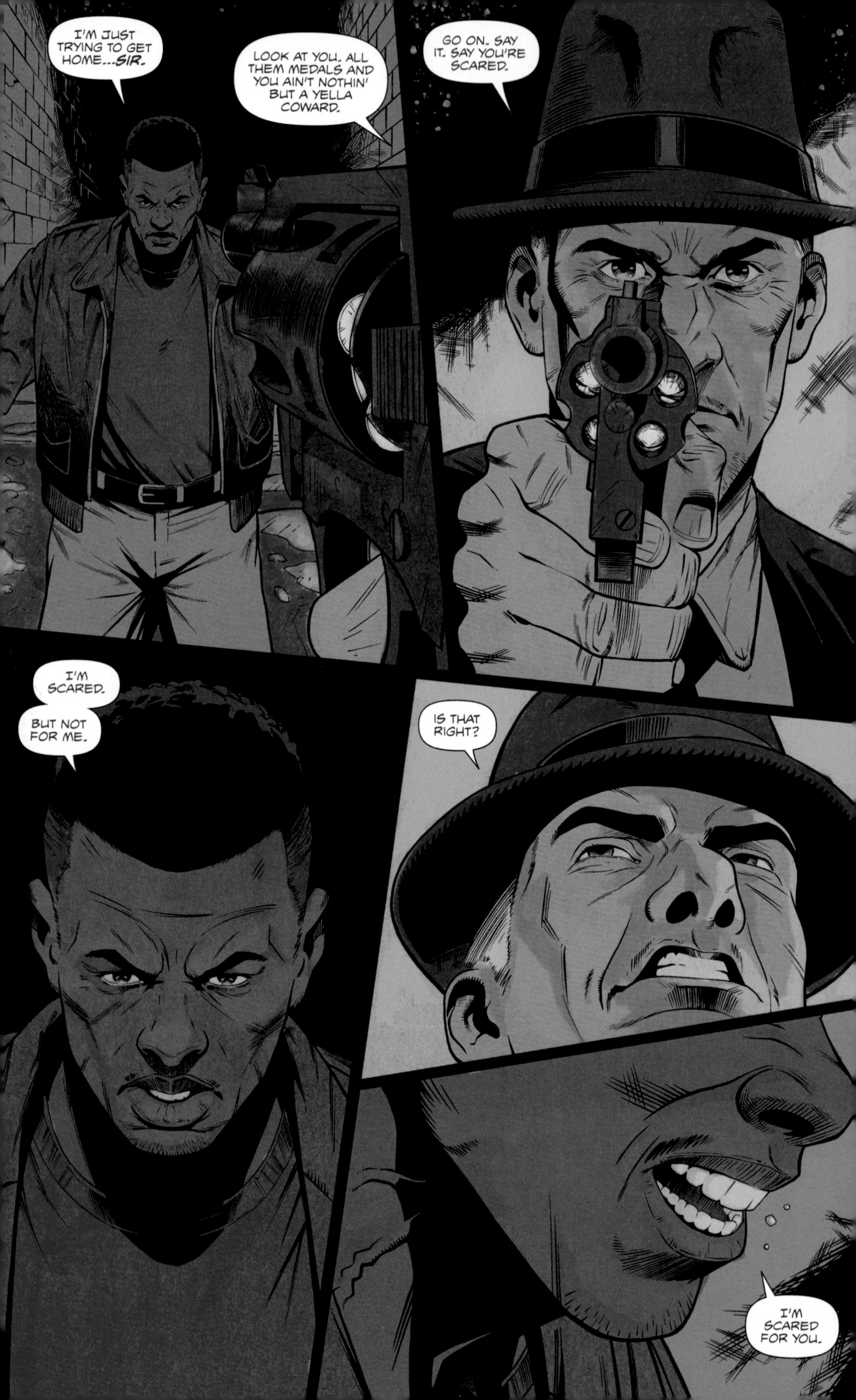
I'M JUST TRYING TO GET HOME... SIR.
LOOK AT YOU. ALL THEM MEDALS AND YOU AIN'T NOTHIN' BUT A YELLA COWARD.
GO ON. SAY IT. SAY YOU'RE SCARED.
I'M SCARED.
BUT NOT FOR ME.
IS THAT RIGHT?
I'M SCARED FOR YOU.

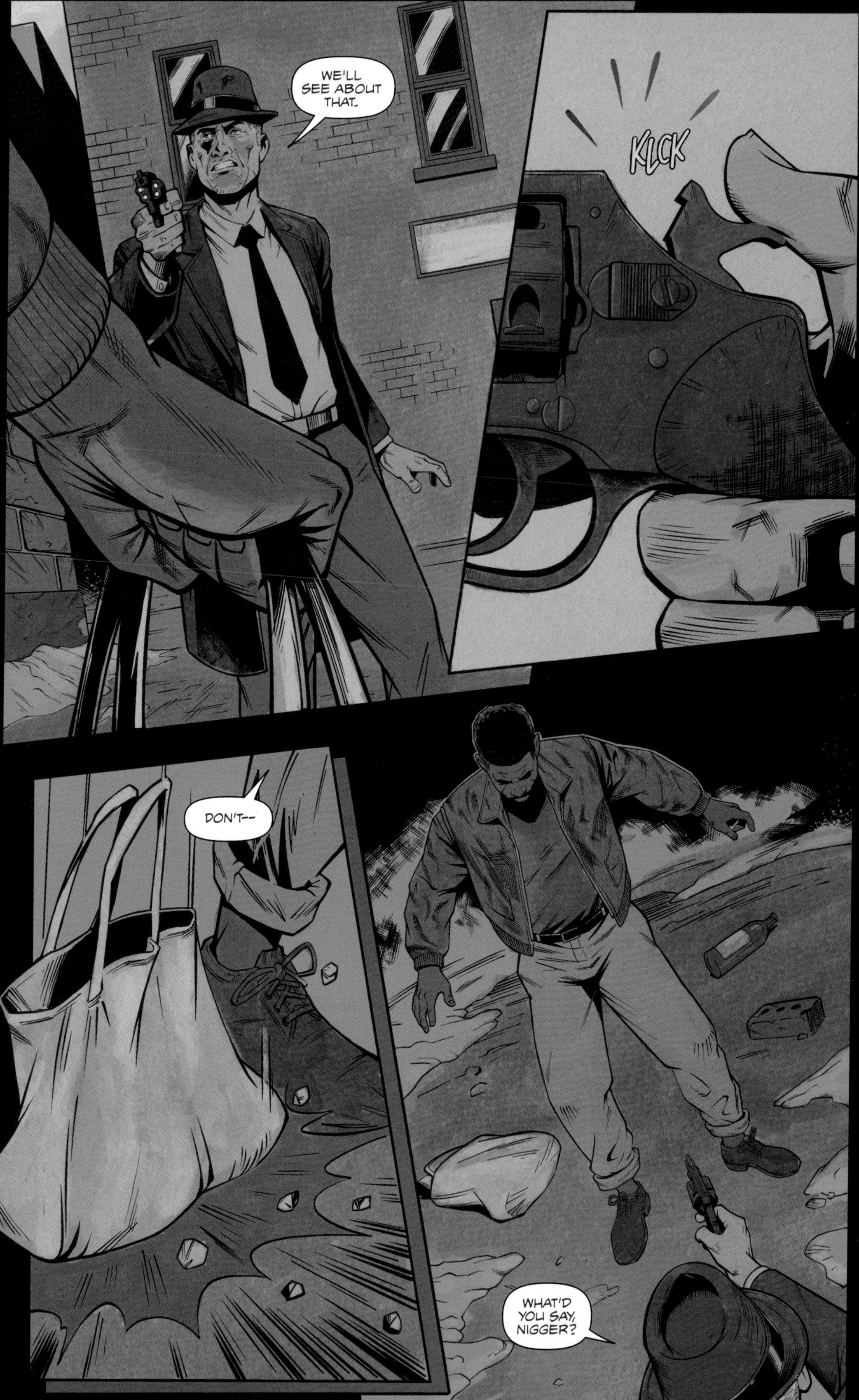
WE'LL SEE ABOUT THAT.
KLCK
DON'T--
WHAT'D YOU SAY, NIGGER?

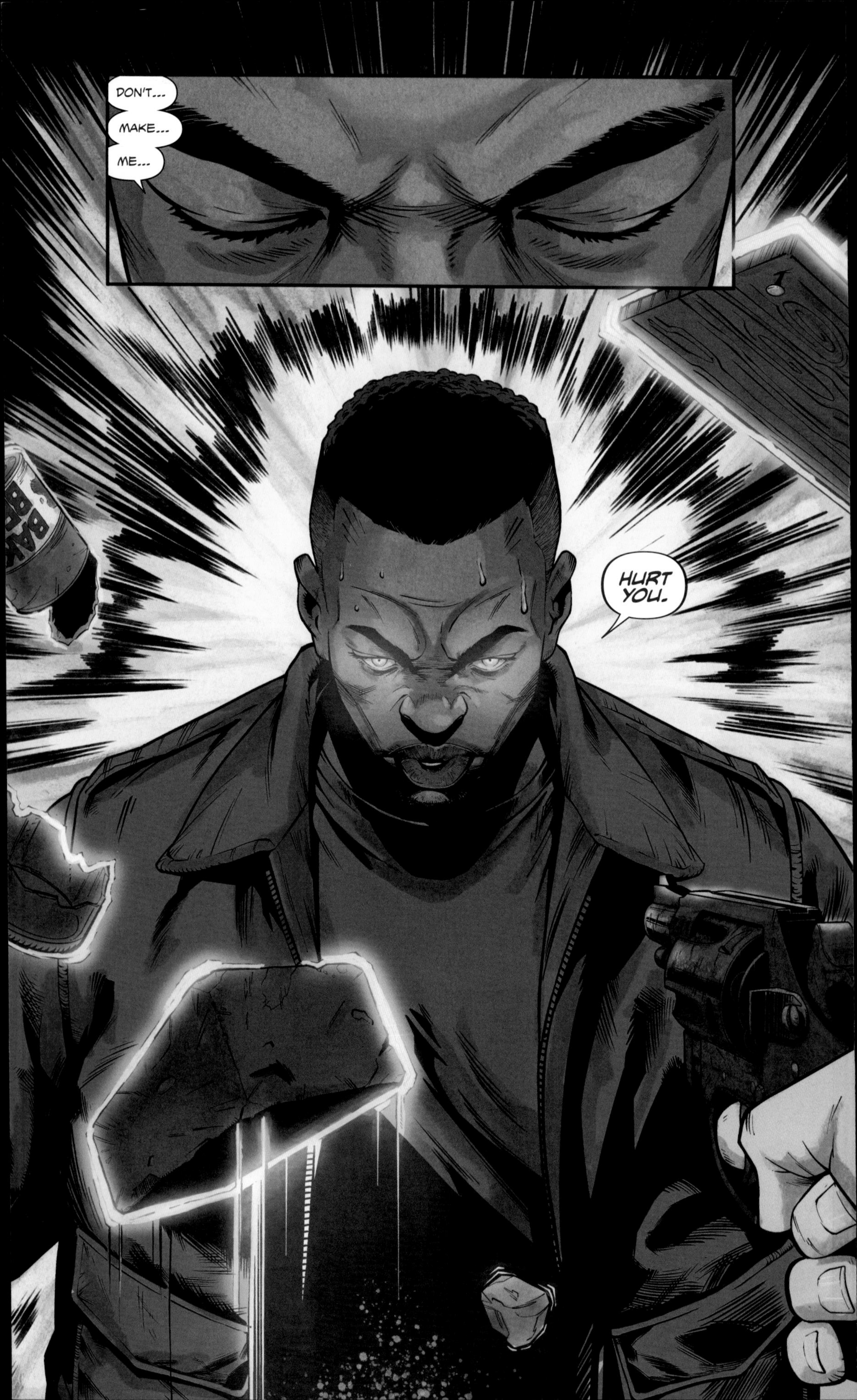
DON'T...
MAKE...
ME...
HURT YOU.

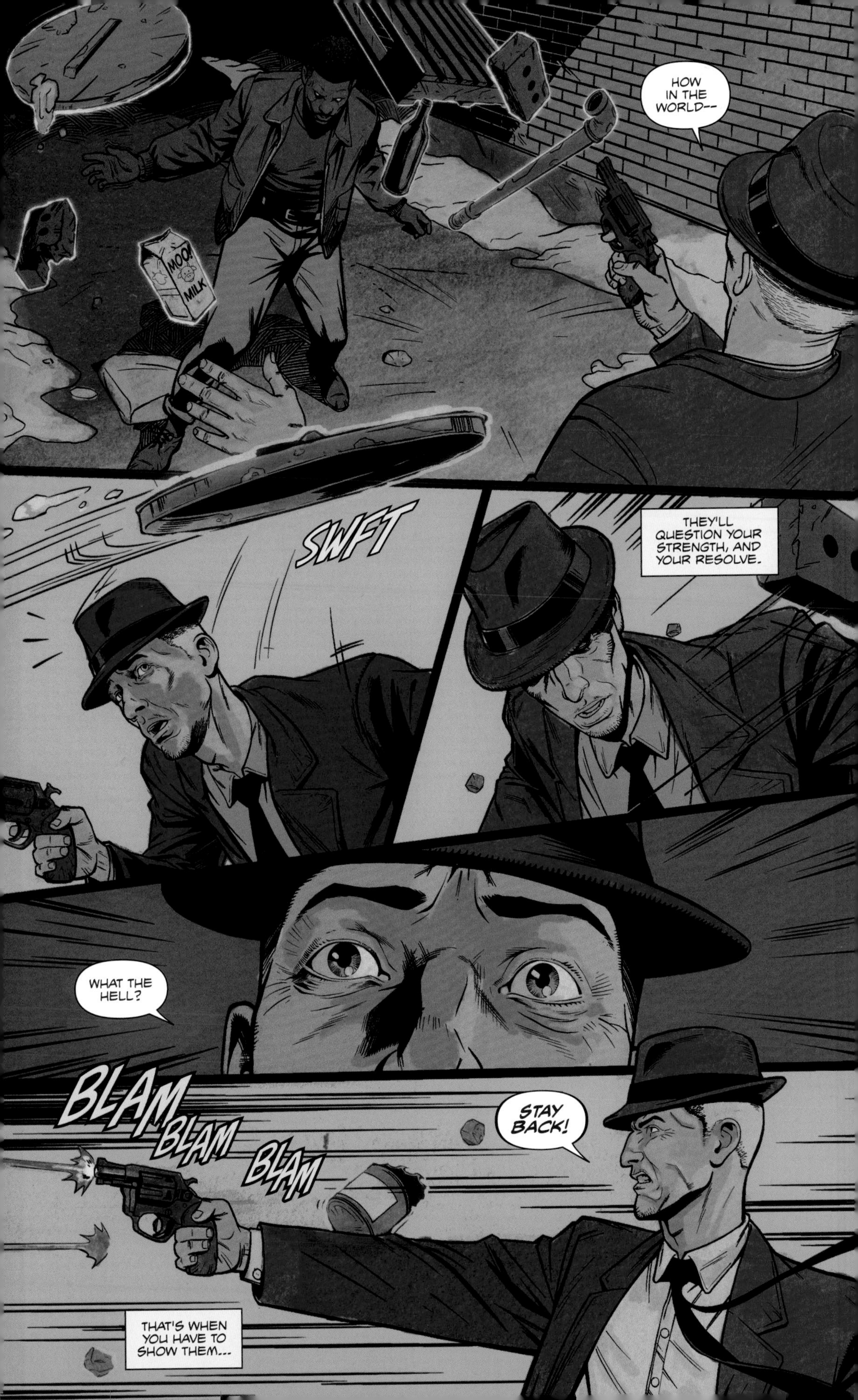
MOO!
MILK
HOW IN THE WORLD--
SWFT
THEY'LL QUESTION YOUR STRENGTH, AND YOUR RESOLVE.
WHAT THE HELL?
BLAM
BLAM
BLAM
STAY BACK!
THAT'S WHEN YOU HAVE TO SHOW THEM...

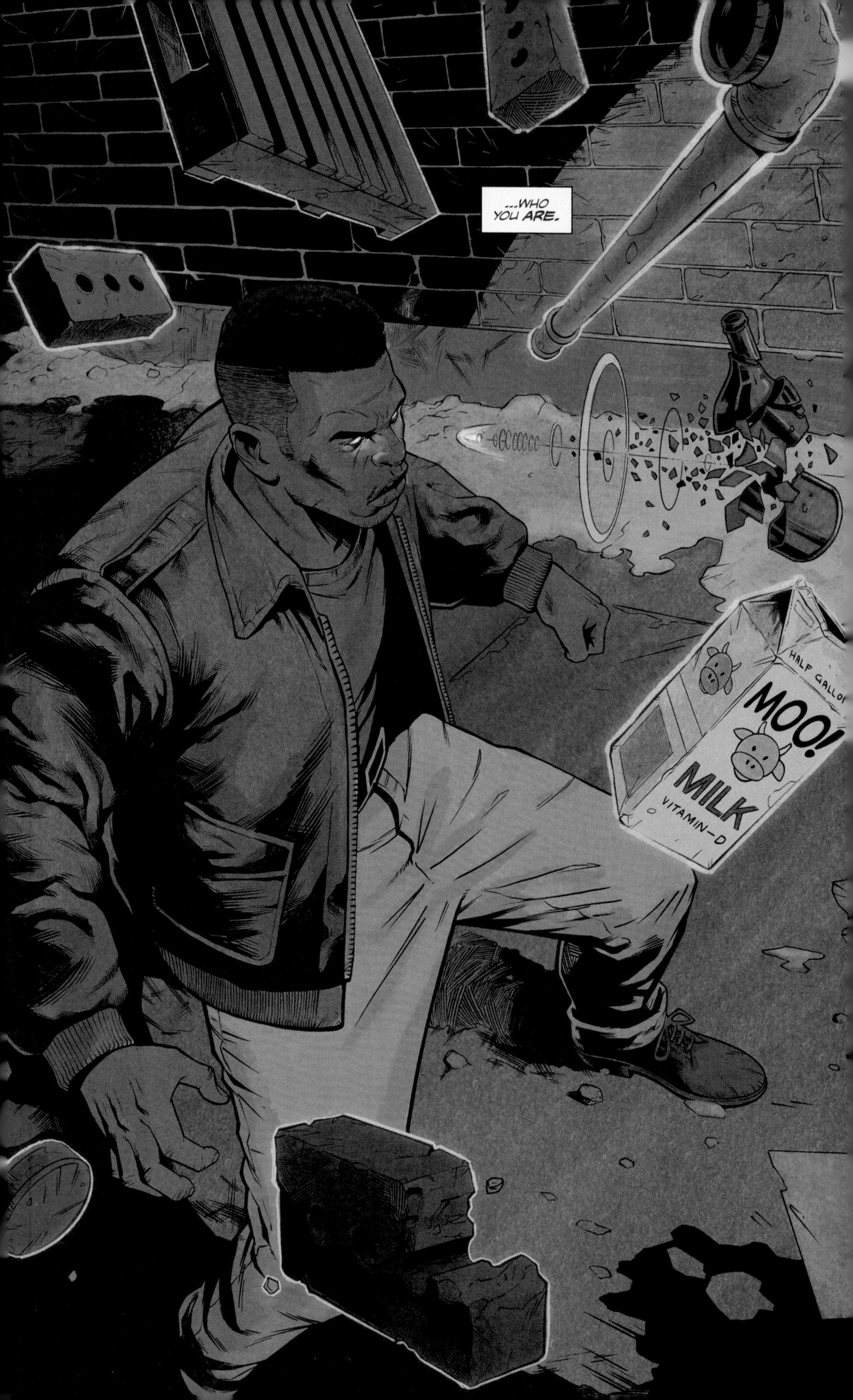
...WHO YOU ARE.
HALF GALLO
MOO!
MILK
VITAMIN-D

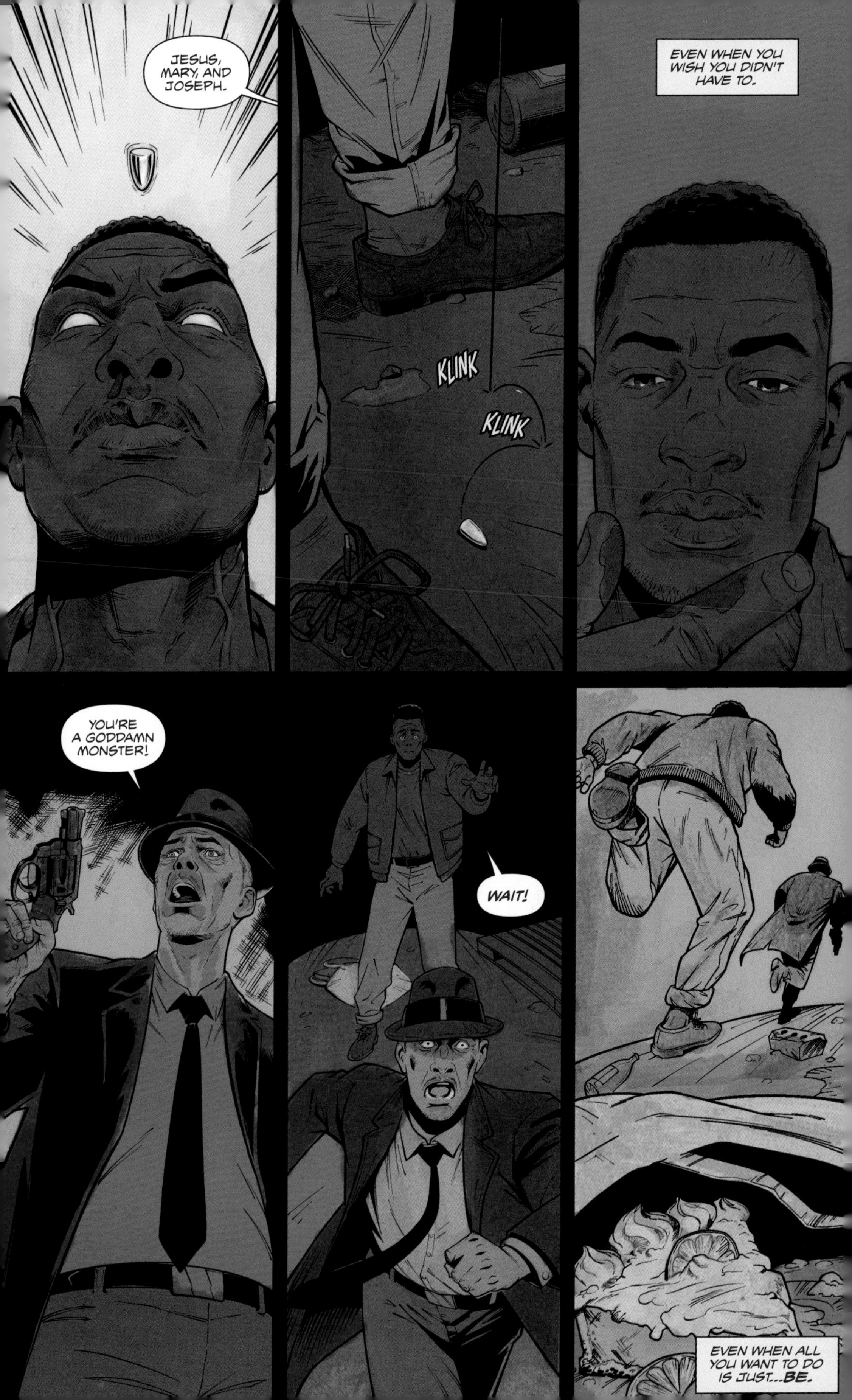
JESUS, MARY, AND JOSEPH.
KLINK
KLINK
EVEN WHEN YOU WISH YOU DIDN'T HAVE TO.
YOU'RE A GODDAMN MONSTER!
WAIT!
EVEN WHEN ALL YOU WANT TO DO IS JUST...BE.

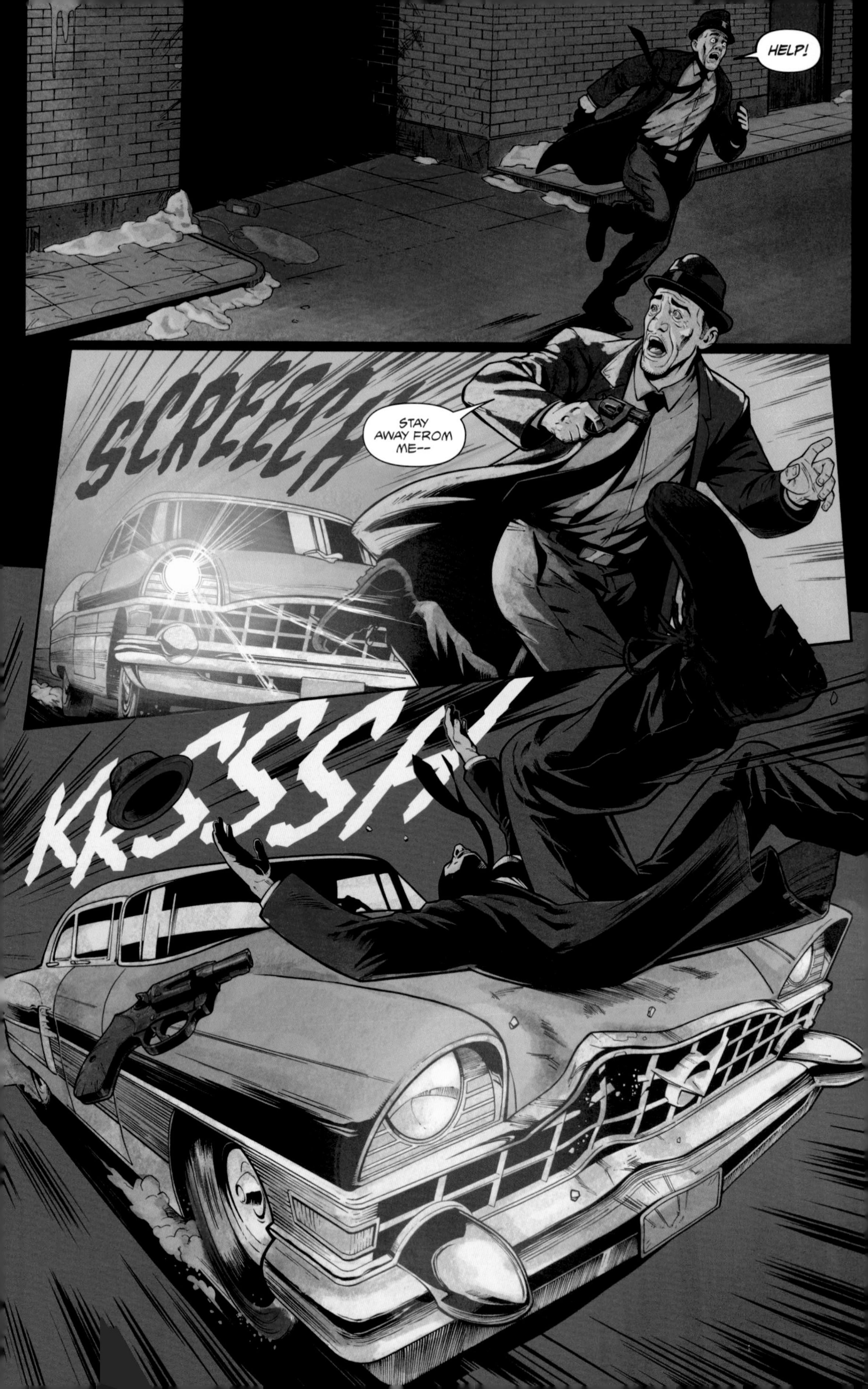
HELP!
SCREECH
STAY AWAY FROM ME--
KRSSSH

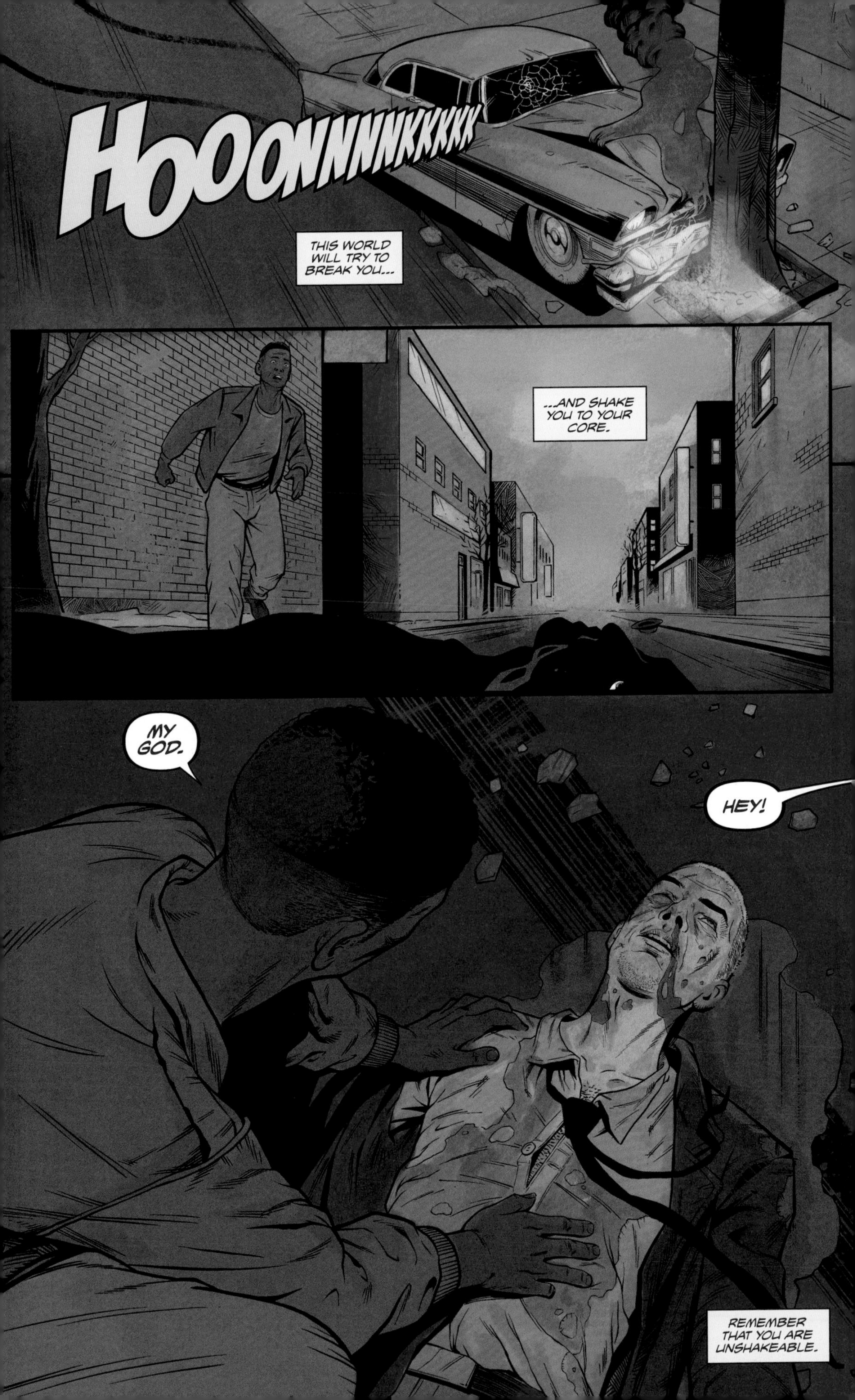
HOOONNNNKKKKK
THIS WORLD WILL TRY TO BREAK YOU...
...AND SHAKE YOU TO YOUR CORE.
MY GOD.
HEY!
REMEMBER THAT YOU ARE UNSHAKEABLE.

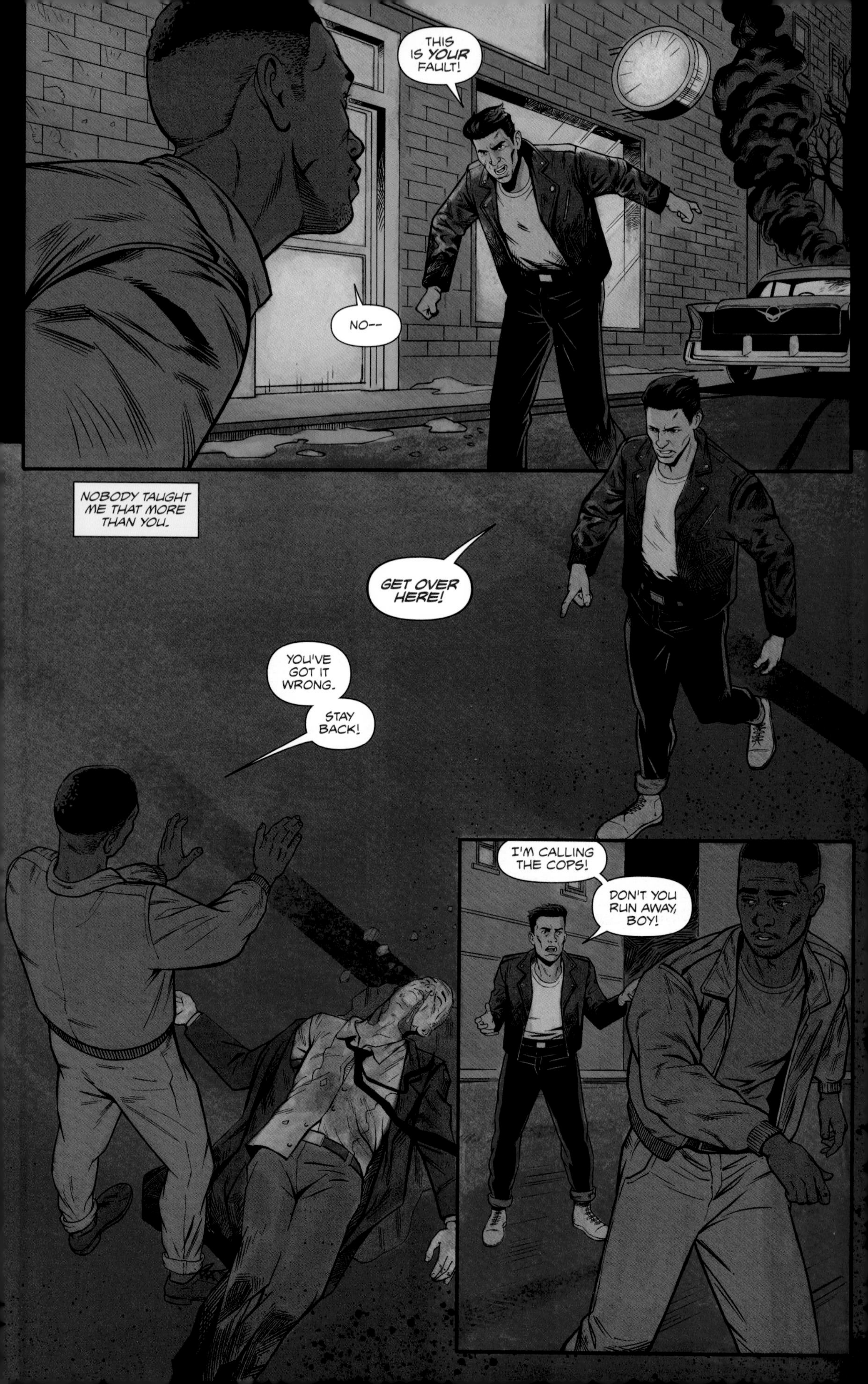
THIS IS YOUR FAULT!
NO--
NOBODY TAUGHT ME THAT MORE THAN YOU.
GET OVER HERE!
YOU'VE GOT IT WRONG.
STAY BACK!
I'M CALLING THE COPS!
DON'T YOU RUN AWAY, BOY!

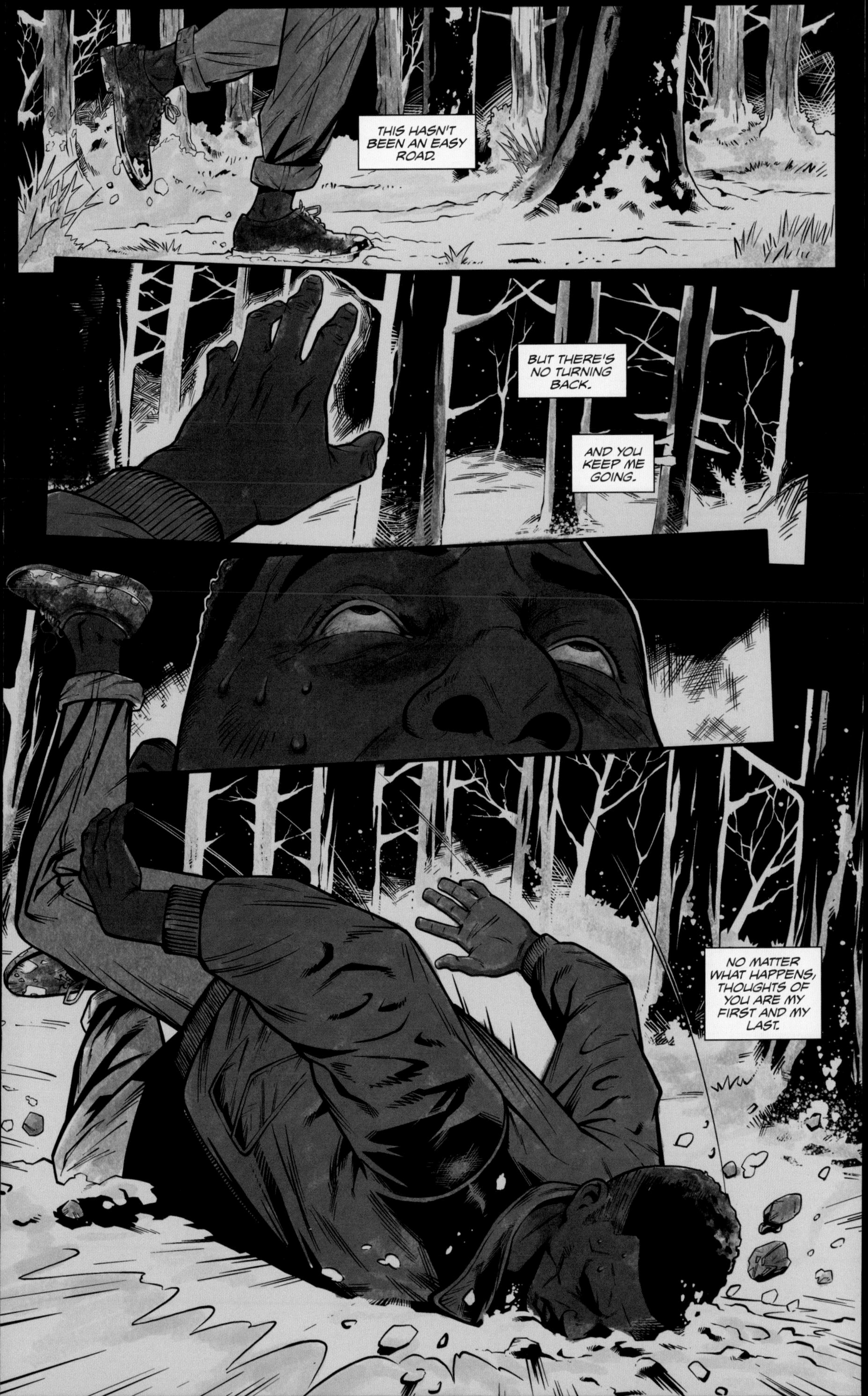

THIS HASN'T BEEN AN EASY ROAD.
BUT THERE'S NO TURNING BACK.
AND YOU KEEP ME GOING.
NO MATTER WHAT HAPPENS, THOUGHTS OF YOU ARE MY FIRST AND MY LAST.

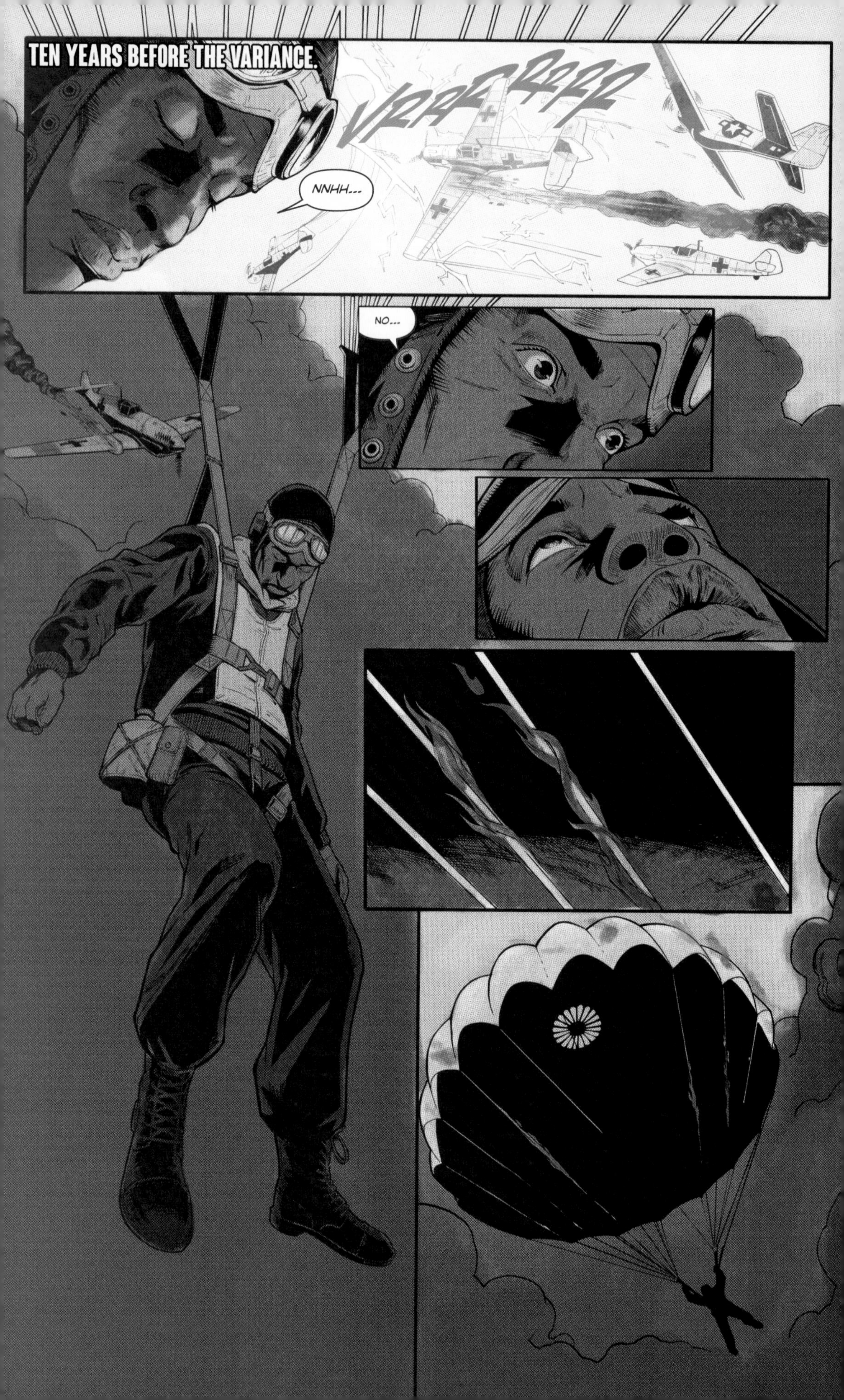
TEN YEARS BEFORE THE VARIANCE.
VRRRRRRR
NNHH...
NO...

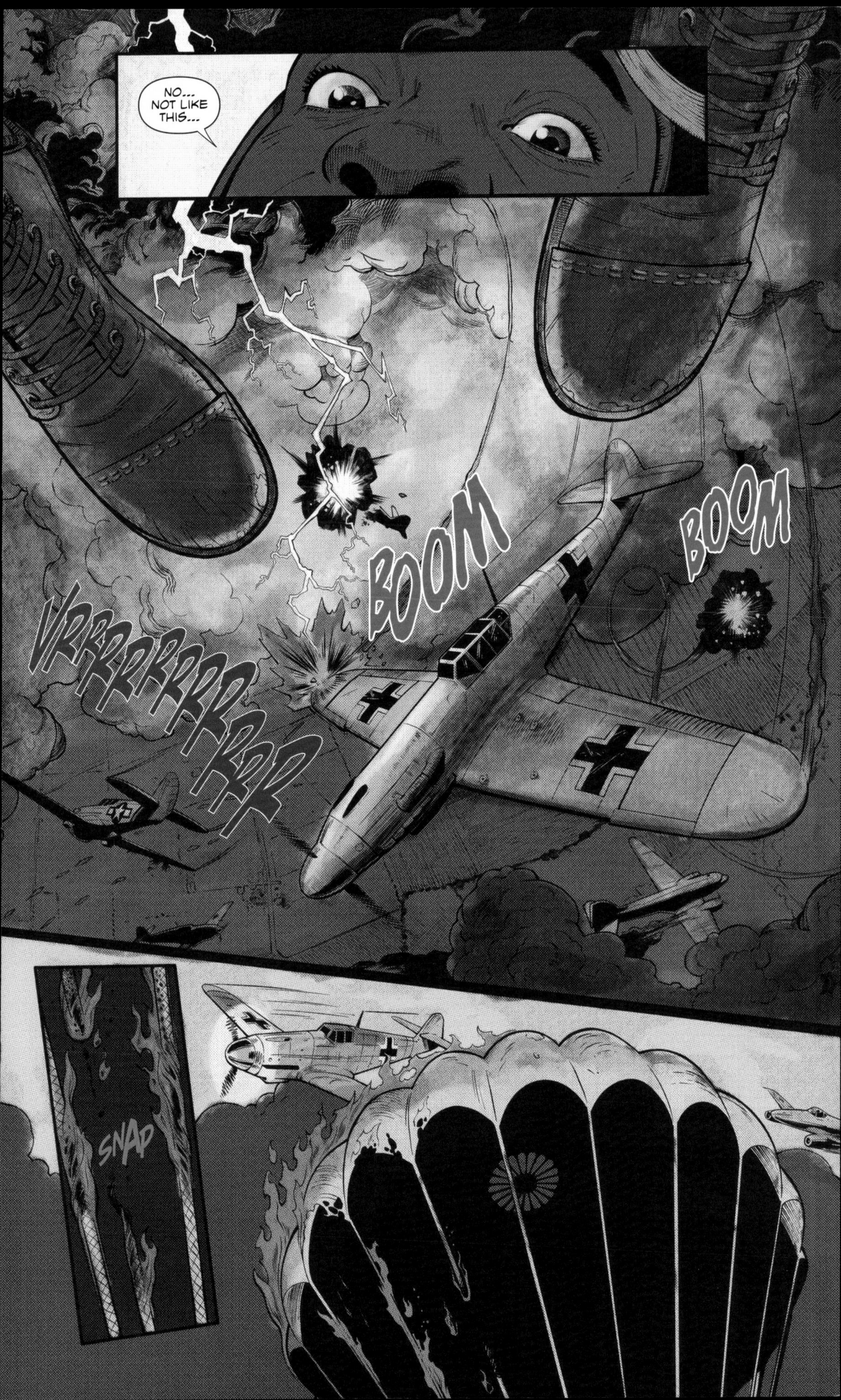
NO... NOT LIKE THIS...
BOOM
BOOM
VRRRRRRRRRRRR
SNAP

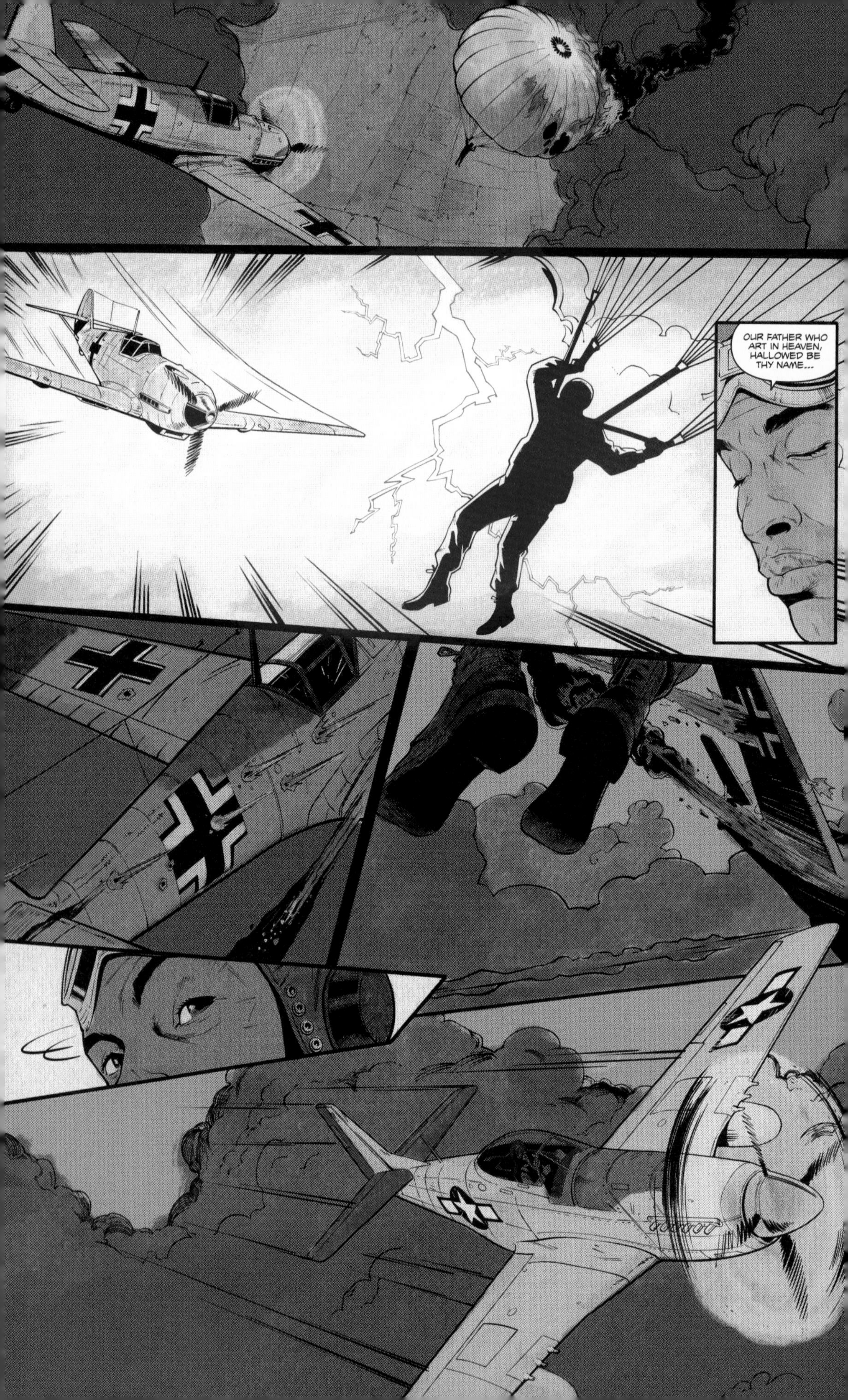
OUR FATHER WHO ART IN HEAVEN, HALLOWED BE THY NAME...

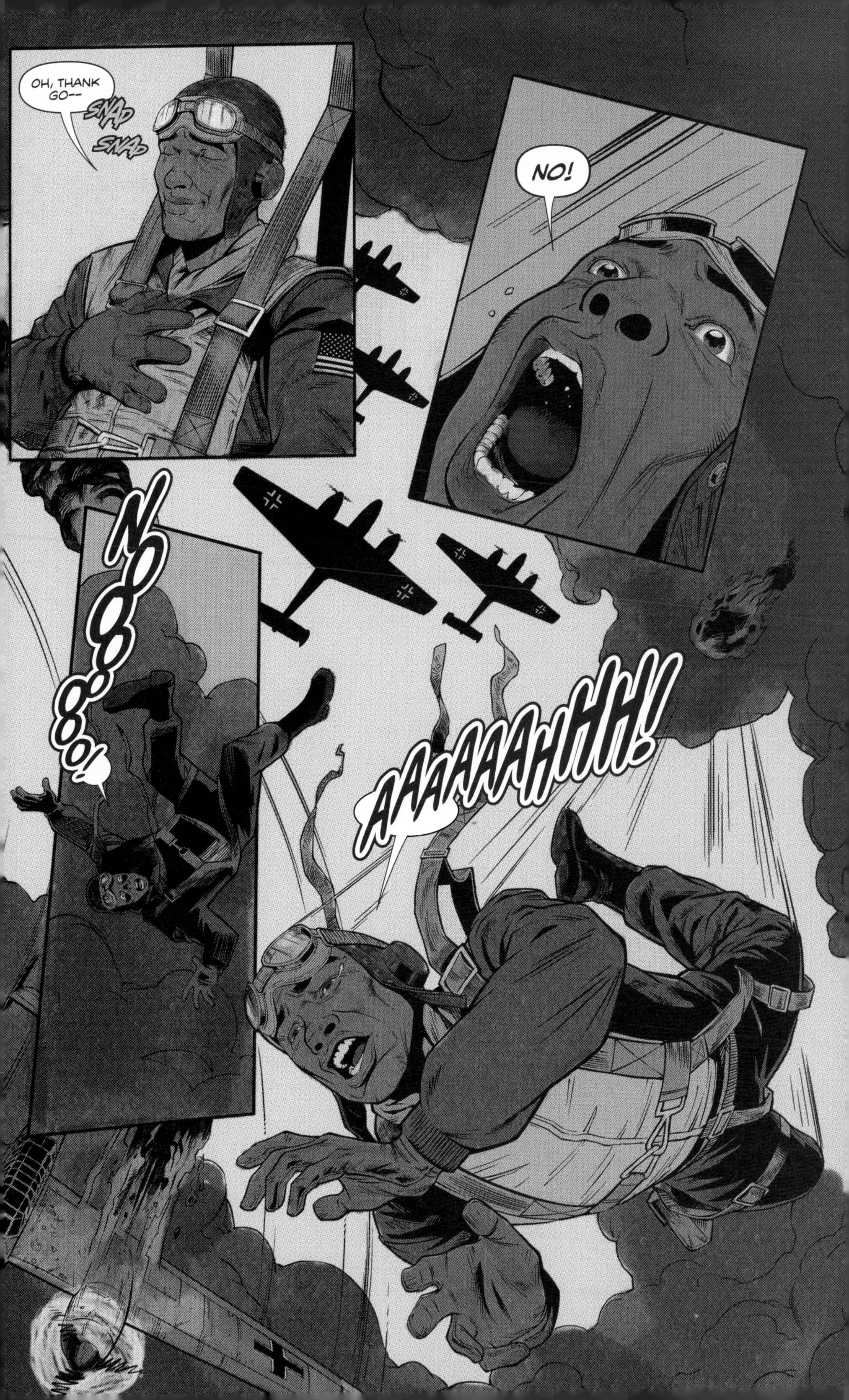
OH, THANK GO--
SNAP SNAP
NO!
NOOOOOOOO!
AAAAAAHHHH!

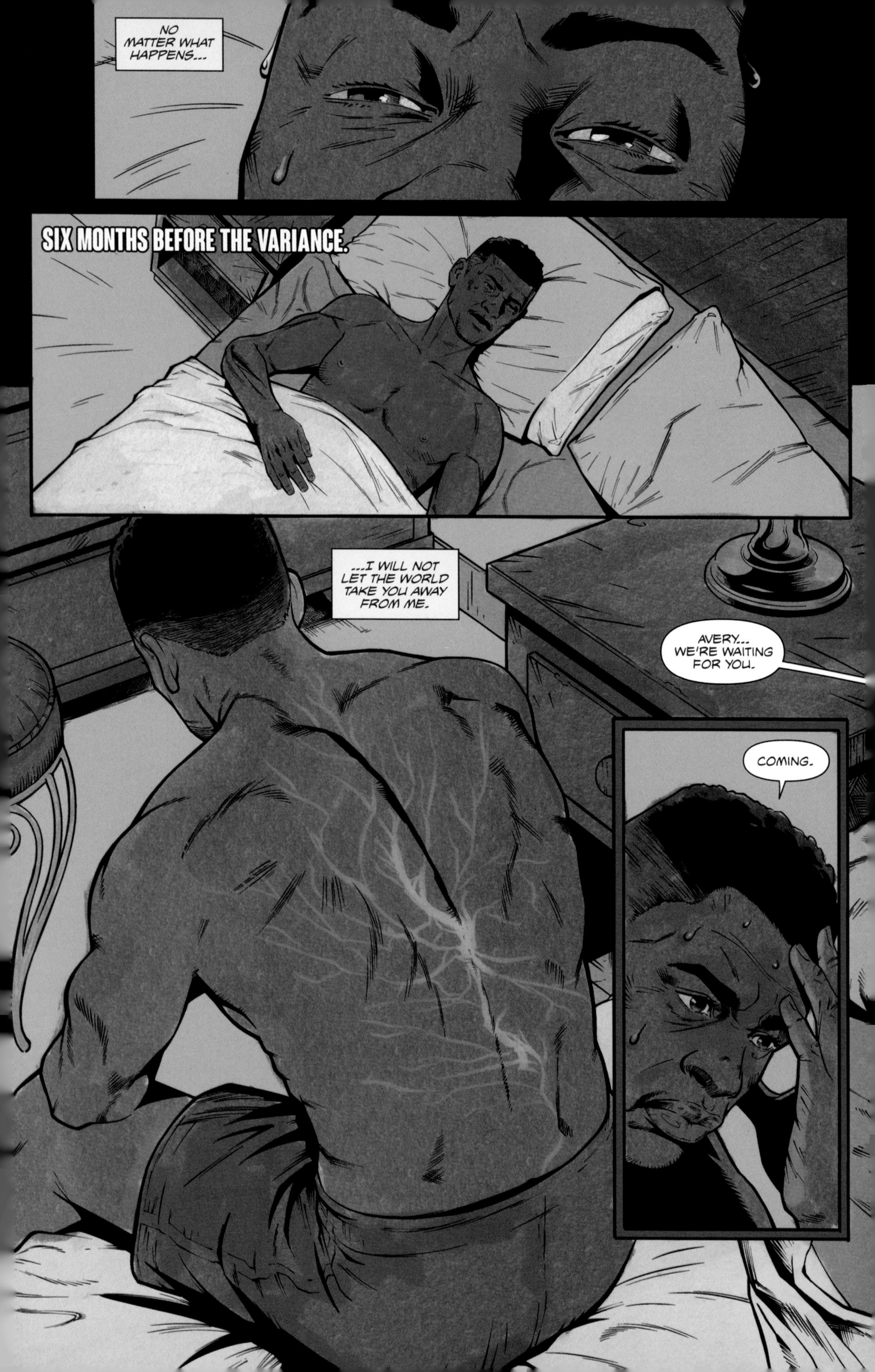
NO MATTER WHAT HAPPENS...
SIX MONTHS BEFORE THE VARIANCE.
...I WILL NOT LET THE WORLD TAKE YOU AWAY FROM ME.
AVERY... WE'RE WAITING FOR YOU.
COMING.

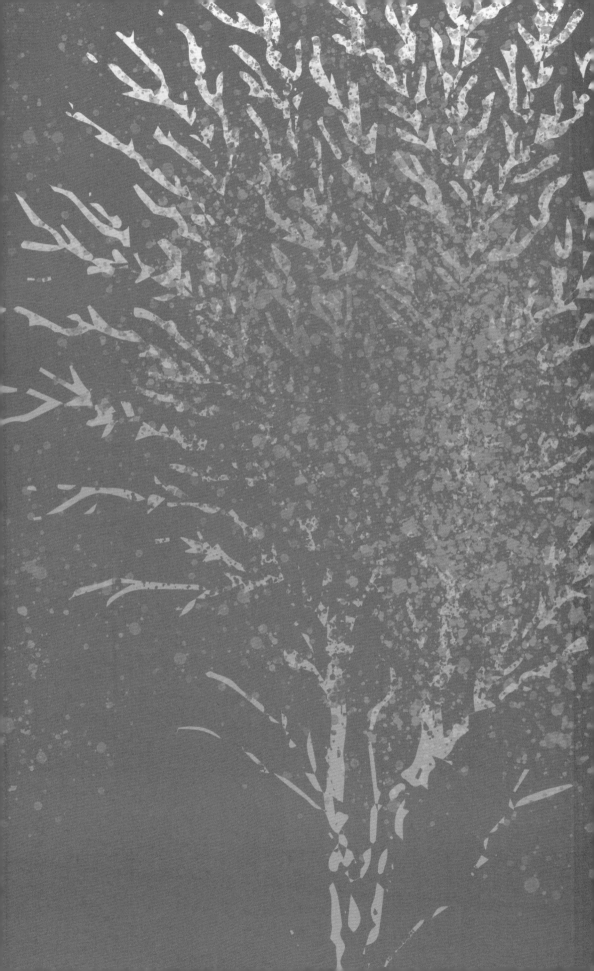

CHAPTER TWO

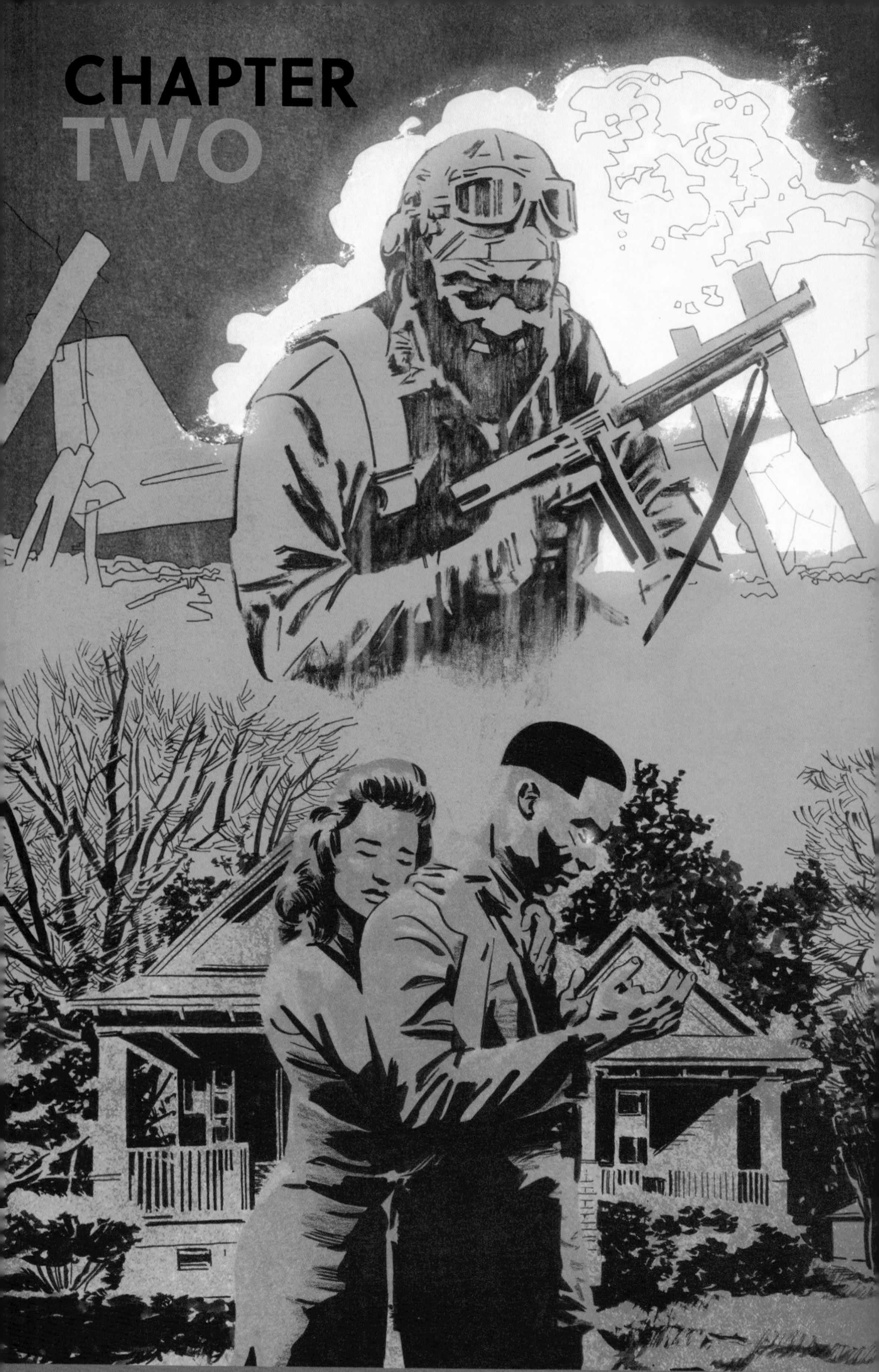

Issue #2 Cover

VALENTINE DE LANDRO

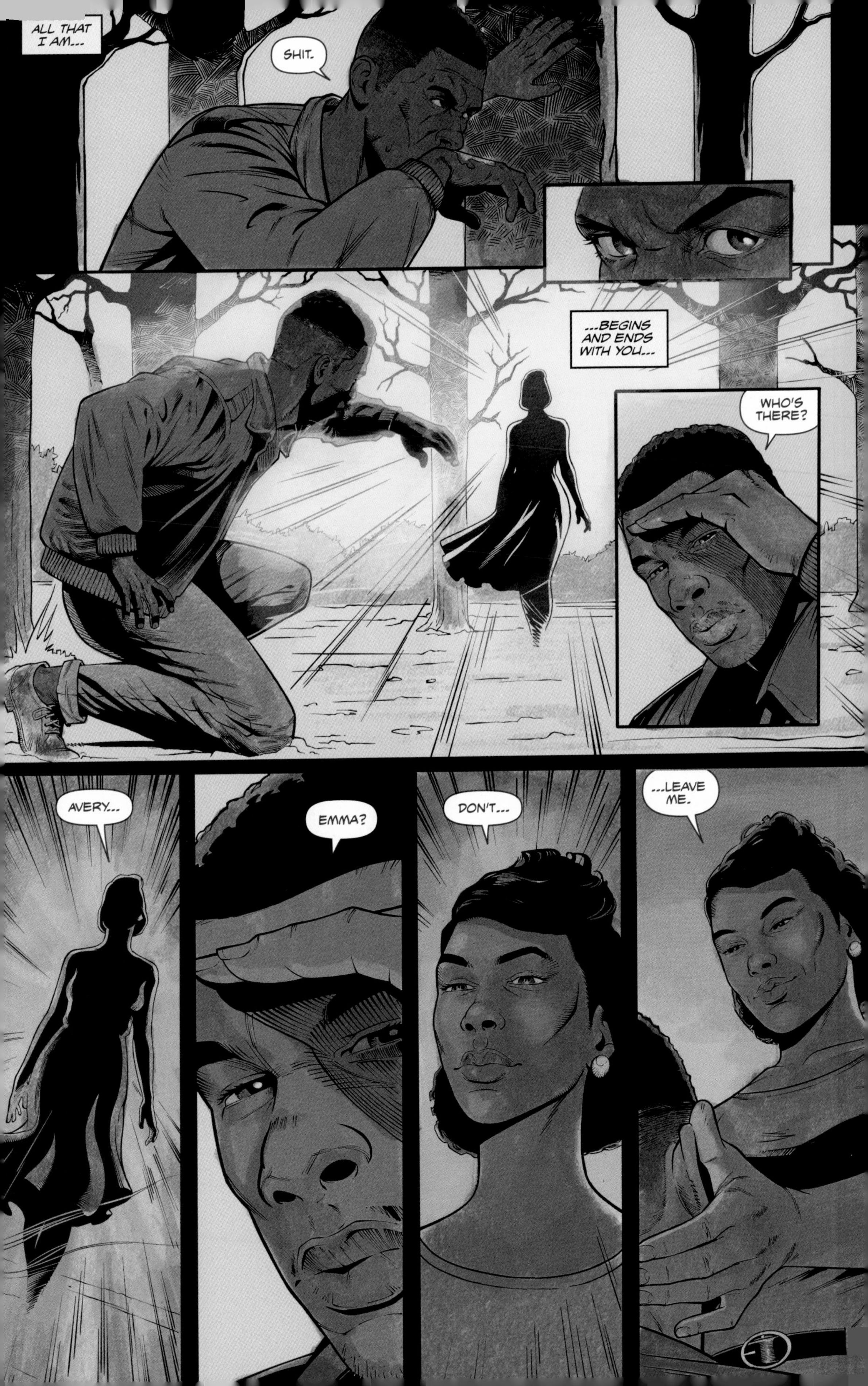
ALL THAT I AM...
SHIT.
...BEGINS AND ENDS WITH YOU...
WHO'S THERE?
AVERY...
EMMA?
DON'T...
...LEAVE ME.

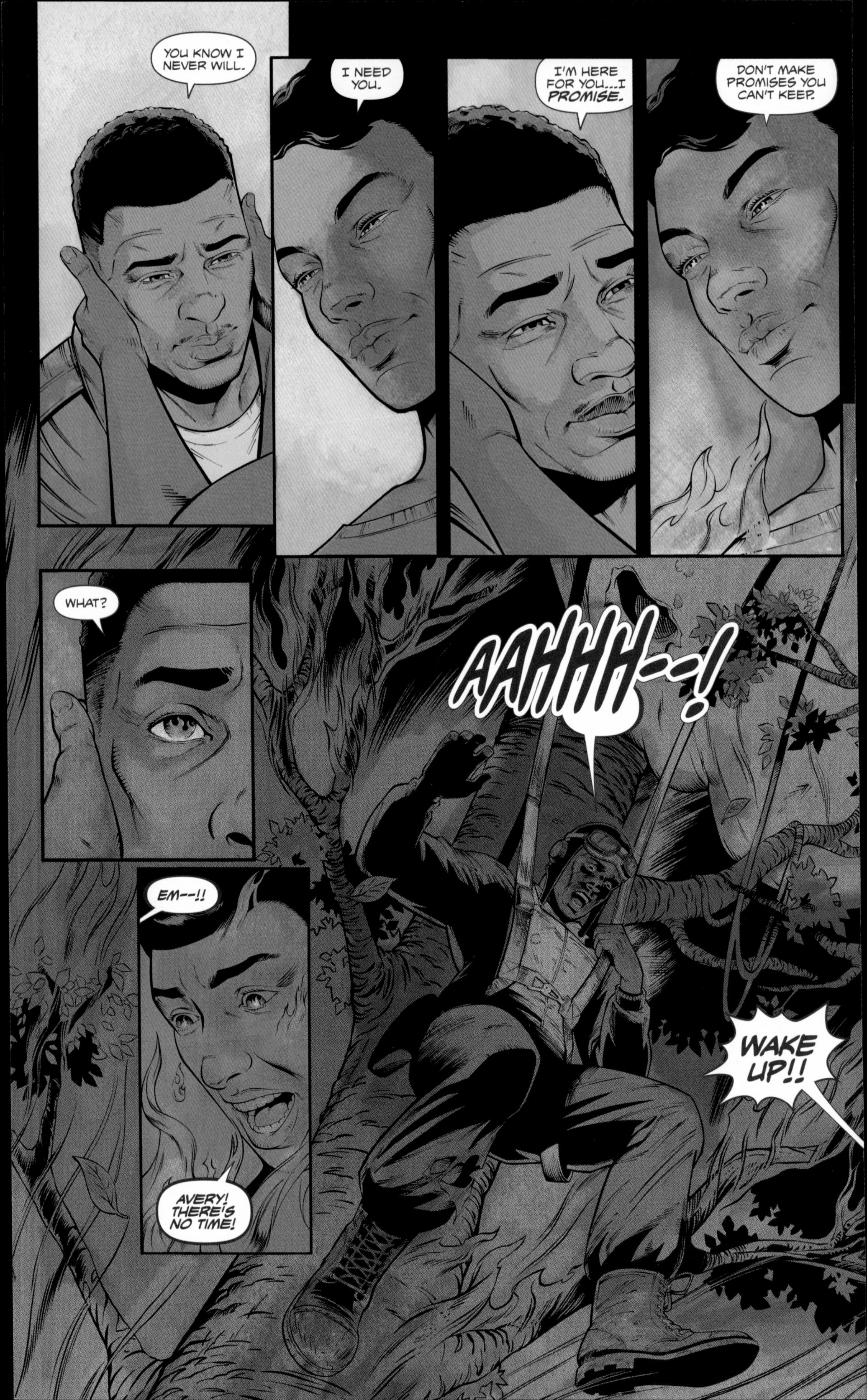
YOU KNOW I NEVER WILL.
I NEED YOU.
I'M HERE FOR YOU...I PROMISE.
DON'T MAKE PROMISES YOU CAN'T KEEP.
WHAT?
AAHHH--!
EM--!!
AVERY! THERE'S NO TIME!
WAKE UP!!

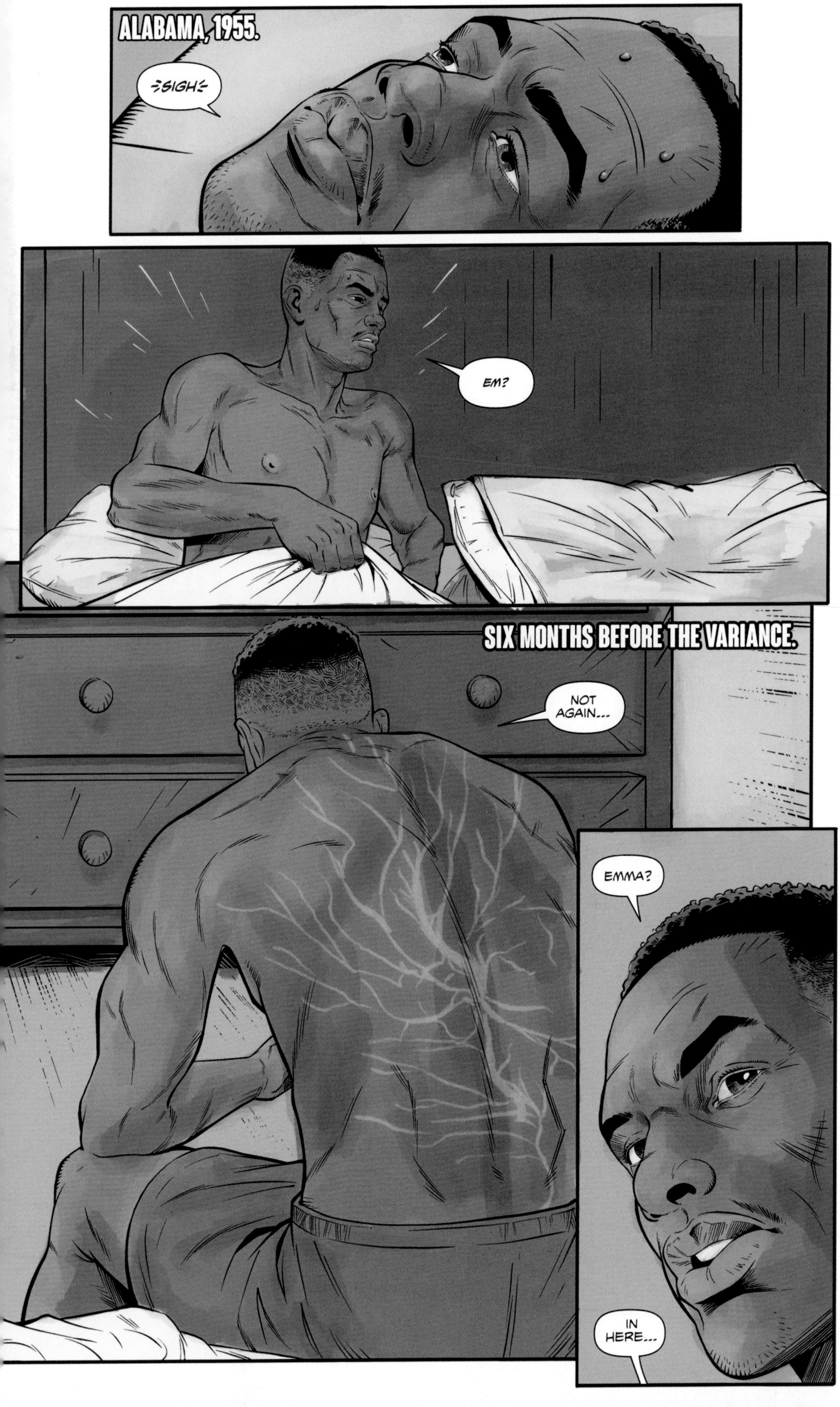
ALABAMA, 1955.
-SIGH-
EM?
SIX MONTHS BEFORE THE VARIANCE.
NOT AGAIN...
EMMA?
IN HERE...

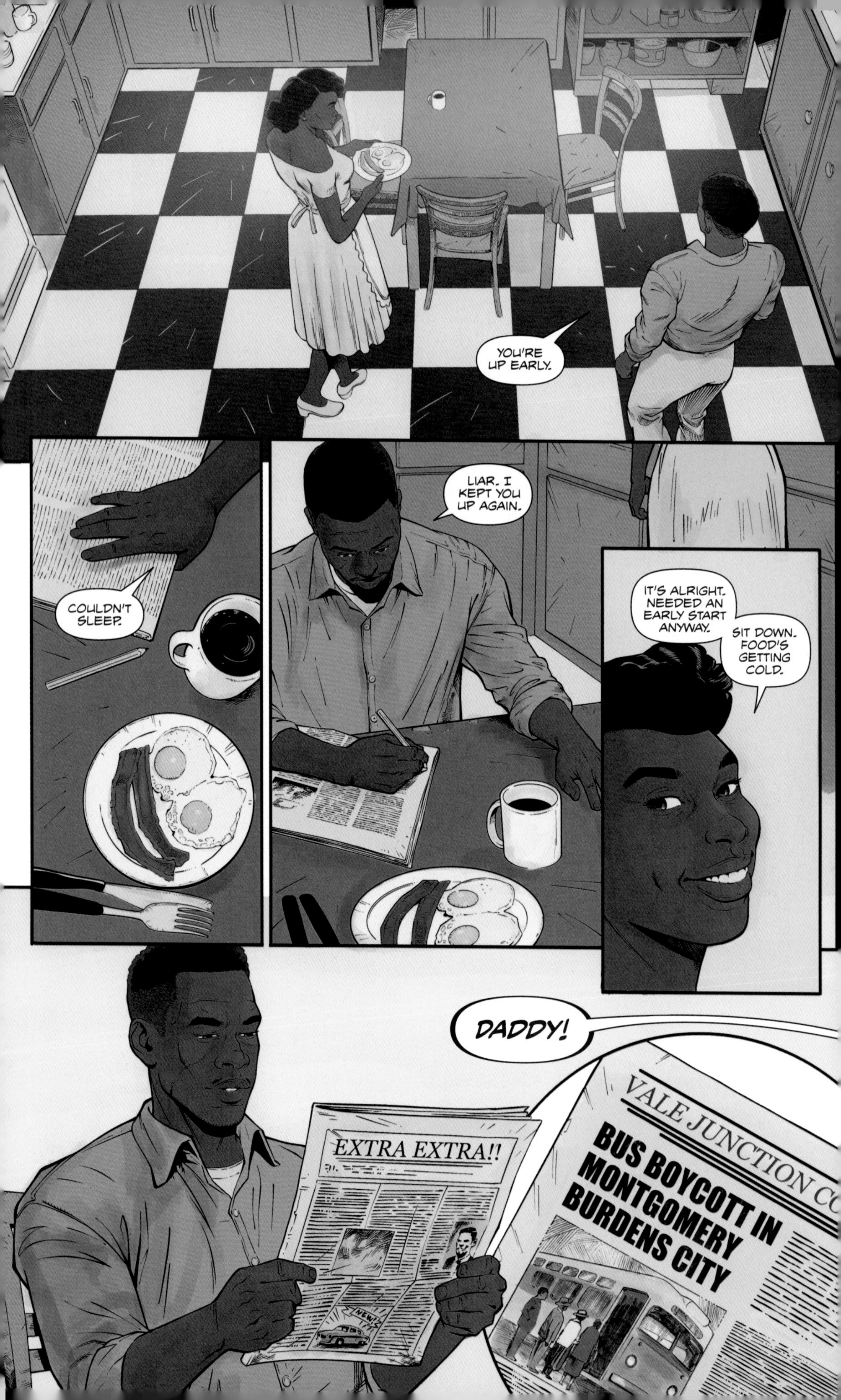
YOU'RE UP EARLY.
COULDN'T SLEEP.
LIAR. I KEPT YOU UP AGAIN.
IT'S ALRIGHT. NEEDED AN EARLY START ANYWAY.
SIT DOWN. FOOD'S GETTING COLD.
DADDY!
EXTRA EXTRA!!
VALE JUNCTION C
BUS BOYCOTT IN MONTGOMERY BURDENS CITY

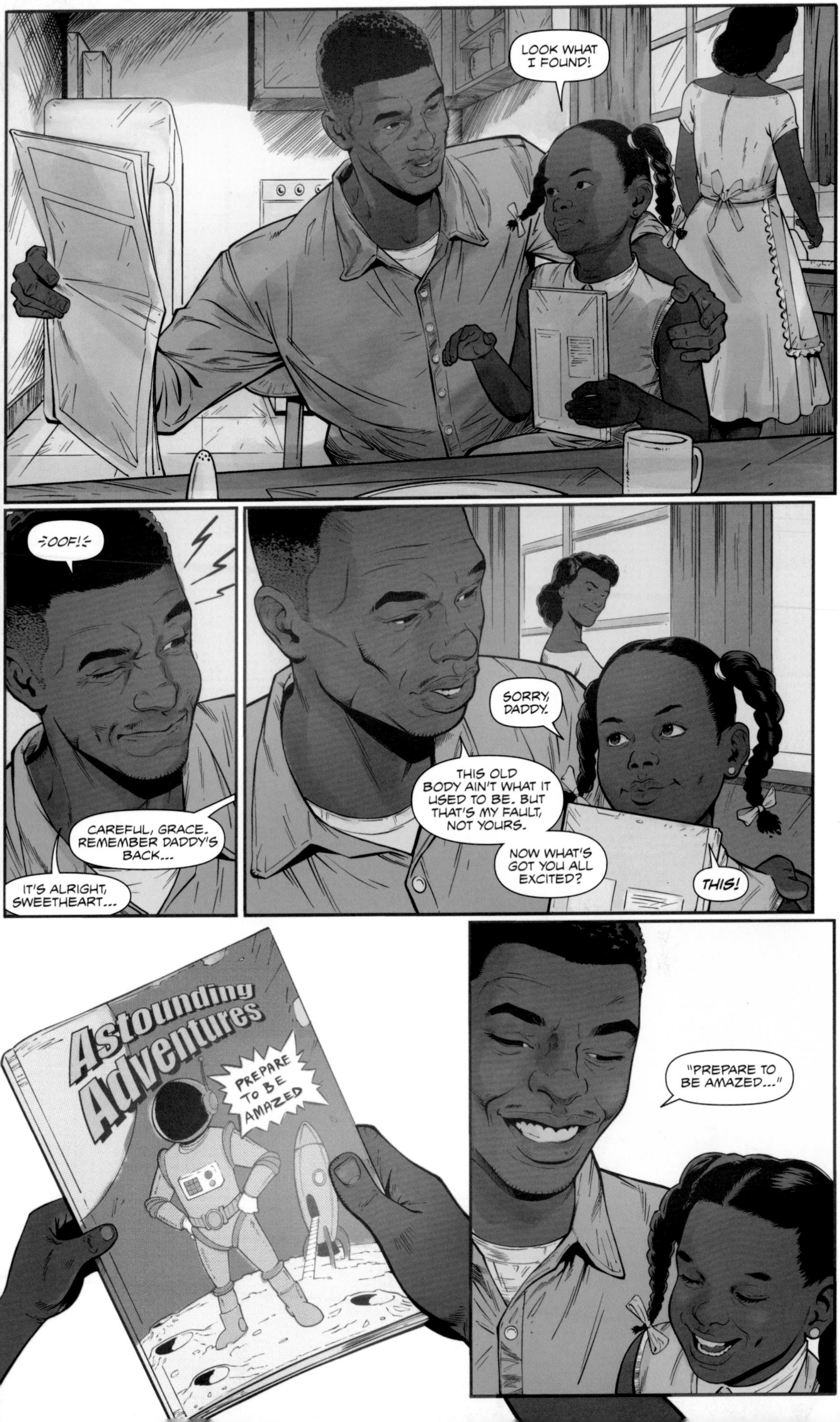
LOOK WHAT I FOUND!
OOF!
CAREFUL, GRACE. REMEMBER DADDY'S BACK...
IT'S ALRIGHT, SWEETHEART...
SORRY, DADDY.
THIS OLD BODY AIN'T WHAT IT USED TO BE. BUT THAT'S MY FAULT, NOT YOURS.
NOW WHAT'S GOT YOU ALL EXCITED?
THIS!
Astounding Adventures
PREPARE TO BE AMAZED
"PREPARE TO BE AMAZED..."

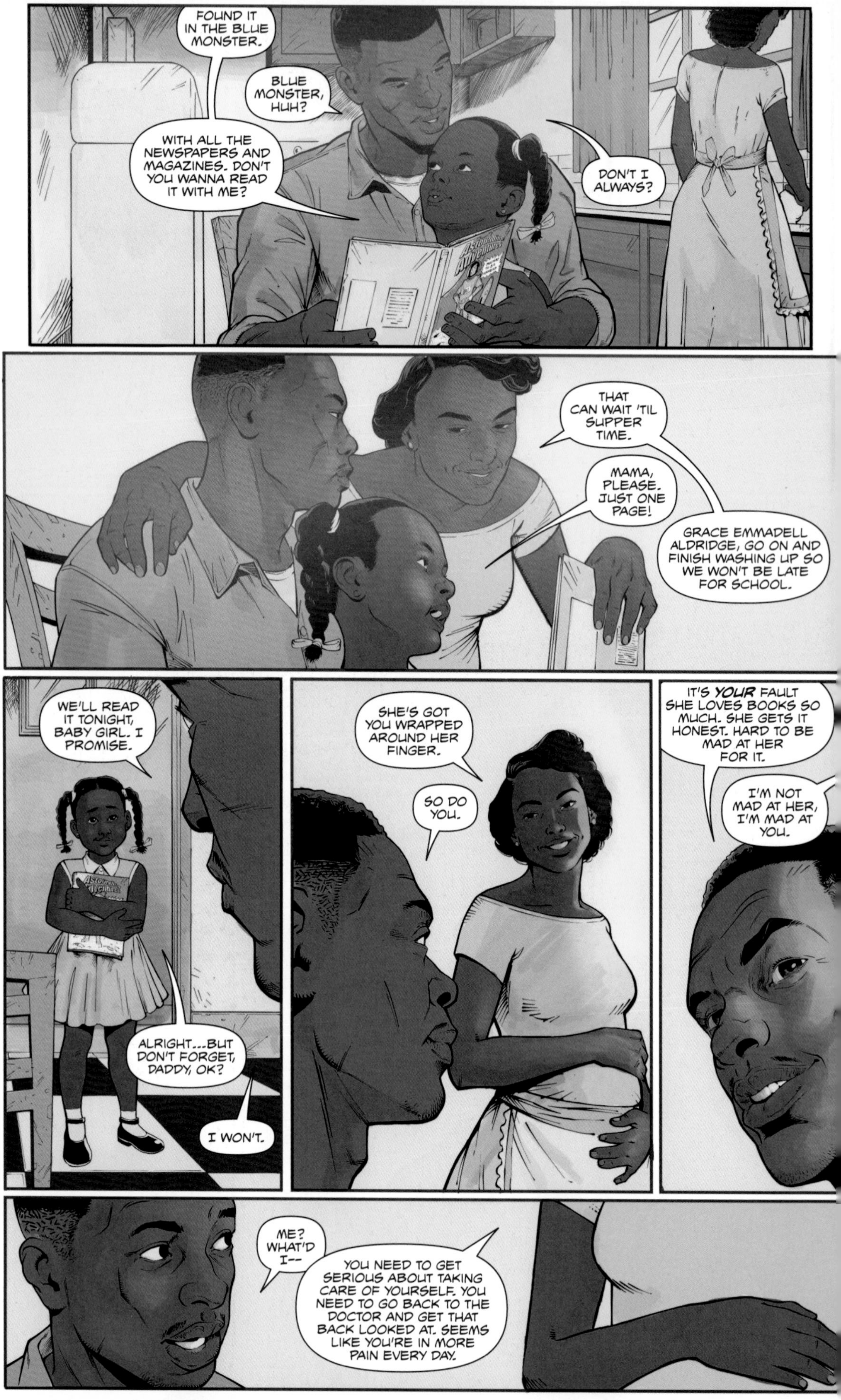
FOUND IT IN THE BLUE MONSTER.
BLUE MONSTER, HUH?
WITH ALL THE NEWSPAPERS AND MAGAZINES. DON'T YOU WANNA READ IT WITH ME?
DON'T I ALWAYS?
THAT CAN WAIT 'TIL SUPPER TIME.
MAMA, PLEASE. JUST ONE PAGE!
GRACE EMMADELL ALDRIDGE, GO ON AND FINISH WASHING UP SO WE WON'T BE LATE FOR SCHOOL.
WE'LL READ IT TONIGHT, BABY GIRL. I PROMISE.
ALRIGHT...BUT DON'T FORGET, DADDY, OK?
I WON'T.
SHE'S GOT YOU WRAPPED AROUND HER FINGER.
SO DO YOU.
IT'S *YOUR* FAULT SHE LOVES BOOKS SO MUCH. SHE GETS IT HONEST. HARD TO BE MAD AT HER FOR IT.
I'M NOT MAD AT HER, I'M MAD AT YOU.
ME? WHAT'D I--
YOU NEED TO GET SERIOUS ABOUT TAKING CARE OF YOURSELF. YOU NEED TO GO BACK TO THE DOCTOR AND GET THAT BACK LOOKED AT. SEEMS LIKE YOU'RE IN MORE PAIN EVERY DAY.

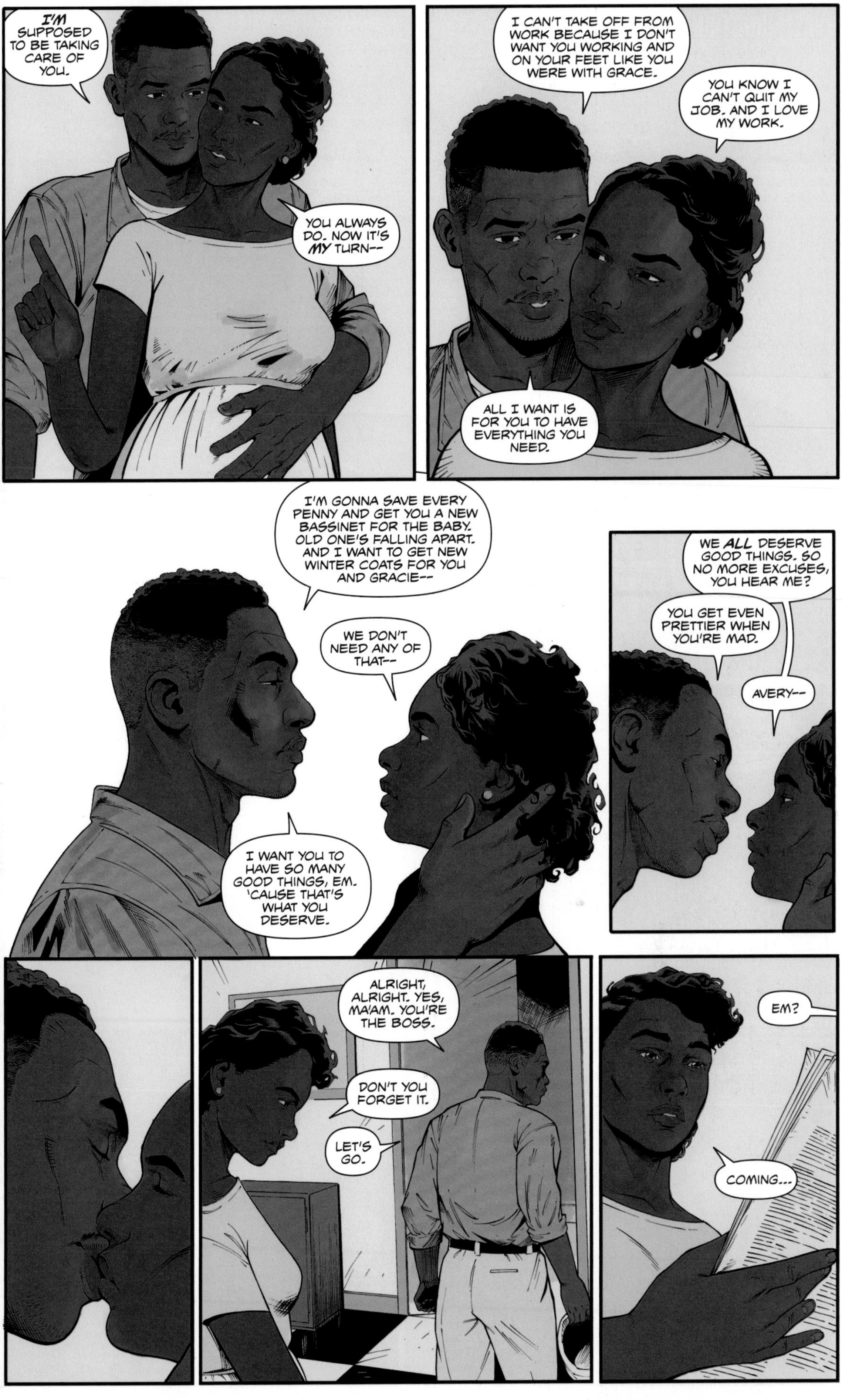
I'M SUPPOSED TO BE TAKING CARE OF YOU.
YOU ALWAYS DO. NOW IT'S MY TURN--
I CAN'T TAKE OFF FROM WORK BECAUSE I DON'T WANT YOU WORKING AND ON YOUR FEET LIKE YOU WERE WITH GRACE.
YOU KNOW I CAN'T QUIT MY JOB. AND I LOVE MY WORK.
ALL I WANT IS FOR YOU TO HAVE EVERYTHING YOU NEED.
I'M GONNA SAVE EVERY PENNY AND GET YOU A NEW BASSINET FOR THE BABY. OLD ONE'S FALLING APART. AND I WANT TO GET NEW WINTER COATS FOR YOU AND GRACIE--
WE DON'T NEED ANY OF THAT--
I WANT YOU TO HAVE SO MANY GOOD THINGS, EM. 'CAUSE THAT'S WHAT YOU DESERVE.
WE ALL DESERVE GOOD THINGS. SO NO MORE EXCUSES, YOU HEAR ME?
YOU GET EVEN PRETTIER WHEN YOU'RE MAD.
AVERY--
ALRIGHT, ALRIGHT. YES, MA'AM. YOU'RE THE BOSS.
DON'T YOU FORGET IT.
LET'S GO.
EM?
COMING...

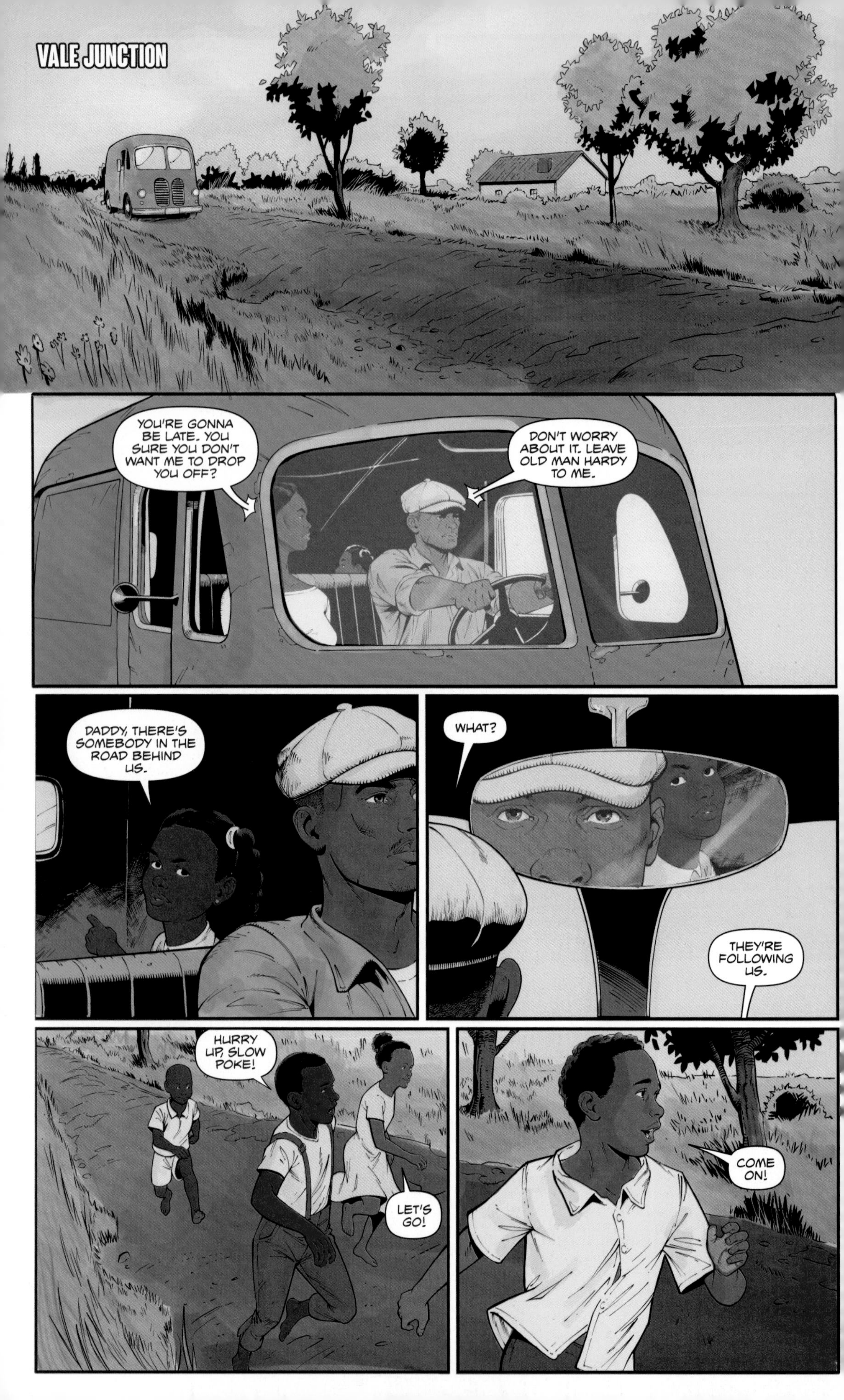
VALE JUNCTION
YOU'RE GONNA BE LATE. YOU SURE YOU DON'T WANT ME TO DROP YOU OFF?
DON'T WORRY ABOUT IT. LEAVE OLD MAN HARDY TO ME.
DADDY, THERE'S SOMEBODY IN THE ROAD BEHIND US.
WHAT?
THEY'RE FOLLOWING US.
HURRY UP, SLOW POKE!
LET'S GO!
COME ON!

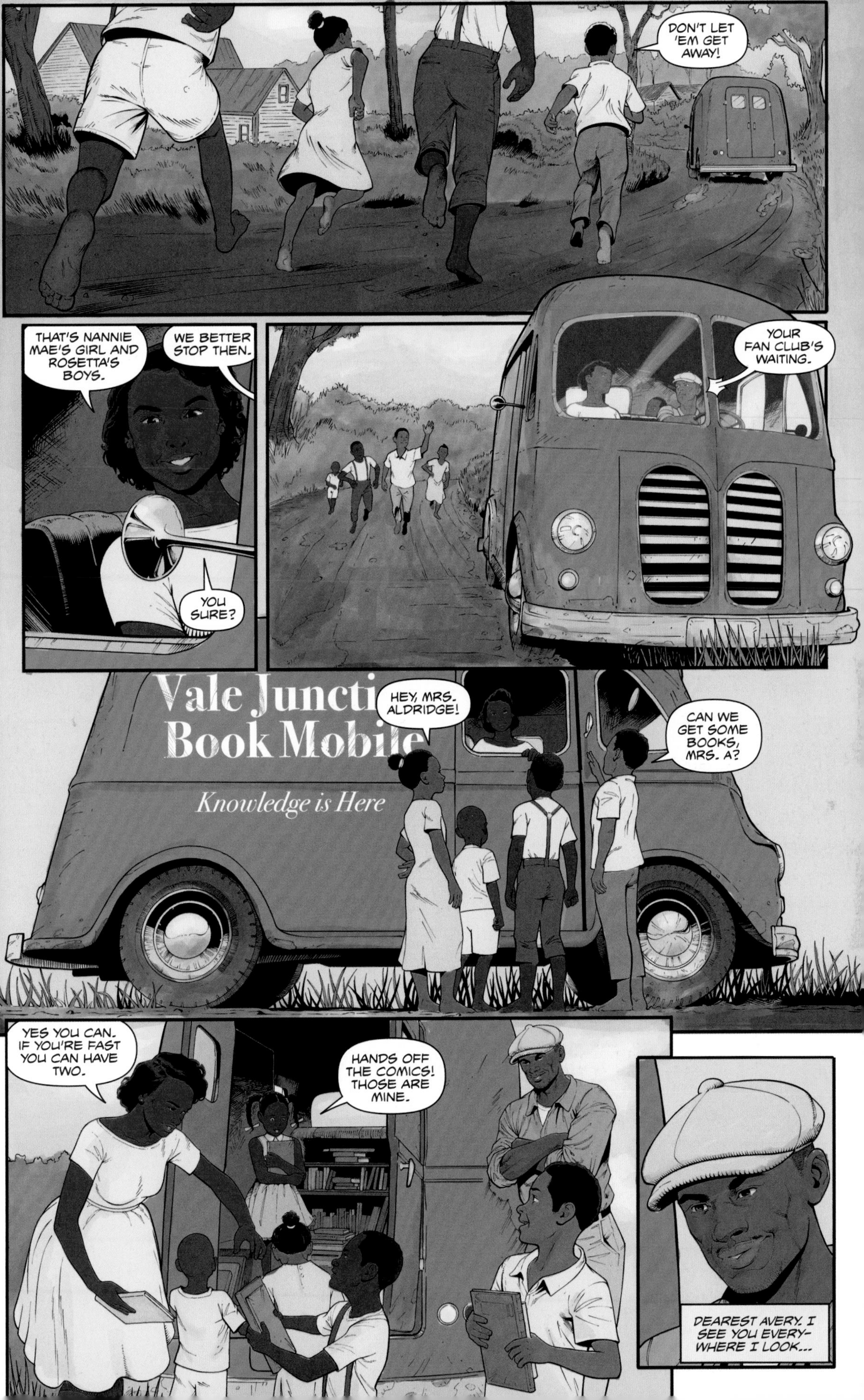
DON'T LET 'EM GET AWAY!
THAT'S NANNIE MAE'S GIRL AND ROSETTA'S BOYS.
WE BETTER STOP THEN.
YOU SURE?
YOUR FAN CLUB'S WAITING.
Vale Juncti
Book Mobile
Knowledge is Here
HEY, MRS. ALDRIDGE!
CAN WE GET SOME BOOKS, MRS. A?
YES YOU CAN. IF YOU'RE FAST YOU CAN HAVE TWO.
HANDS OFF THE COMICS! THOSE ARE MINE.
DEAREST AVERY. I SEE YOU EVERYWHERE I LOOK...

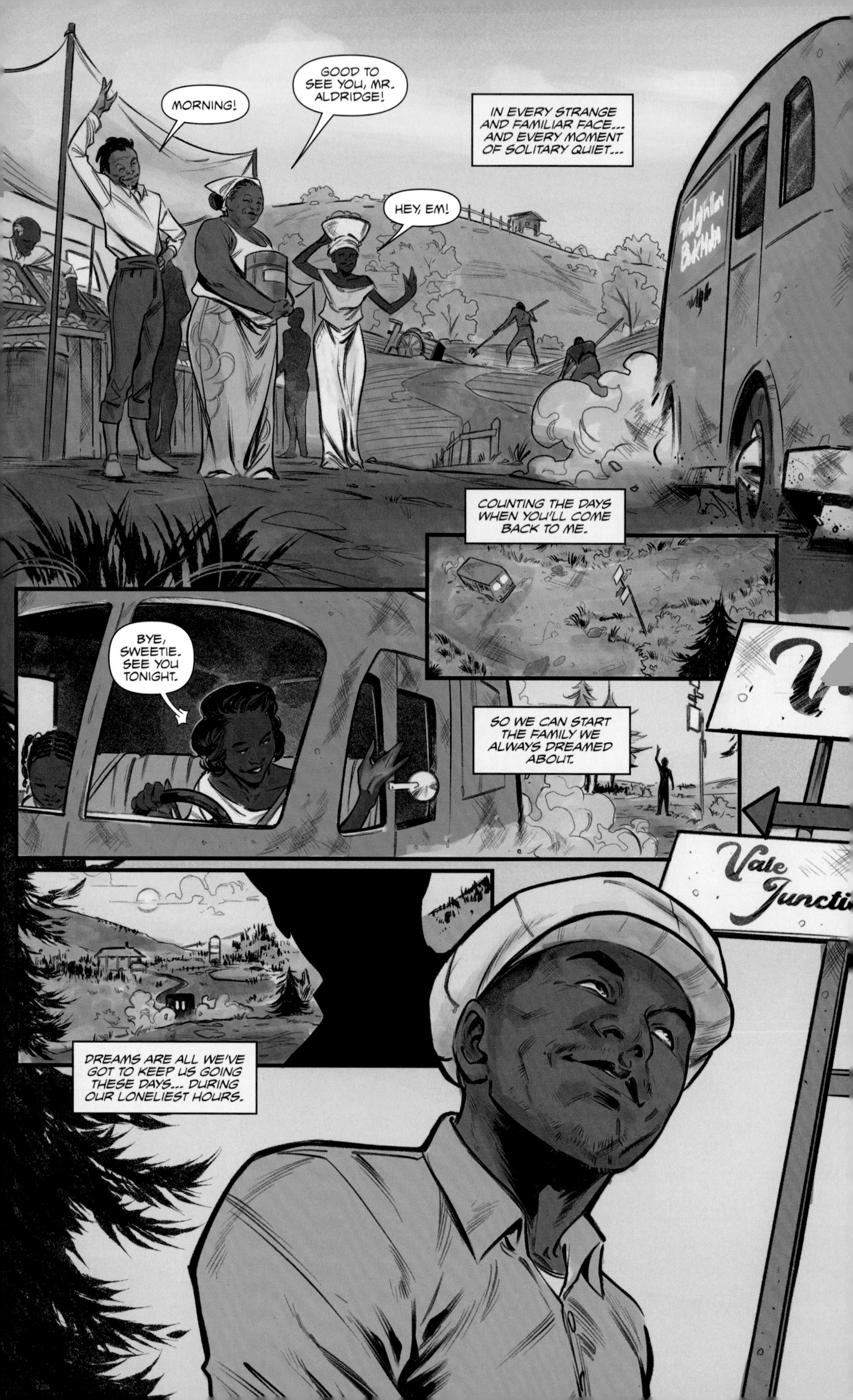
MORNING!
GOOD TO SEE YOU, MR. ALDRIDGE!
IN EVERY STRANGE AND FAMILIAR FACE... AND EVERY MOMENT OF SOLITARY QUIET...
HEY, EM!
COUNTING THE DAYS WHEN YOU'LL COME BACK TO ME.
BYE, SWEETIE. SEE YOU TONIGHT.
SO WE CAN START THE FAMILY WE ALWAYS DREAMED ABOUT.
Vale Juncti
DREAMS ARE ALL WE'VE GOT TO KEEP US GOING THESE DAYS... DURING OUR LONELIEST HOURS.

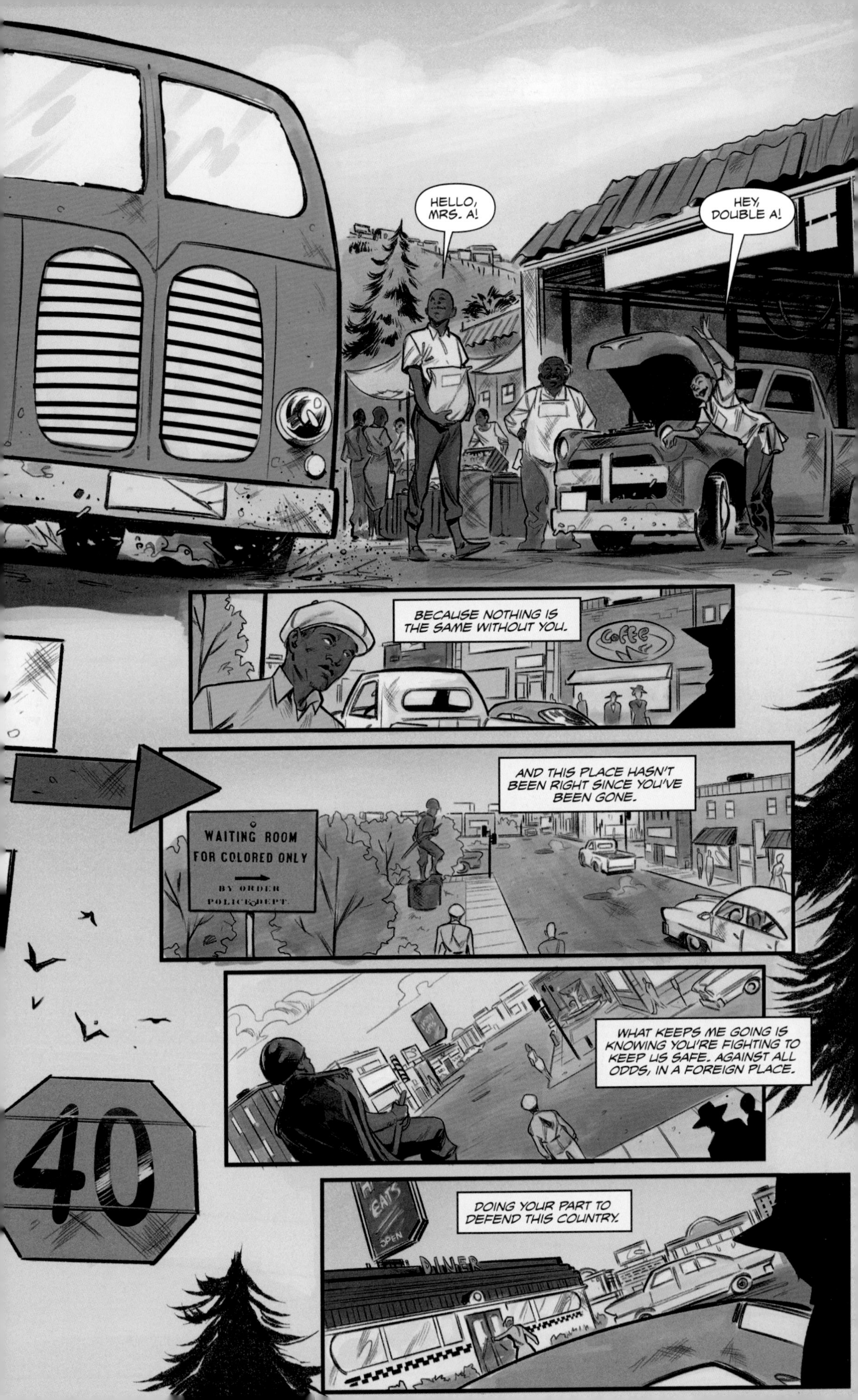
HELLO, MRS. A!
HEY, DOUBLE A!
BECAUSE NOTHING IS THE SAME WITHOUT YOU.
COFFEE
AND THIS PLACE HASN'T BEEN RIGHT SINCE YOU'VE BEEN GONE.
WAITING ROOM FOR COLORED ONLY
BY ORDER POLICE DEPT.
WHAT KEEPS ME GOING IS KNOWING YOU'RE FIGHTING TO KEEP US SAFE. AGAINST ALL ODDS, IN A FOREIGN PLACE.
40
DOING YOUR PART TO DEFEND THIS COUNTRY.
EATS
OPEN
DINER

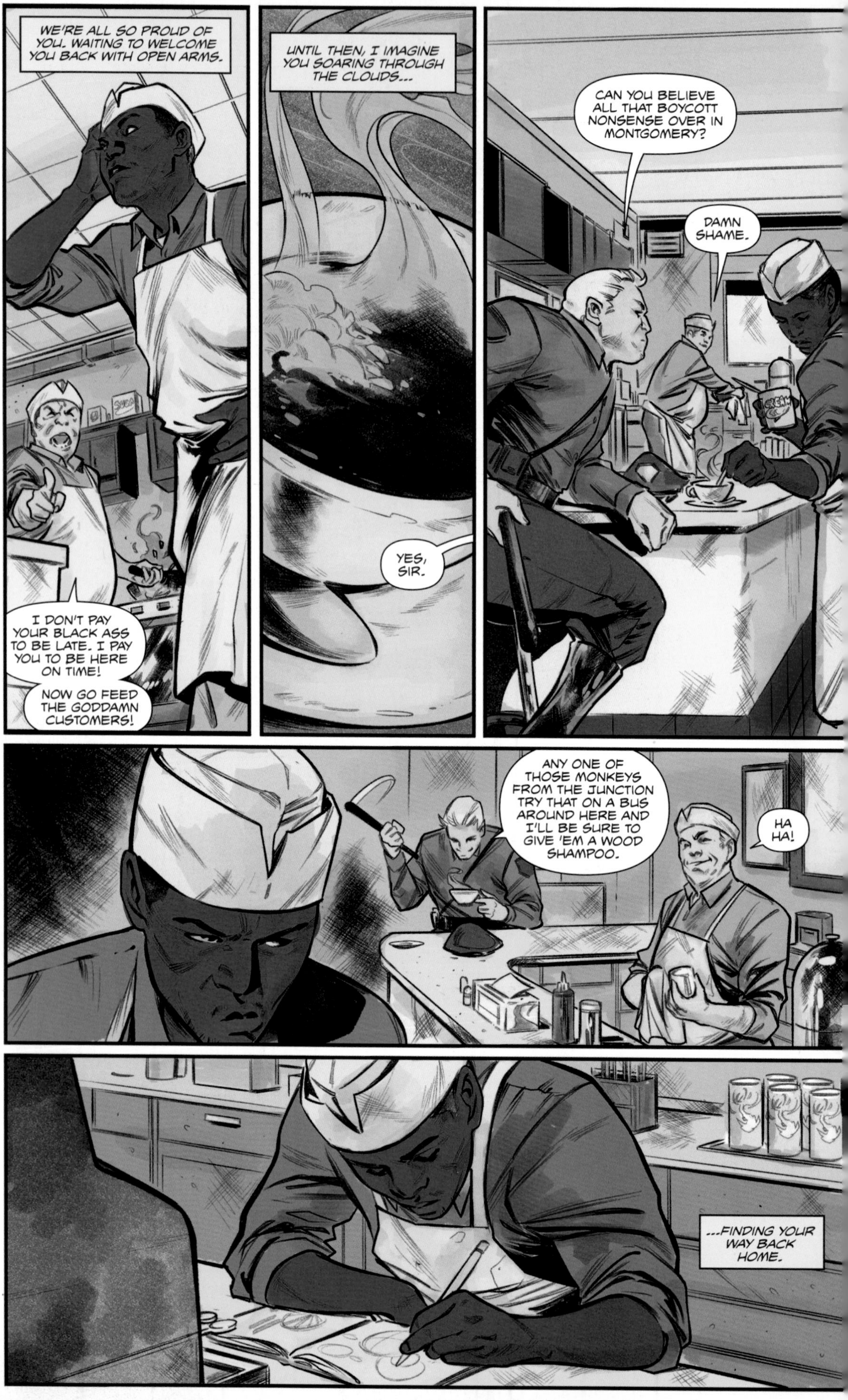
WE'RE ALL SO PROUD OF YOU. WAITING TO WELCOME YOU BACK WITH OPEN ARMS.
I DON'T PAY YOUR BLACK ASS TO BE LATE. I PAY YOU TO BE HERE ON TIME!
NOW GO FEED THE GODDAMN CUSTOMERS!
UNTIL THEN, I IMAGINE YOU SOARING THROUGH THE CLOUDS...
YES, SIR.
CAN YOU BELIEVE ALL THAT BOYCOTT NONSENSE OVER IN MONTGOMERY?
DAMN SHAME.
ANY ONE OF THOSE MONKEYS FROM THE JUNCTION TRY THAT ON A BUS AROUND HERE AND I'LL BE SURE TO GIVE 'EM A WOOD SHAMPOO.
HA HA!
...FINDING YOUR WAY BACK HOME.

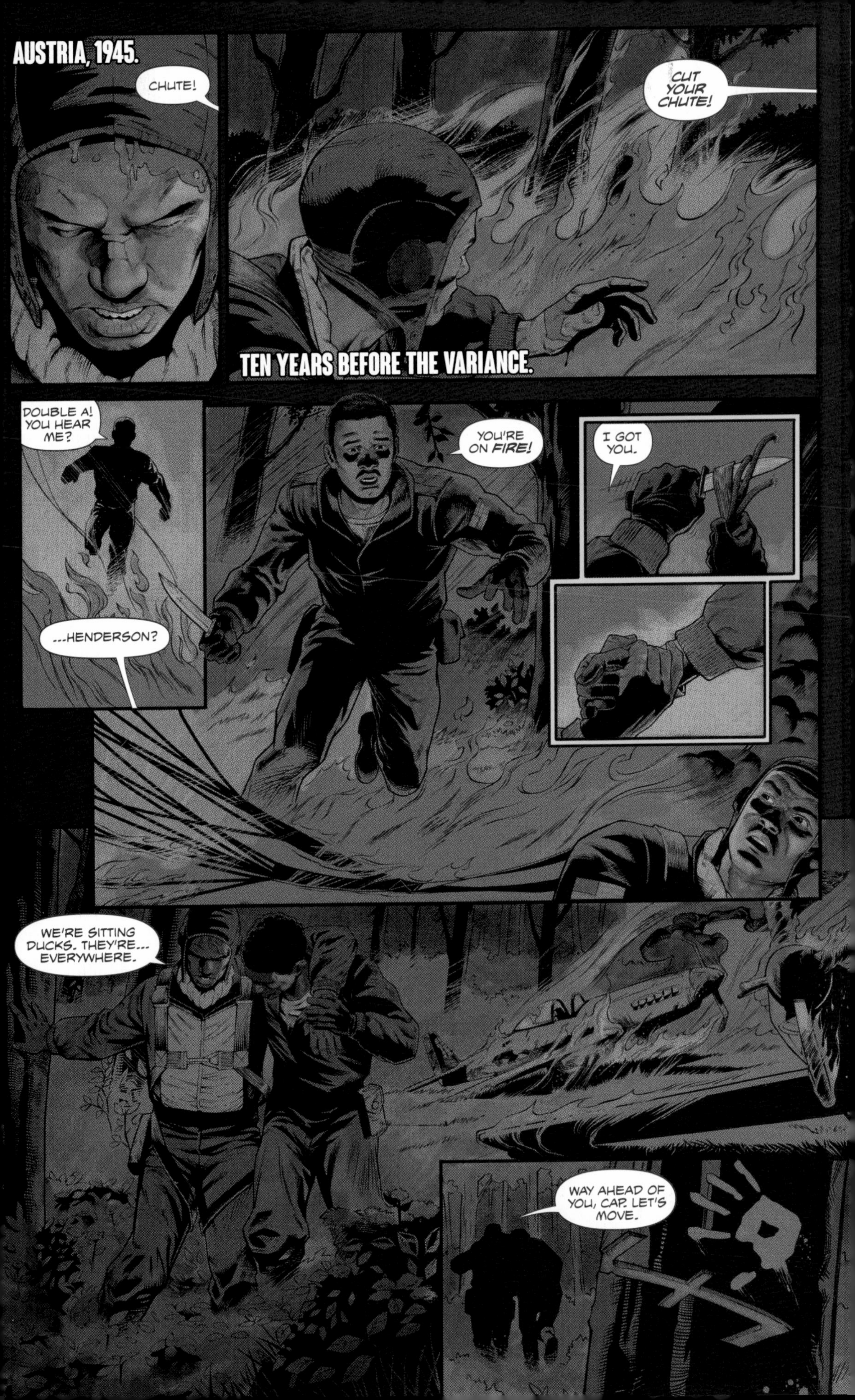
AUSTRIA, 1945.
CHUTE!
CUT YOUR CHUTE!
TEN YEARS BEFORE THE VARIANCE.
DOUBLE A! YOU HEAR ME?
...HENDERSON?
YOU'RE ON FIRE!
I GOT YOU.
WE'RE SITTING DUCKS. THEY'RE... EVERYWHERE.
WAY AHEAD OF YOU, CAP. LET'S MOVE.

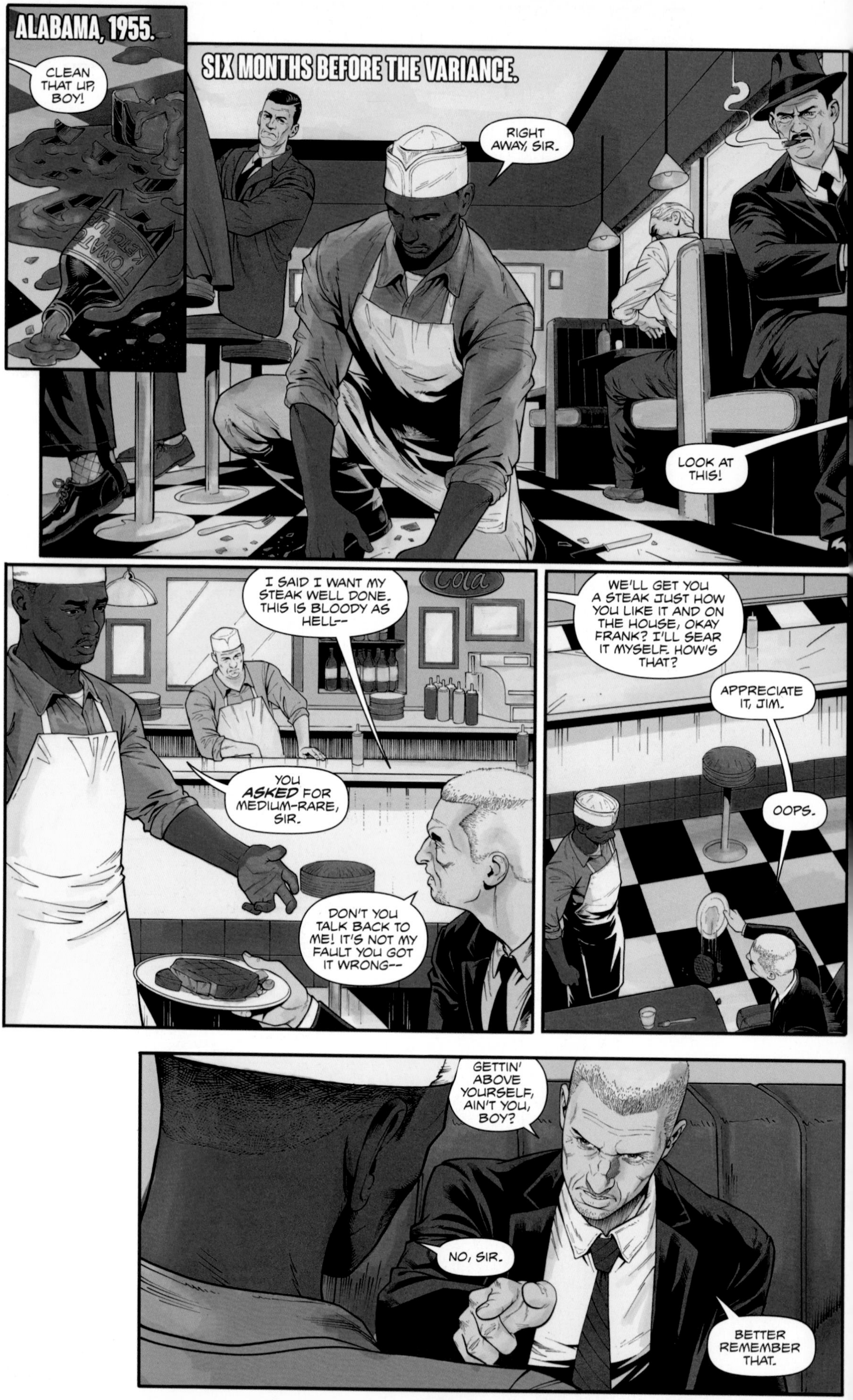
ALABAMA, 1955.
CLEAN THAT UP, BOY!
TOMATO KETCHUP
SIX MONTHS BEFORE THE VARIANCE.
RIGHT AWAY, SIR.
LOOK AT THIS!
Cola
I SAID I WANT MY STEAK WELL DONE. THIS IS BLOODY AS HELL--
YOU ASKED FOR MEDIUM-RARE, SIR.
DON'T YOU TALK BACK TO ME! IT'S NOT MY FAULT YOU GOT IT WRONG--
WE'LL GET YOU A STEAK JUST HOW YOU LIKE IT AND ON THE HOUSE, OKAY FRANK? I'LL SEAR IT MYSELF. HOW'S THAT?
APPRECIATE IT, JIM.
OOPS.
GETTIN' ABOVE YOURSELF, AIN'T YOU, BOY?
NO, SIR.
BETTER REMEMBER THAT.

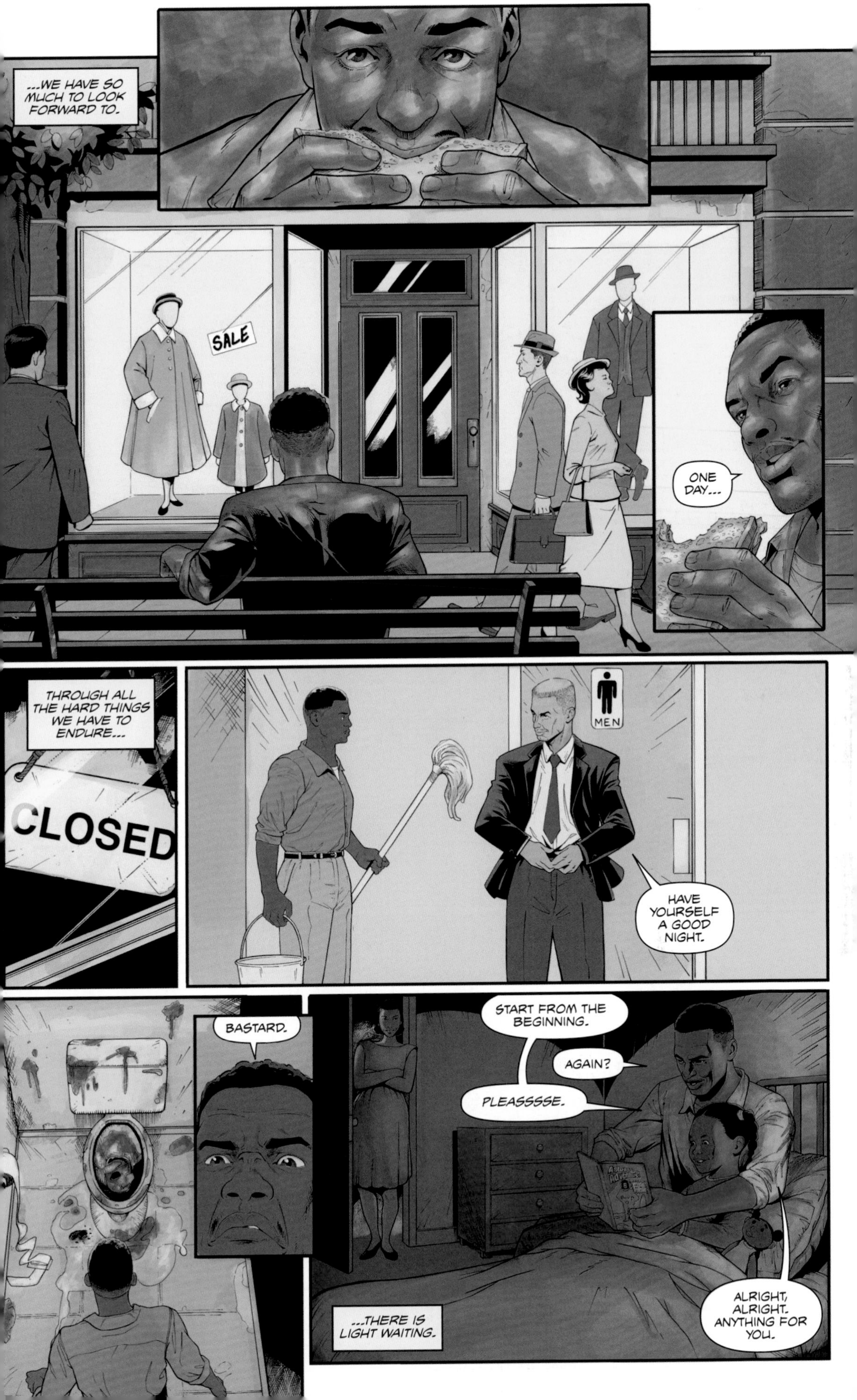
...WE HAVE SO MUCH TO LOOK FORWARD TO.
SALE
ONE DAY...
THROUGH ALL THE HARD THINGS WE HAVE TO ENDURE...
CLOSED
MEN
HAVE YOURSELF A GOOD NIGHT.
BASTARD.
START FROM THE BEGINNING.
AGAIN?
PLEASSSSE.
ALRIGHT, ALRIGHT. ANYTHING FOR YOU.
...THERE IS LIGHT WAITING.

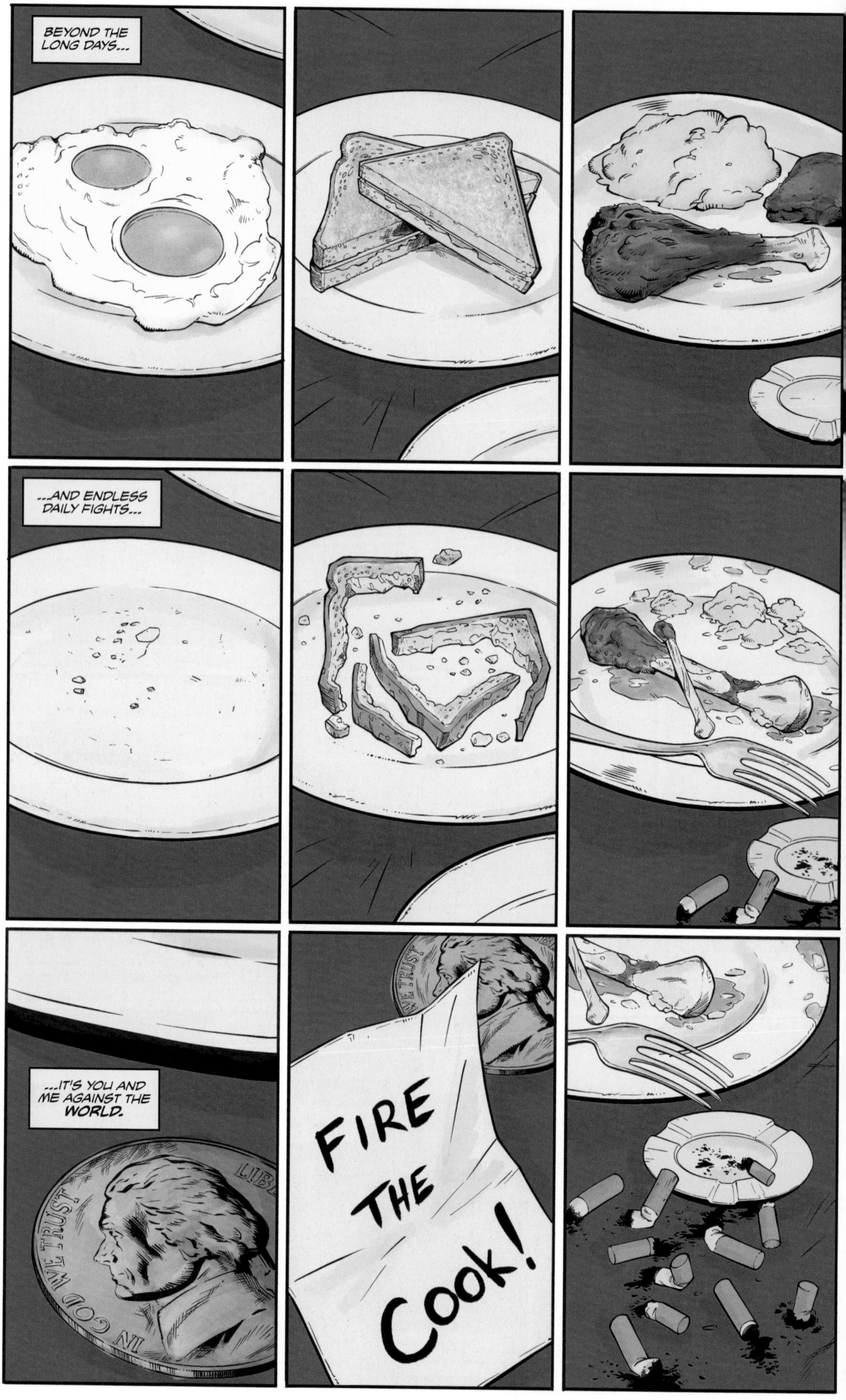
BEYOND THE LONG DAYS...
...AND ENDLESS DAILY FIGHTS...
...IT'S YOU AND ME AGAINST THE WORLD.
IN GOD WE TRUST
LIBE
FIRE THE COOK!

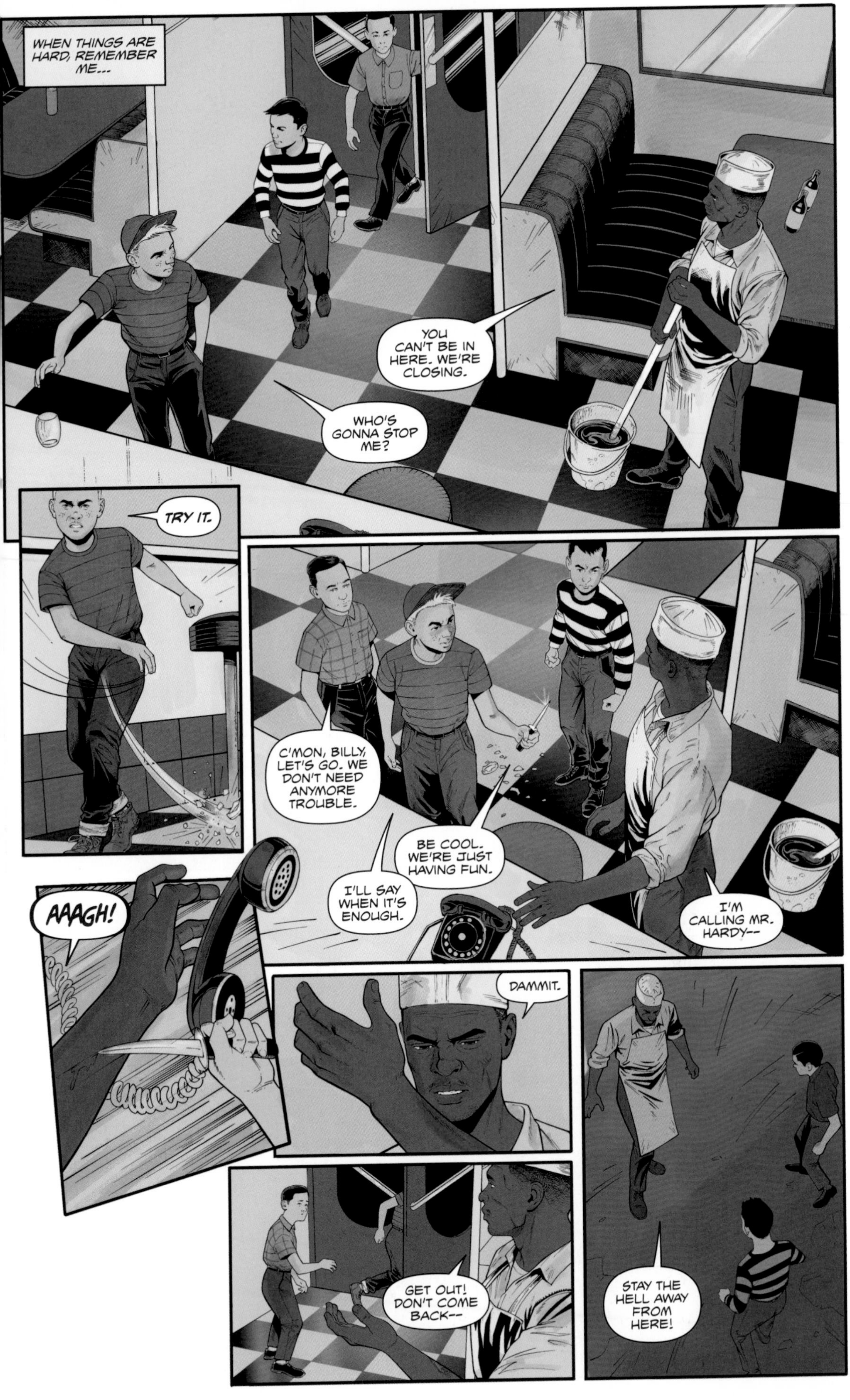
WHEN THINGS ARE HARD, REMEMBER ME...
YOU CAN'T BE IN HERE. WE'RE CLOSING.
WHO'S GONNA STOP ME?
TRY IT.
C'MON, BILLY, LET'S GO. WE DON'T NEED ANYMORE TROUBLE.
I'LL SAY WHEN IT'S ENOUGH.
BE COOL. WE'RE JUST HAVING FUN.
I'M CALLING MR. HARDY--
AAAGH!
DAMMIT.
GET OUT! DON'T COME BACK--
STAY THE HELL AWAY FROM HERE!

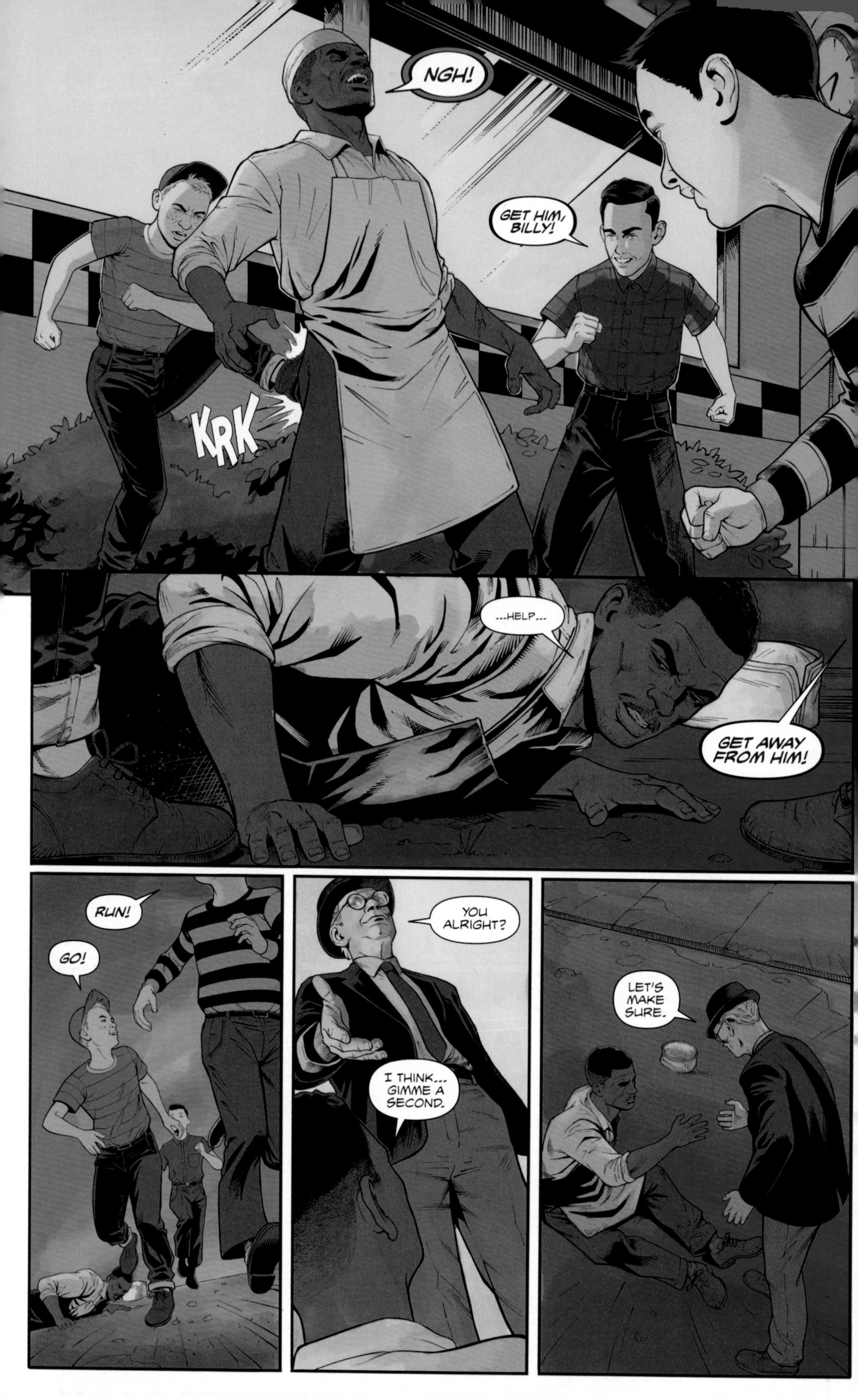
NGH!
GET HIM, BILLY!
KRK
...HELP...
GET AWAY FROM HIM!
RUN!
GO!
YOU ALRIGHT?
I THINK... GIMME A SECOND.
LET'S MAKE SURE.

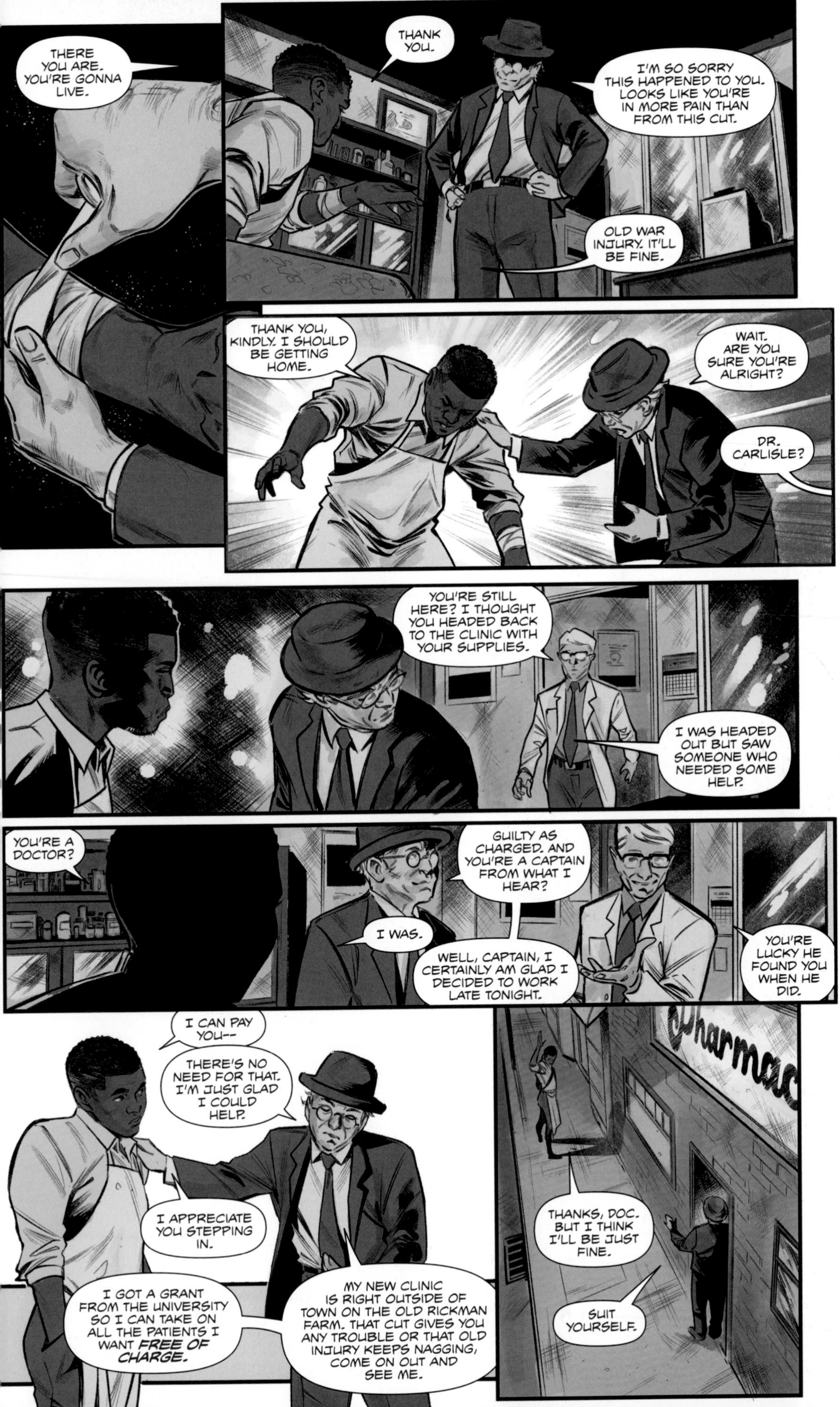
THERE YOU ARE. YOU'RE GONNA LIVE.
THANK YOU.
I'M SO SORRY THIS HAPPENED TO YOU. LOOKS LIKE YOU'RE IN MORE PAIN THAN FROM THIS CUT.
OLD WAR INJURY. IT'LL BE FINE.
THANK YOU, KINDLY. I SHOULD BE GETTING HOME.
WAIT. ARE YOU SURE YOU'RE ALRIGHT?
DR. CARLISLE?
YOU'RE STILL HERE? I THOUGHT YOU HEADED BACK TO THE CLINIC WITH YOUR SUPPLIES.
I WAS HEADED OUT BUT SAW SOMEONE WHO NEEDED SOME HELP.
YOU'RE A DOCTOR?
GUILTY AS CHARGED. AND YOU'RE A CAPTAIN FROM WHAT I HEAR?
I WAS.
WELL, CAPTAIN, I CERTAINLY AM GLAD I DECIDED TO WORK LATE TONIGHT.
YOU'RE LUCKY HE FOUND YOU WHEN HE DID.
I CAN PAY YOU--
THERE'S NO NEED FOR THAT. I'M JUST GLAD I COULD HELP.
I APPRECIATE YOU STEPPING IN.
I GOT A GRANT FROM THE UNIVERSITY SO I CAN TAKE ON ALL THE PATIENTS I WANT ***FREE OF CHARGE.***
MY NEW CLINIC IS RIGHT OUTSIDE OF TOWN ON THE OLD RICKMAN FARM. THAT CUT GIVES YOU ANY TROUBLE OR THAT OLD INJURY KEEPS NAGGING, COME ON OUT AND SEE ME.
Pharmac
THANKS, DOC. BUT I THINK I'LL BE JUST FINE.
SUIT YOURSELF.

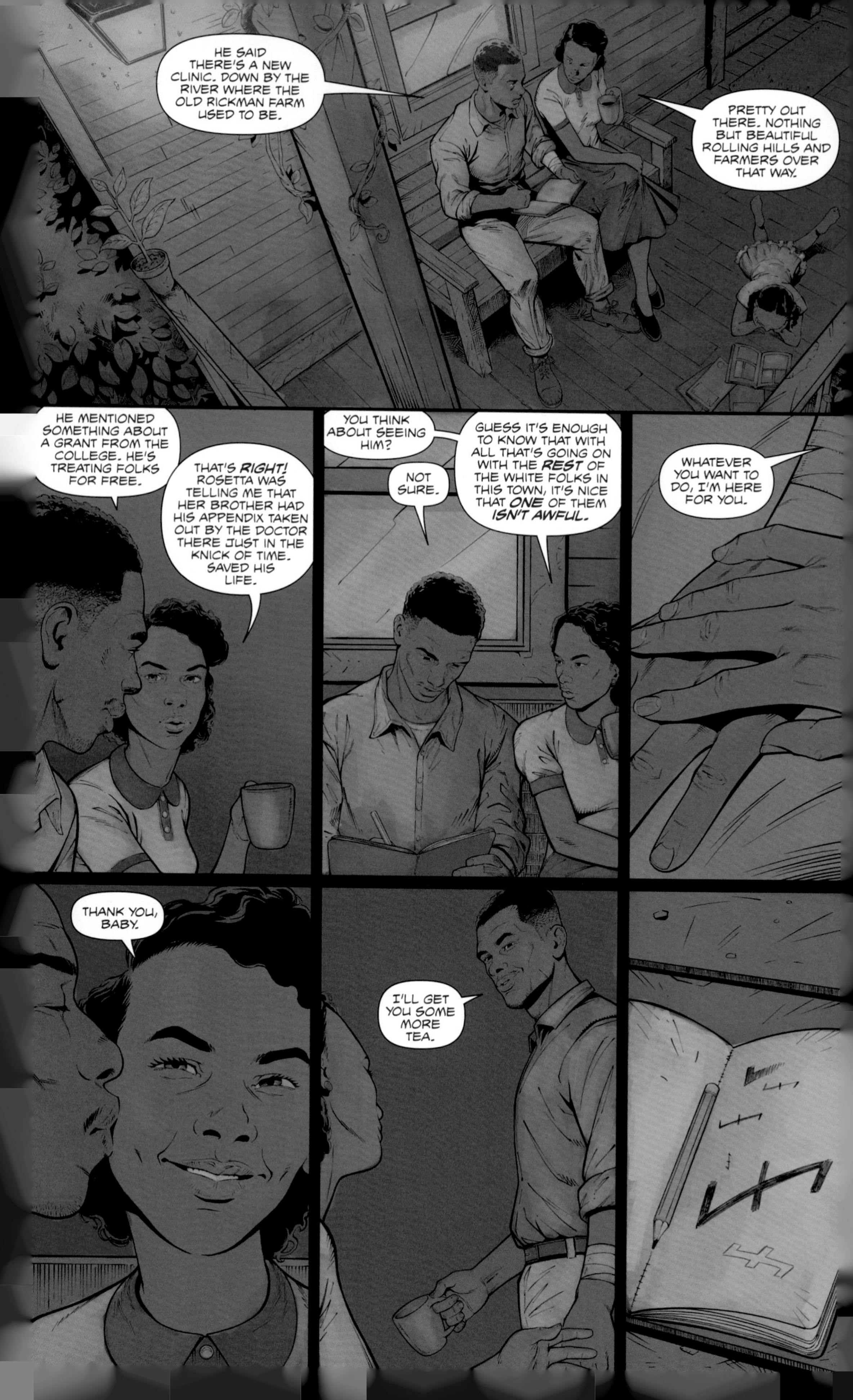

HE SAID THERE'S A NEW CLINIC. DOWN BY THE RIVER WHERE THE OLD RICKMAN FARM USED TO BE.
PRETTY OUT THERE. NOTHING BUT BEAUTIFUL ROLLING HILLS AND FARMERS OVER THAT WAY.
HE MENTIONED SOMETHING ABOUT A GRANT FROM THE COLLEGE. HE'S TREATING FOLKS FOR FREE.
THAT'S RIGHT! ROSETTA WAS TELLING ME THAT HER BROTHER HAD HIS APPENDIX TAKEN OUT BY THE DOCTOR THERE JUST IN THE KNICK OF TIME. SAVED HIS LIFE.
YOU THINK ABOUT SEEING HIM?
NOT SURE.
GUESS IT'S ENOUGH TO KNOW THAT WITH ALL THAT'S GOING ON WITH THE REST OF THE WHITE FOLKS IN THIS TOWN, IT'S NICE THAT ONE OF THEM ISN'T AWFUL.
WHATEVER YOU WANT TO DO, I'M HERE FOR YOU.
THANK YOU, BABY.
I'LL GET YOU SOME MORE TEA.

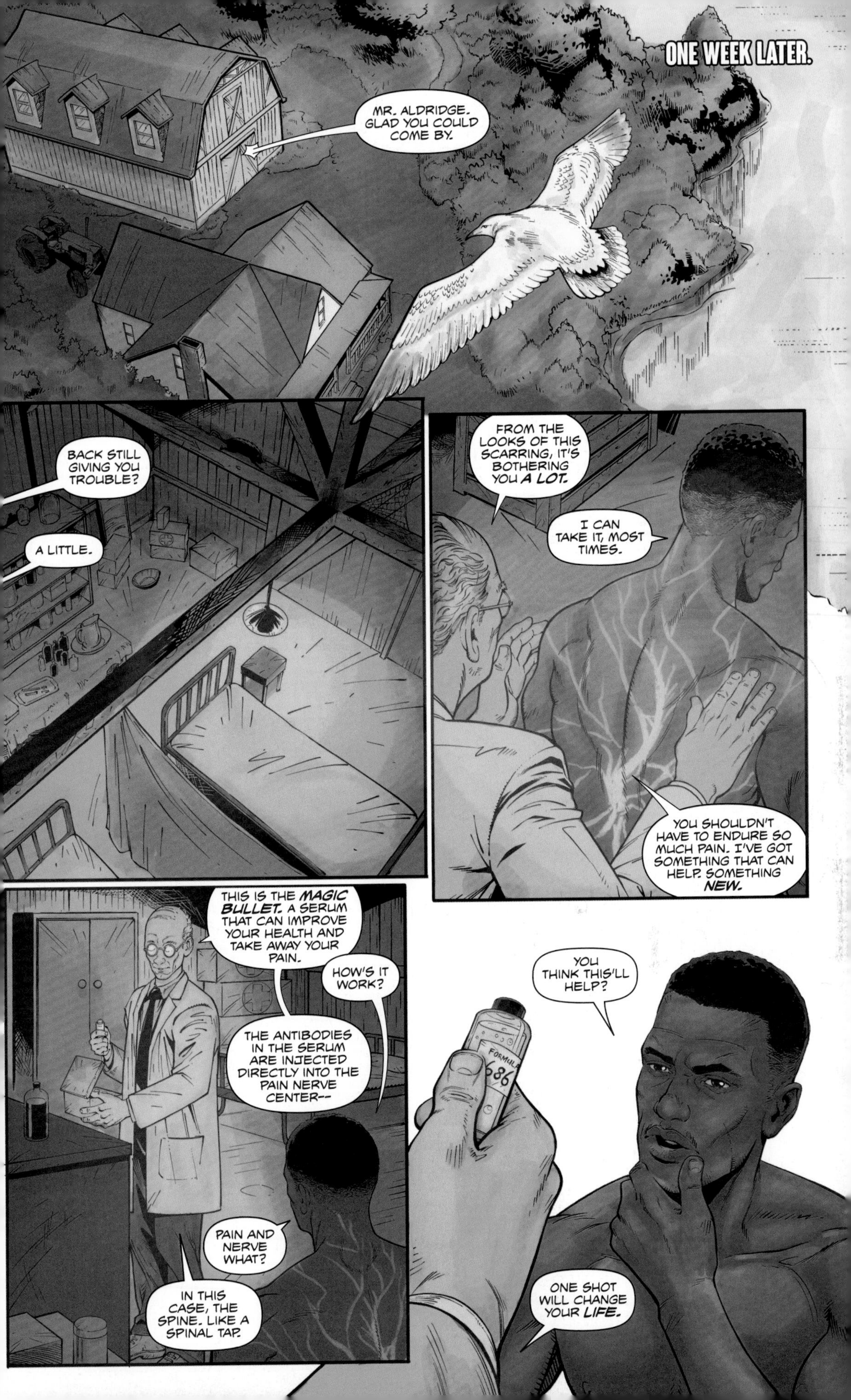
ONE WEEK LATER.
MR. ALDRIDGE. GLAD YOU COULD COME BY.
BACK STILL GIVING YOU TROUBLE?
A LITTLE.
FROM THE LOOKS OF THIS SCARRING, IT'S BOTHERING YOU *A LOT.*
I CAN TAKE IT, MOST TIMES.
YOU SHOULDN'T HAVE TO ENDURE SO MUCH PAIN. I'VE GOT SOMETHING THAT CAN HELP. SOMETHING *NEW.*
THIS IS THE *MAGIC BULLET.* A SERUM THAT CAN IMPROVE YOUR HEALTH AND TAKE AWAY YOUR PAIN.
HOW'S IT WORK?
THE ANTIBODIES IN THE SERUM ARE INJECTED DIRECTLY INTO THE PAIN NERVE CENTER--
PAIN AND NERVE WHAT?
IN THIS CASE, THE SPINE. LIKE A SPINAL TAP.
YOU THINK THIS'LL HELP?
FORMULA 686
ONE SHOT WILL CHANGE YOUR *LIFE.*

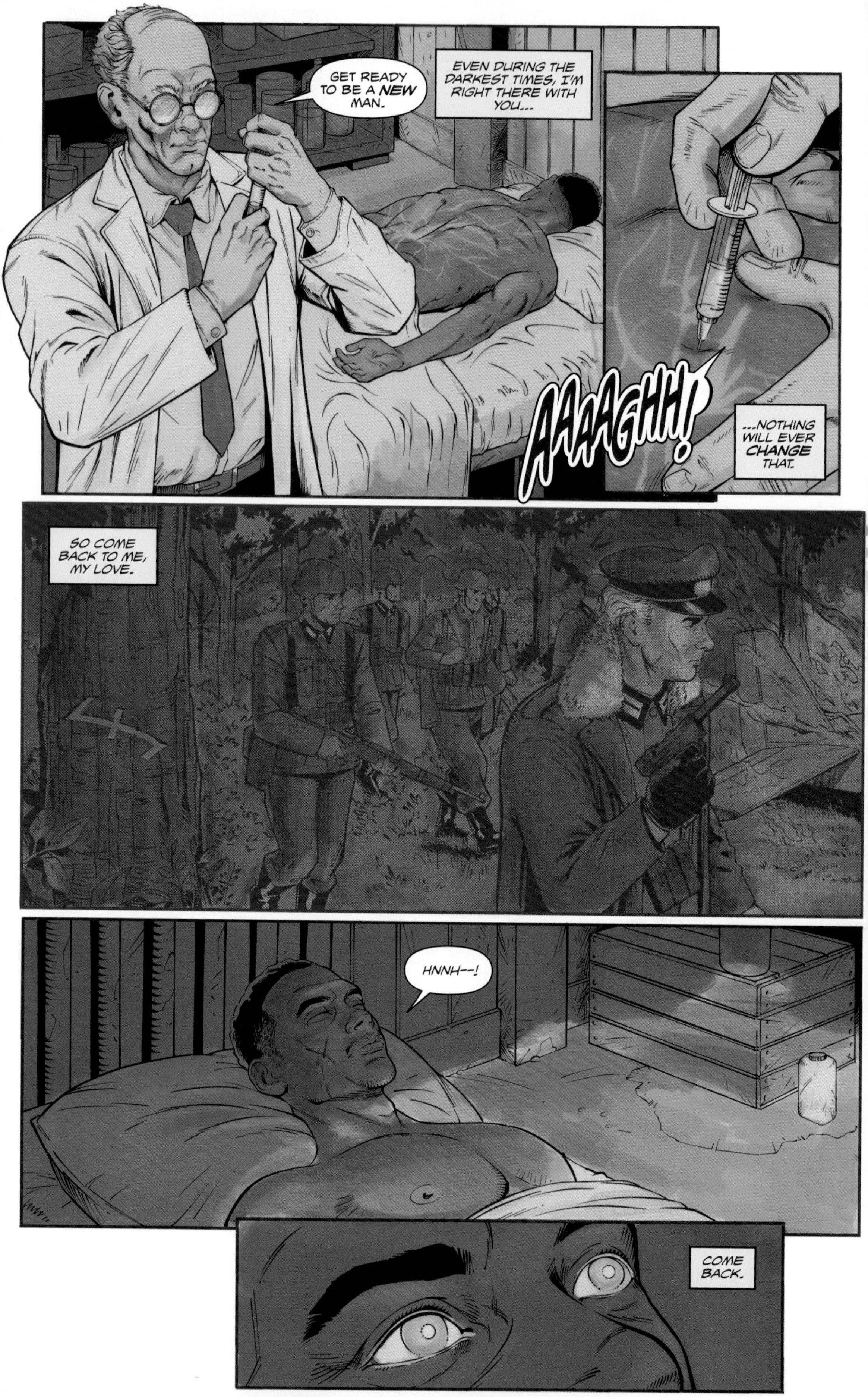
GET READY TO BE A **NEW** MAN.
EVEN DURING THE DARKEST TIMES, I'M RIGHT THERE WITH YOU...
AAAAGHH!
...NOTHING WILL EVER **CHANGE** THAT.
SO COME BACK TO ME, MY LOVE.
HNNH--!
COME BACK.

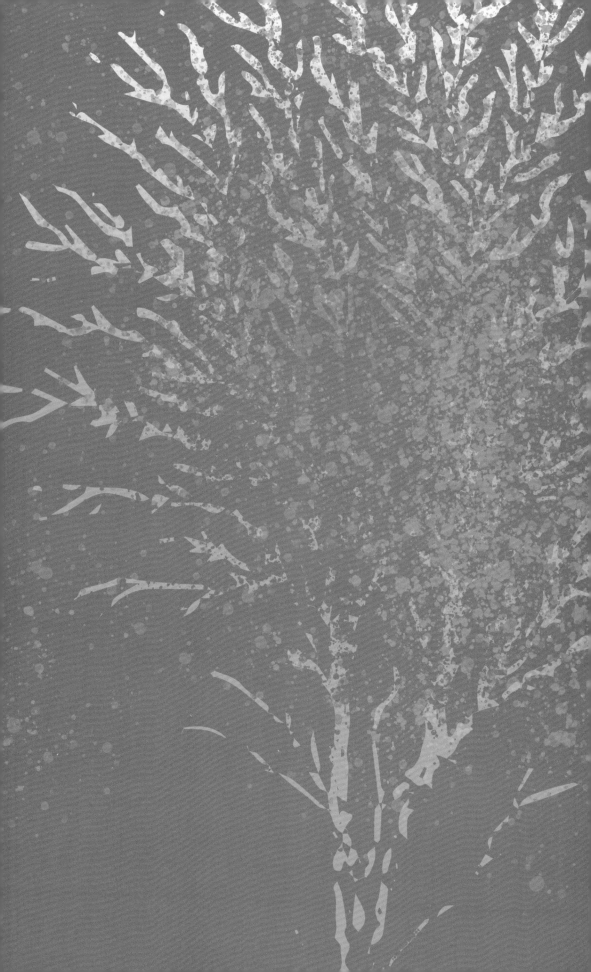

CHAPTER THREE

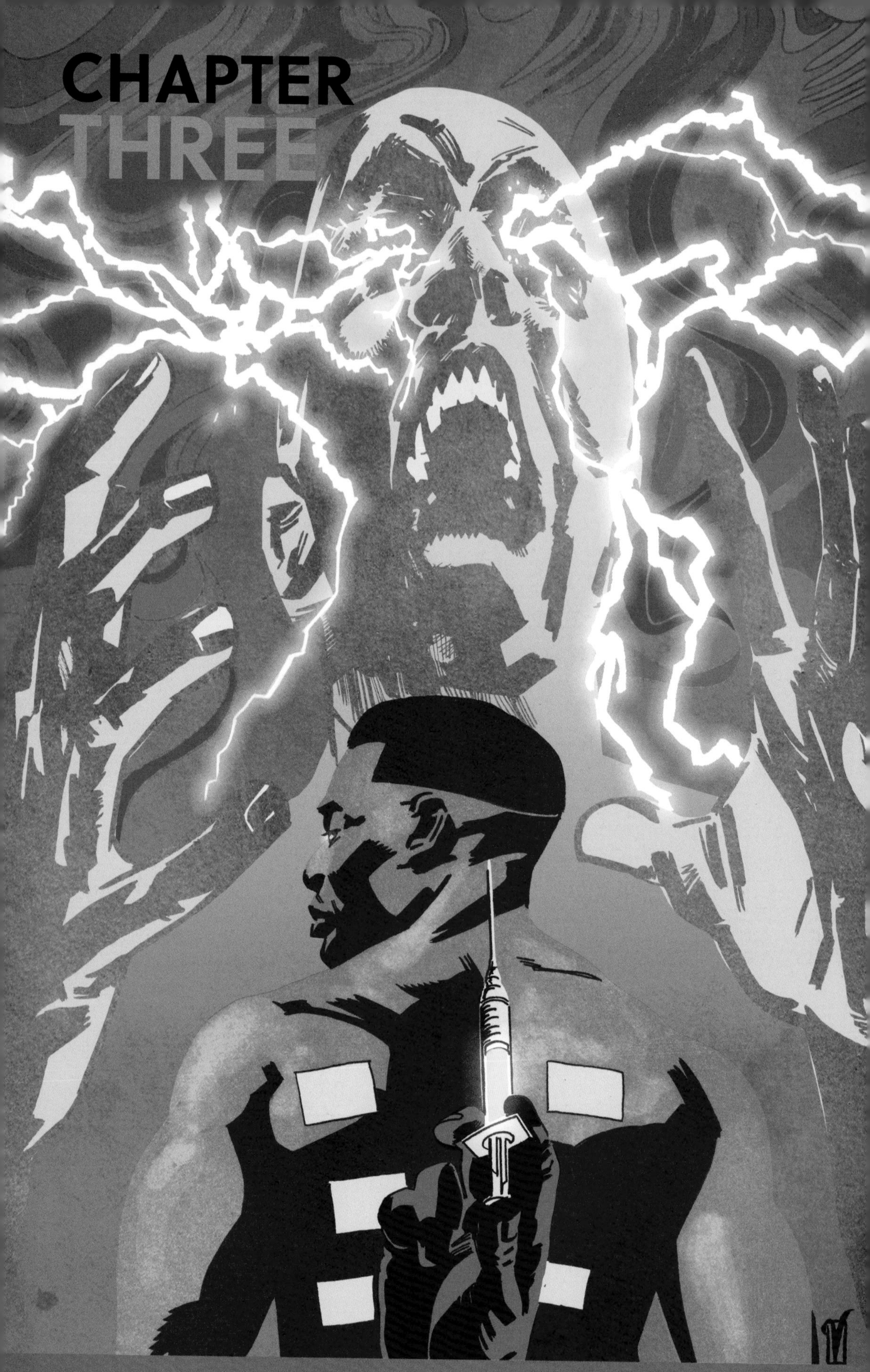

Issue #3 Cover
VALENTINE DE LANDRO

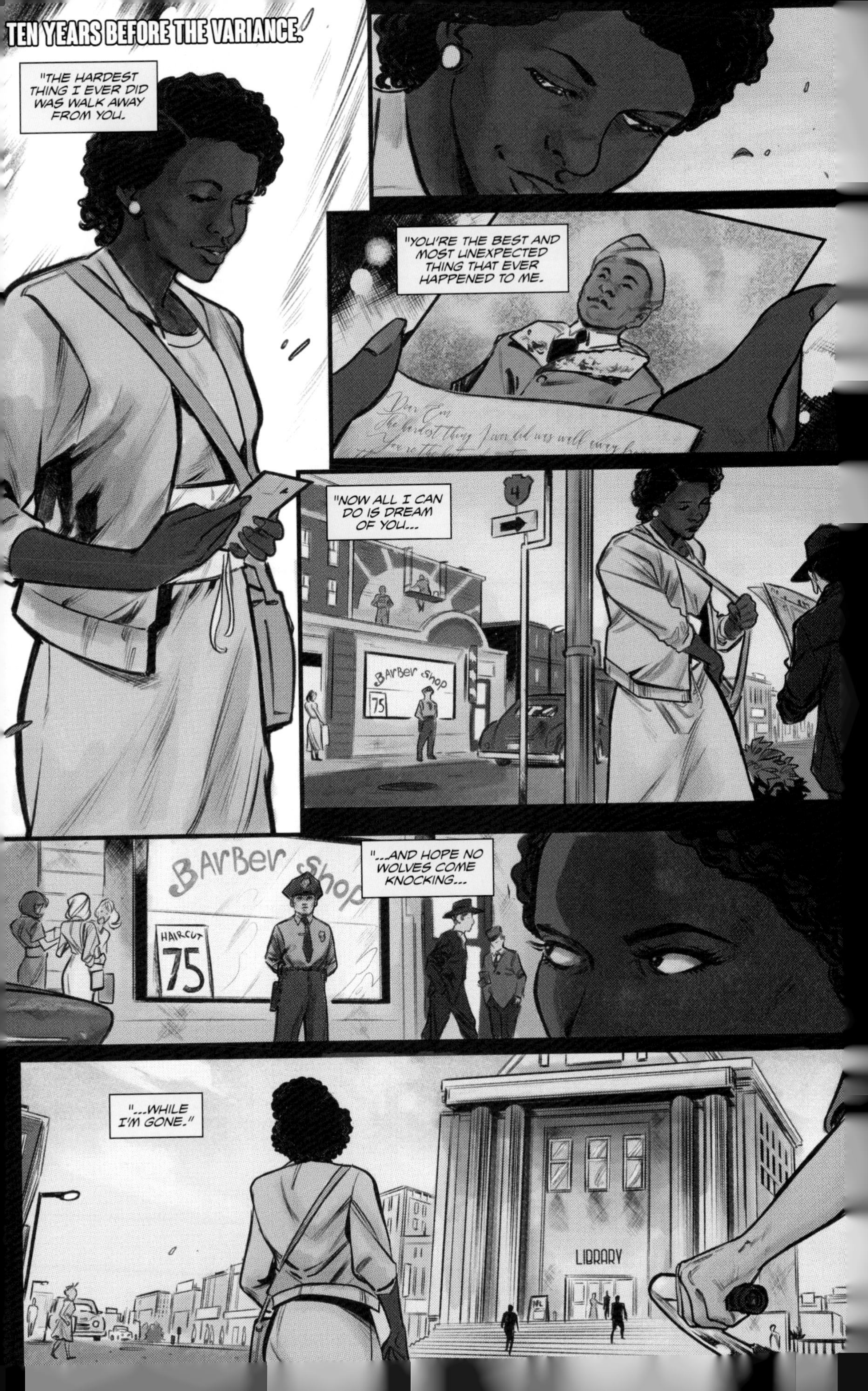
TEN YEARS BEFORE THE VARIANCE.
"THE HARDEST THING I EVER DID WAS WALK AWAY FROM YOU.
"YOU'RE THE BEST AND MOST UNEXPECTED THING THAT EVER HAPPENED TO ME.
"NOW ALL I CAN DO IS DREAM OF YOU...
4
BArBer Shop
75
BArBer Shop
HAIRCUT
75
"...AND HOPE NO WOLVES COME KNOCKING...
"...WHILE I'M GONE."
LIBRARY

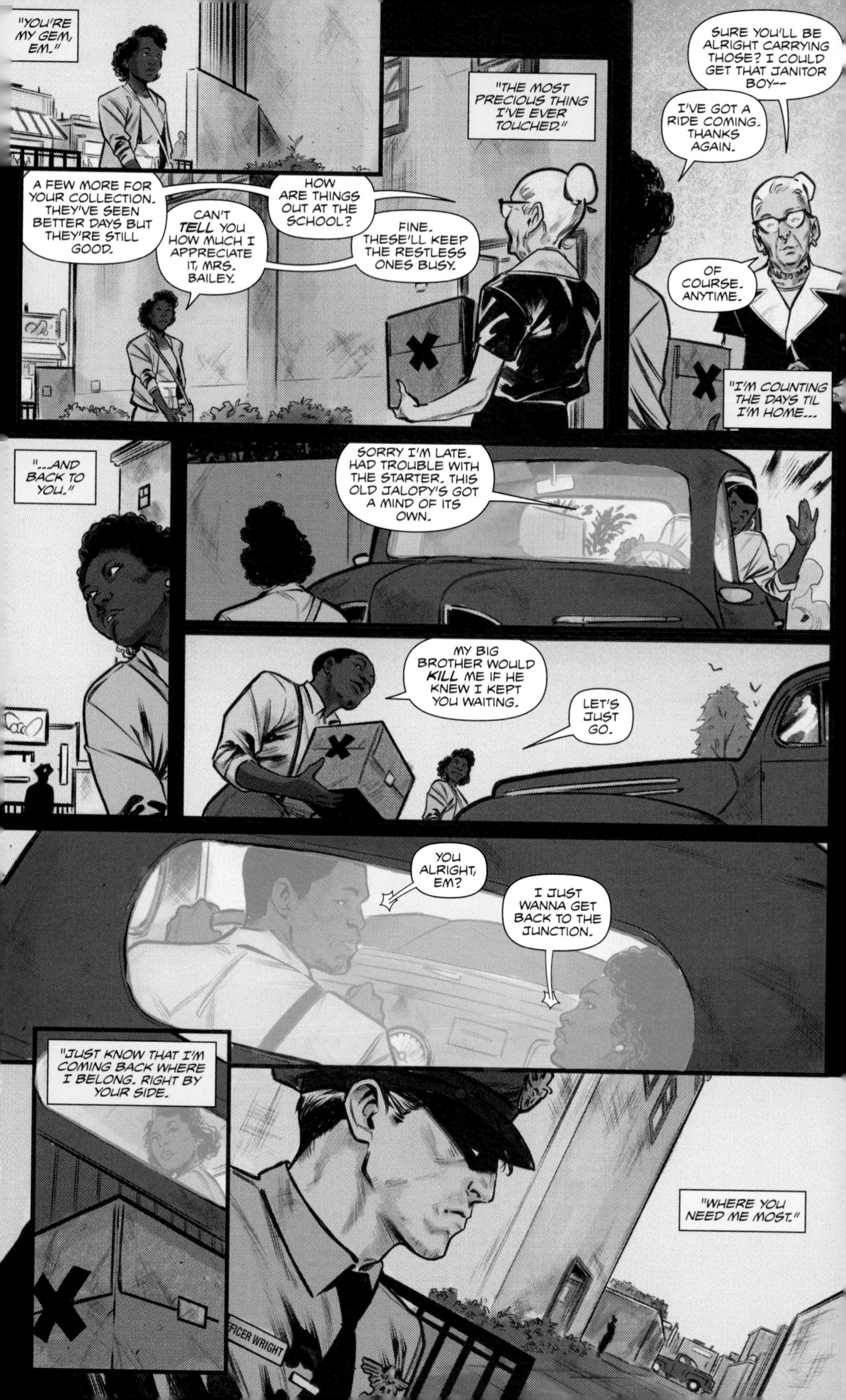
"YOU'RE MY GEM, EM."
"THE MOST PRECIOUS THING I'VE EVER TOUCHED."
A FEW MORE FOR YOUR COLLECTION. THEY'VE SEEN BETTER DAYS BUT THEY'RE STILL GOOD.
CAN'T TELL YOU HOW MUCH I APPRECIATE IT, MRS. BAILEY.
HOW ARE THINGS OUT AT THE SCHOOL?
FINE. THESE'LL KEEP THE RESTLESS ONES BUSY.
SURE YOU'LL BE ALRIGHT CARRYING THOSE? I COULD GET THAT JANITOR BOY--
I'VE GOT A RIDE COMING. THANKS AGAIN.
OF COURSE. ANYTIME.
"I'M COUNTING THE DAYS TIL I'M HOME...
"...AND BACK TO YOU."
SORRY I'M LATE. HAD TROUBLE WITH THE STARTER. THIS OLD JALOPY'S GOT A MIND OF ITS OWN.
MY BIG BROTHER WOULD KILL ME IF HE KNEW I KEPT YOU WAITING.
LET'S JUST GO.
YOU ALRIGHT, EM?
I JUST WANNA GET BACK TO THE JUNCTION.
"JUST KNOW THAT I'M COMING BACK WHERE I BELONG. RIGHT BY YOUR SIDE.
"WHERE YOU NEED ME MOST."
FFICER WRIGHT

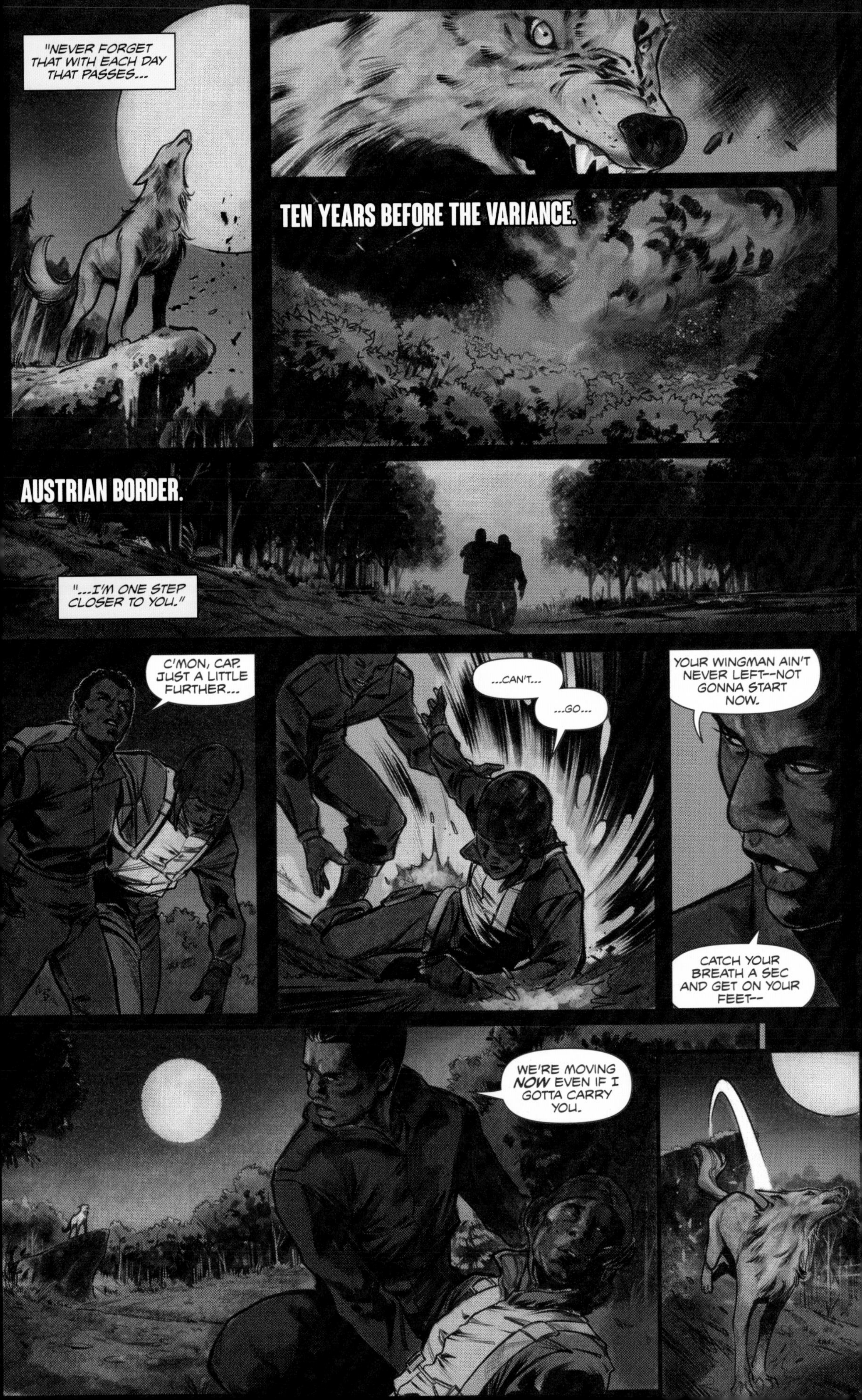
"NEVER FORGET THAT WITH EACH DAY THAT PASSES...
TEN YEARS BEFORE THE VARIANCE.
AUSTRIAN BORDER.
"...I'M ONE STEP CLOSER TO YOU."
C'MON, CAP. JUST A LITTLE FURTHER...
...CAN'T...
...GO...
YOUR WINGMAN AIN'T NEVER LEFT--NOT GONNA START NOW.
CATCH YOUR BREATH A SEC AND GET ON YOUR FEET--
WE'RE MOVING NOW EVEN IF I GOTTA CARRY YOU.

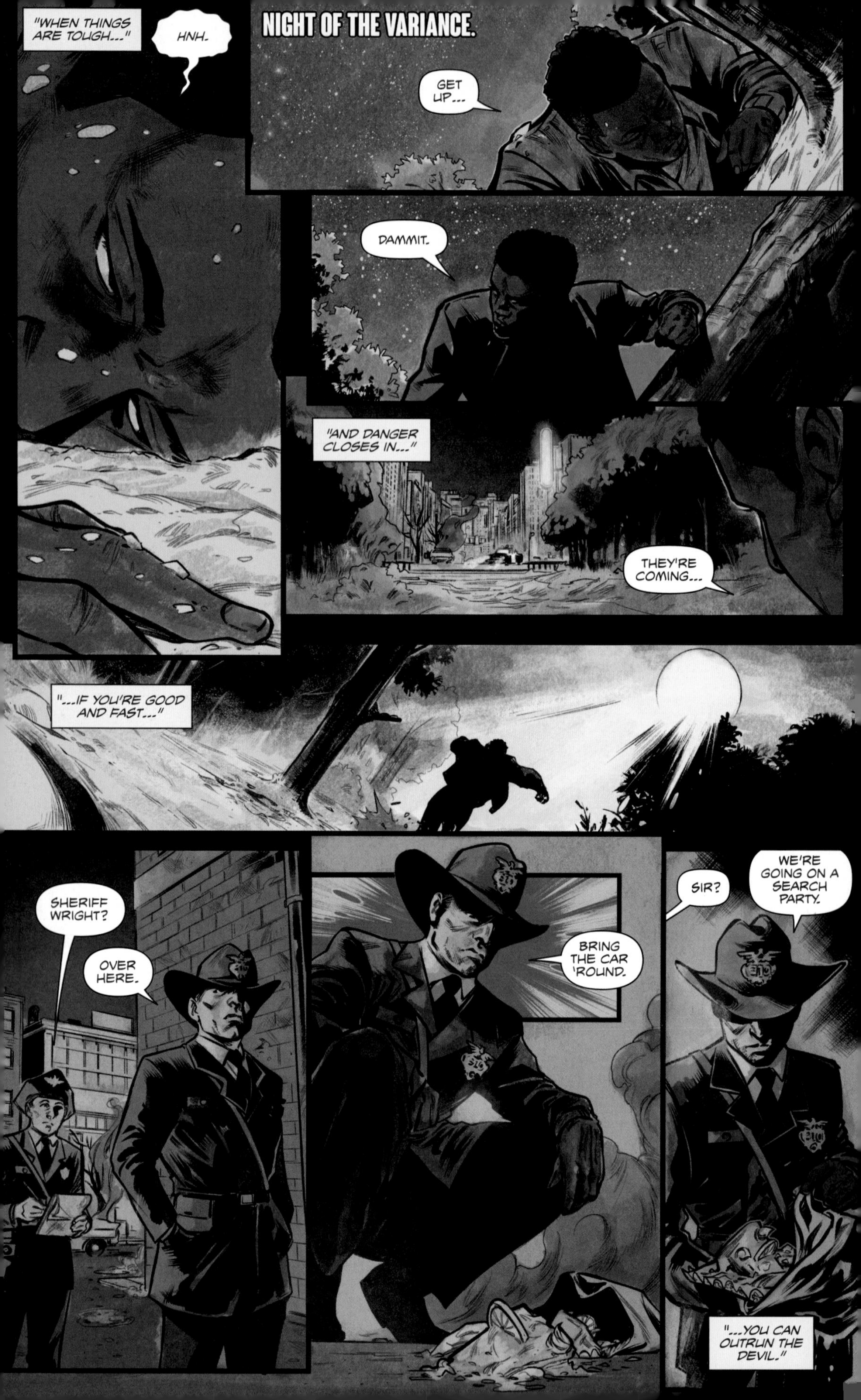
"WHEN THINGS ARE TOUGH..."
HNH.
NIGHT OF THE VARIANCE.
GET UP...
DAMMIT.
"AND DANGER CLOSES IN..."
THEY'RE COMING...
"...IF YOU'RE GOOD AND FAST..."
SHERIFF WRIGHT?
OVER HERE.
BRING THE CAR 'ROUND.
SIR?
WE'RE GOING ON A SEARCH PARTY.
"...YOU CAN OUTRUN THE DEVIL."

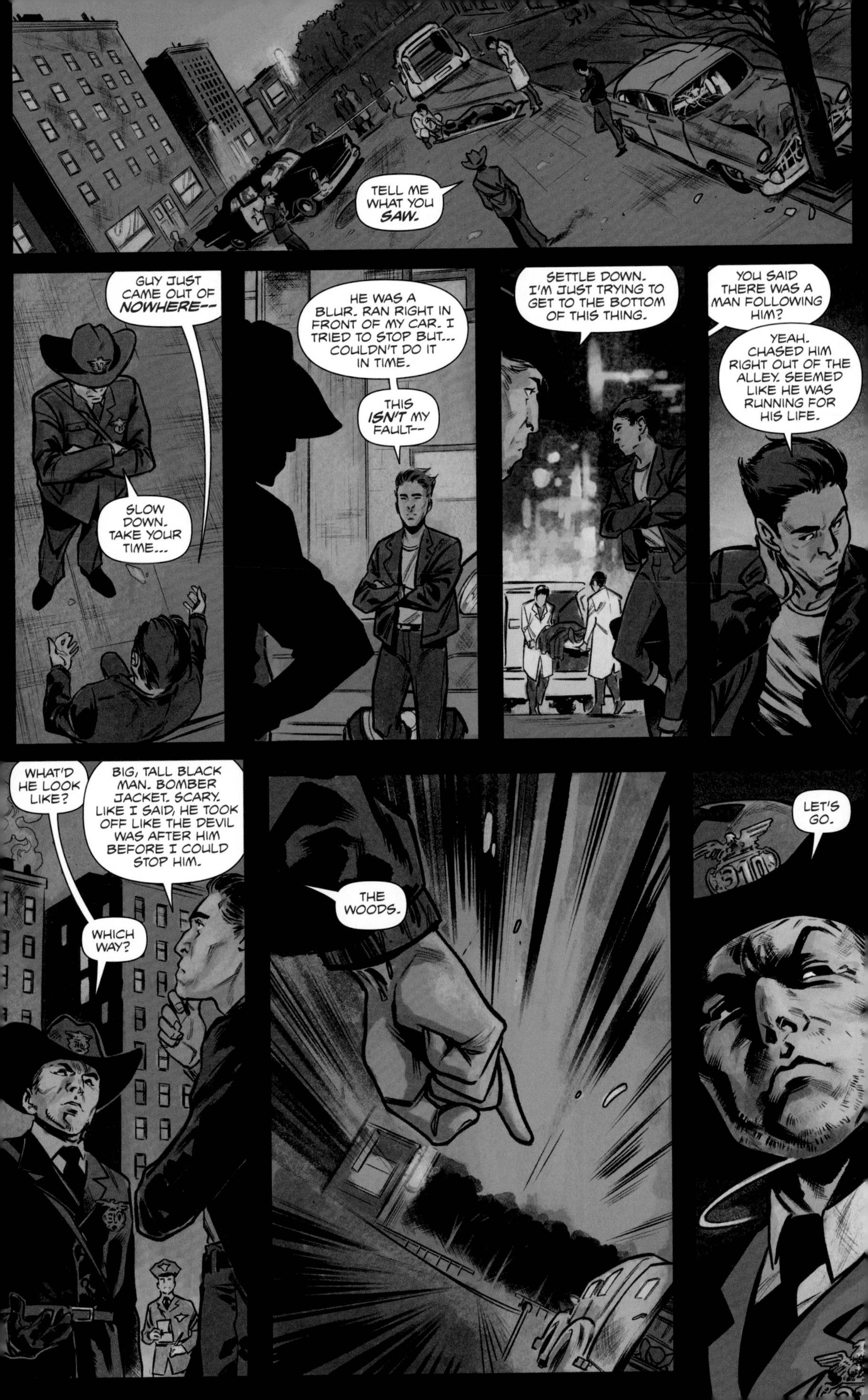
TELL ME WHAT YOU *SAW.*
GUY JUST CAME OUT OF *NOWHERE--*
SLOW DOWN. TAKE YOUR TIME...
HE WAS A BLUR. RAN RIGHT IN FRONT OF MY CAR. I TRIED TO STOP BUT... COULDN'T DO IT IN TIME.
THIS *ISN'T* MY FAULT--
SETTLE DOWN. I'M JUST TRYING TO GET TO THE BOTTOM OF THIS THING.
YOU SAID THERE WAS A MAN FOLLOWING HIM?
YEAH. CHASED HIM RIGHT OUT OF THE ALLEY. SEEMED LIKE HE WAS RUNNING FOR HIS LIFE.
WHAT'D HE LOOK LIKE?
BIG, TALL BLACK MAN. BOMBER JACKET. SCARY. LIKE I SAID, HE TOOK OFF LIKE THE DEVIL WAS AFTER HIM BEFORE I COULD STOP HIM.
WHICH WAY?
THE WOODS.
LET'S GO.

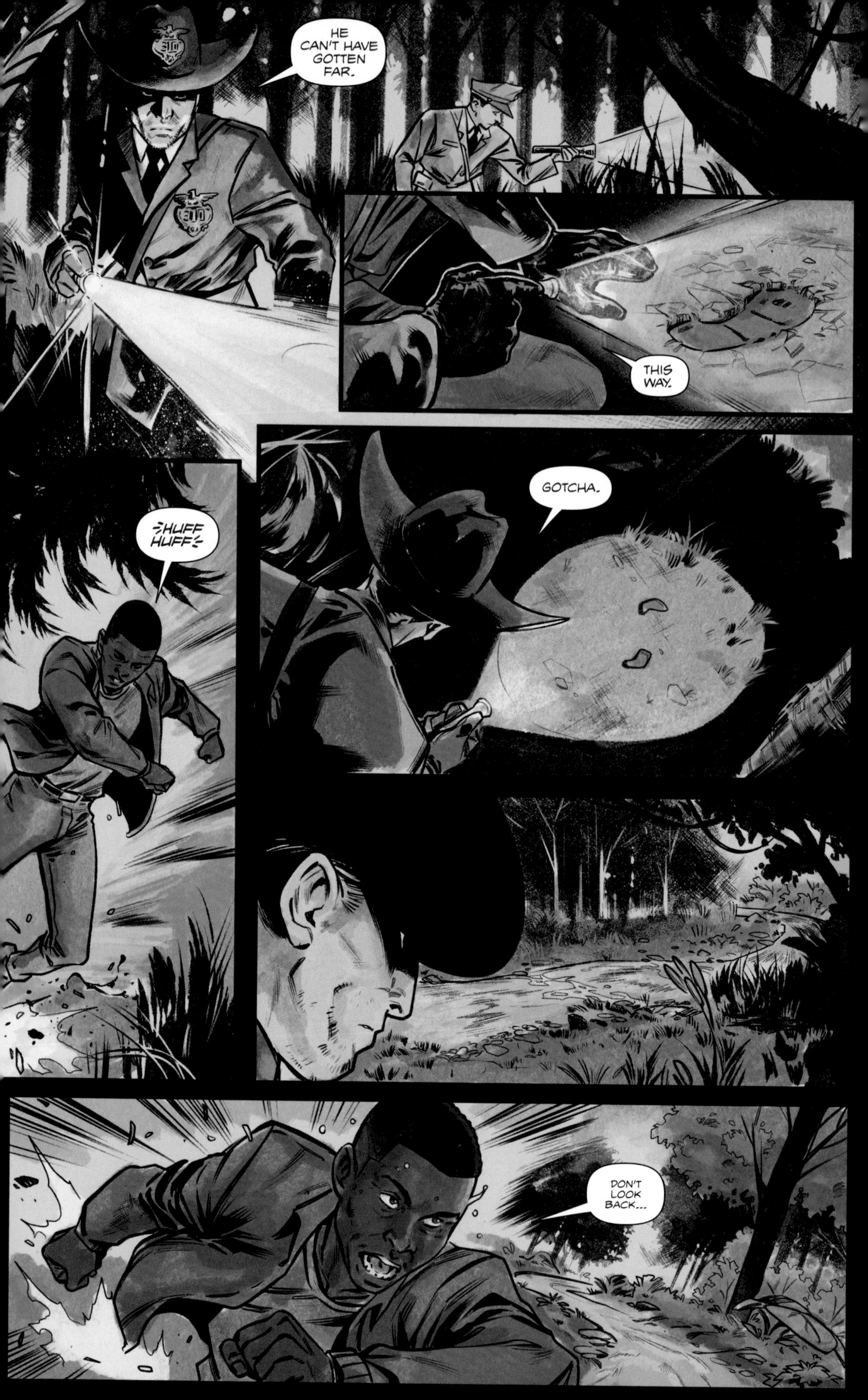
HE CAN'T HAVE GOTTEN FAR.
THIS WAY.
HUFF HUFF
GOTCHA.
DON'T LOOK BACK...

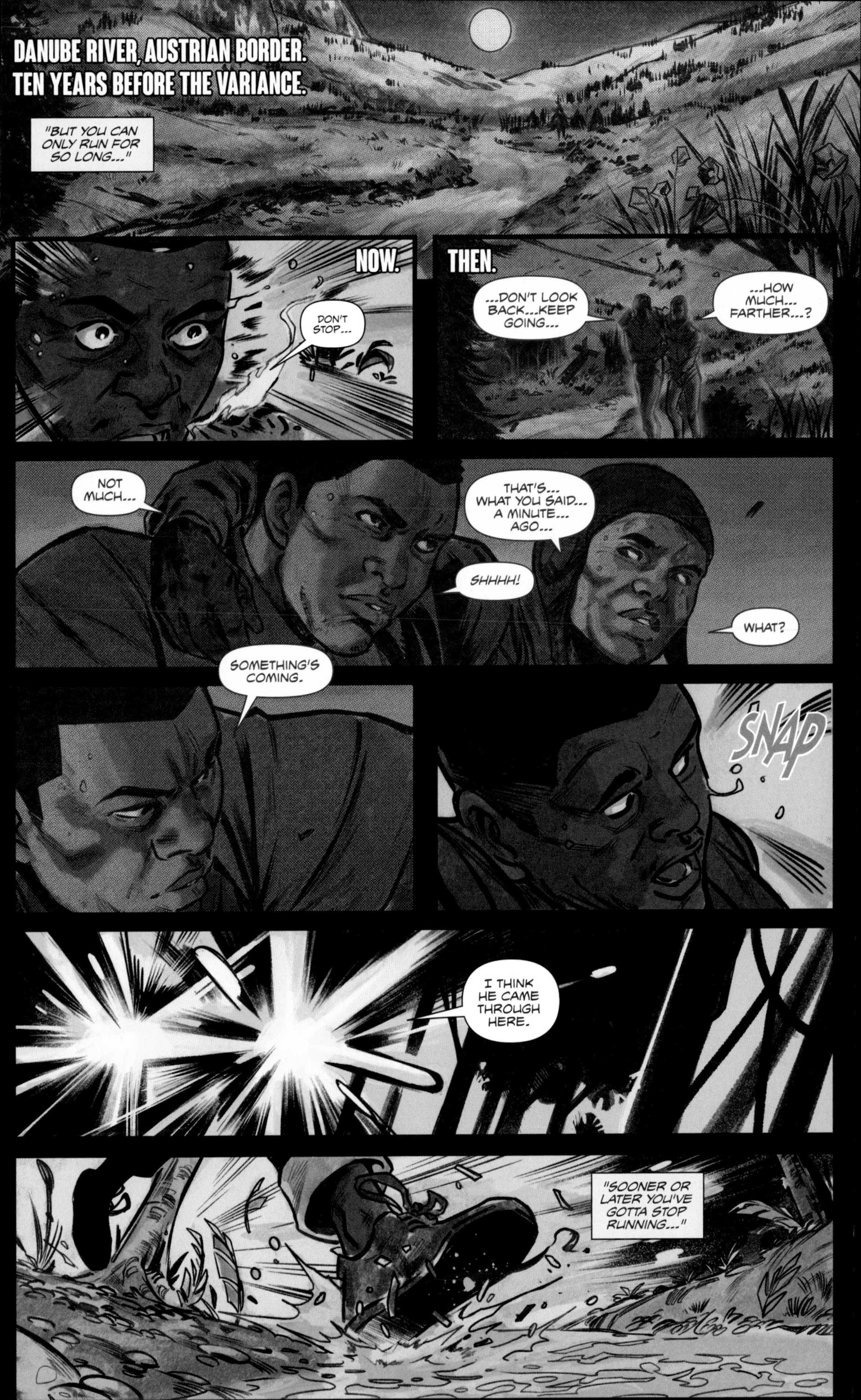

DANUBE RIVER, AUSTRIAN BORDER.
TEN YEARS BEFORE THE VARIANCE.
"BUT YOU CAN ONLY RUN FOR SO LONG..."
NOW.
DON'T STOP...
THEN.
...DON'T LOOK BACK...KEEP GOING...
...HOW MUCH... FARTHER...?
NOT MUCH...
THAT'S... WHAT YOU SAID... A MINUTE... AGO...
SHHHH!
WHAT?
SOMETHING'S COMING.
SNAP
I THINK HE CAME THROUGH HERE.
"SOONER OR LATER YOU'VE GOTTA STOP RUNNING..."

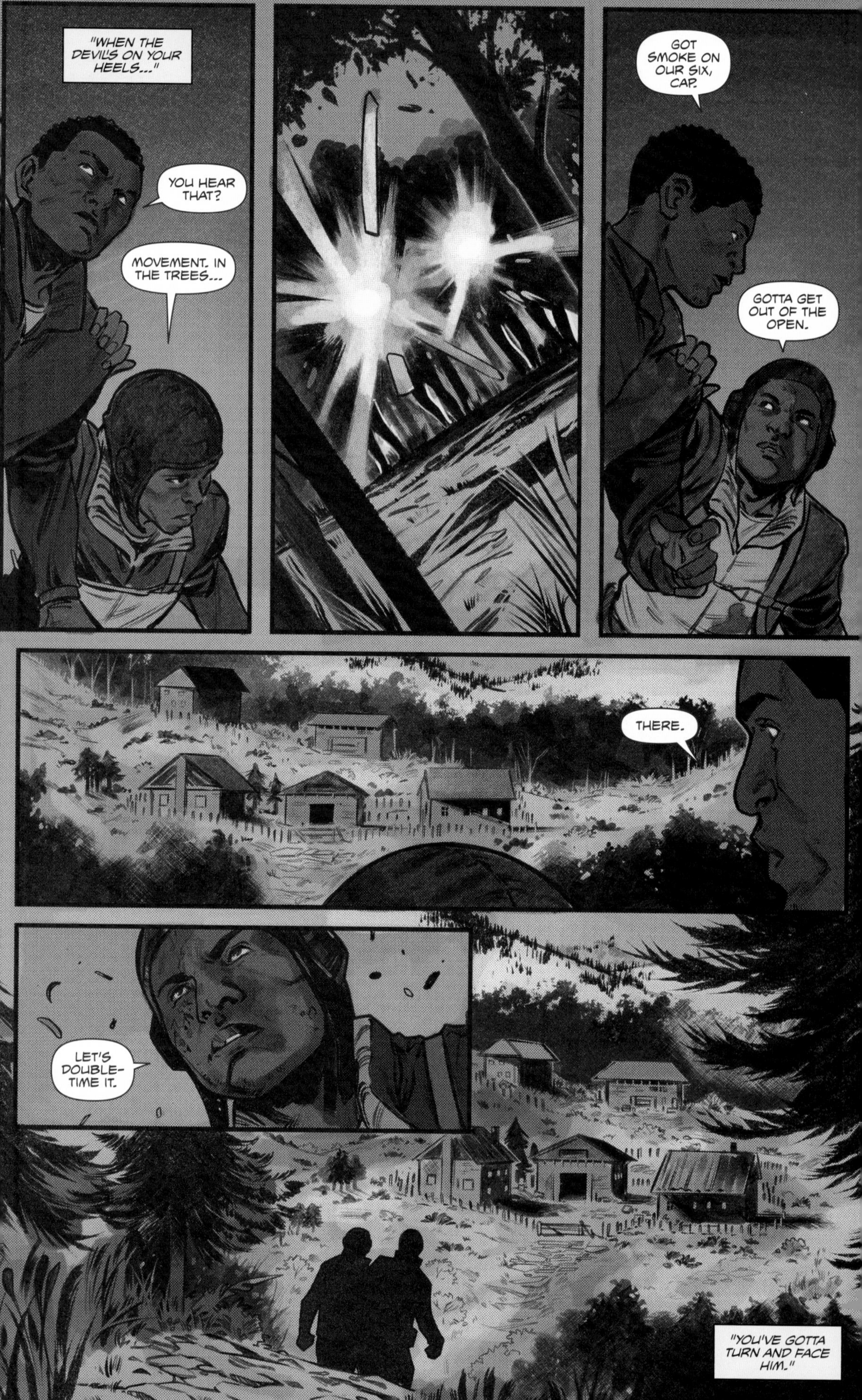
"WHEN THE DEVIL'S ON YOUR HEELS..."
YOU HEAR THAT?
MOVEMENT. IN THE TREES...
GOT SMOKE ON OUR SIX, CAP.
GOTTA GET OUT OF THE OPEN.
THERE.
LET'S DOUBLE-TIME IT.
"YOU'VE GOTTA TURN AND FACE HIM."

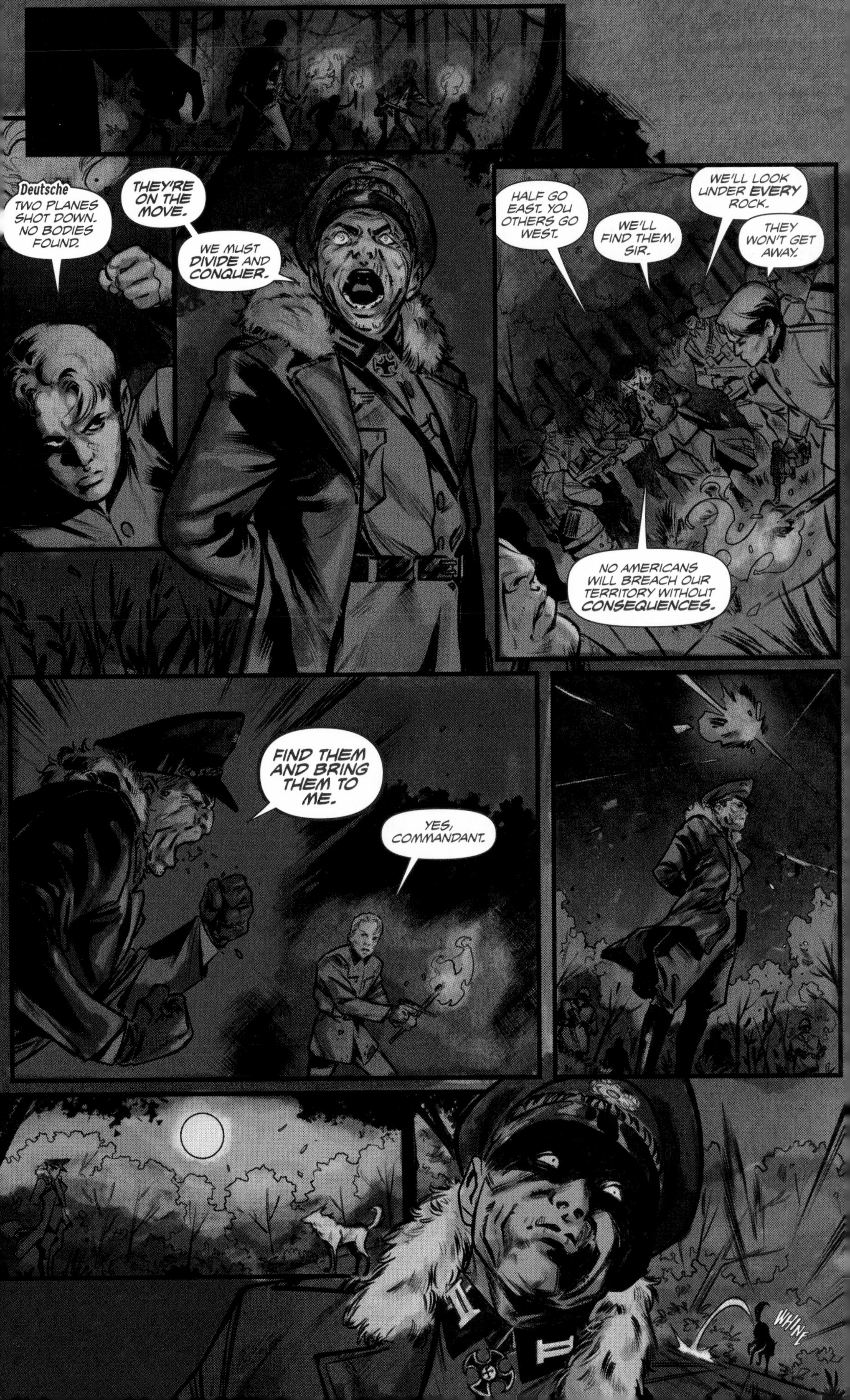
Deutsche
TWO PLANES SHOT DOWN. NO BODIES FOUND.
THEY'RE ON THE MOVE.
WE MUST DIVIDE AND CONQUER.
HALF GO EAST. YOU OTHERS GO WEST.
WE'LL FIND THEM, SIR.
WE'LL LOOK UNDER EVERY ROCK.
THEY WON'T GET AWAY.
NO AMERICANS WILL BREACH OUR TERRITORY WITHOUT CONSEQUENCES.
FIND THEM AND BRING THEM TO ME.
YES, COMMANDANT.
WHINE

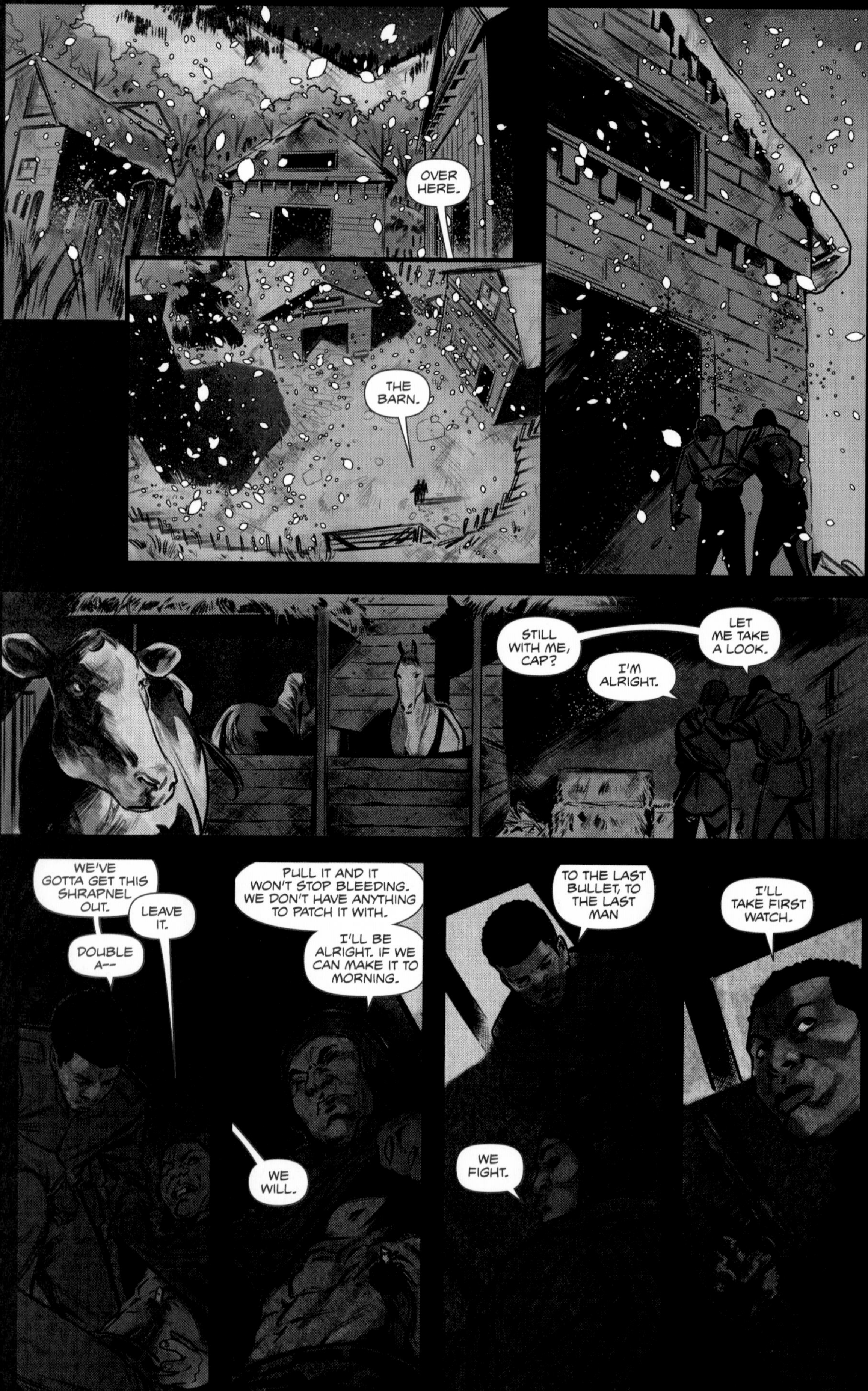
OVER HERE.
THE BARN.
STILL WITH ME, CAP?
LET ME TAKE A LOOK.
I'M ALRIGHT.
WE'VE GOTTA GET THIS SHRAPNEL OUT.
LEAVE IT.
DOUBLE A--
PULL IT AND IT WON'T STOP BLEEDING. WE DON'T HAVE ANYTHING TO PATCH IT WITH.
I'LL BE ALRIGHT. IF WE CAN MAKE IT TO MORNING.
WE WILL.
TO THE LAST BULLET, TO THE LAST MAN
WE FIGHT.
I'LL TAKE FIRST WATCH.

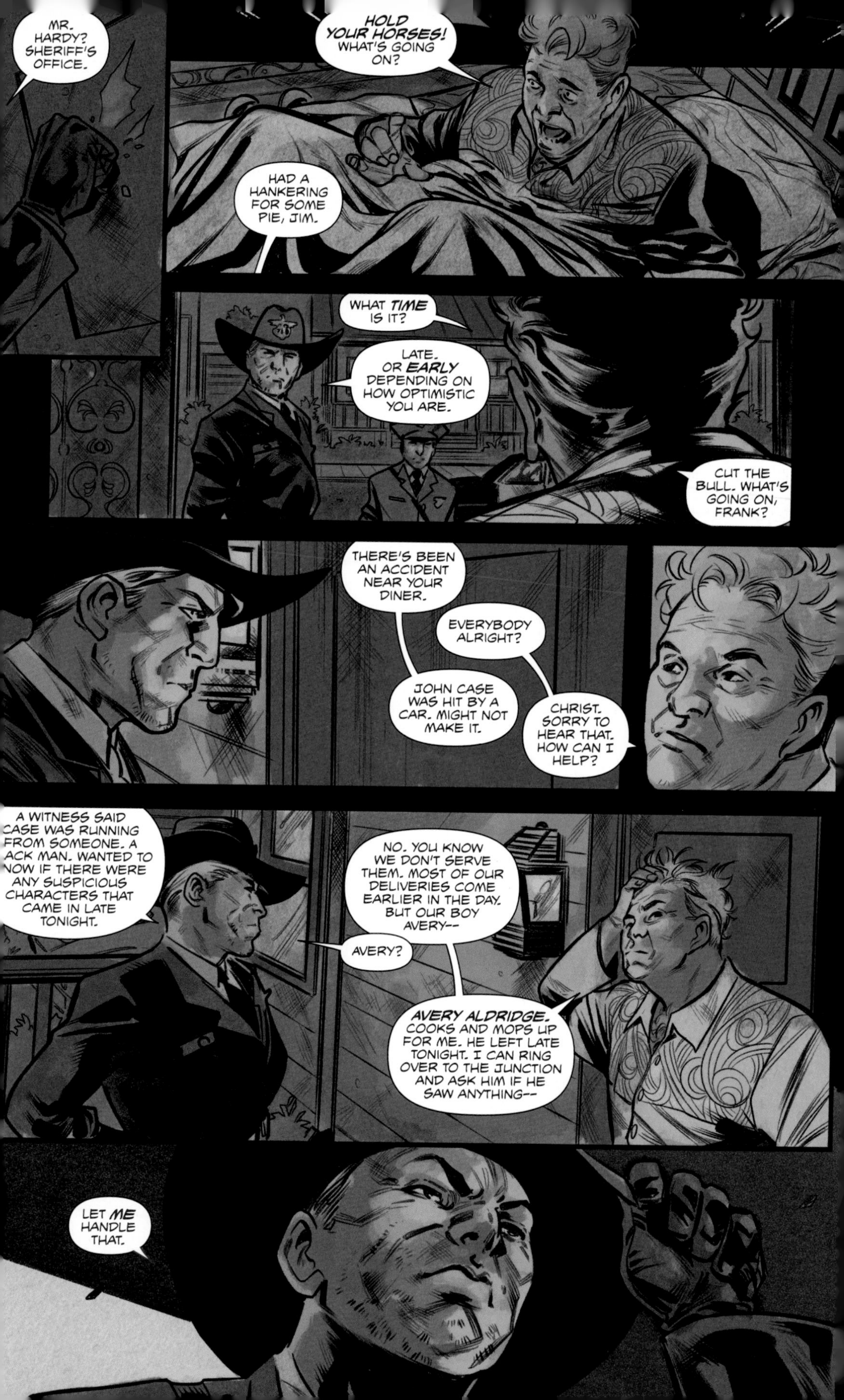
MR. HARDY? SHERIFF'S OFFICE.
HOLD YOUR HORSES! WHAT'S GOING ON?
HAD A HANKERING FOR SOME PIE, JIM.
WHAT TIME IS IT?
LATE. OR EARLY DEPENDING ON HOW OPTIMISTIC YOU ARE.
CUT THE BULL. WHAT'S GOING ON, FRANK?
THERE'S BEEN AN ACCIDENT NEAR YOUR DINER.
EVERYBODY ALRIGHT?
JOHN CASE WAS HIT BY A CAR. MIGHT NOT MAKE IT.
CHRIST. SORRY TO HEAR THAT. HOW CAN I HELP?
A WITNESS SAID CASE WAS RUNNING FROM SOMEONE. A ACK MAN. WANTED TO NOW IF THERE WERE ANY SUSPICIOUS CHARACTERS THAT CAME IN LATE TONIGHT.
NO. YOU KNOW WE DON'T SERVE THEM. MOST OF OUR DELIVERIES COME EARLIER IN THE DAY. BUT OUR BOY AVERY--
AVERY?
AVERY ALDRIDGE. COOKS AND MOPS UP FOR ME. HE LEFT LATE TONIGHT. I CAN RING OVER TO THE JUNCTION AND ASK HIM IF HE SAW ANYTHING--
LET ME HANDLE THAT.

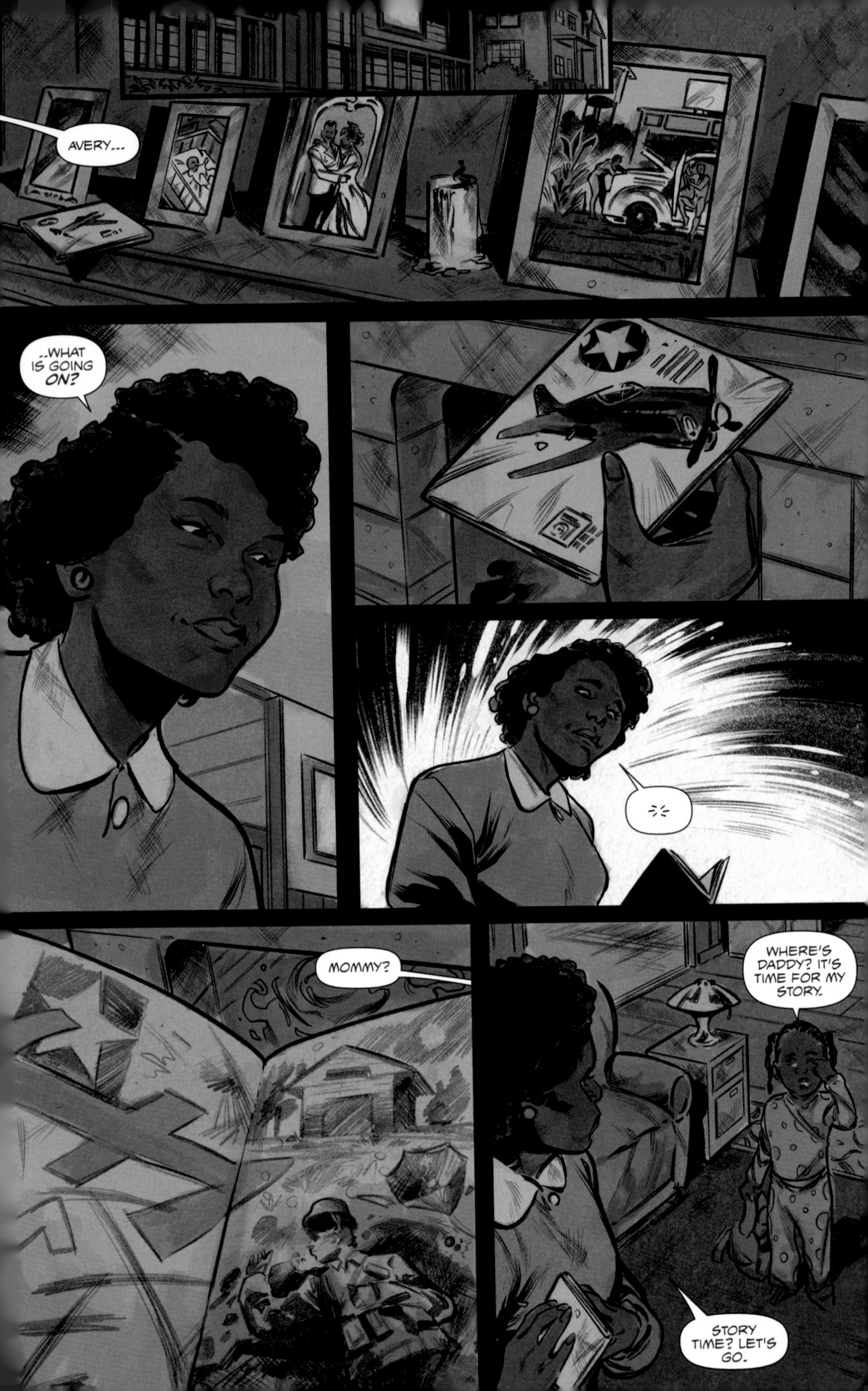
AVERY...
..WHAT IS GOING ON?
...
MOMMY?
WHERE'S DADDY? IT'S TIME FOR MY STORY.
STORY TIME? LET'S GO.

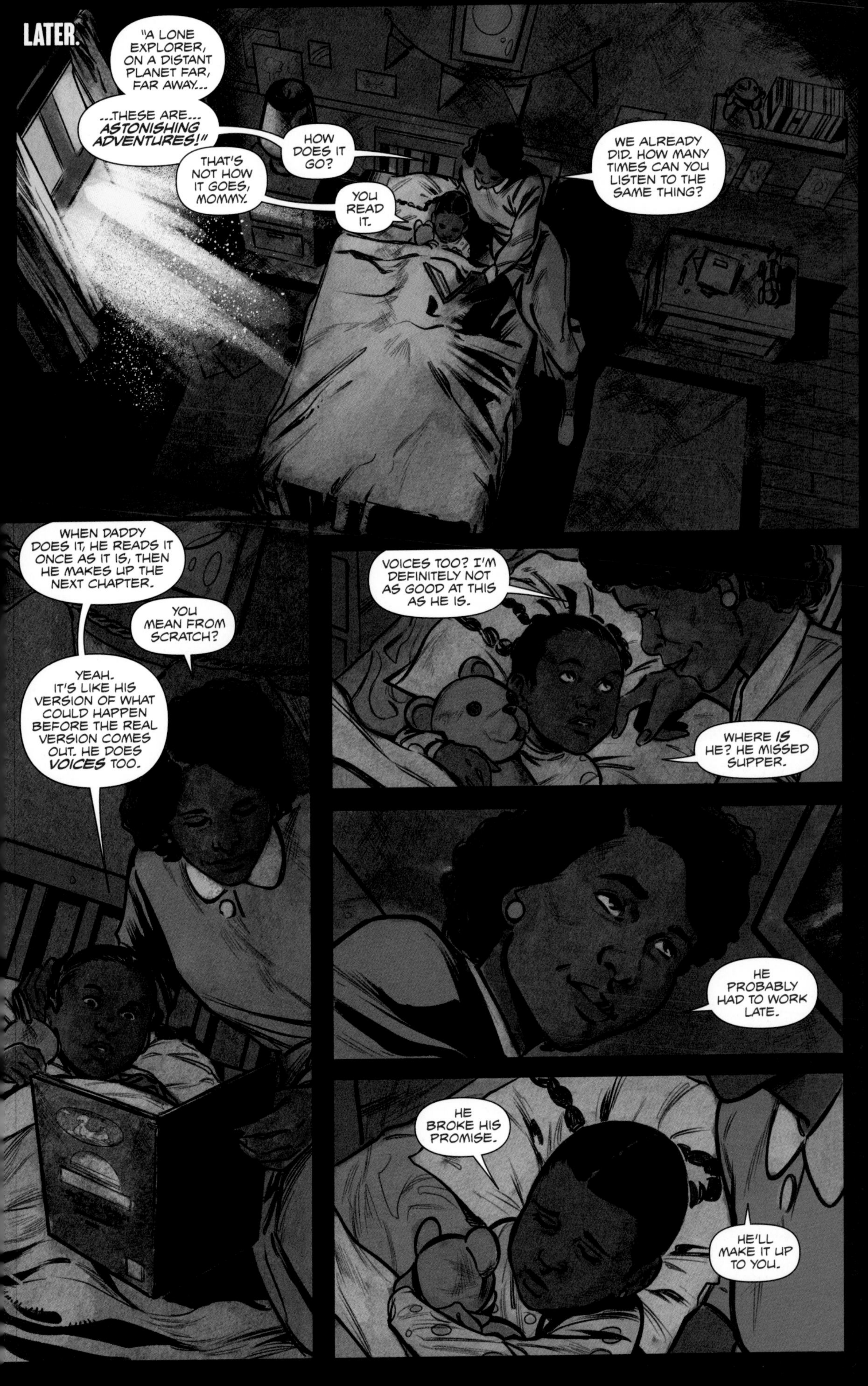
LATER.
"A LONE EXPLORER, ON A DISTANT PLANET FAR, FAR AWAY...
...THESE ARE... ASTONISHING ADVENTURES!"
HOW DOES IT GO?
THAT'S NOT HOW IT GOES, MOMMY.
YOU READ IT.
WE ALREADY DID. HOW MANY TIMES CAN YOU LISTEN TO THE SAME THING?
WHEN DADDY DOES IT, HE READS IT ONCE AS IT IS, THEN HE MAKES UP THE NEXT CHAPTER.
YOU MEAN FROM SCRATCH?
YEAH. IT'S LIKE HIS VERSION OF WHAT COULD HAPPEN BEFORE THE REAL VERSION COMES OUT. HE DOES VOICES TOO.
VOICES TOO? I'M DEFINITELY NOT AS GOOD AT THIS AS HE IS.
WHERE IS HE? HE MISSED SUPPER.
HE PROBABLY HAD TO WORK LATE.
HE BROKE HIS PROMISE.
HE'LL MAKE IT UP TO YOU.

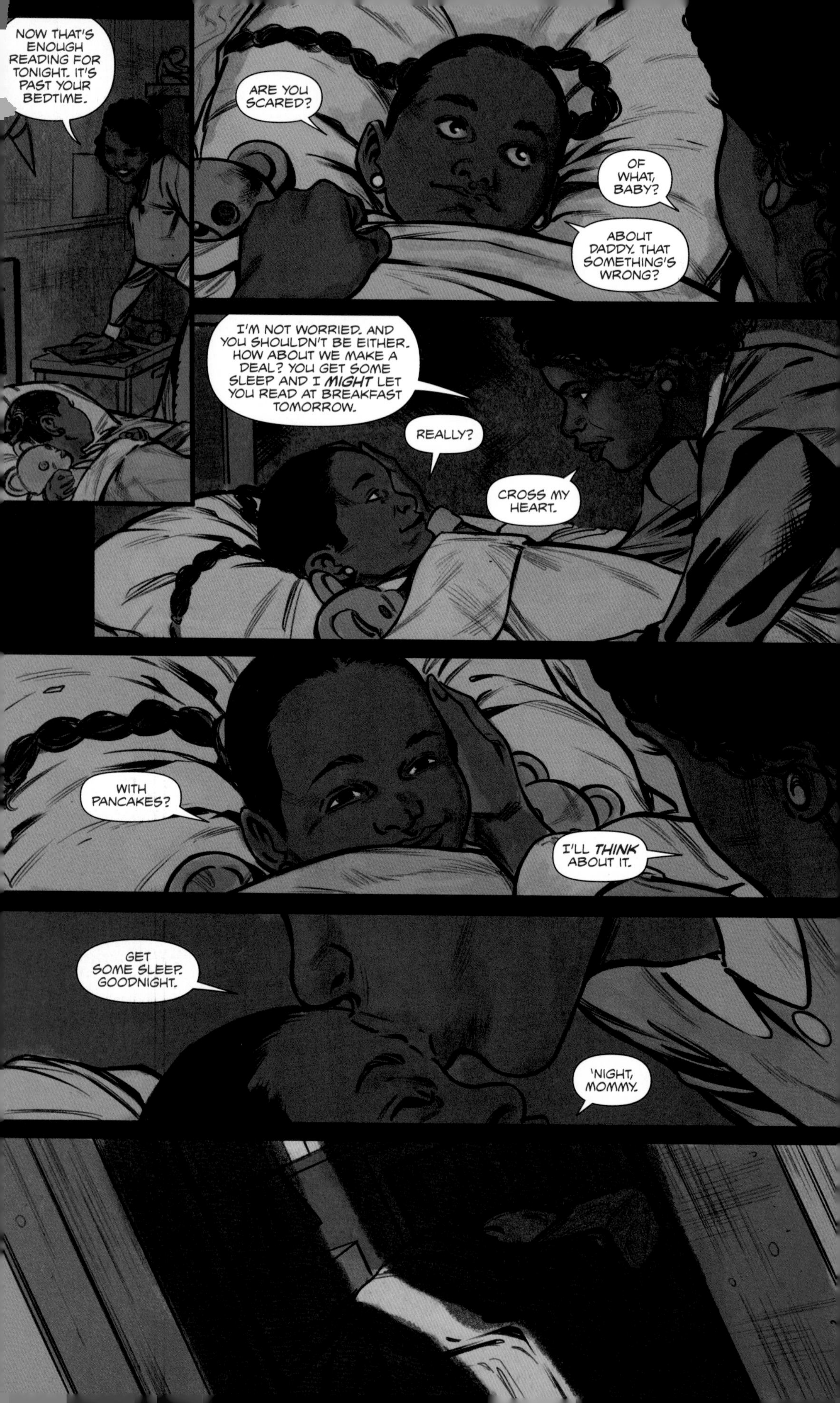
NOW THAT'S ENOUGH READING FOR TONIGHT. IT'S PAST YOUR BEDTIME.
ARE YOU SCARED?
OF WHAT, BABY?
ABOUT DADDY. THAT SOMETHING'S WRONG?
I'M NOT WORRIED. AND YOU SHOULDN'T BE EITHER. HOW ABOUT WE MAKE A DEAL? YOU GET SOME SLEEP AND I *MIGHT* LET YOU READ AT BREAKFAST TOMORROW.
REALLY?
CROSS MY HEART.
WITH PANCAKES?
I'LL *THINK* ABOUT IT.
GET SOME SLEEP. GOODNIGHT.
'NIGHT, MOMMY.

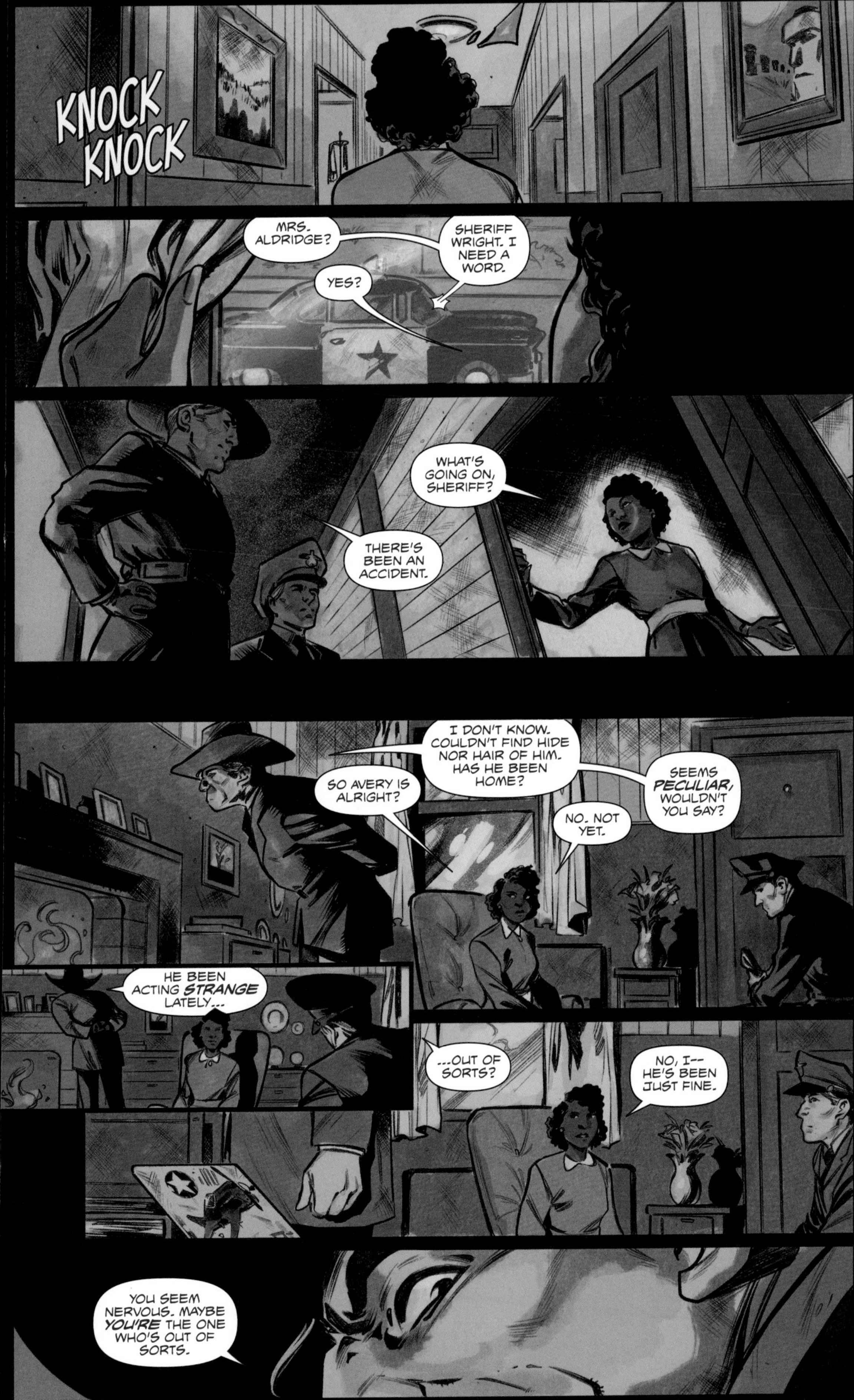
KNOCK KNOCK
MRS. ALDRIDGE?
SHERIFF WRIGHT. I NEED A WORD.
YES?
WHAT'S GOING ON, SHERIFF?
THERE'S BEEN AN ACCIDENT.
SO AVERY IS ALRIGHT?
I DON'T KNOW. COULDN'T FIND HIDE NOR HAIR OF HIM. HAS HE BEEN HOME?
NO. NOT YET.
SEEMS PECULIAR, WOULDN'T YOU SAY?
HE BEEN ACTING STRANGE LATELY...
...OUT OF SORTS?
NO, I-- HE'S BEEN JUST FINE.
YOU SEEM NERVOUS. MAYBE YOU'RE THE ONE WHO'S OUT OF SORTS.

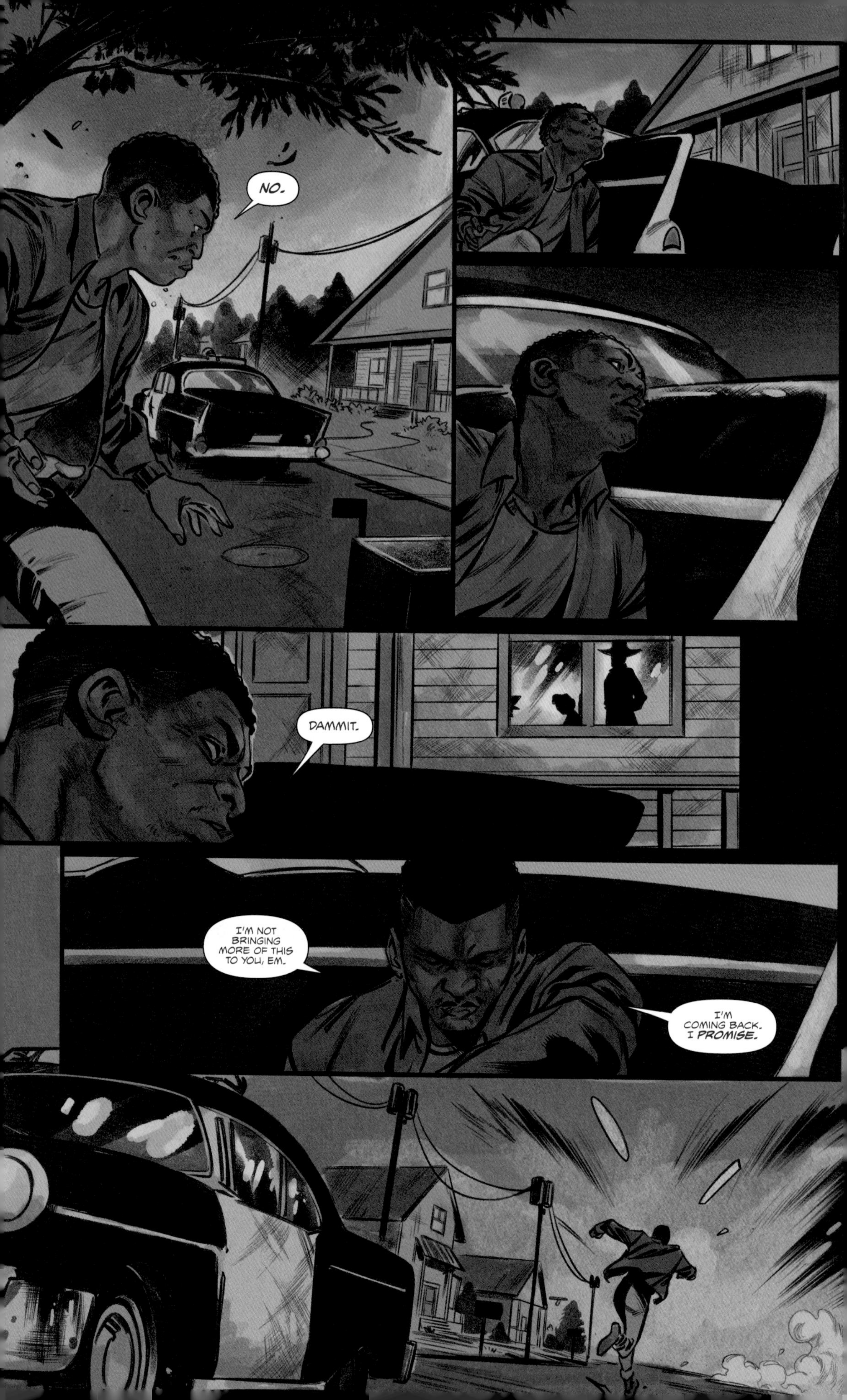
NO.
DAMMIT.
I'M NOT BRINGING MORE OF THIS TO YOU, EM.
I'M COMING BACK. I PROMISE.

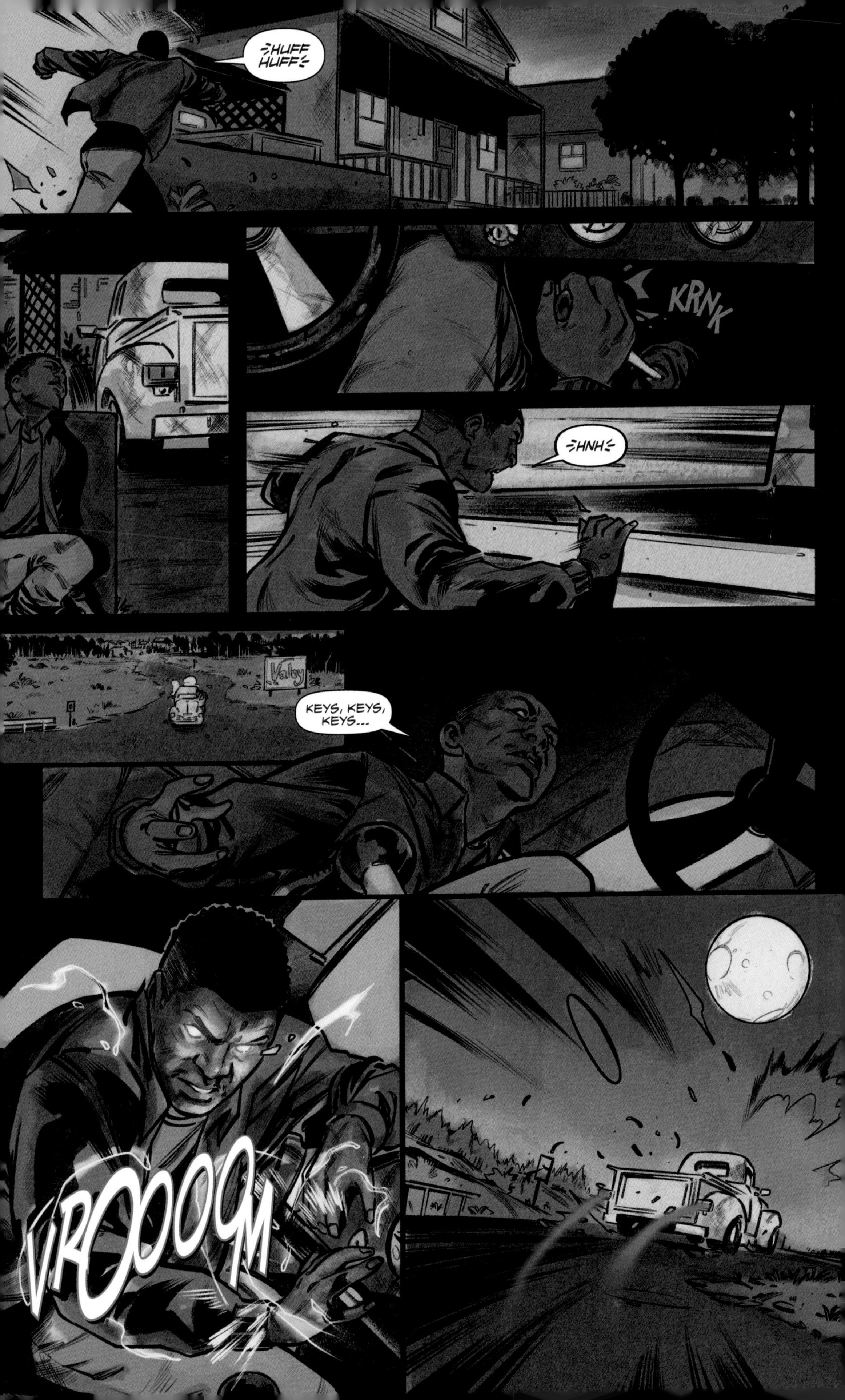
HUFF HUFF
KRNK
HNH
KEYS, KEYS, KEYS...
VROOOOM

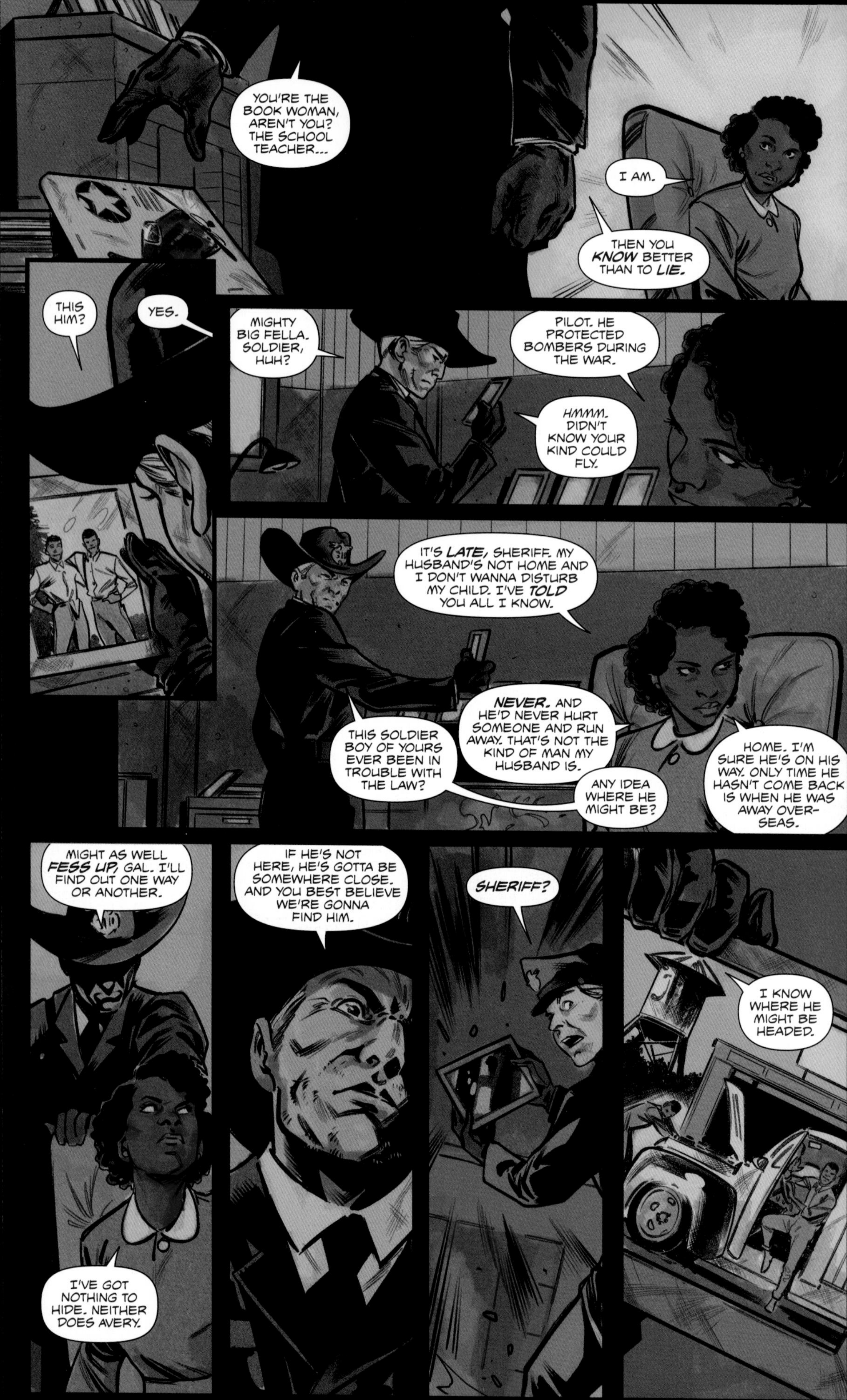

YOU'RE THE BOOK WOMAN, AREN'T YOU? THE SCHOOL TEACHER...
I AM.
THEN YOU KNOW BETTER THAN TO LIE.
THIS HIM?
YES.
MIGHTY BIG FELLA. SOLDIER, HUH?
PILOT. HE PROTECTED BOMBERS DURING THE WAR.
HMMM. DIDN'T KNOW YOUR KIND COULD FLY.
IT'S LATE, SHERIFF. MY HUSBAND'S NOT HOME AND I DON'T WANNA DISTURB MY CHILD. I'VE TOLD YOU ALL I KNOW.
THIS SOLDIER BOY OF YOURS EVER BEEN IN TROUBLE WITH THE LAW?
NEVER. AND HE'D NEVER HURT SOMEONE AND RUN AWAY. THAT'S NOT THE KIND OF MAN MY HUSBAND IS.
ANY IDEA WHERE HE MIGHT BE?
HOME. I'M SURE HE'S ON HIS WAY. ONLY TIME HE HASN'T COME BACK IS WHEN HE WAS AWAY OVER-SEAS.
MIGHT AS WELL FESS UP, GAL. I'LL FIND OUT ONE WAY OR ANOTHER.
I'VE GOT NOTHING TO HIDE. NEITHER DOES AVERY.
IF HE'S NOT HERE, HE'S GOTTA BE SOMEWHERE CLOSE. AND YOU BEST BELIEVE WE'RE GONNA FIND HIM.
SHERIFF?
I KNOW WHERE HE MIGHT BE HEADED.

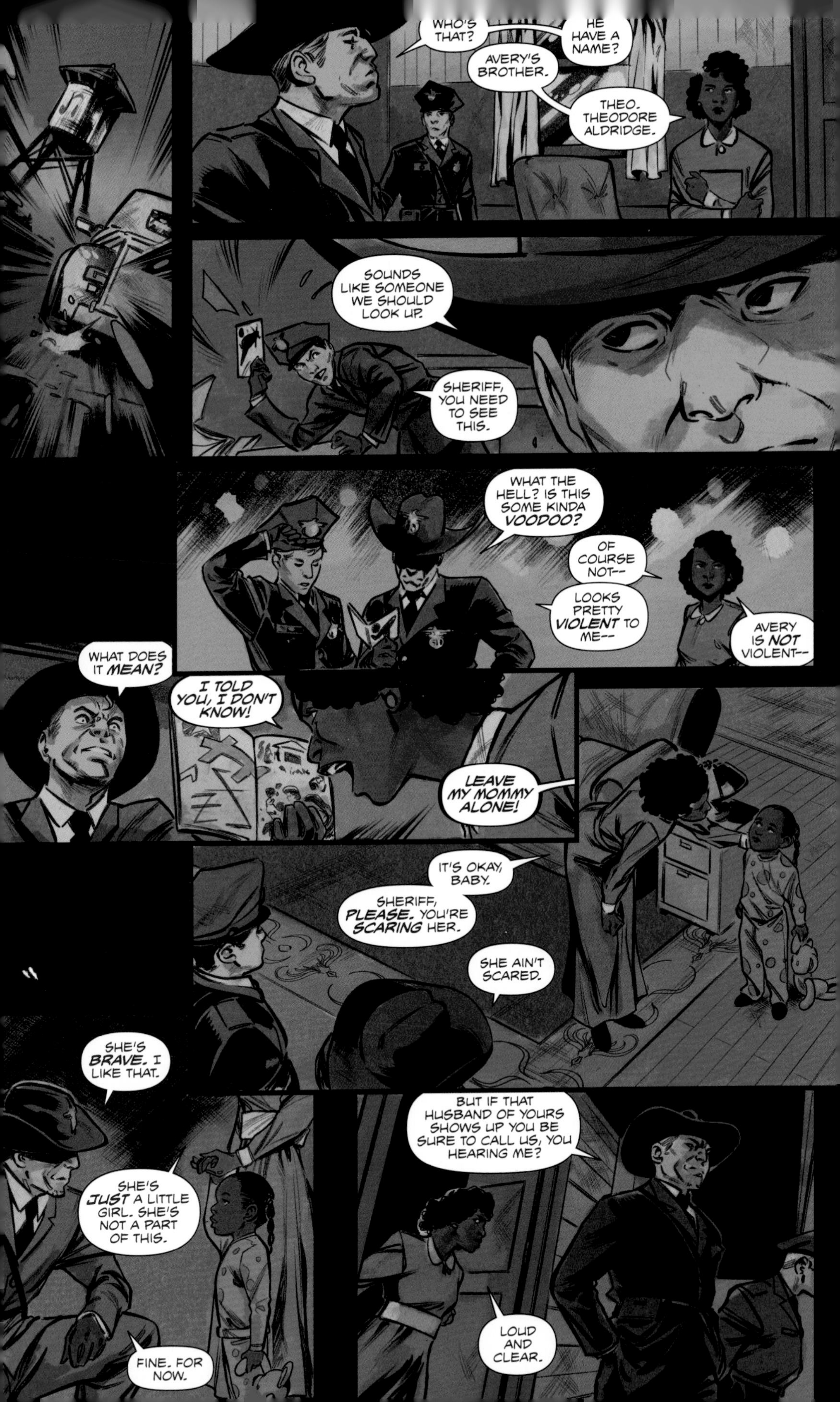

WHO'S THAT?
HE HAVE A NAME?
AVERY'S BROTHER.
THEO. THEODORE ALDRIDGE.
SOUNDS LIKE SOMEONE WE SHOULD LOOK UP.
SHERIFF, YOU NEED TO SEE THIS.
WHAT THE HELL? IS THIS SOME KINDA VOODOO?
OF COURSE NOT--
LOOKS PRETTY VIOLENT TO ME--
AVERY IS NOT VIOLENT--
WHAT DOES IT MEAN?
I TOLD YOU, I DON'T KNOW!
LEAVE MY MOMMY ALONE!
IT'S OKAY, BABY.
SHERIFF, PLEASE. YOU'RE SCARING HER.
SHE AIN'T SCARED.
SHE'S BRAVE. I LIKE THAT.
SHE'S JUST A LITTLE GIRL. SHE'S NOT A PART OF THIS.
FINE. FOR NOW.
BUT IF THAT HUSBAND OF YOURS SHOWS UP YOU BE SURE TO CALL US, YOU HEARING ME?
LOUD AND CLEAR.

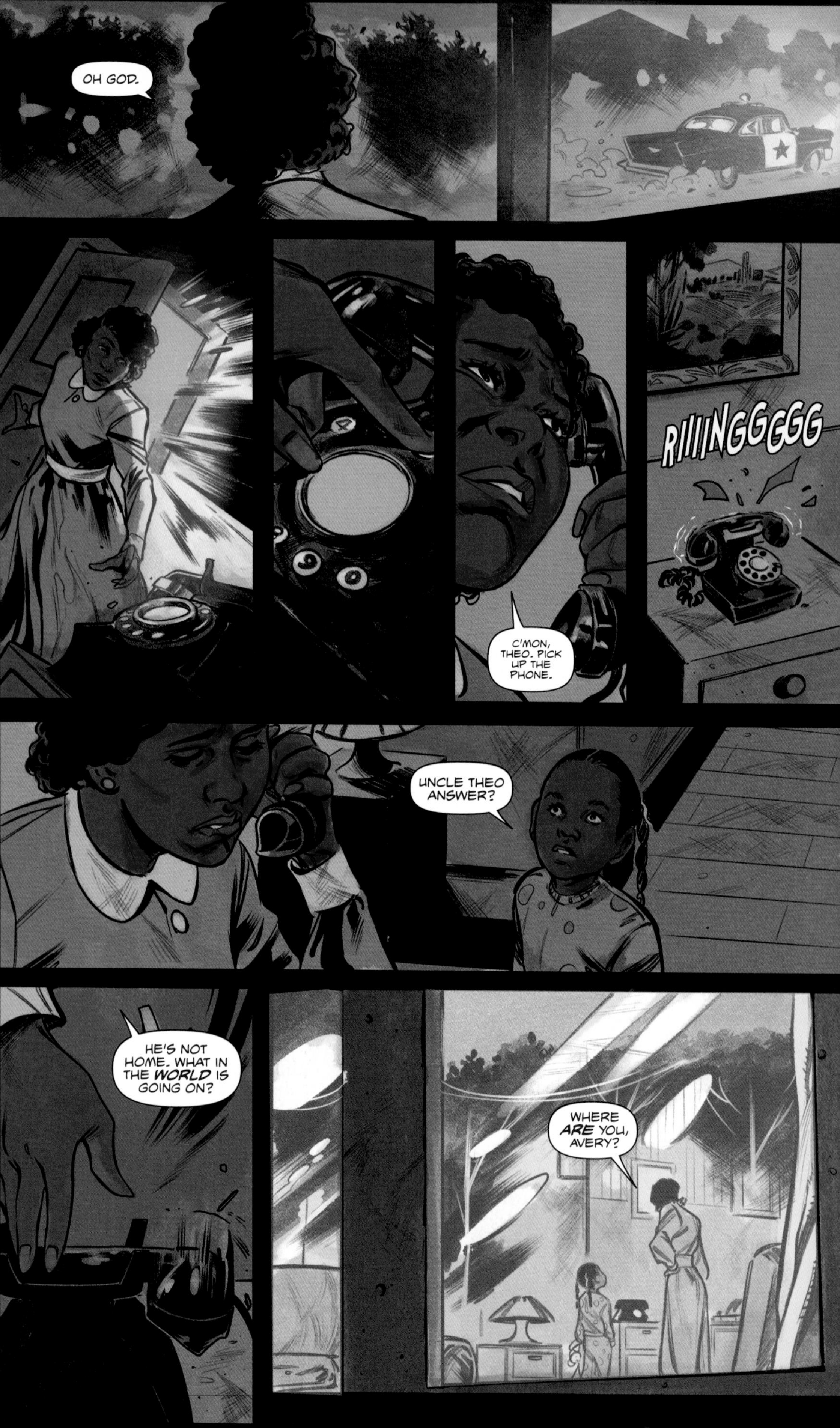
OH GOD.
RIIIINGGGGG
C'MON, THEO. PICK UP THE PHONE.
UNCLE THEO ANSWER?
HE'S NOT HOME. WHAT IN THE *WORLD* IS GOING ON?
WHERE *ARE* YOU, AVERY?

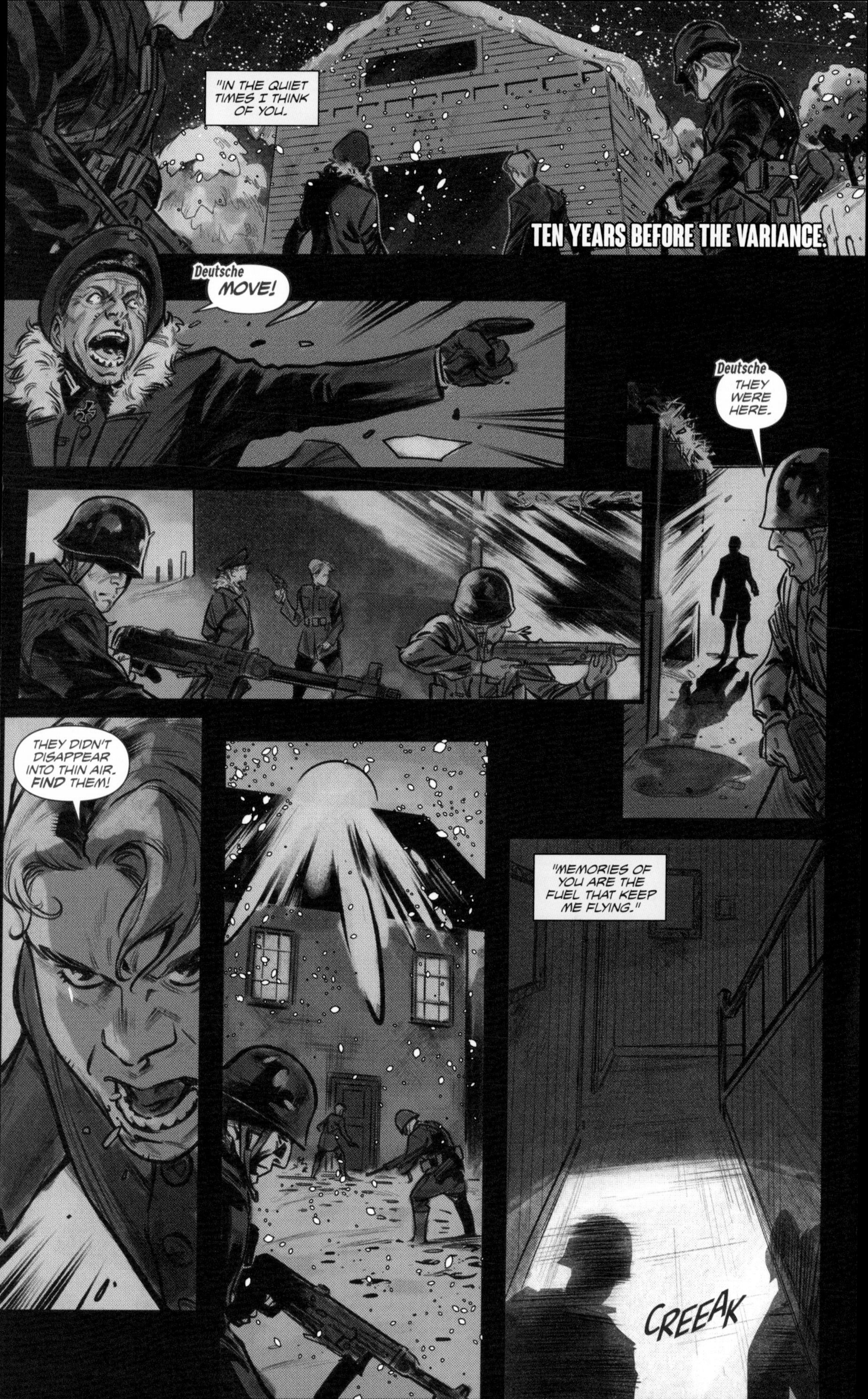
"IN THE QUIET TIMES I THINK OF YOU.
TEN YEARS BEFORE THE VARIANCE.
Deutsche MOVE!
Deutsche THEY WERE HERE.
THEY DIDN'T DISAPPEAR INTO THIN AIR. FIND THEM!
"MEMORIES OF YOU ARE THE FUEL THAT KEEP ME FLYING."
CREEAK

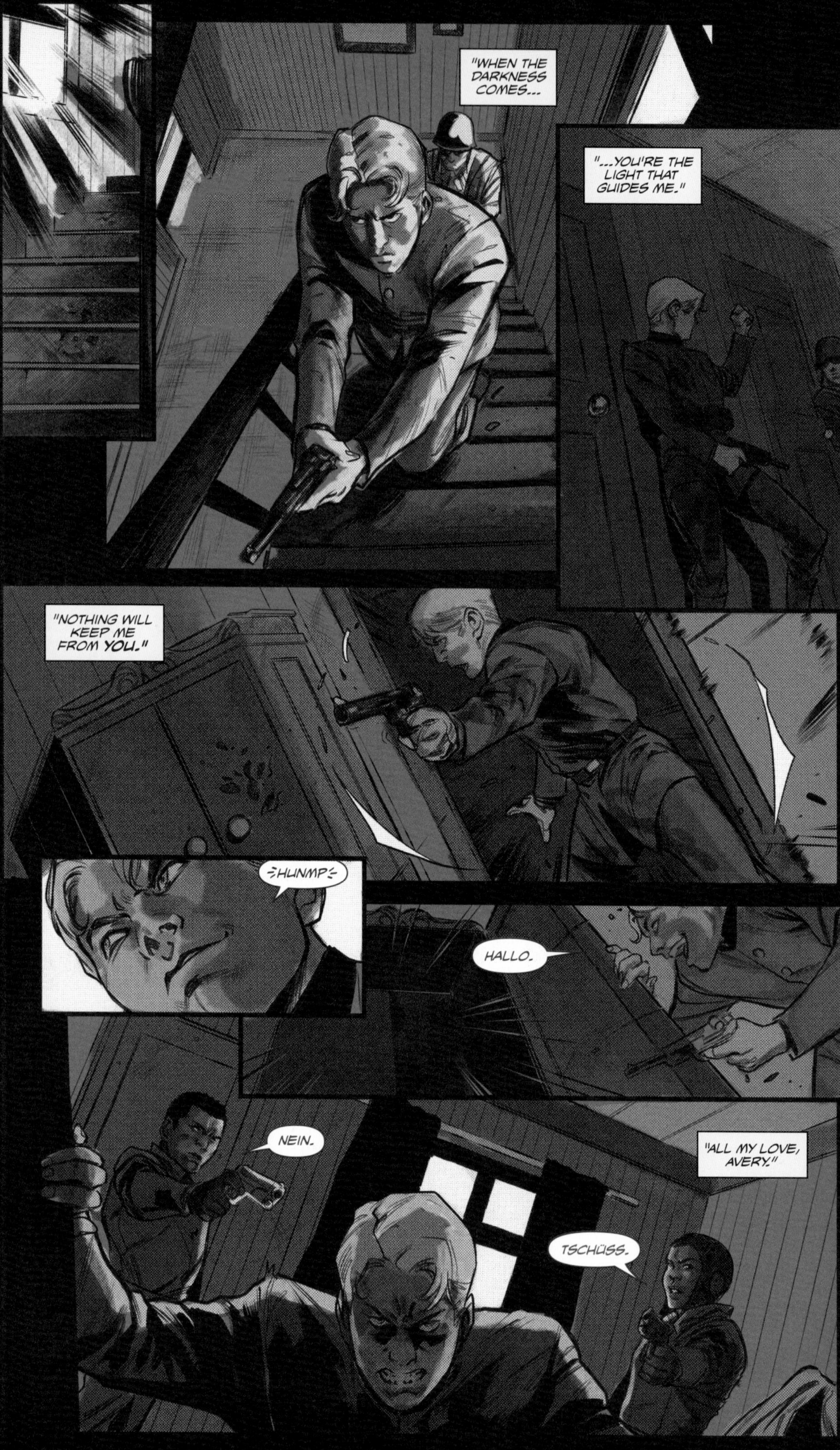
"WHEN THE DARKNESS COMES...
"...YOU'RE THE LIGHT THAT GUIDES ME."
"NOTHING WILL KEEP ME FROM YOU."
HUNMP
HALLO.
NEIN.
"ALL MY LOVE, AVERY."
TSCHÜSS.

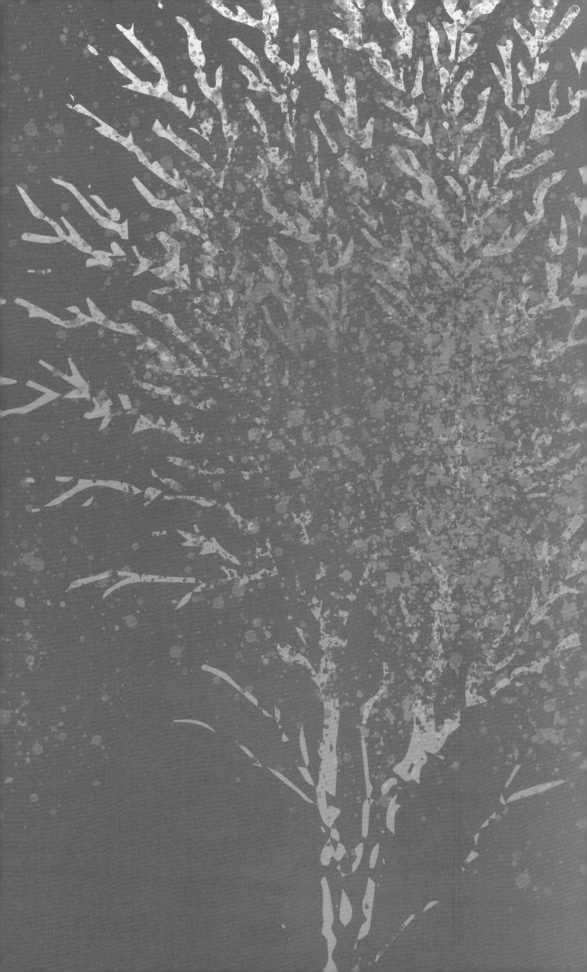

CHAPTER FOUR

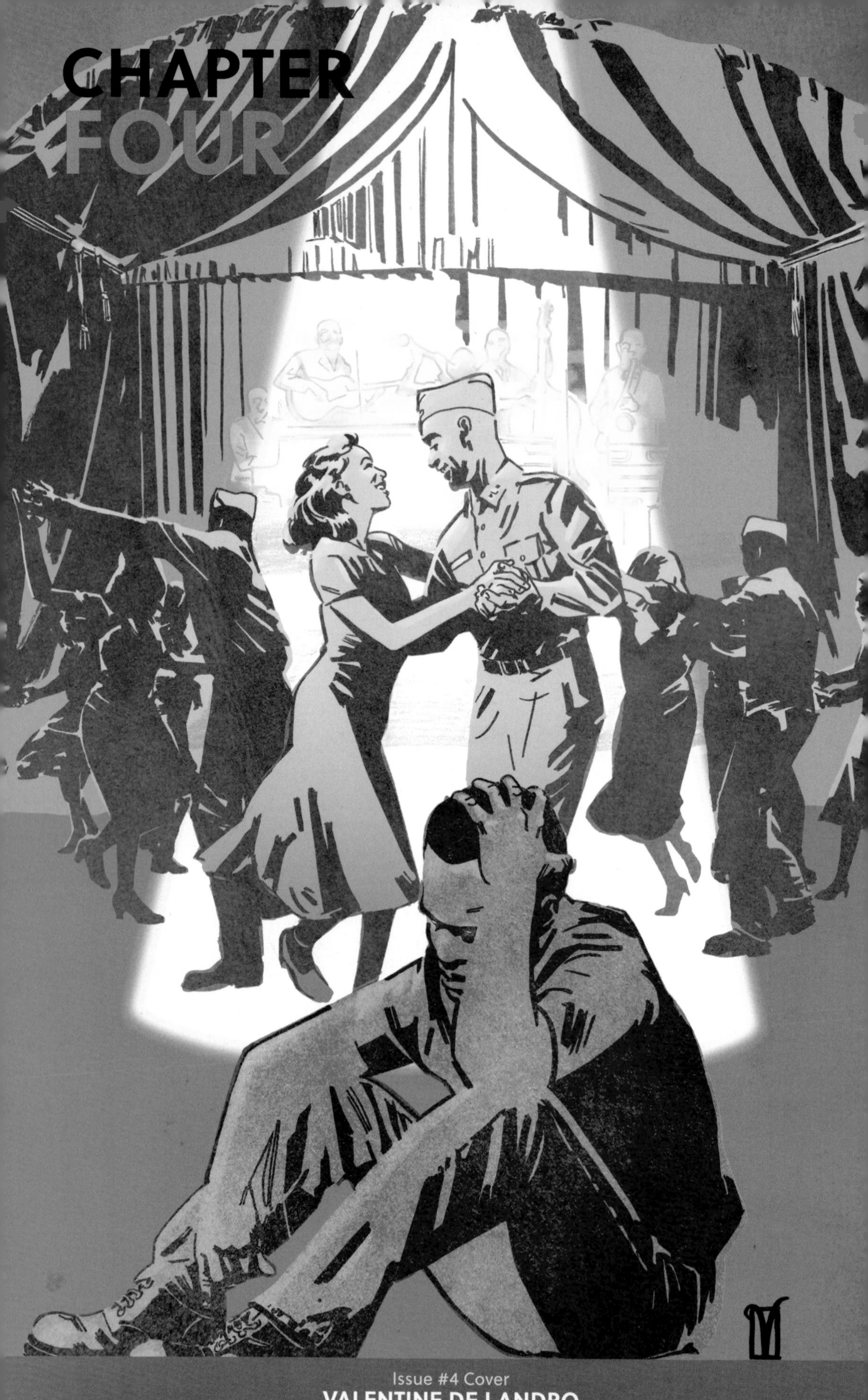

Issue #4 Cover
VALENTINE DE LANDRO

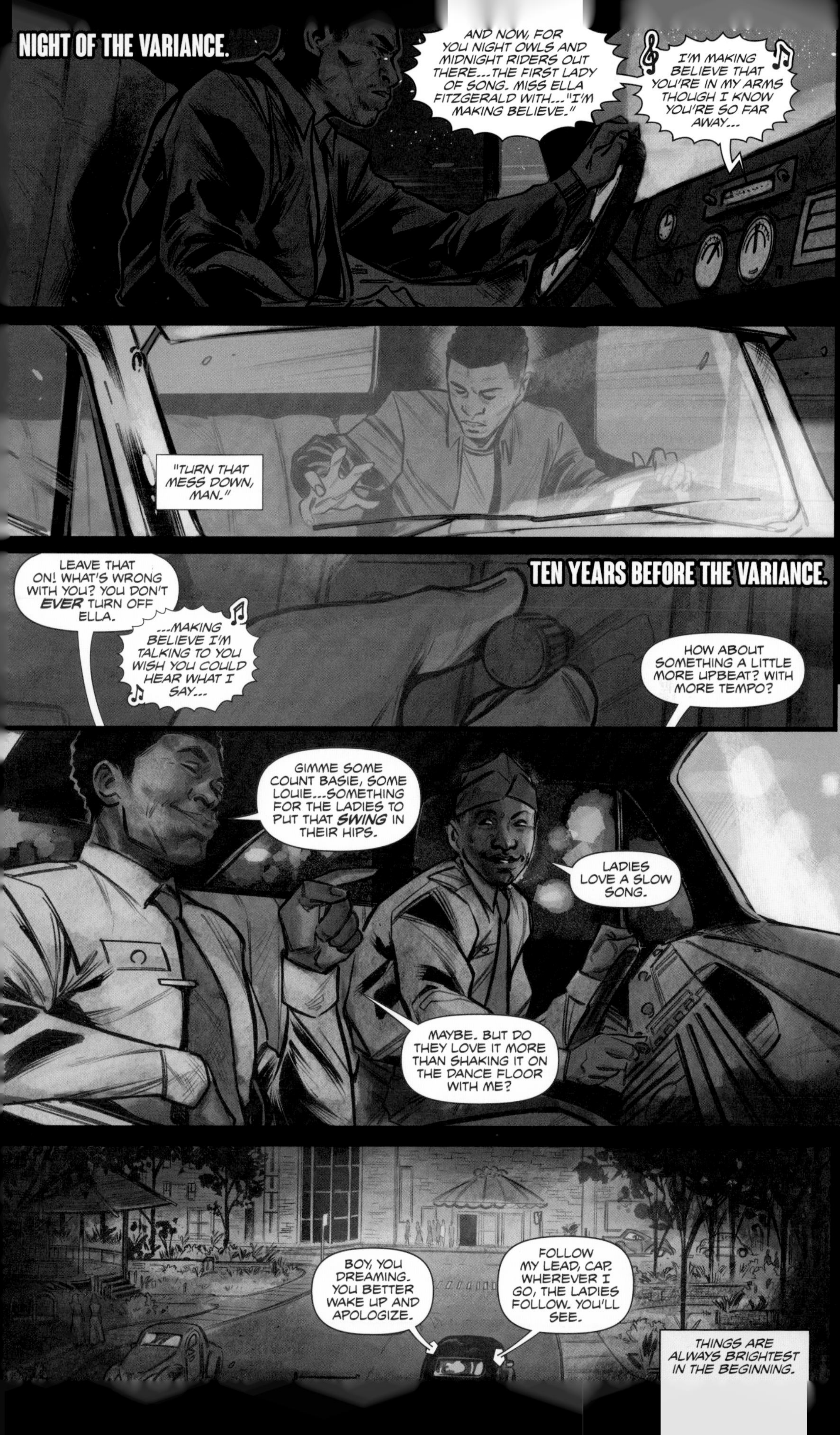
NIGHT OF THE VARIANCE.
AND NOW, FOR YOU NIGHT OWLS AND MIDNIGHT RIDERS OUT THERE...THE FIRST LADY OF SONG. MISS ELLA FITZGERALD WITH..."I'M MAKING BELIEVE."
I'M MAKING BELIEVE THAT YOU'RE IN MY ARMS THOUGH I KNOW YOU'RE SO FAR AWAY...
"TURN THAT MESS DOWN, MAN."
TEN YEARS BEFORE THE VARIANCE.
LEAVE THAT ON! WHAT'S WRONG WITH YOU? YOU DON'T EVER TURN OFF ELLA.
...MAKING BELIEVE I'M TALKING TO YOU WISH YOU COULD HEAR WHAT I SAY...
HOW ABOUT SOMETHING A LITTLE MORE UPBEAT? WITH MORE TEMPO?
GIMME SOME COUNT BASIE, SOME LOUIE...SOMETHING FOR THE LADIES TO PUT THAT SWING IN THEIR HIPS.
LADIES LOVE A SLOW SONG.
MAYBE. BUT DO THEY LOVE IT MORE THAN SHAKING IT ON THE DANCE FLOOR WITH ME?
BOY, YOU DREAMING. YOU BETTER WAKE UP AND APOLOGIZE.
FOLLOW MY LEAD, CAP. WHEREVER I GO, THE LADIES FOLLOW. YOU'LL SEE.
THINGS ARE ALWAYS BRIGHTEST IN THE BEGINNING.

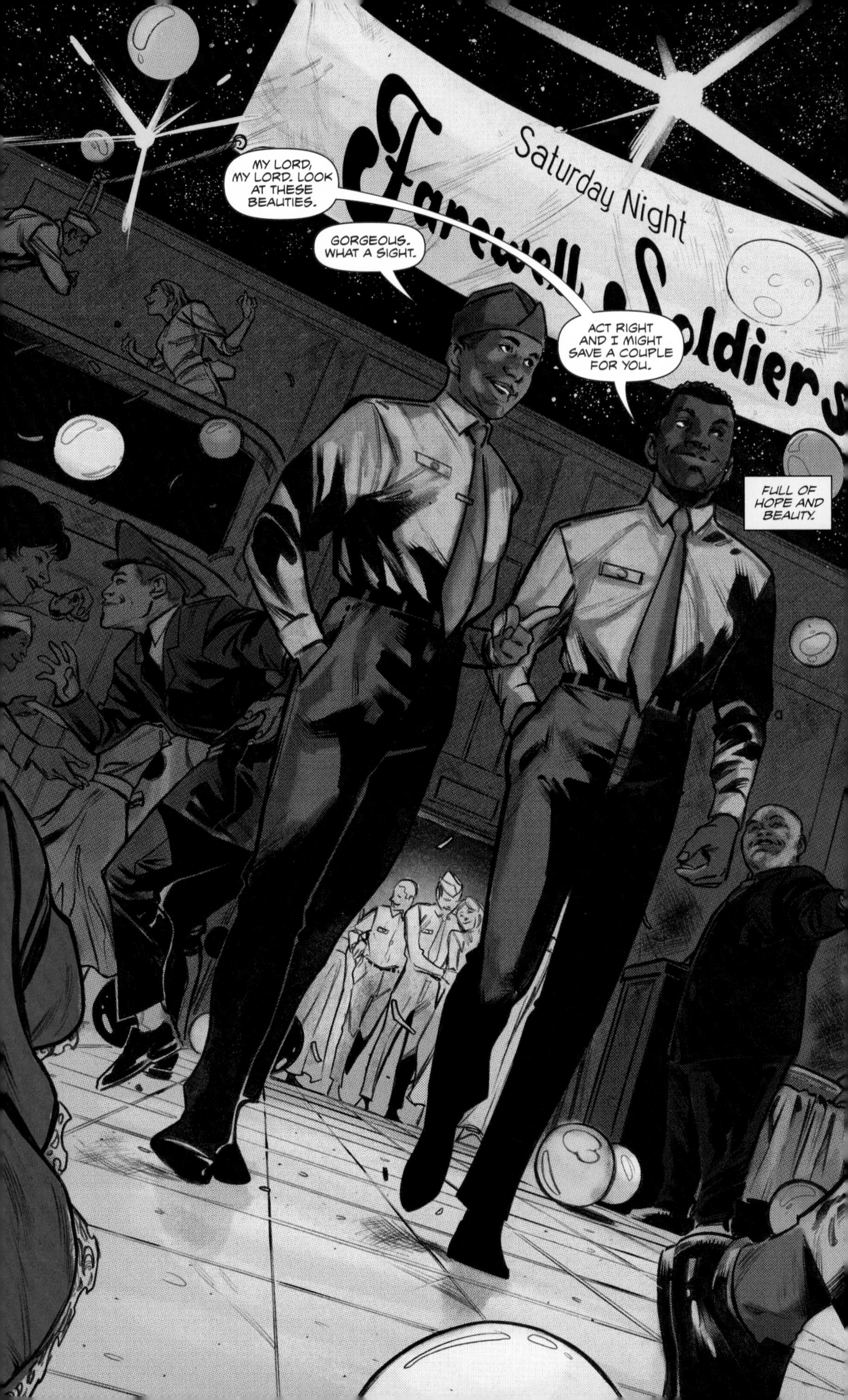
Saturday Night
Farewell Soldiers
MY LORD, MY LORD. LOOK AT THESE BEAUTIES.
GORGEOUS. WHAT A SIGHT.
ACT RIGHT AND I MIGHT SAVE A COUPLE FOR YOU.
FULL OF HOPE AND BEAUTY.

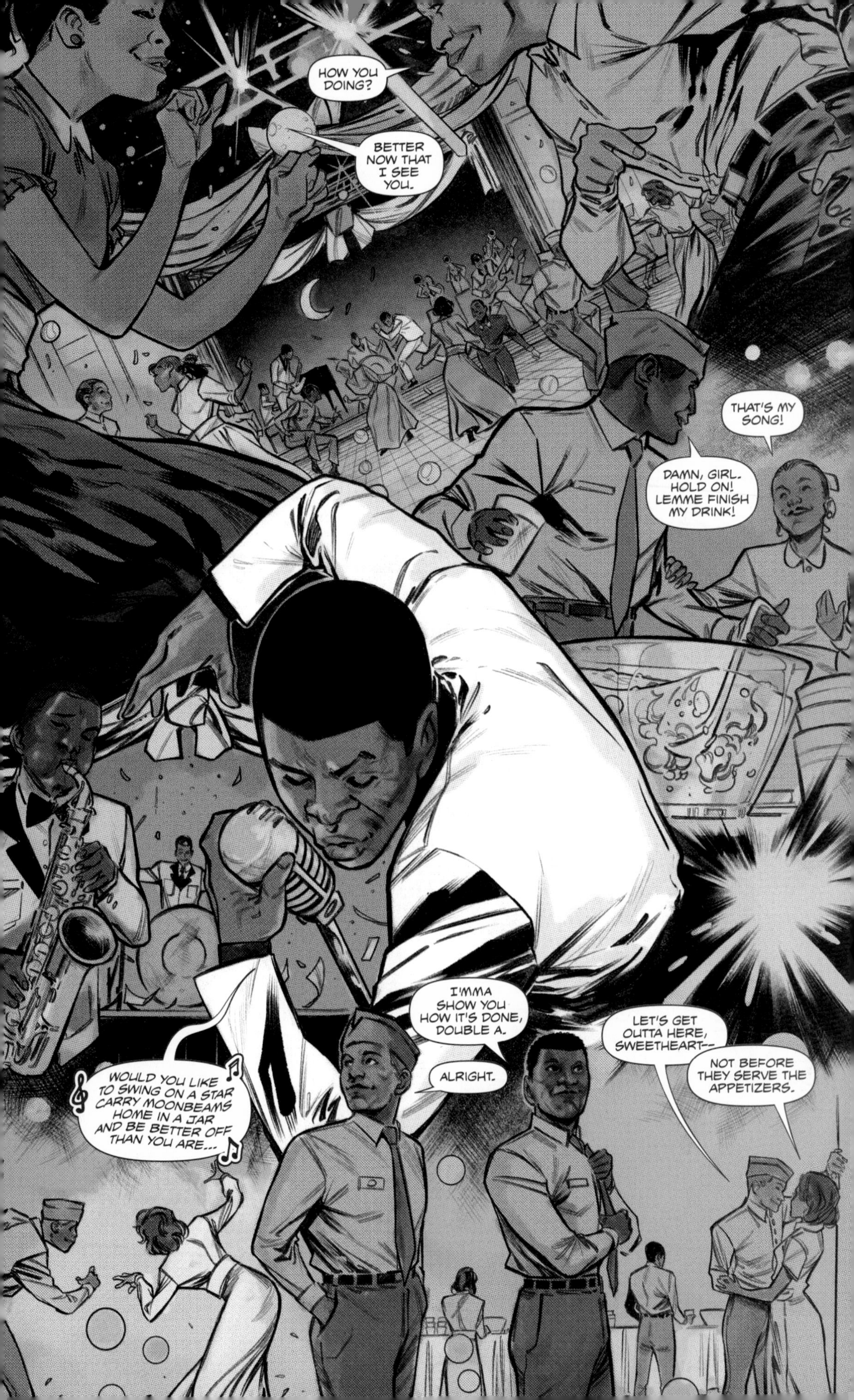
HOW YOU DOING?
BETTER NOW THAT I SEE YOU.
THAT'S MY SONG!
DAMN, GIRL. HOLD ON! LEMME FINISH MY DRINK!
I'MMA SHOW YOU HOW IT'S DONE, DOUBLE A.
ALRIGHT.
WOULD YOU LIKE TO SWING ON A STAR CARRY MOONBEAMS HOME IN A JAR AND BE BETTER OFF THAN YOU ARE...
LET'S GET OUTTA HERE, SWEETHEART--
NOT BEFORE THEY SERVE THE APPETIZERS.

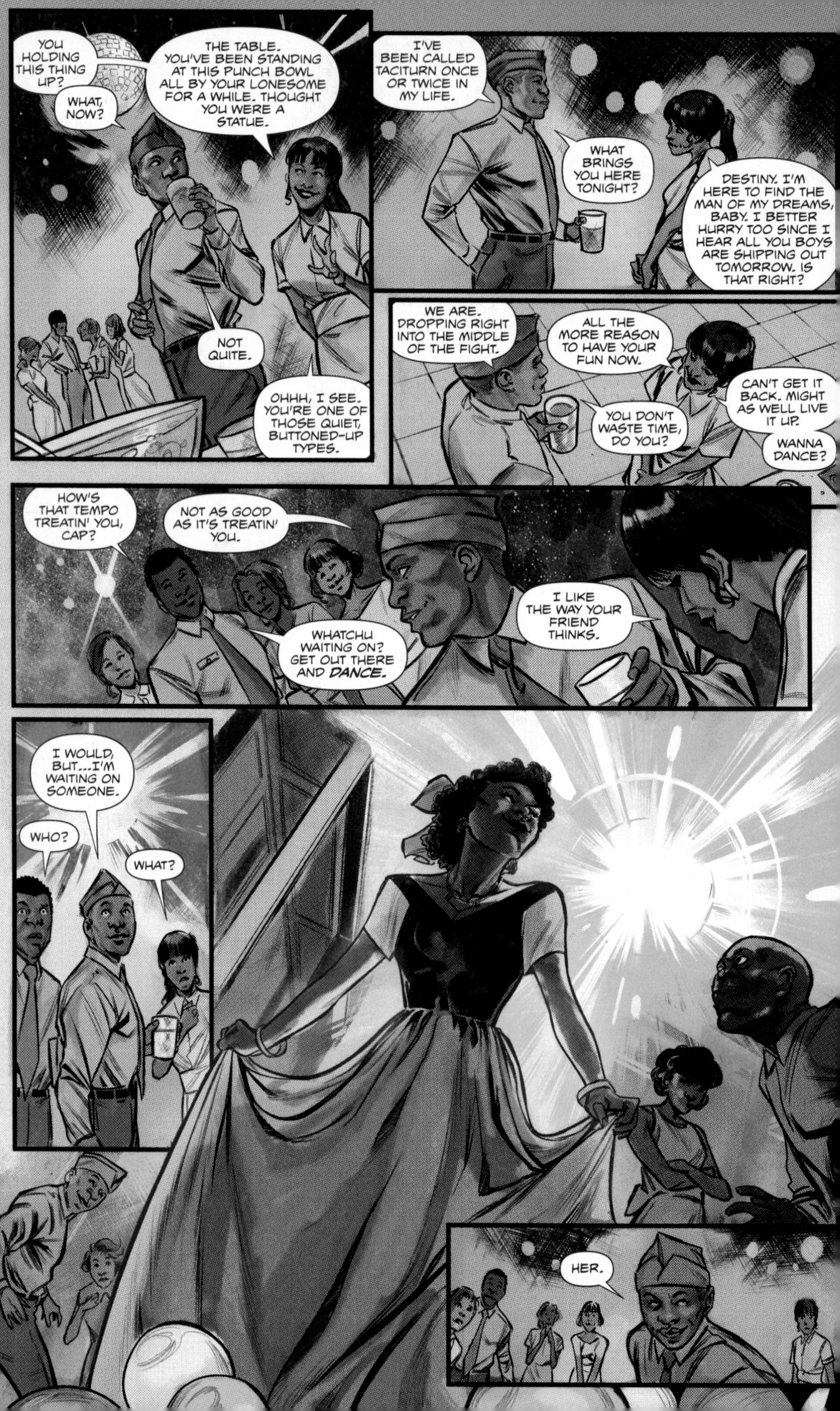
YOU HOLDING THIS THING UP?
WHAT, NOW?
THE TABLE. YOU'VE BEEN STANDING AT THIS PUNCH BOWL ALL BY YOUR LONESOME FOR A WHILE. THOUGHT YOU WERE A STATUE.
NOT QUITE.
OHHH, I SEE. YOU'RE ONE OF THOSE QUIET, BUTTONED-UP TYPES.
I'VE BEEN CALLED TACITURN ONCE OR TWICE IN MY LIFE.
WHAT BRINGS YOU HERE TONIGHT?
DESTINY. I'M HERE TO FIND THE MAN OF MY DREAMS, BABY. I BETTER HURRY TOO SINCE I HEAR ALL YOU BOYS ARE SHIPPING OUT TOMORROW. IS THAT RIGHT?
WE ARE. DROPPING RIGHT INTO THE MIDDLE OF THE FIGHT.
ALL THE MORE REASON TO HAVE YOUR FUN NOW.
YOU DON'T WASTE TIME, DO YOU?
CAN'T GET IT BACK. MIGHT AS WELL LIVE IT UP.
WANNA DANCE?
HOW'S THAT TEMPO TREATIN' YOU, CAP?
NOT AS GOOD AS IT'S TREATIN' YOU.
WHATCHU WAITING ON? GET OUT THERE AND DANCE.
I LIKE THE WAY YOUR FRIEND THINKS.
I WOULD, BUT...I'M WAITING ON SOMEONE.
WHO?
WHAT?
HER.

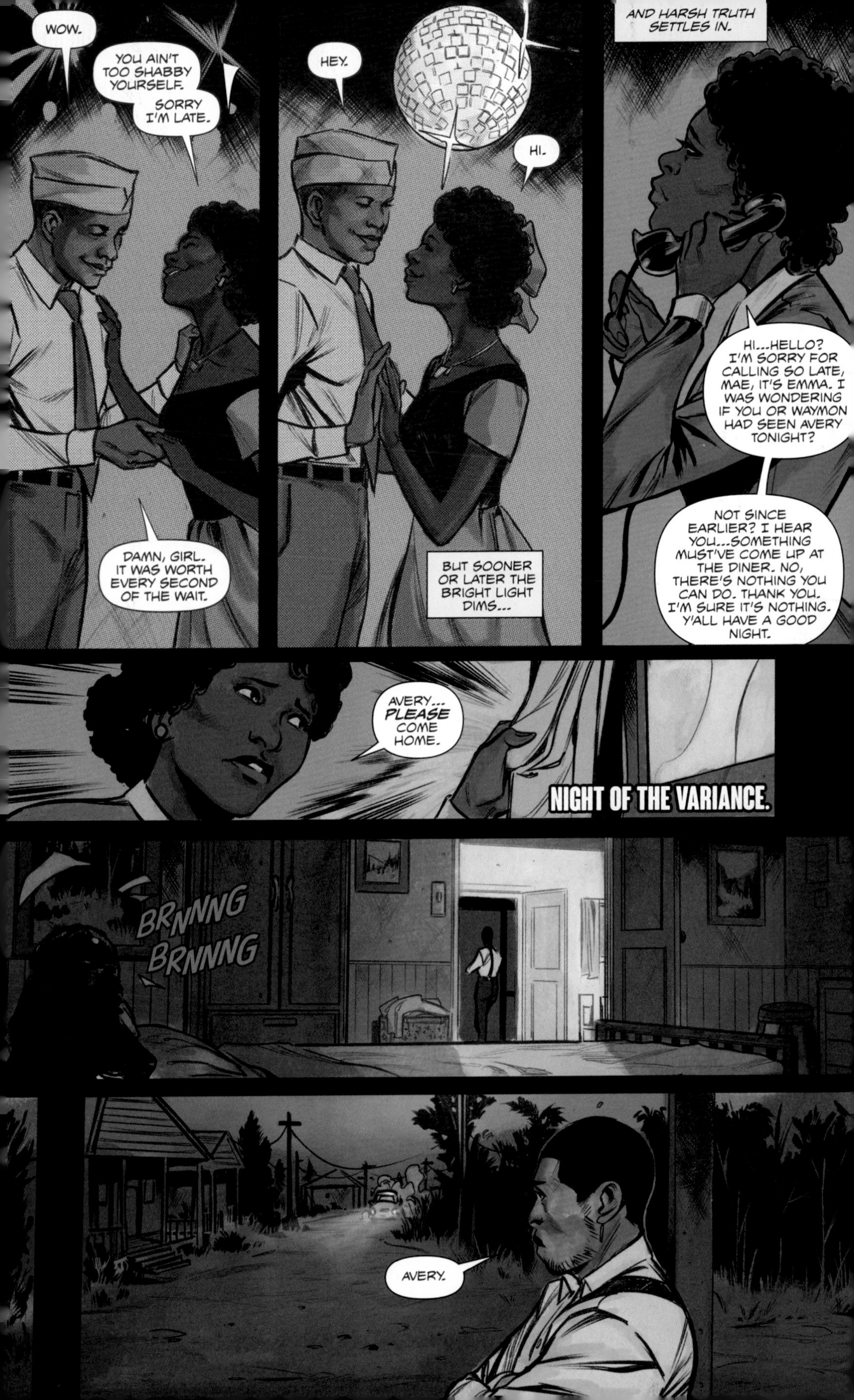
WOW.
YOU AIN'T TOO SHABBY YOURSELF.
SORRY I'M LATE.
DAMN, GIRL. IT WAS WORTH EVERY SECOND OF THE WAIT.
HEY.
HI.
BUT SOONER OR LATER THE BRIGHT LIGHT DIMS...
AND HARSH TRUTH SETTLES IN.
HI...HELLO? I'M SORRY FOR CALLING SO LATE, MAE, IT'S EMMA. I WAS WONDERING IF YOU OR WAYMON HAD SEEN AVERY TONIGHT?
NOT SINCE EARLIER? I HEAR YOU...SOMETHING MUST'VE COME UP AT THE DINER. NO, THERE'S NOTHING YOU CAN DO. THANK YOU. I'M SURE IT'S NOTHING. Y'ALL HAVE A GOOD NIGHT.
AVERY... PLEASE COME HOME.
NIGHT OF THE VARIANCE.
BRNNNG BRNNNG
AVERY.

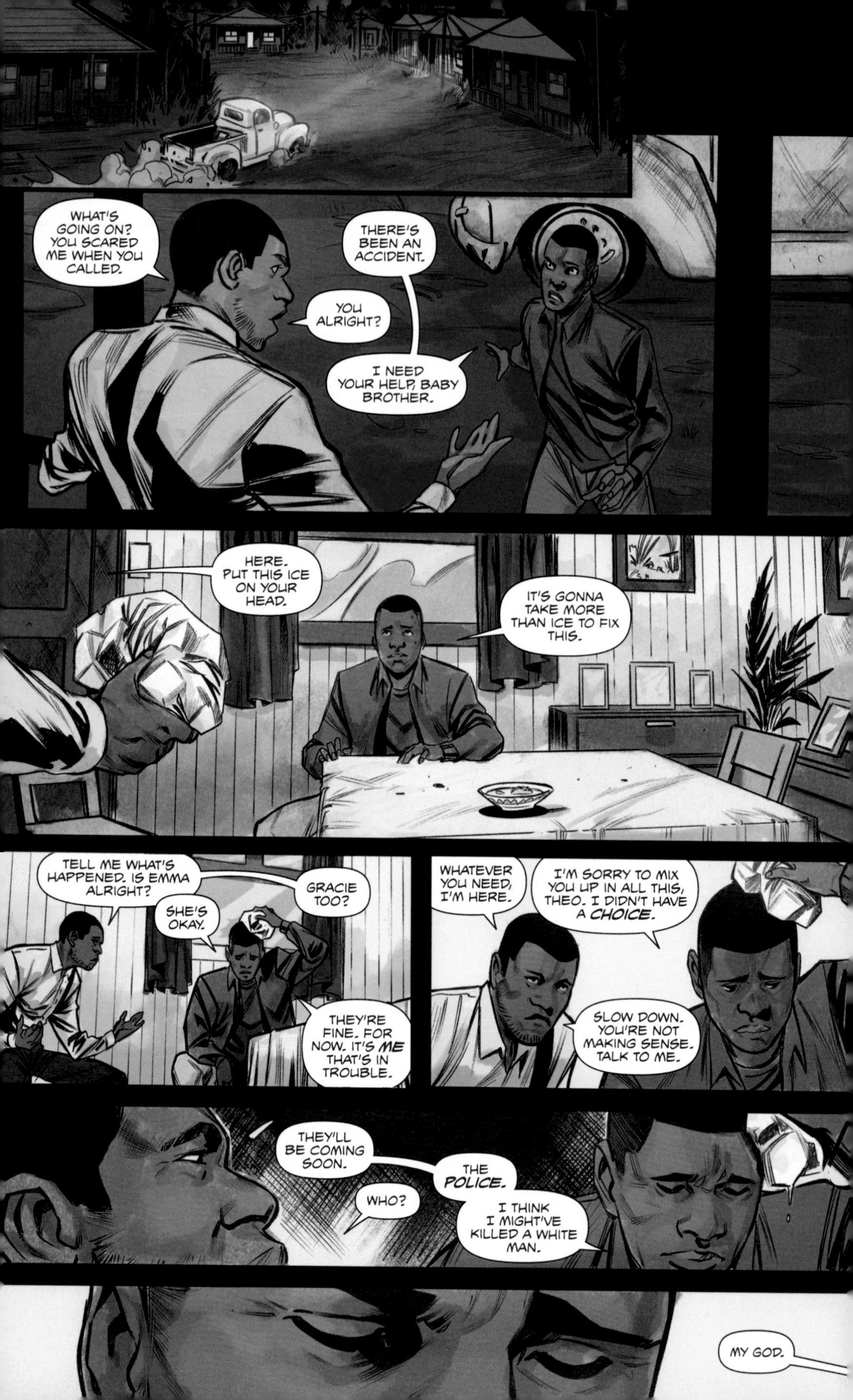
WHAT'S GOING ON? YOU SCARED ME WHEN YOU CALLED.
THERE'S BEEN AN ACCIDENT.
YOU ALRIGHT?
I NEED YOUR HELP, BABY BROTHER.
HERE. PUT THIS ICE ON YOUR HEAD.
IT'S GONNA TAKE MORE THAN ICE TO FIX THIS.
TELL ME WHAT'S HAPPENED. IS EMMA ALRIGHT?
SHE'S OKAY.
GRACIE TOO?
THEY'RE FINE. FOR NOW. IT'S ME THAT'S IN TROUBLE.
WHATEVER YOU NEED, I'M HERE.
I'M SORRY TO MIX YOU UP IN ALL THIS, THEO. I DIDN'T HAVE A CHOICE.
SLOW DOWN. YOU'RE NOT MAKING SENSE. TALK TO ME.
THEY'LL BE COMING SOON.
WHO?
THE POLICE.
I THINK I MIGHT'VE KILLED A WHITE MAN.
MY GOD.

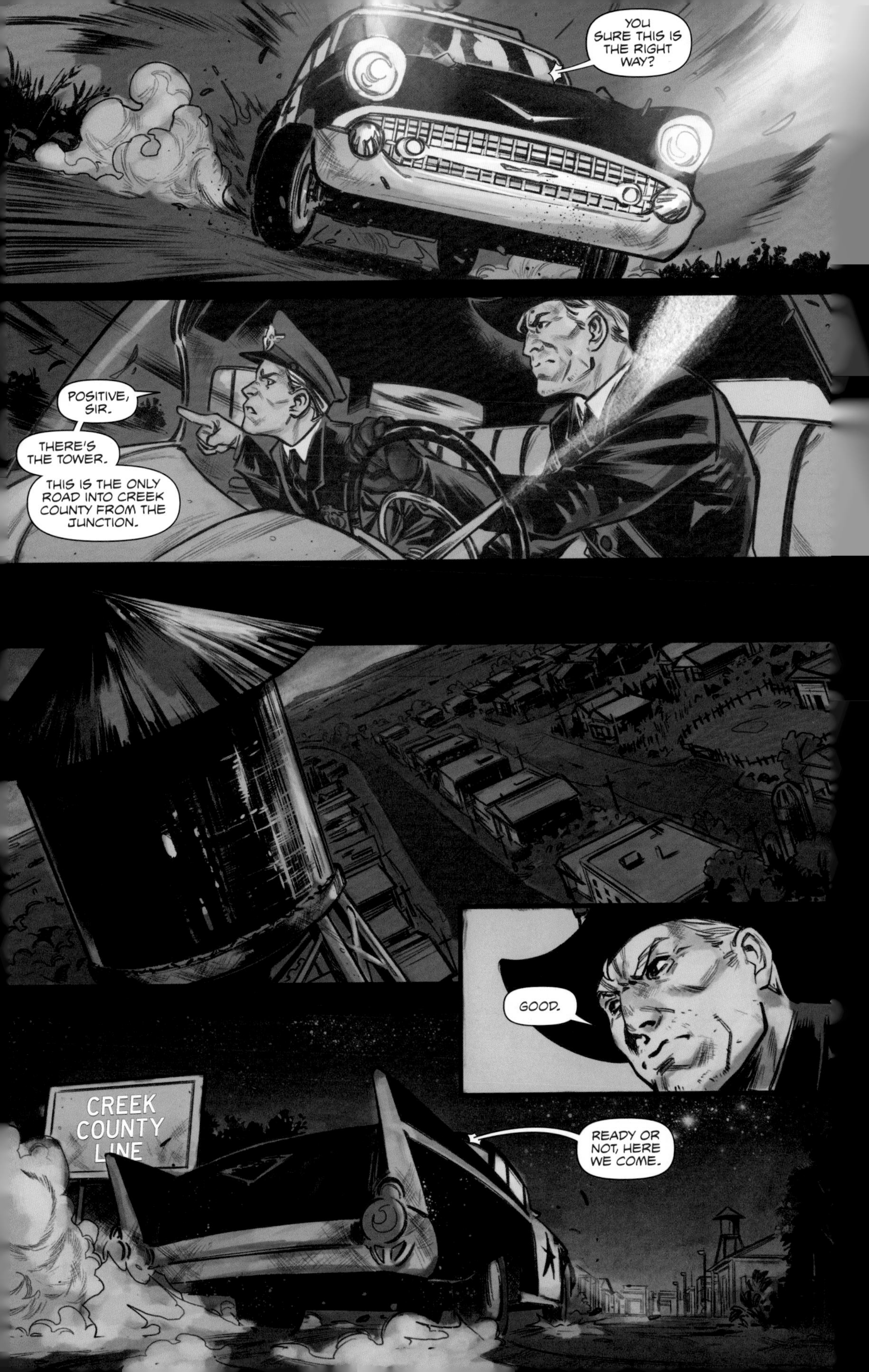
YOU SURE THIS IS THE RIGHT WAY?
POSITIVE, SIR.
THERE'S THE TOWER.
THIS IS THE ONLY ROAD INTO CREEK COUNTY FROM THE JUNCTION.
GOOD.
CREEK COUNTY LINE
READY OR NOT, HERE WE COME.

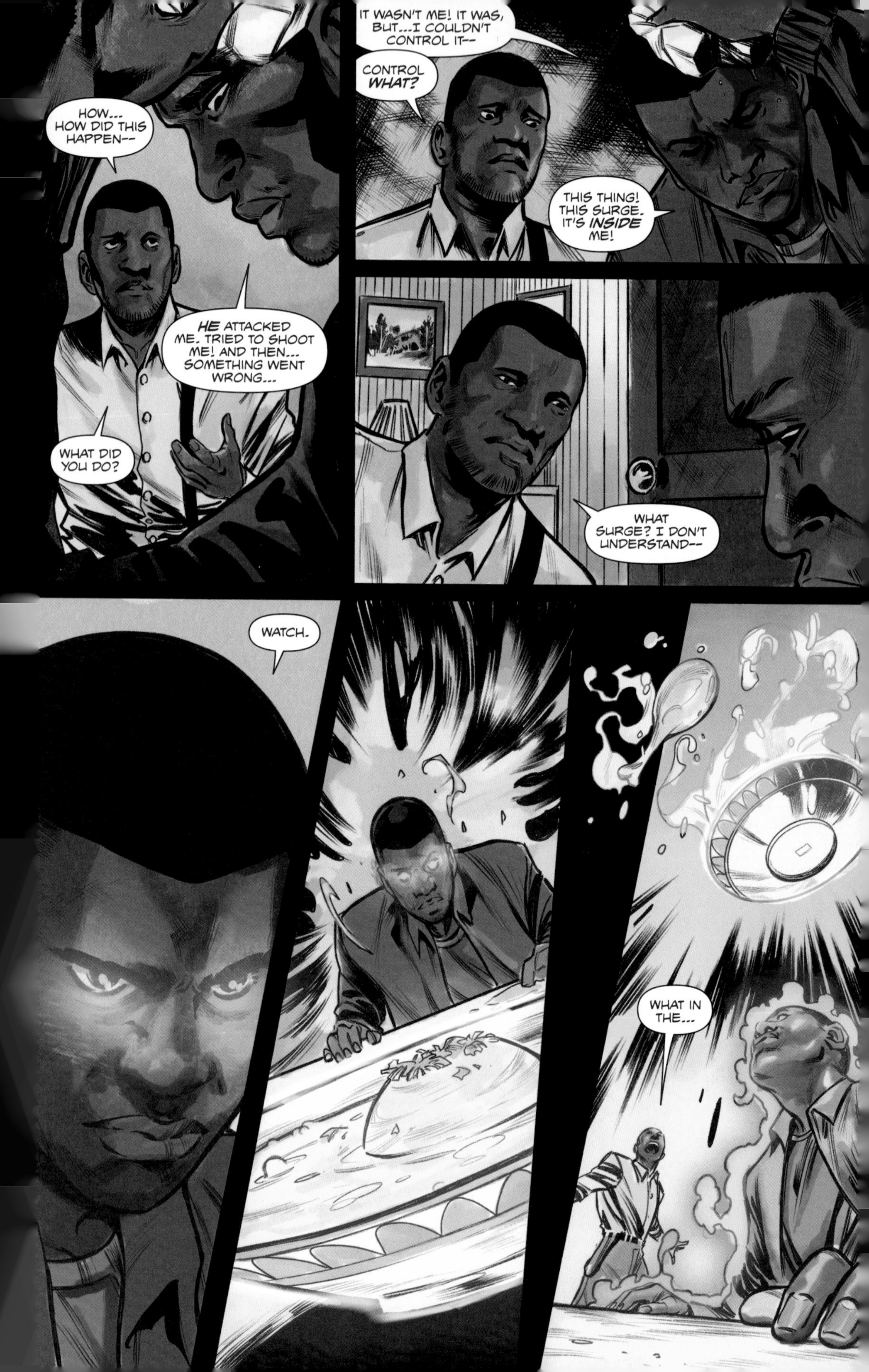
HOW... HOW DID THIS HAPPEN--
HE ATTACKED ME. TRIED TO SHOOT ME! AND THEN... SOMETHING WENT WRONG...
WHAT DID YOU DO?
IT WASN'T ME! IT WAS, BUT... I COULDN'T CONTROL IT--
CONTROL WHAT?
THIS THING! THIS SURGE. IT'S INSIDE ME!
WHAT SURGE? I DON'T UNDERSTAND--
WATCH.
WHAT IN THE...

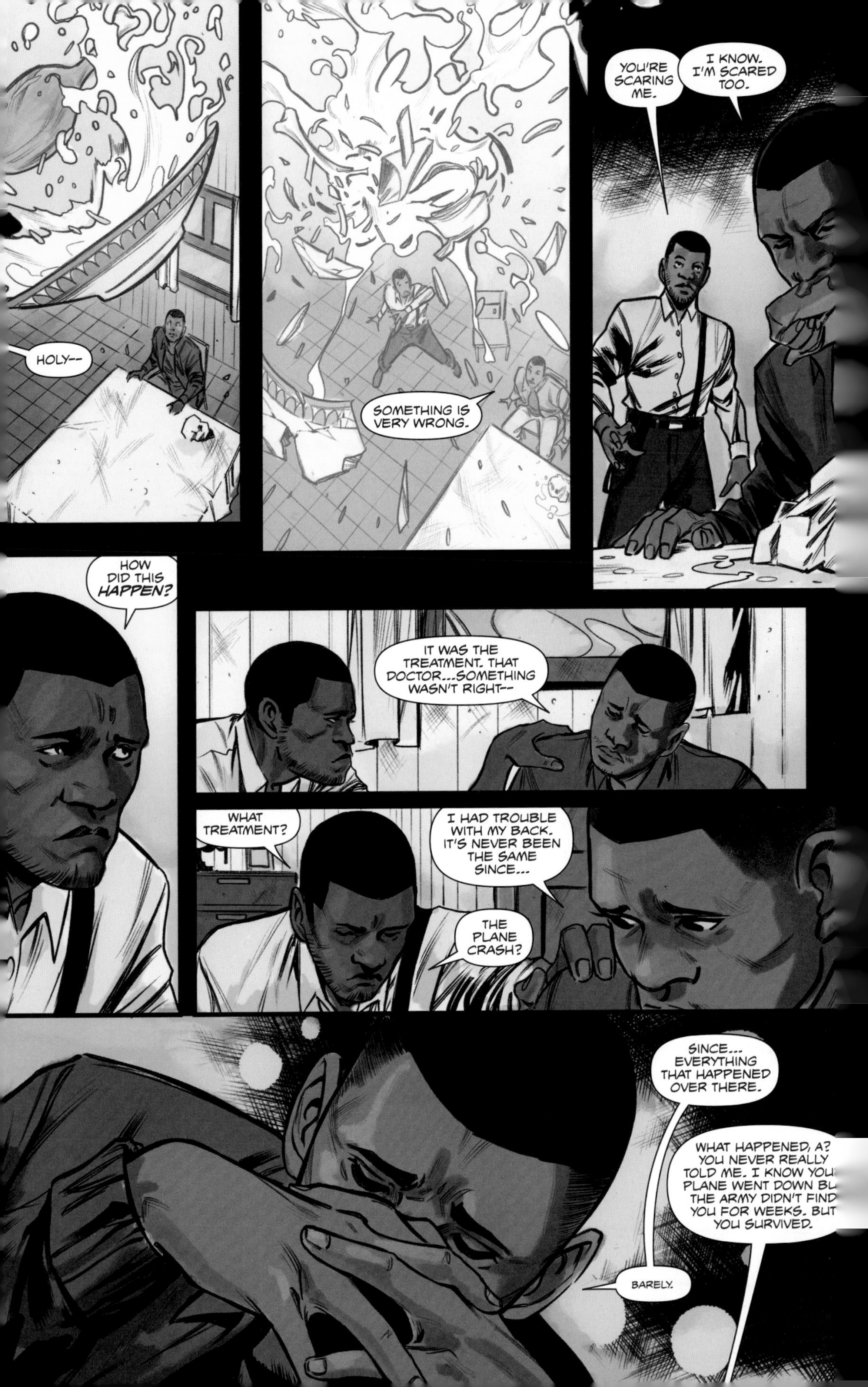
HOLY--
SOMETHING IS VERY WRONG.
YOU'RE SCARING ME.
I KNOW. I'M SCARED TOO.
HOW DID THIS *HAPPEN?*
IT WAS THE TREATMENT. THAT DOCTOR...SOMETHING WASN'T RIGHT--
WHAT TREATMENT?
I HAD TROUBLE WITH MY BACK. IT'S NEVER BEEN THE SAME SINCE...
THE PLANE CRASH?
SINCE... EVERYTHING THAT HAPPENED OVER THERE.
WHAT HAPPENED, A? YOU NEVER REALLY TOLD ME. I KNOW YOU PLANE WENT DOWN BU THE ARMY DIDN'T FIND YOU FOR WEEKS. BUT YOU SURVIVED.
BARELY.

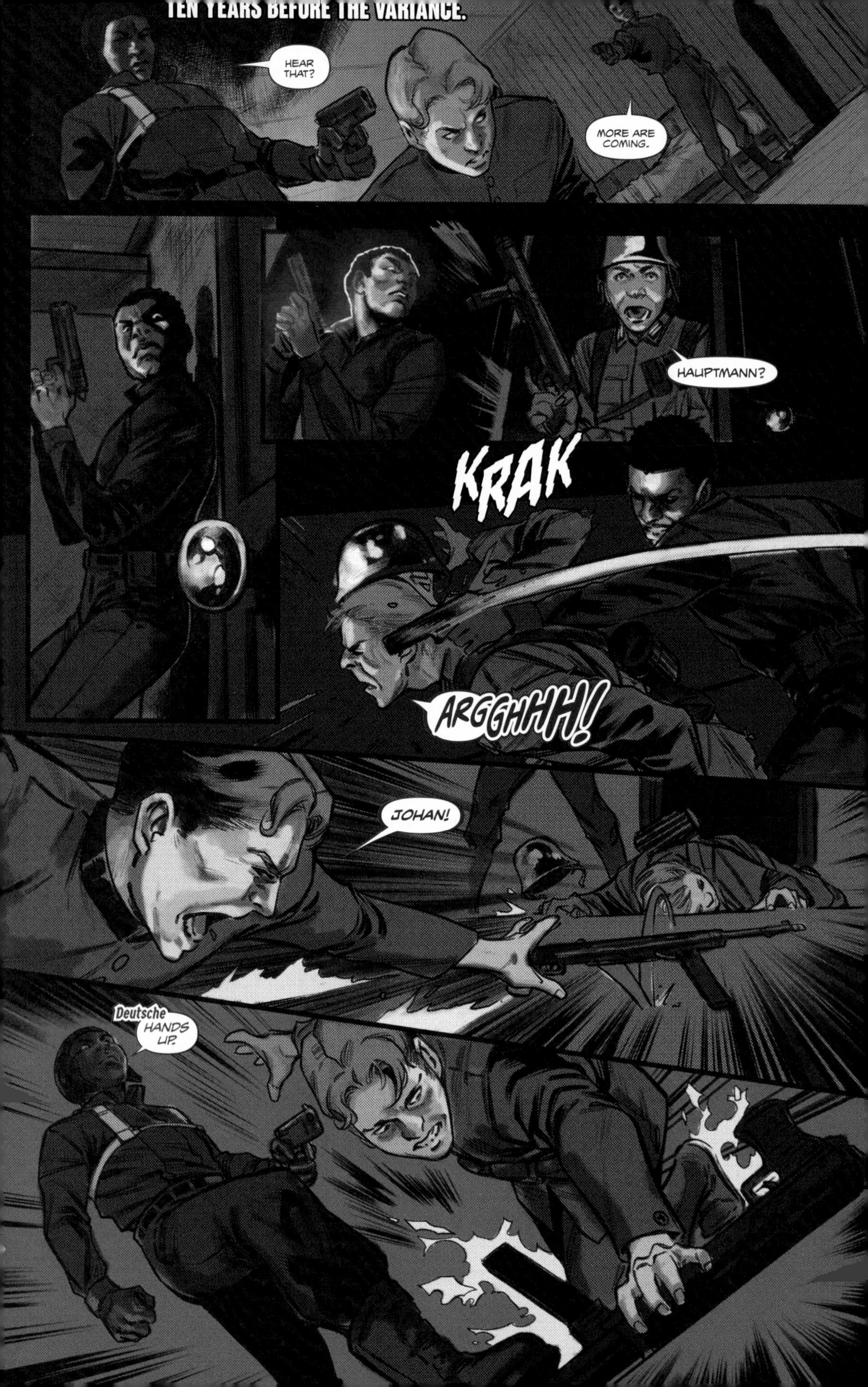
TEN YEARS BEFORE THE VARIANCE.
HEAR THAT?
MORE ARE COMING.
HAUPTMANN?
KRAK
ARGGHHH!
JOHAN!
Deutsche
HANDS UP.

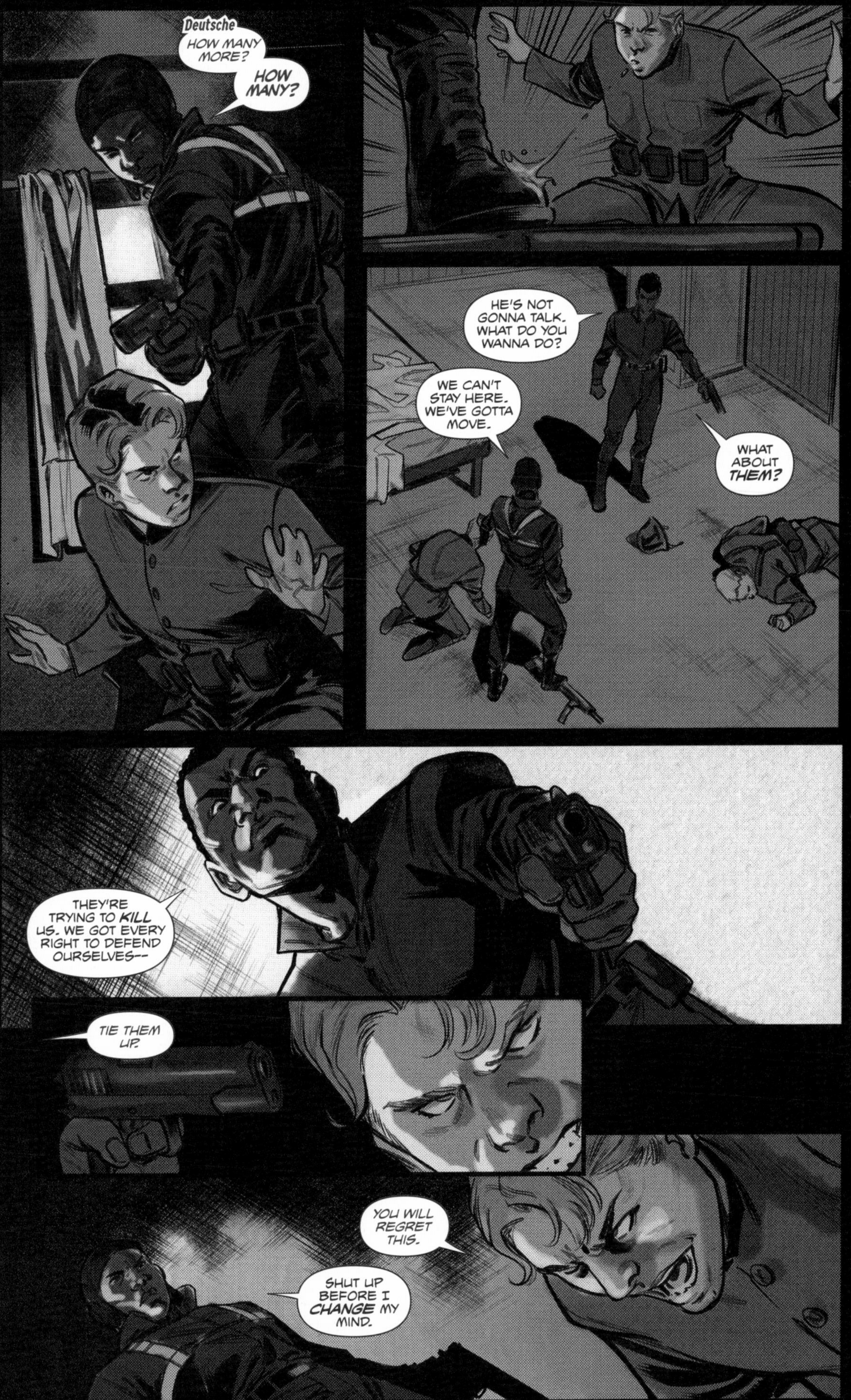
Deutsche
HOW MANY MORE?
HOW MANY?
HE'S NOT GONNA TALK. WHAT DO YOU WANNA DO?
WE CAN'T STAY HERE. WE'VE GOTTA MOVE.
WHAT ABOUT THEM?
THEY'RE TRYING TO KILL US. WE GOT EVERY RIGHT TO DEFEND OURSELVES--
TIE THEM UP?
YOU WILL REGRET THIS.
SHUT UP BEFORE I CHANGE MY MIND.

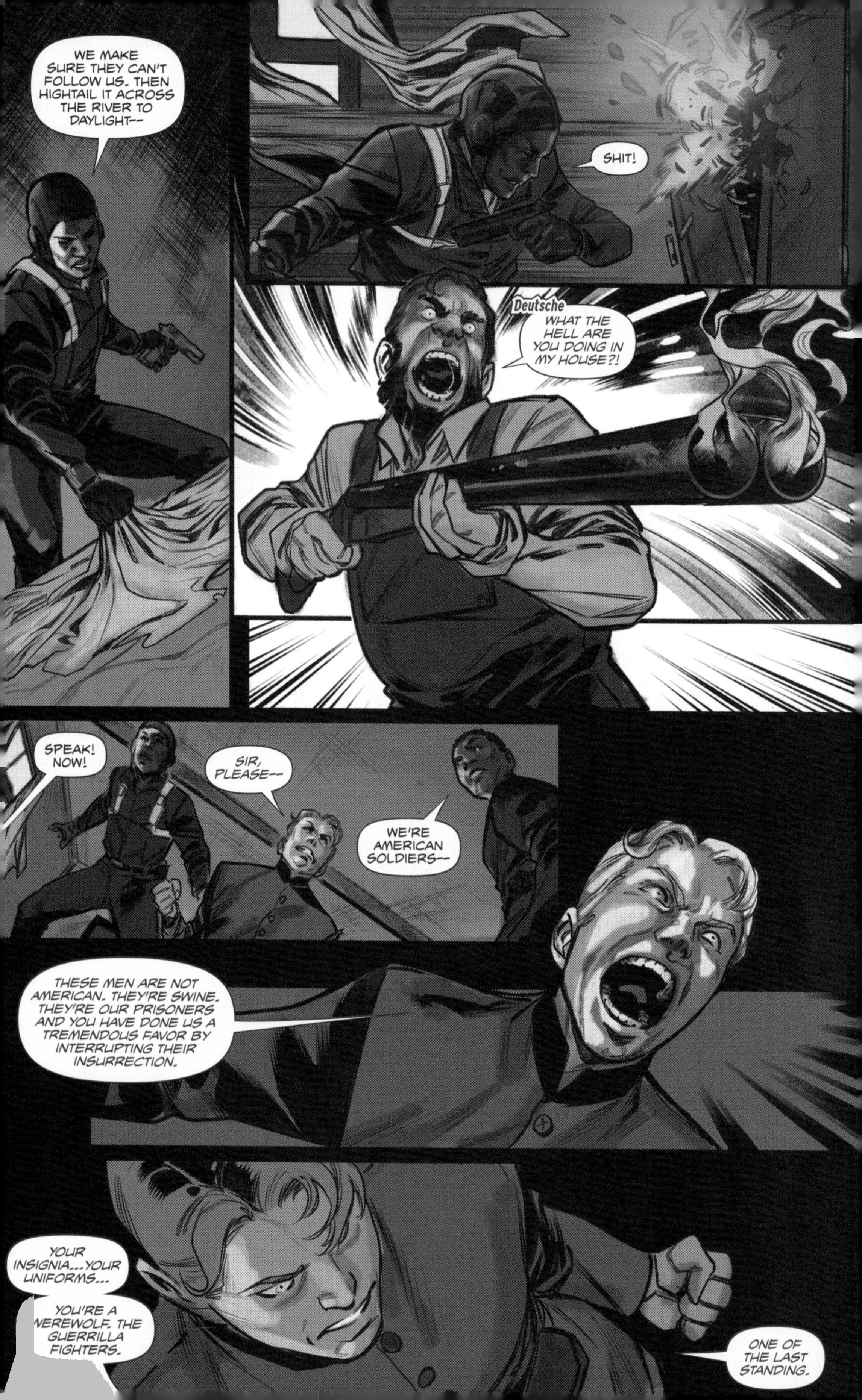
WE MAKE SURE THEY CAN'T FOLLOW US. THEN HIGHTAIL IT ACROSS THE RIVER TO DAYLIGHT--
SHIT!
Deutsche
WHAT THE HELL ARE YOU DOING IN MY HOUSE?!
SPEAK! NOW!
SIR, PLEASE--
WE'RE AMERICAN SOLDIERS--
THESE MEN ARE NOT AMERICAN. THEY'RE SWINE. THEY'RE OUR PRISONERS AND YOU HAVE DONE US A TREMENDOUS FAVOR BY INTERRUPTING THEIR INSURRECTION.
YOUR INSIGNIA...YOUR UNIFORMS...
YOU'RE A WEREWOLF. THE GUERRILLA FIGHTERS.
ONE OF THE LAST STANDING.

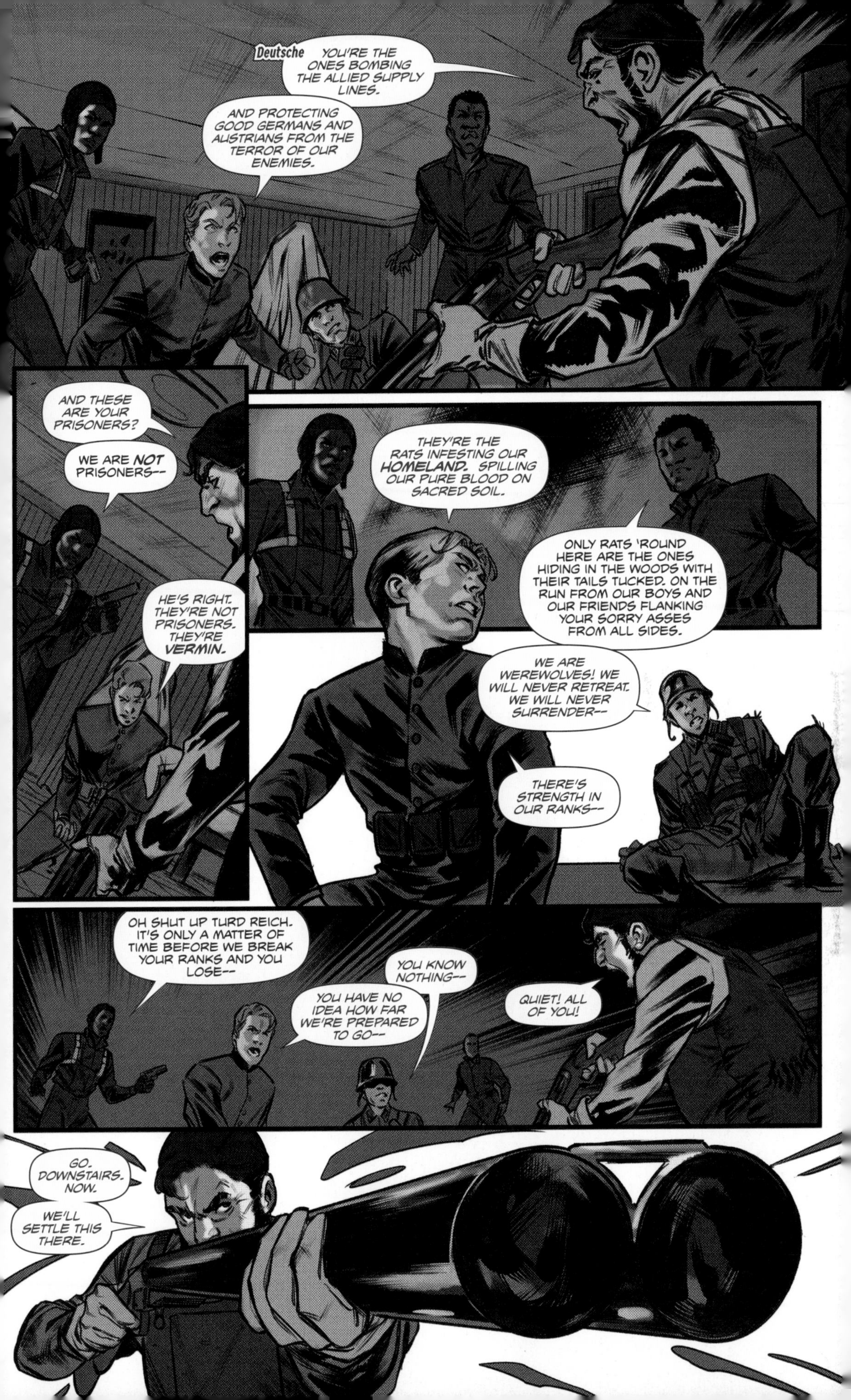
Deutsche
YOU'RE THE ONES BOMBING THE ALLIED SUPPLY LINES.
AND PROTECTING GOOD GERMANS AND AUSTRIANS FROM THE TERROR OF OUR ENEMIES.
AND THESE ARE YOUR PRISONERS?
WE ARE NOT PRISONERS--
HE'S RIGHT. THEY'RE NOT PRISONERS. THEY'RE VERMIN.
THEY'RE THE RATS INFESTING OUR HOMELAND. SPILLING OUR PURE BLOOD ON SACRED SOIL.
ONLY RATS 'ROUND HERE ARE THE ONES HIDING IN THE WOODS WITH THEIR TAILS TUCKED. ON THE RUN FROM OUR BOYS AND OUR FRIENDS FLANKING YOUR SORRY ASSES FROM ALL SIDES.
WE ARE WEREWOLVES! WE WILL NEVER RETREAT. WE WILL NEVER SURRENDER--
THERE'S STRENGTH IN OUR RANKS--
OH SHUT UP TURD REICH. IT'S ONLY A MATTER OF TIME BEFORE WE BREAK YOUR RANKS AND YOU LOSE--
YOU KNOW NOTHING--
YOU HAVE NO IDEA HOW FAR WE'RE PREPARED TO GO--
QUIET! ALL OF YOU!
GO. DOWNSTAIRS. NOW.
WE'LL SETTLE THIS THERE.

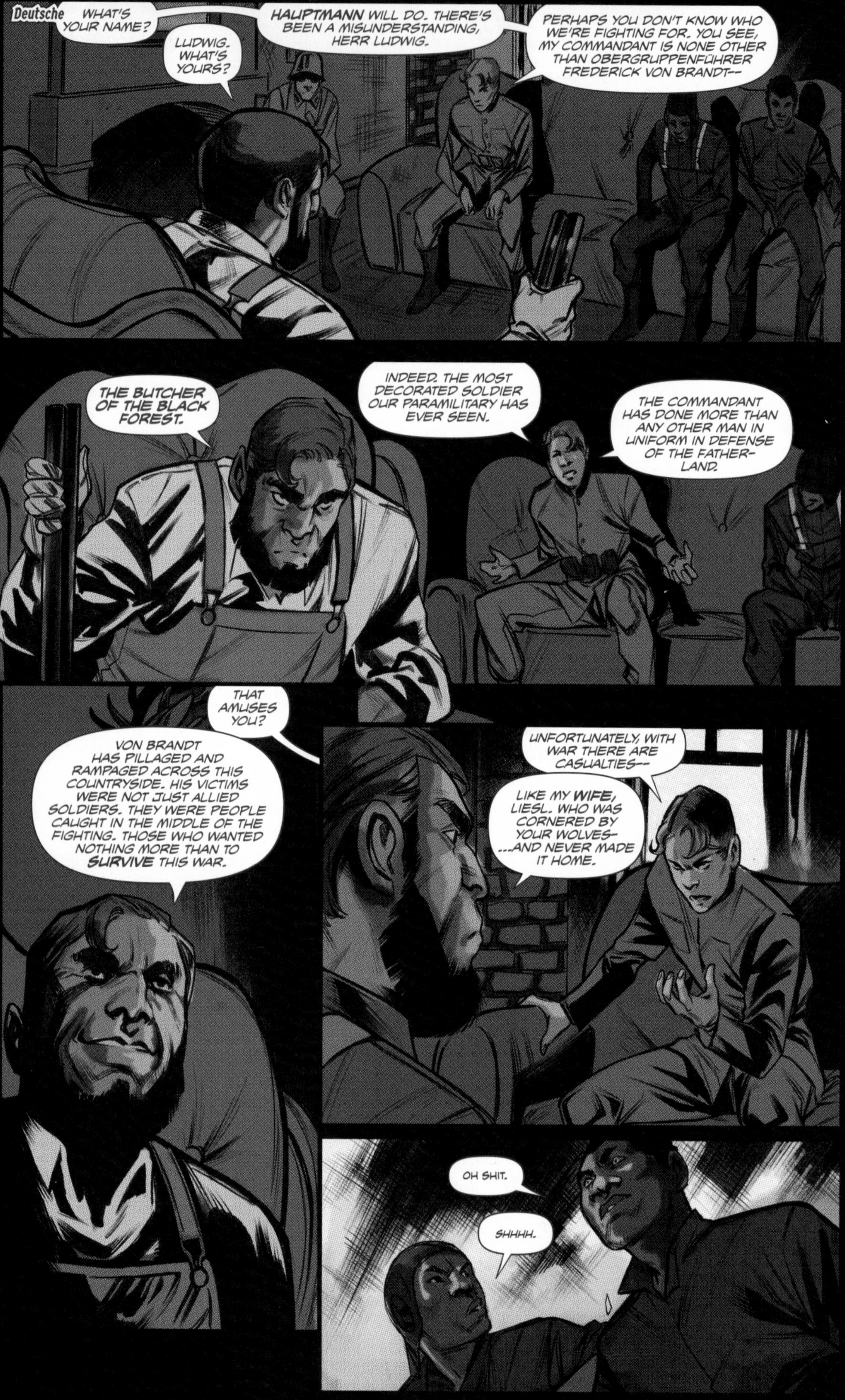
Deutsche
WHAT'S YOUR NAME?
LUDWIG. WHAT'S YOURS?
HAUPTMANN WILL DO. THERE'S BEEN A MISUNDERSTANDING, HERR LUDWIG.
PERHAPS YOU DON'T KNOW WHO WE'RE FIGHTING FOR. YOU SEE, MY COMMANDANT IS NONE OTHER THAN OBERGRUPPENFÜHRER FREDERICK VON BRANDT--
THE BUTCHER OF THE BLACK FOREST.
INDEED. THE MOST DECORATED SOLDIER OUR PARAMILITARY HAS EVER SEEN.
THE COMMANDANT HAS DONE MORE THAN ANY OTHER MAN IN UNIFORM IN DEFENSE OF THE FATHER-LAND.
THAT AMUSES YOU?
VON BRANDT HAS PILLAGED AND RAMPAGED ACROSS THIS COUNTRYSIDE. HIS VICTIMS WERE NOT JUST ALLIED SOLDIERS. THEY WERE PEOPLE CAUGHT IN THE MIDDLE OF THE FIGHTING. THOSE WHO WANTED NOTHING MORE THAN TO SURVIVE THIS WAR.
UNFORTUNATELY, WITH WAR THERE ARE CASUALTIES--
LIKE MY WIFE, LIESL. WHO WAS CORNERED BY YOUR WOLVES---AND NEVER MADE IT HOME.
OH SHIT.
SHHHH.

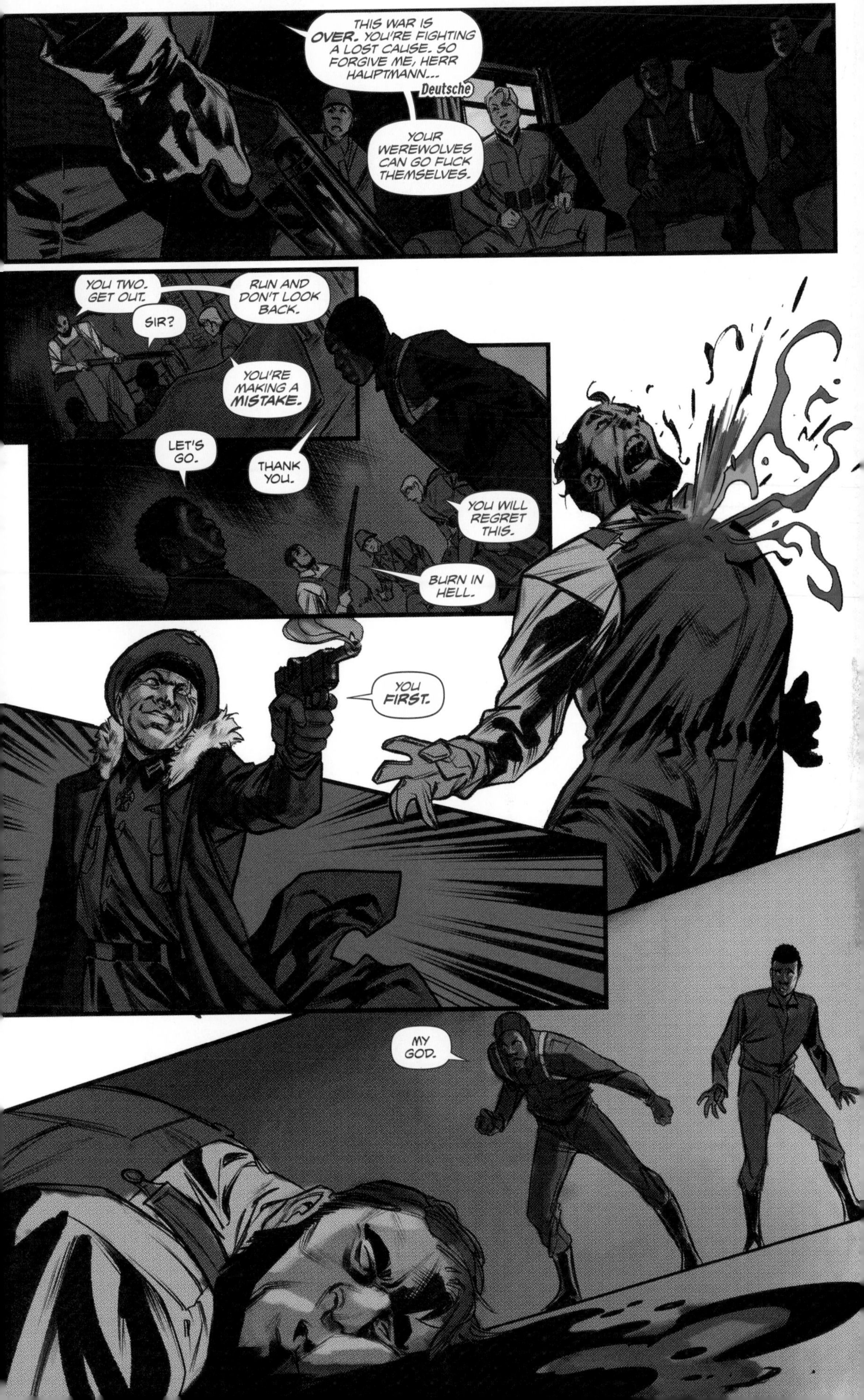
THIS WAR IS OVER. YOU'RE FIGHTING A LOST CAUSE. SO FORGIVE ME, HERR HAUPTMANN...
Deutsche
YOUR WEREWOLVES CAN GO FUCK THEMSELVES.
YOU TWO. GET OUT.
RUN AND DON'T LOOK BACK.
SIR?
YOU'RE MAKING A MISTAKE.
LET'S GO.
THANK YOU.
YOU WILL REGRET THIS.
BURN IN HELL.
YOU FIRST.
MY GOD.

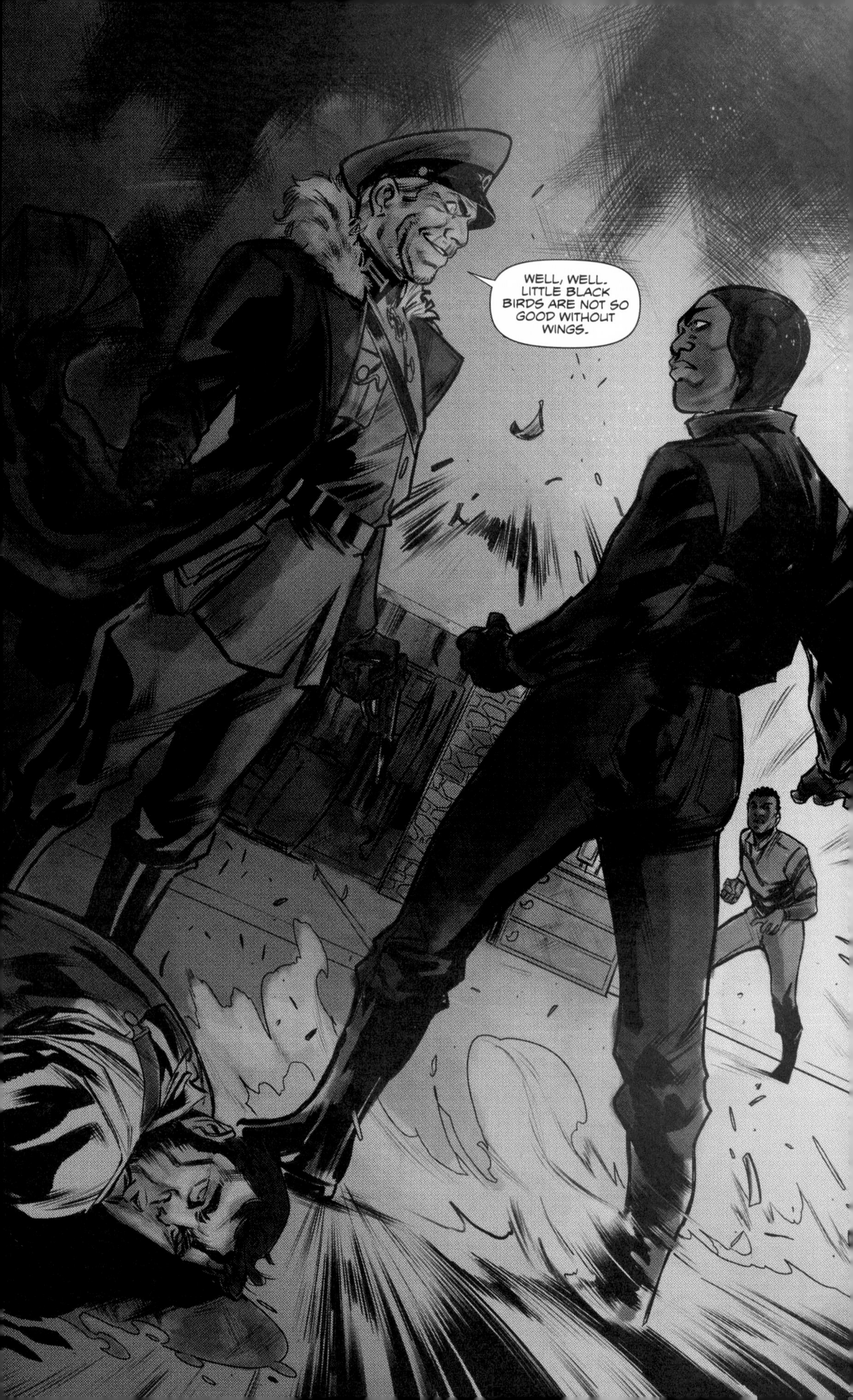
WELL, WELL. LITTLE BLACK BIRDS ARE NOT SO GOOD WITHOUT WINGS.

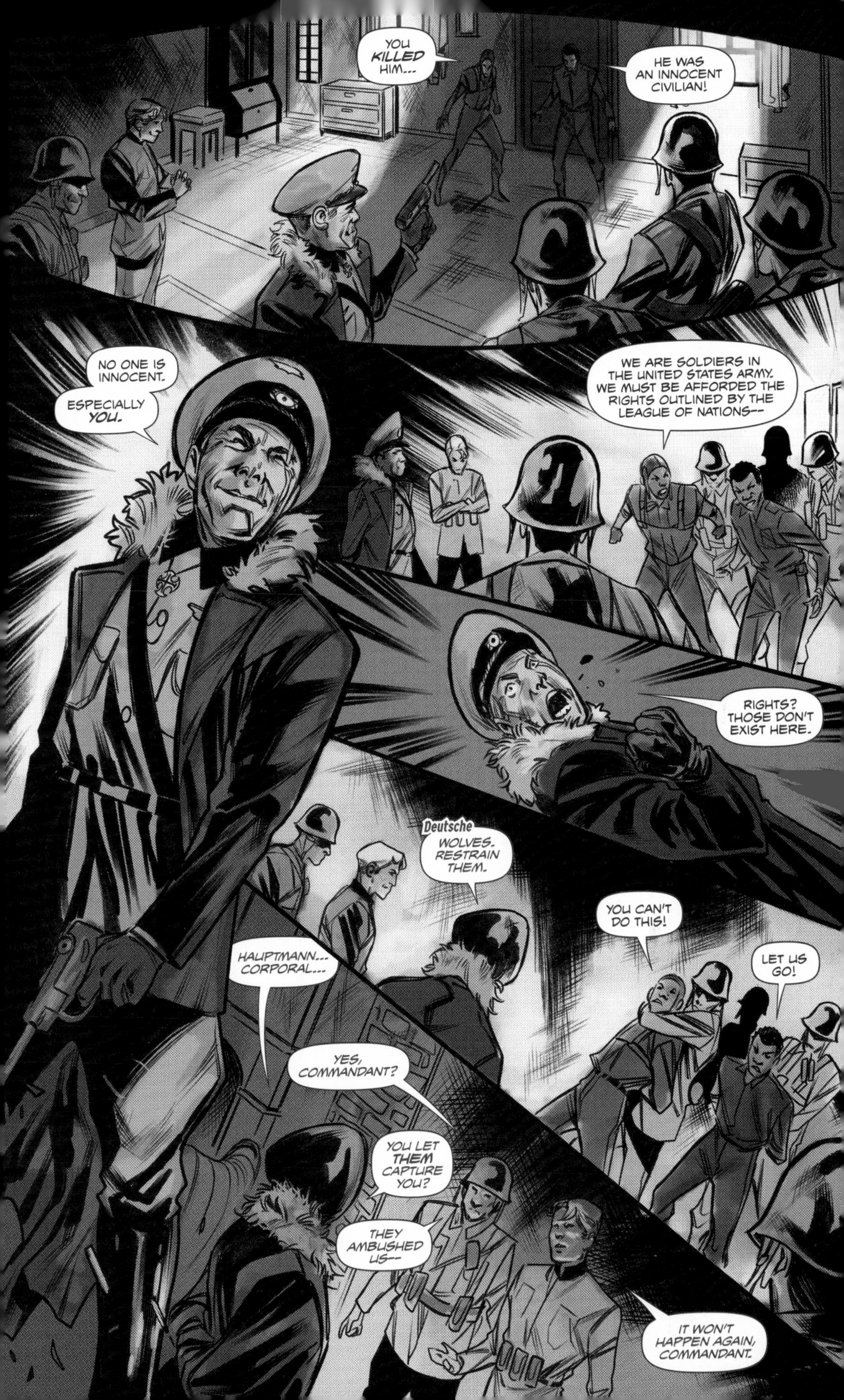
YOU KILLED HIM...
HE WAS AN INNOCENT CIVILIAN!
NO ONE IS INNOCENT.
ESPECIALLY YOU.
WE ARE SOLDIERS IN THE UNITED STATES ARMY. WE MUST BE AFFORDED THE RIGHTS OUTLINED BY THE LEAGUE OF NATIONS--
RIGHTS? THOSE DON'T EXIST HERE.
Deutsche
WOLVES. RESTRAIN THEM.
YOU CAN'T DO THIS!
LET US GO!
HAUPTMANN... CORPORAL...
YES, COMMANDANT?
YOU LET THEM CAPTURE YOU?
THEY AMBUSHED US--
IT WON'T HAPPEN AGAIN, COMMANDANT.

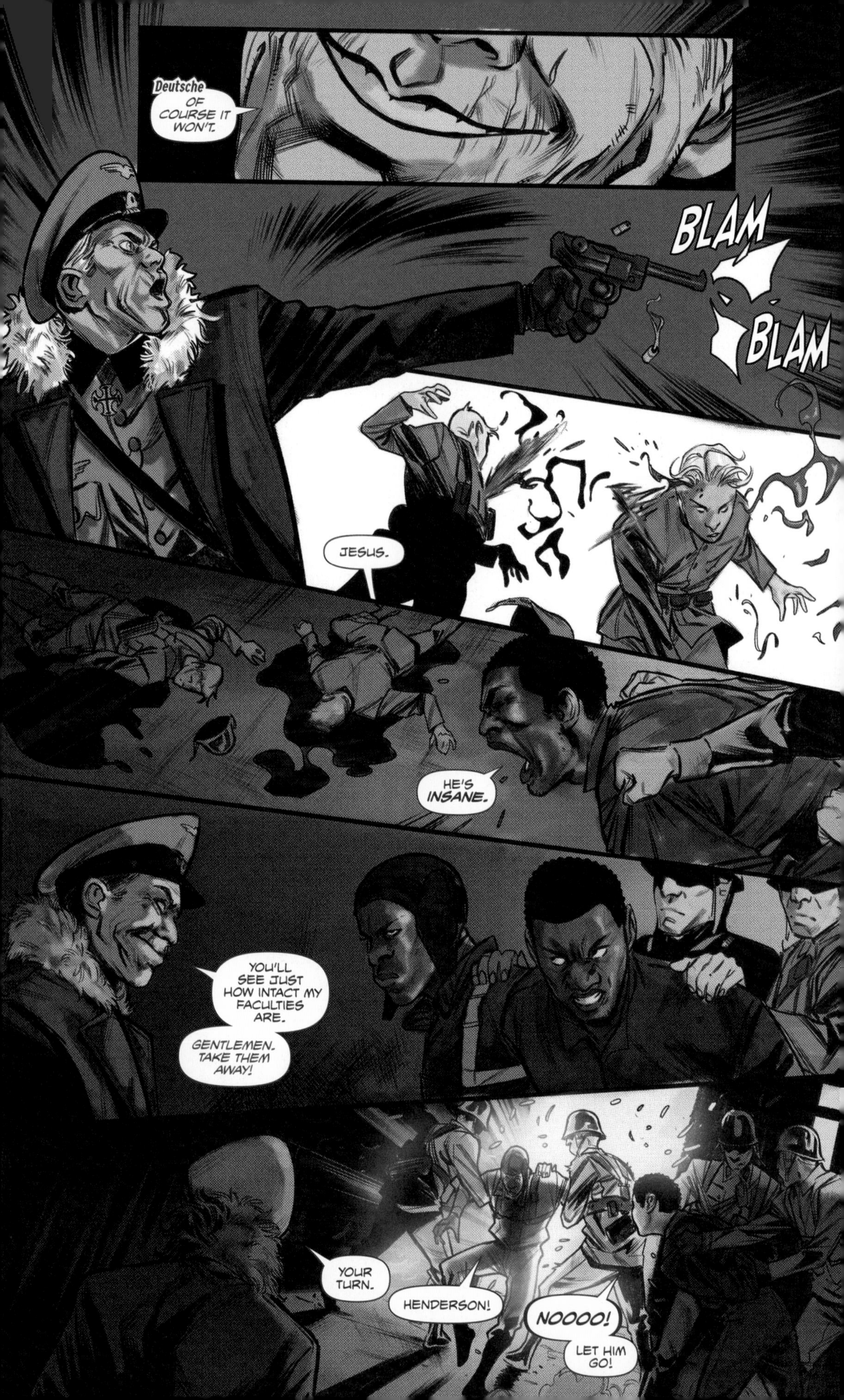
Deutsche
OF COURSE IT WON'T.
BLAM
BLAM
JESUS.
HE'S INSANE.
YOU'LL SEE JUST HOW INTACT MY FACULTIES ARE.
GENTLEMEN. TAKE THEM AWAY!
YOUR TURN.
HENDERSON!
NOOOO!
LET HIM GO!

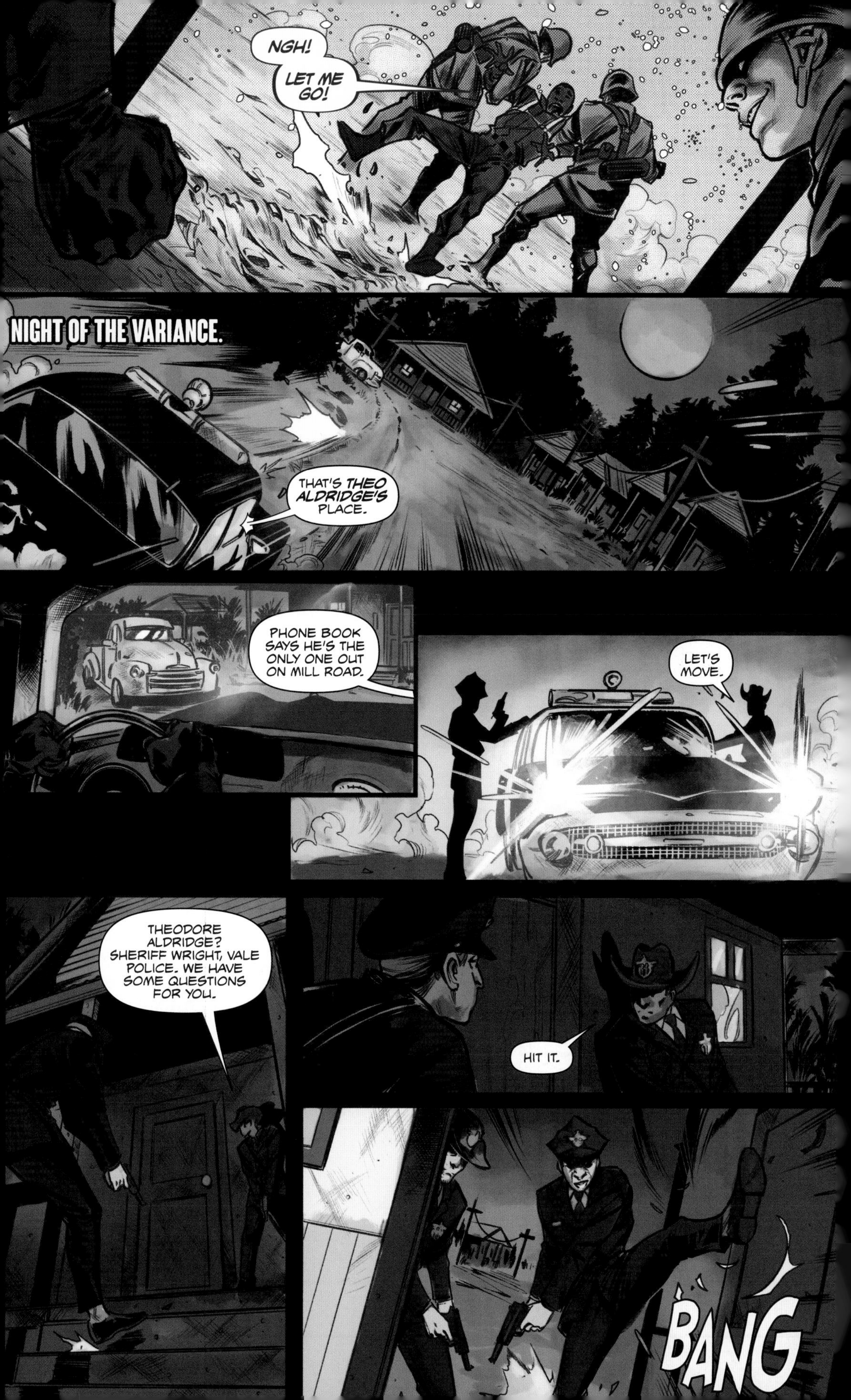
NGH!
LET ME GO!
NIGHT OF THE VARIANCE.
THAT'S THEO ALDRIDGE'S PLACE.
PHONE BOOK SAYS HE'S THE ONLY ONE OUT ON MILL ROAD.
LET'S MOVE.
THEODORE ALDRIDGE? SHERIFF WRIGHT, VALE POLICE. WE HAVE SOME QUESTIONS FOR YOU.
HIT IT.
BANG

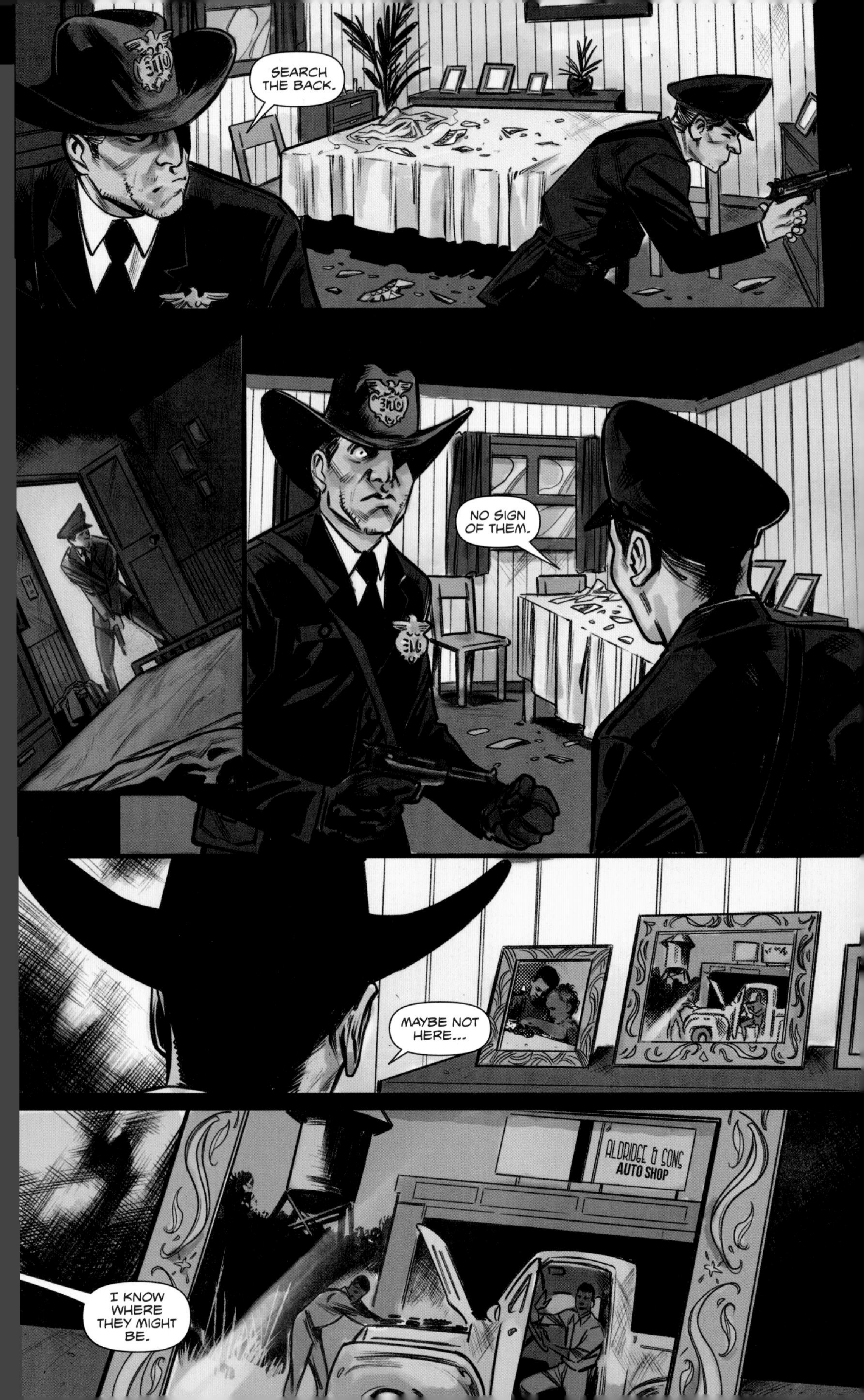
SEARCH THE BACK.
NO SIGN OF THEM.
MAYBE NOT HERE...
ALDRIDGE & SONS
AUTO SHOP
I KNOW WHERE THEY MIGHT BE.

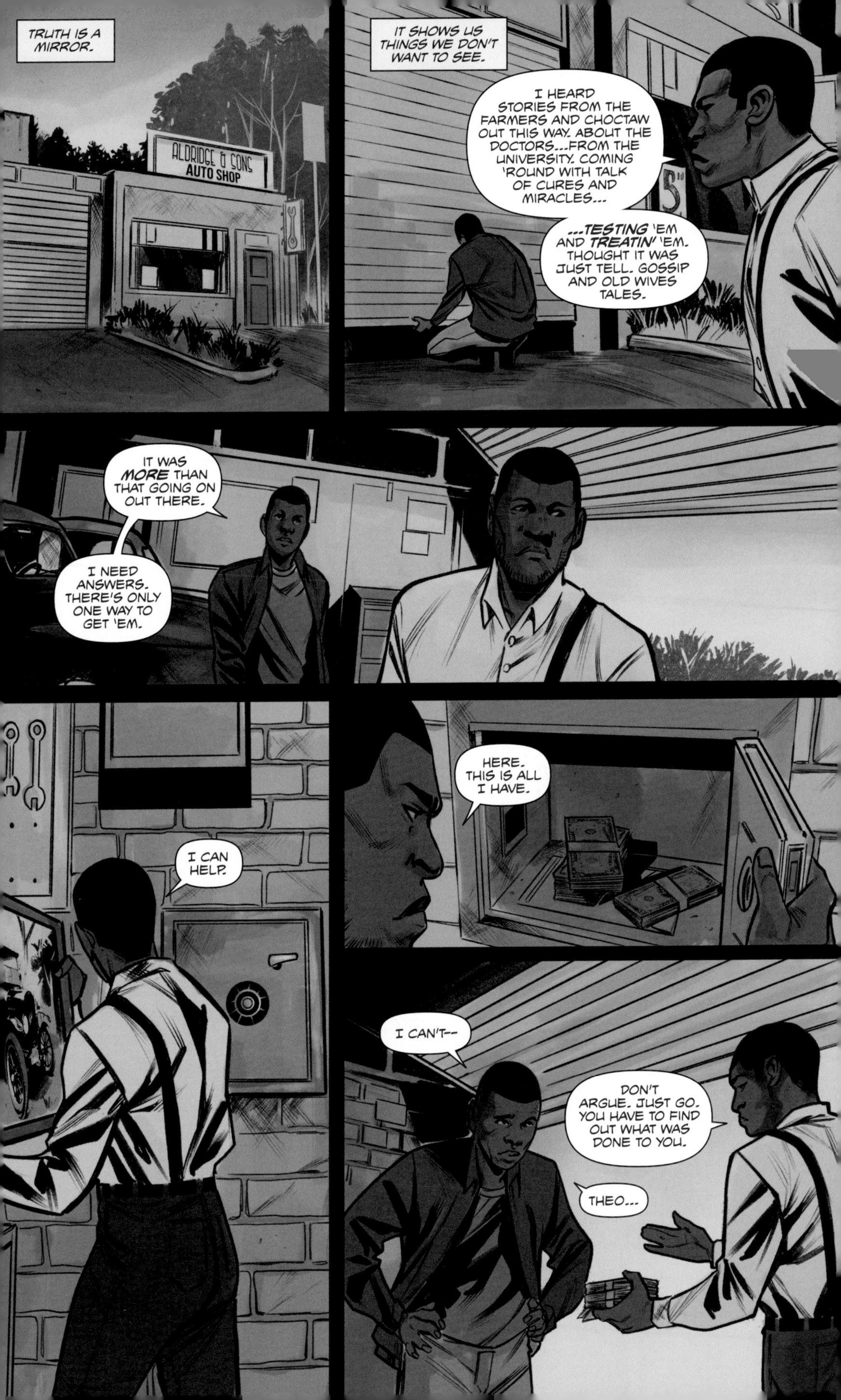
TRUTH IS A MIRROR.
ALDRIDGE & SONS AUTO SHOP
IT SHOWS US THINGS WE DON'T WANT TO SEE.
I HEARD STORIES FROM THE FARMERS AND CHOCTAW OUT THIS WAY. ABOUT THE DOCTORS...FROM THE UNIVERSITY. COMING 'ROUND WITH TALK OF CURES AND MIRACLES...
...TESTING 'EM AND TREATIN' 'EM. THOUGHT IT WAS JUST TELL. GOSSIP AND OLD WIVES TALES.
IT WAS MORE THAN THAT GOING ON OUT THERE.
I NEED ANSWERS. THERE'S ONLY ONE WAY TO GET 'EM.
I CAN HELP.
HERE. THIS IS ALL I HAVE.
I CAN'T--
DON'T ARGUE. JUST GO. YOU HAVE TO FIND OUT WHAT WAS DONE TO YOU.
THEO...

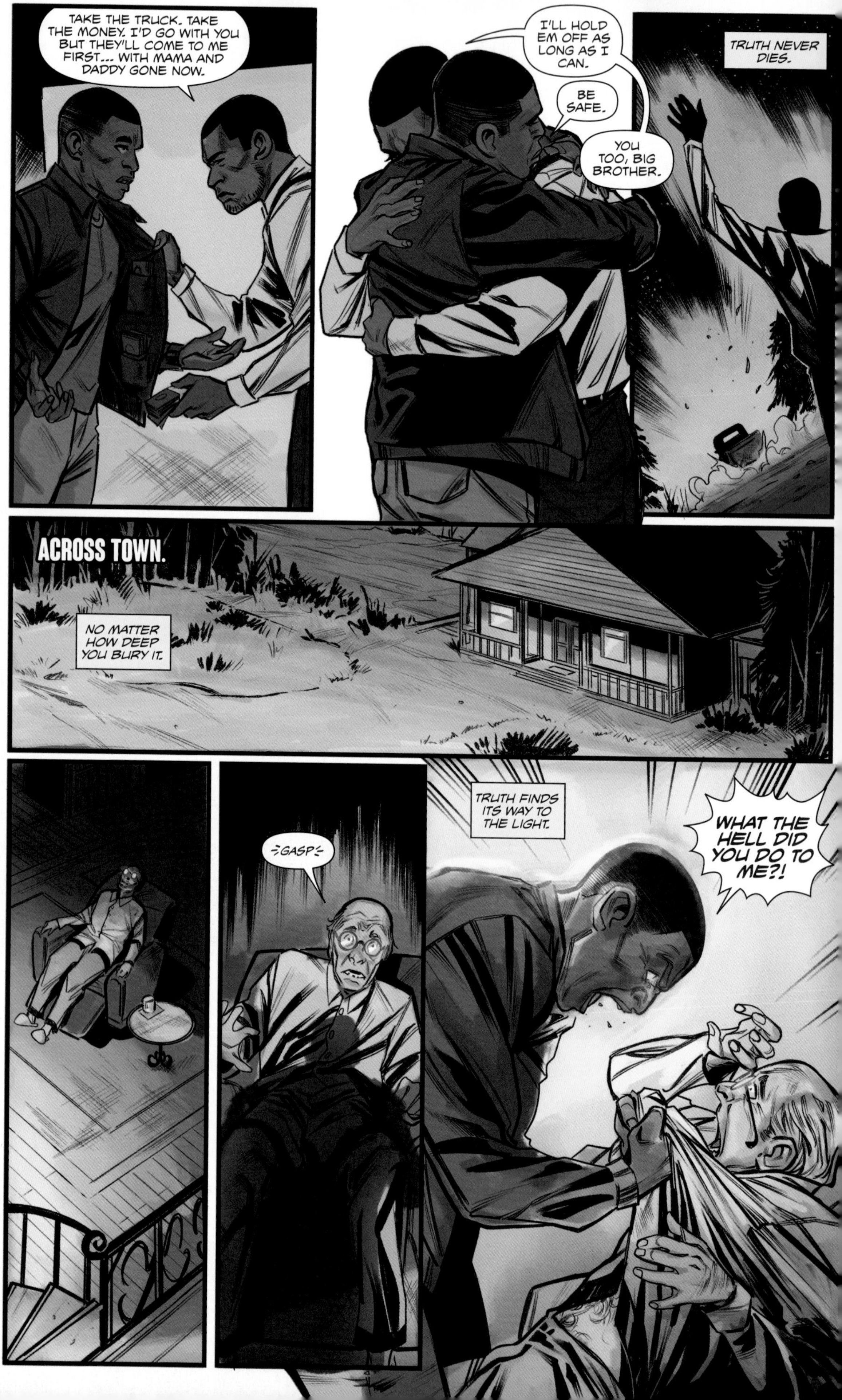

TAKE THE TRUCK. TAKE THE MONEY. I'D GO WITH YOU BUT THEY'LL COME TO ME FIRST... WITH MAMA AND DADDY GONE NOW.
I'LL HOLD EM OFF AS LONG AS I CAN.
BE SAFE.
YOU TOO, BIG BROTHER.
TRUTH NEVER DIES.
ACROSS TOWN.
NO MATTER HOW DEEP YOU BURY IT.
GASP
TRUTH FINDS ITS WAY TO THE LIGHT.
WHAT THE HELL DID YOU DO TO ME?!

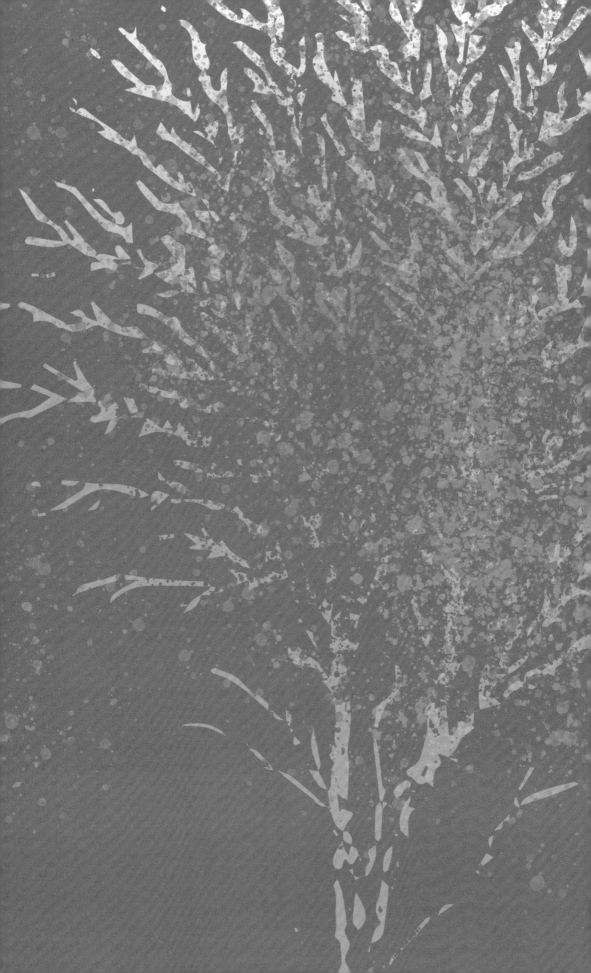

CHAPTER FIVE

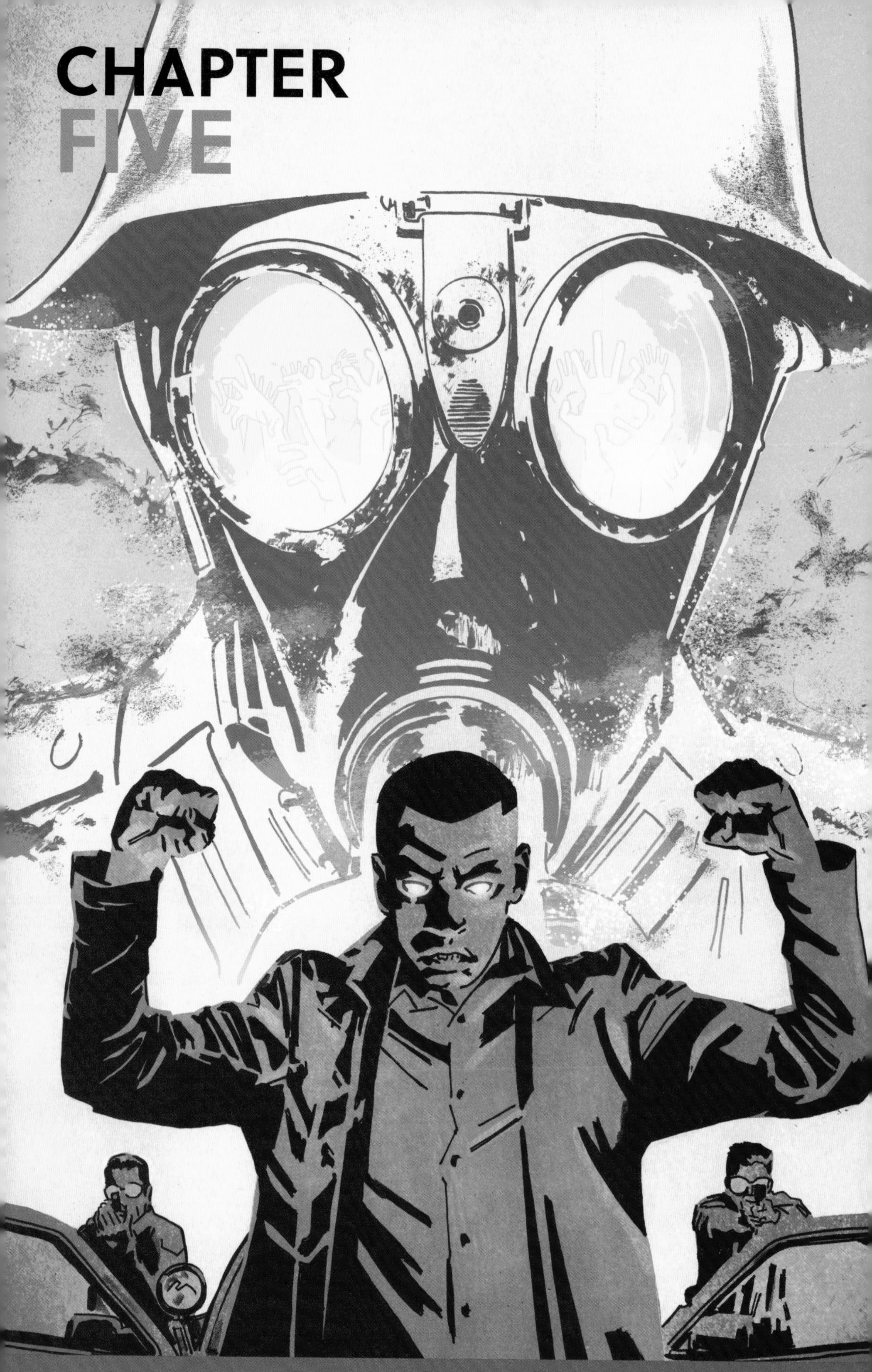

Issue #5 Cover
VALENTINE DE LANDRO

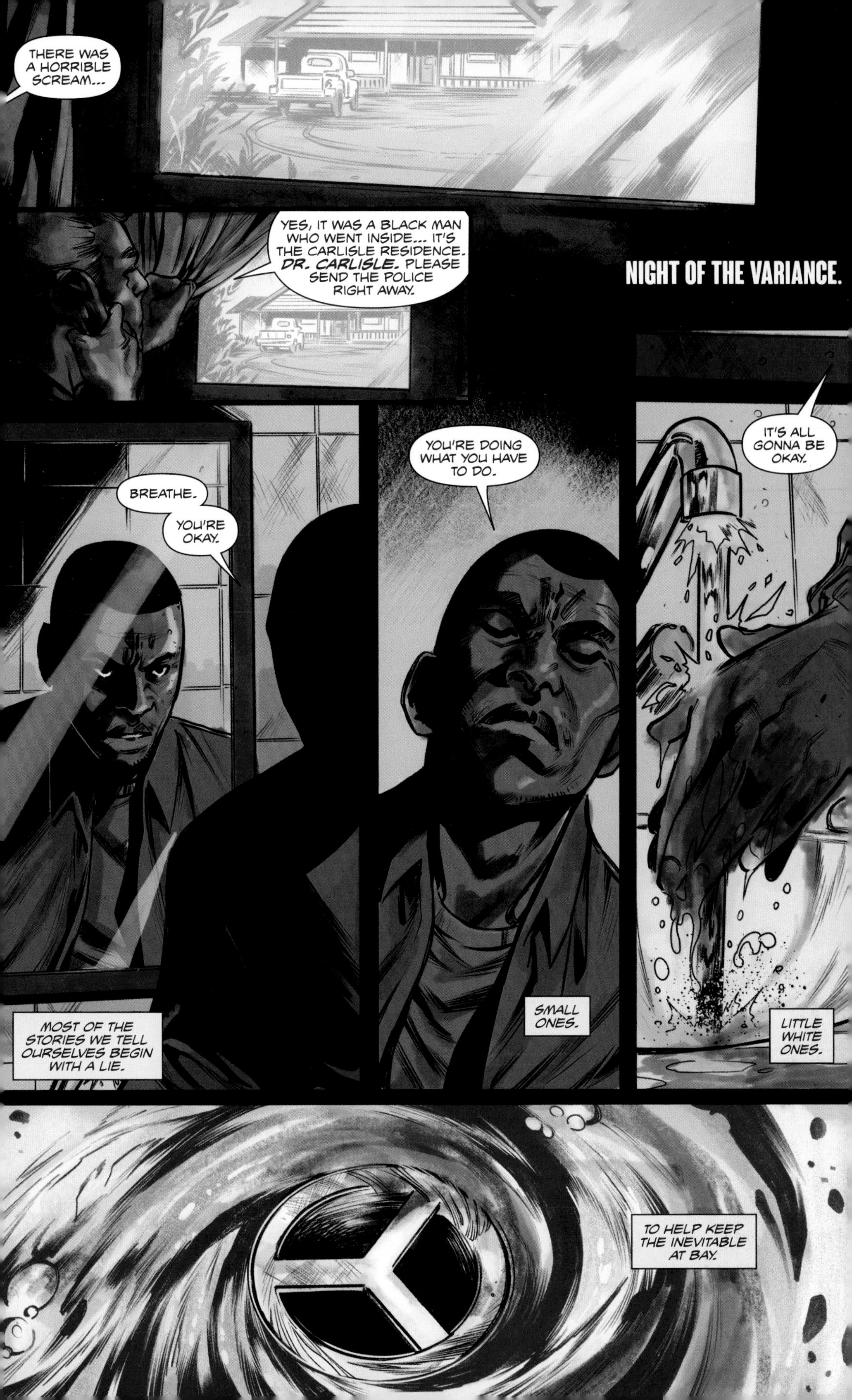
THERE WAS A HORRIBLE SCREAM...
YES, IT WAS A BLACK MAN WHO WENT INSIDE... IT'S THE CARLISLE RESIDENCE. DR. CARLISLE. PLEASE SEND THE POLICE RIGHT AWAY.
NIGHT OF THE VARIANCE.
BREATHE.
YOU'RE OKAY.
MOST OF THE STORIES WE TELL OURSELVES BEGIN WITH A LIE.
YOU'RE DOING WHAT YOU HAVE TO DO.
SMALL ONES.
IT'S ALL GONNA BE OKAY.
LITTLE WHITE ONES.
TO HELP KEEP THE INEVITABLE AT BAY.

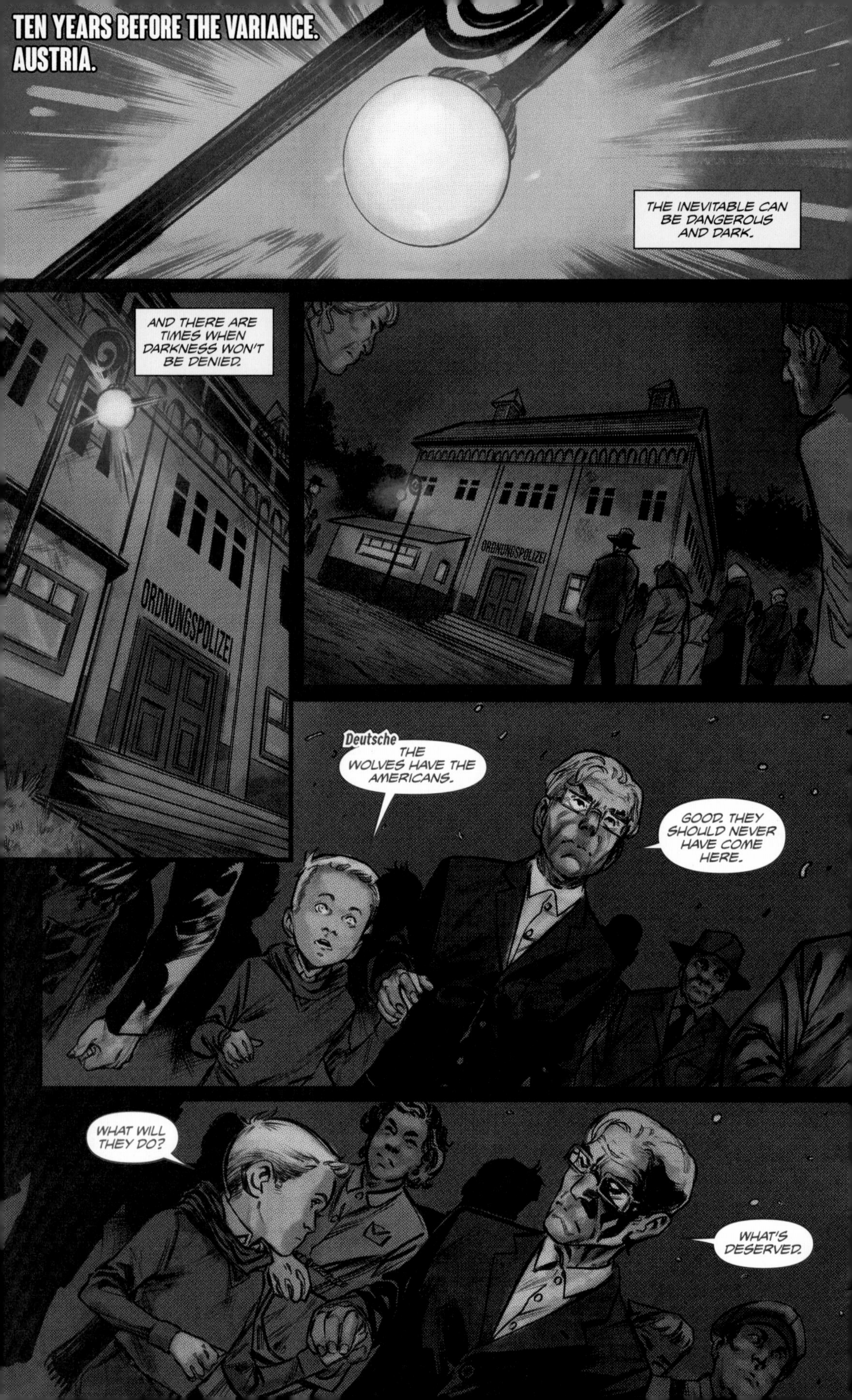
TEN YEARS BEFORE THE VARIANCE.
AUSTRIA.
THE INEVITABLE CAN BE DANGEROUS AND DARK.
AND THERE ARE TIMES WHEN DARKNESS WON'T BE DENIED.
ORDNUNGSPOLIZEI
ORDNUNGSPOLIZEI
Deutsche
THE WOLVES HAVE THE AMERICANS.
GOOD. THEY SHOULD NEVER HAVE COME HERE.
WHAT WILL THEY DO?
WHAT'S DESERVED.

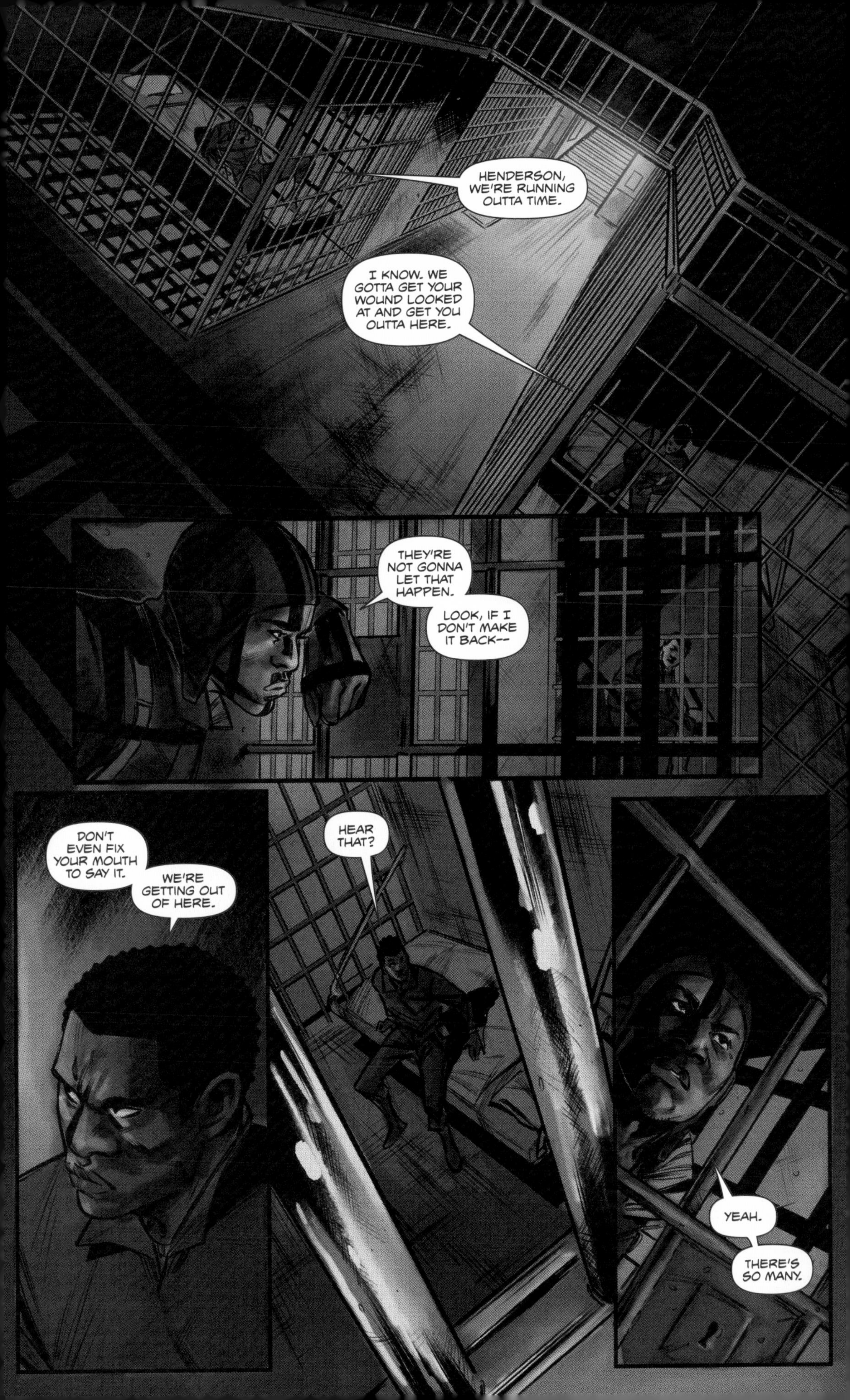
HENDERSON, WE'RE RUNNING OUTTA TIME.
I KNOW. WE GOTTA GET YOUR WOUND LOOKED AT AND GET YOU OUTTA HERE.
THEY'RE NOT GONNA LET THAT HAPPEN.
LOOK, IF I DON'T MAKE IT BACK--
DON'T EVEN FIX YOUR MOUTH TO SAY IT.
WE'RE GETTING OUT OF HERE.
HEAR THAT?
YEAH.
THERE'S SO MANY.

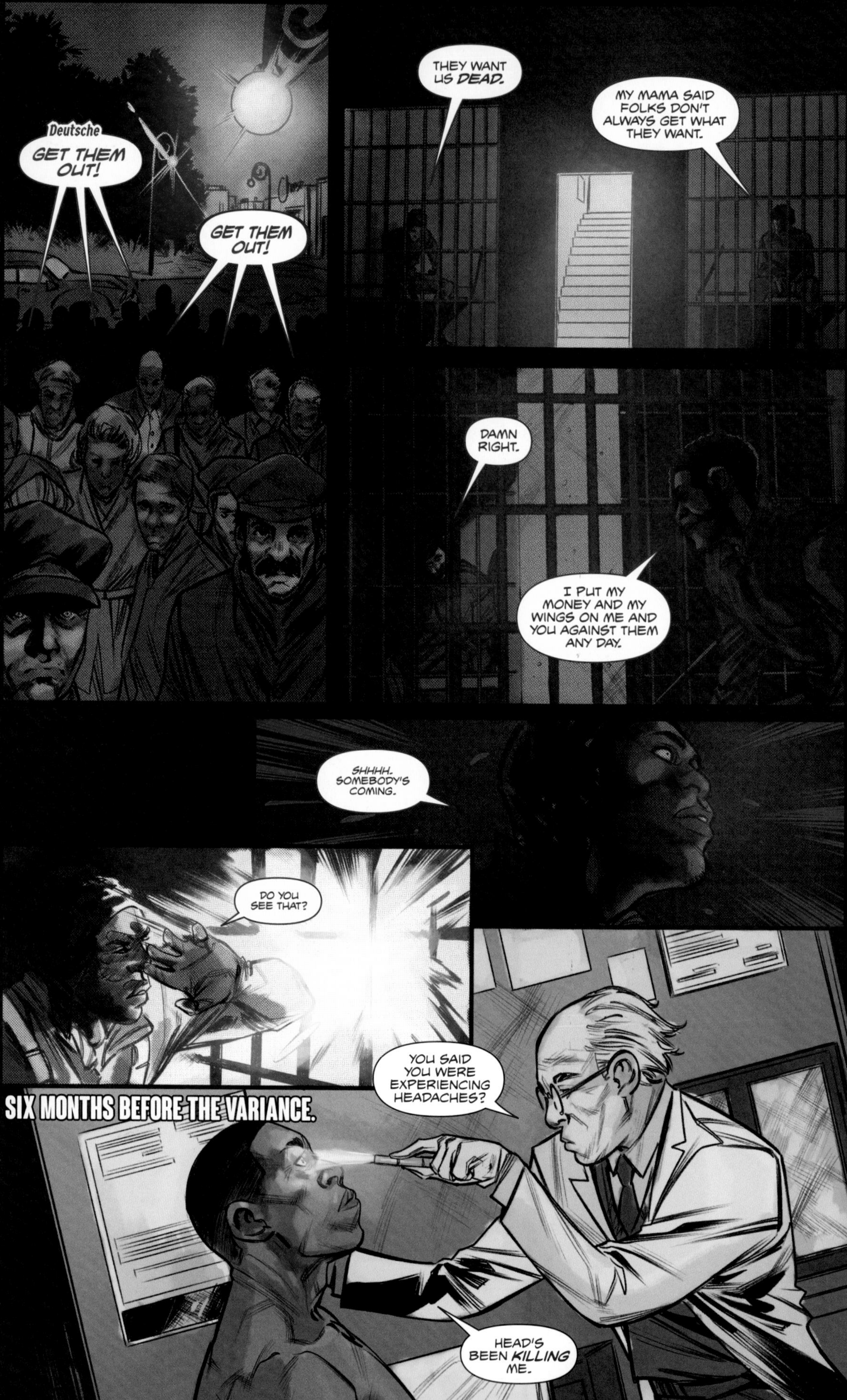
Deutsche
GET THEM OUT!
GET THEM OUT!
THEY WANT US DEAD.
MY MAMA SAID FOLKS DON'T ALWAYS GET WHAT THEY WANT.
DAMN RIGHT.
I PUT MY MONEY AND MY WINGS ON ME AND YOU AGAINST THEM ANY DAY.
SHHHH. SOMEBODY'S COMING.
DO YOU SEE THAT?
SIX MONTHS BEFORE THE VARIANCE.
YOU SAID YOU WERE EXPERIENCING HEADACHES?
HEAD'S BEEN KILLING ME.

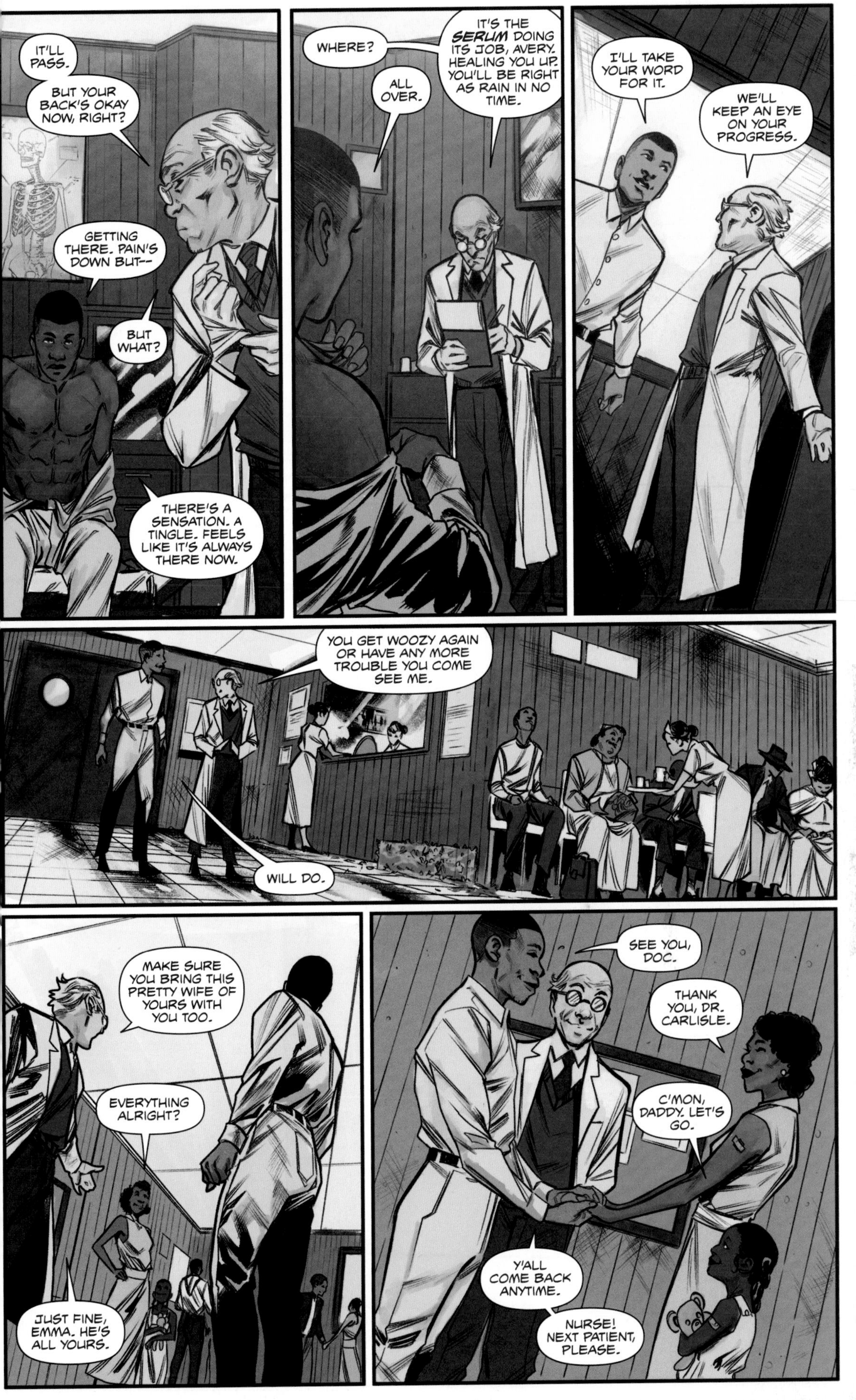
IT'LL PASS.
BUT YOUR BACK'S OKAY NOW, RIGHT?
GETTING THERE. PAIN'S DOWN BUT--
BUT WHAT?
THERE'S A SENSATION. A TINGLE. FEELS LIKE IT'S ALWAYS THERE NOW.
WHERE?
ALL OVER.
IT'S THE SERUM DOING ITS JOB, AVERY. HEALING YOU UP. YOU'LL BE RIGHT AS RAIN IN NO TIME.
I'LL TAKE YOUR WORD FOR IT.
WE'LL KEEP AN EYE ON YOUR PROGRESS.
YOU GET WOOZY AGAIN OR HAVE ANY MORE TROUBLE YOU COME SEE ME.
WILL DO.
MAKE SURE YOU BRING THIS PRETTY WIFE OF YOURS WITH YOU TOO.
EVERYTHING ALRIGHT?
JUST FINE, EMMA. HE'S ALL YOURS.
SEE YOU, DOC.
THANK YOU, DR. CARLISLE.
C'MON, DADDY. LET'S GO.
Y'ALL COME BACK ANYTIME.
NURSE! NEXT PATIENT, PLEASE.

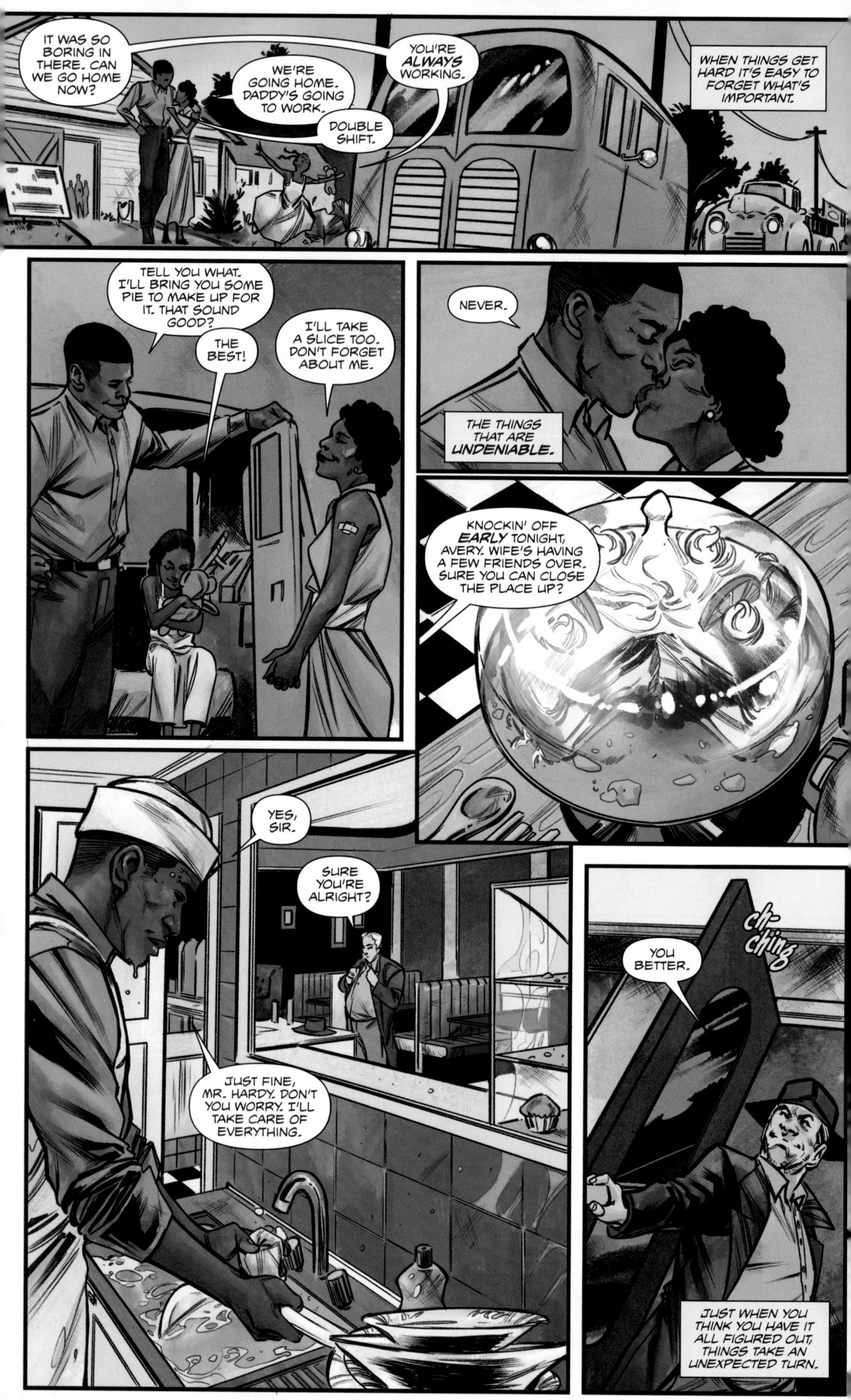

IT WAS SO BORING IN THERE. CAN WE GO HOME NOW?
WE'RE GOING HOME. DADDY'S GOING TO WORK.
YOU'RE ALWAYS WORKING.
DOUBLE SHIFT.
WHEN THINGS GET HARD IT'S EASY TO FORGET WHAT'S IMPORTANT.
TELL YOU WHAT. I'LL BRING YOU SOME PIE TO MAKE UP FOR IT. THAT SOUND GOOD?
THE BEST!
I'LL TAKE A SLICE TOO. DON'T FORGET ABOUT ME.
NEVER.
THE THINGS THAT ARE UNDENIABLE.
KNOCKIN' OFF EARLY TONIGHT, AVERY. WIFE'S HAVING A FEW FRIENDS OVER. SURE YOU CAN CLOSE THE PLACE UP?
YES, SIR.
SURE YOU'RE ALRIGHT?
JUST FINE, MR. HARDY. DON'T YOU WORRY. I'LL TAKE CARE OF EVERYTHING.
YOU BETTER.
CH-CHING
JUST WHEN YOU THINK YOU HAVE IT ALL FIGURED OUT, THINGS TAKE AN UNEXPECTED TURN.

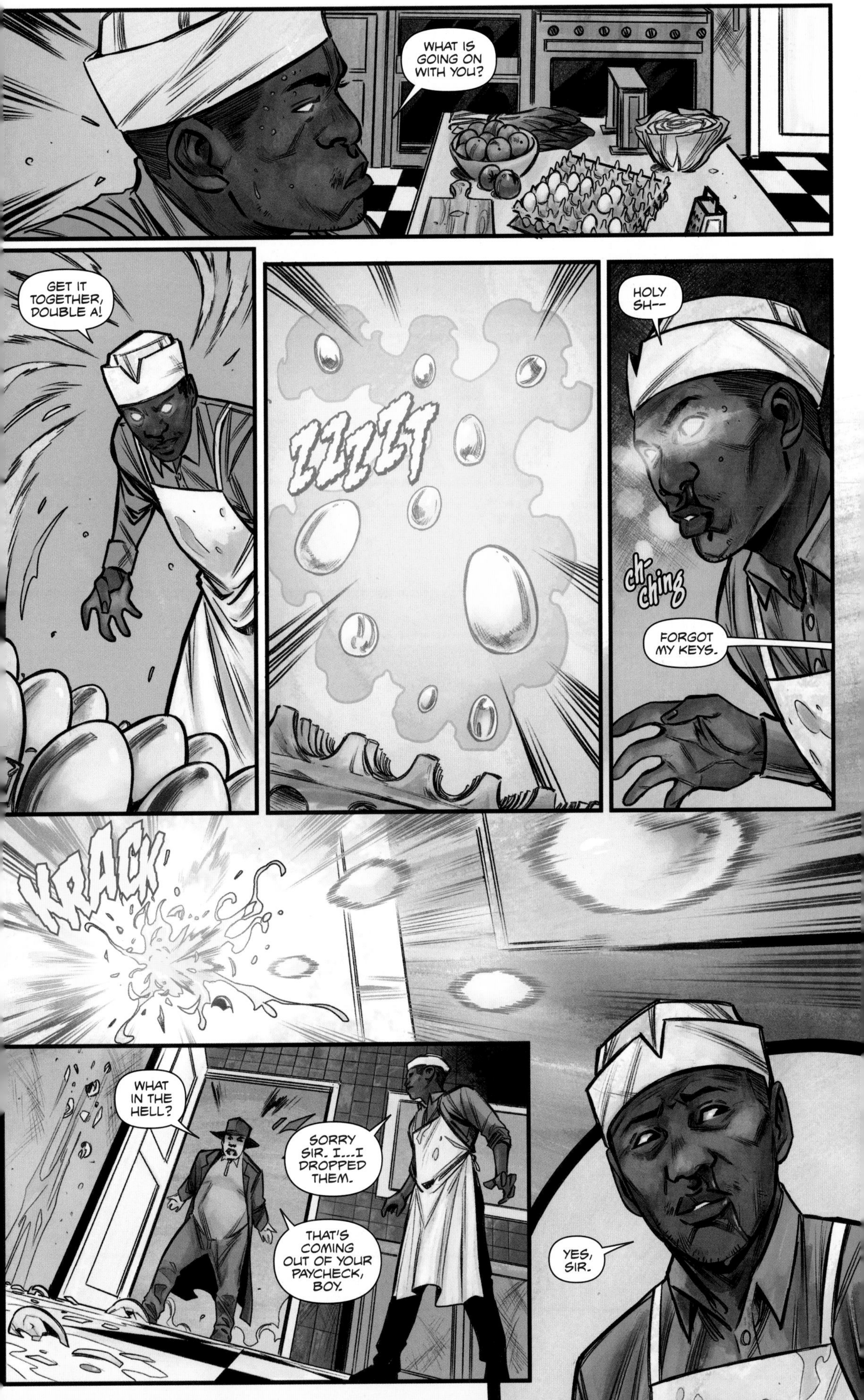
WHAT IS GOING ON WITH YOU?
GET IT TOGETHER, DOUBLE A!
ZZZZT
HOLY SH--
CH-CHING
FORGOT MY KEYS.
KRACK
WHAT IN THE HELL?
SORRY SIR. I...I DROPPED THEM.
THAT'S COMING OUT OF YOUR PAYCHECK, BOY.
YES, SIR.

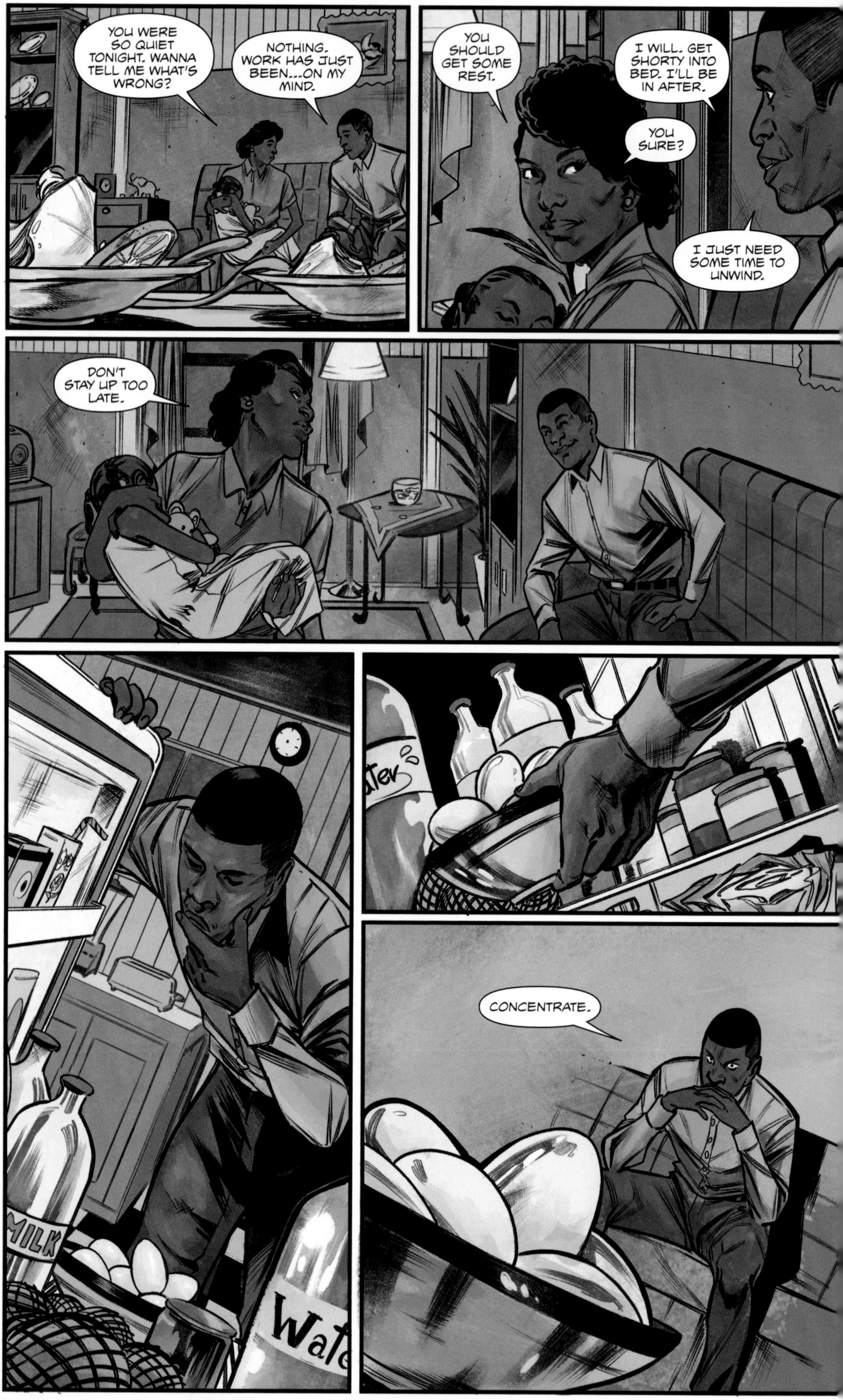
YOU WERE SO QUIET TONIGHT. WANNA TELL ME WHAT'S WRONG?
NOTHING. WORK HAS JUST BEEN...ON MY MIND.
YOU SHOULD GET SOME REST.
I WILL. GET SHORTY INTO BED. I'LL BE IN AFTER.
YOU SURE?
I JUST NEED SOME TIME TO UNWIND.
DON'T STAY UP TOO LATE.
MILK
Water
Wate
CONCENTRATE.

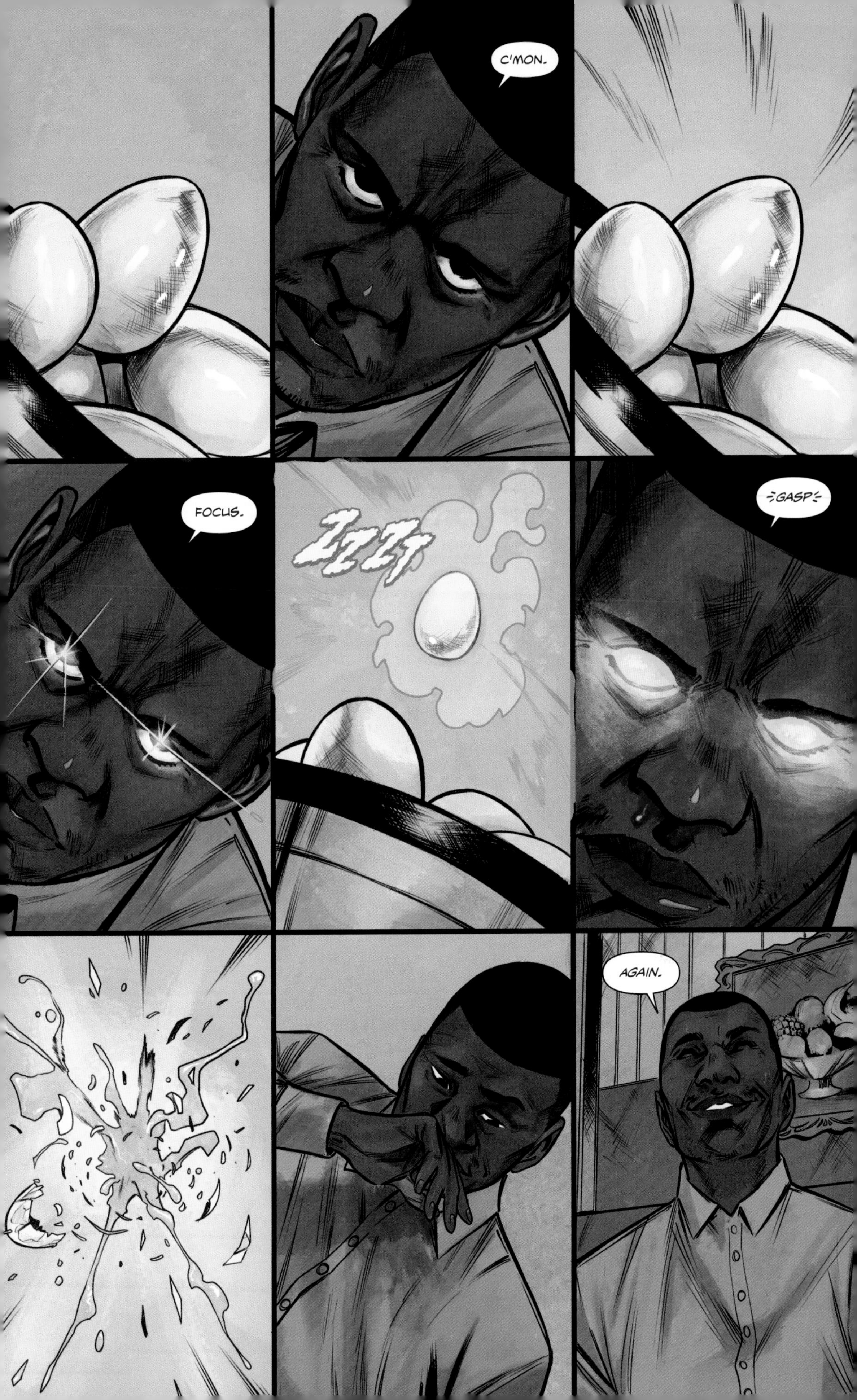
C'MON.
FOCUS.
ZZZT
GASP
AGAIN.

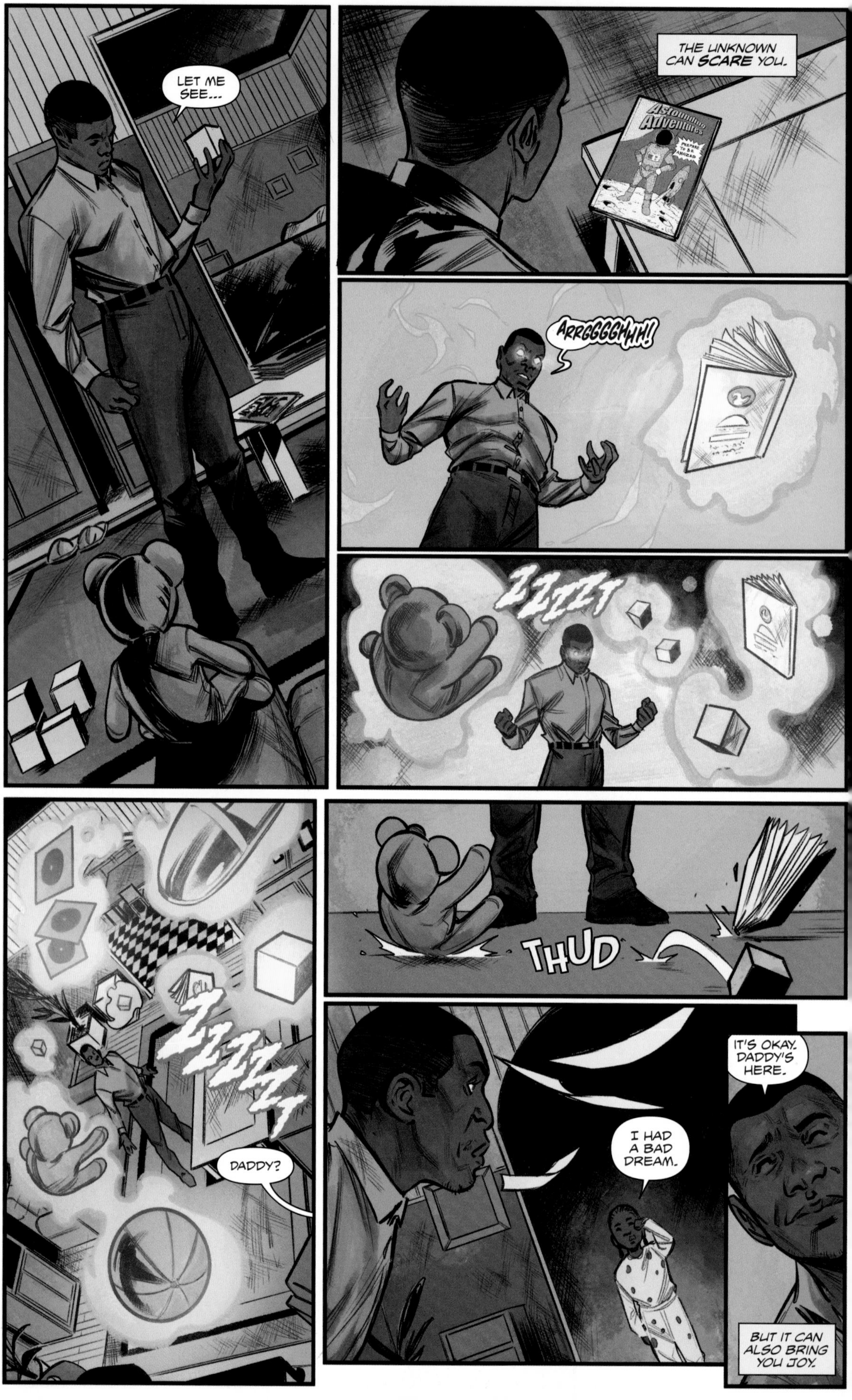
LET ME SEE...
THE UNKNOWN CAN SCARE YOU.
Astounding Adventures
ARRGGGGHHH!
ZZZZZ
ZZZZZ
DADDY?
THUD
IT'S OKAY. DADDY'S HERE.
I HAD A BAD DREAM.
BUT IT CAN ALSO BRING YOU JOY.

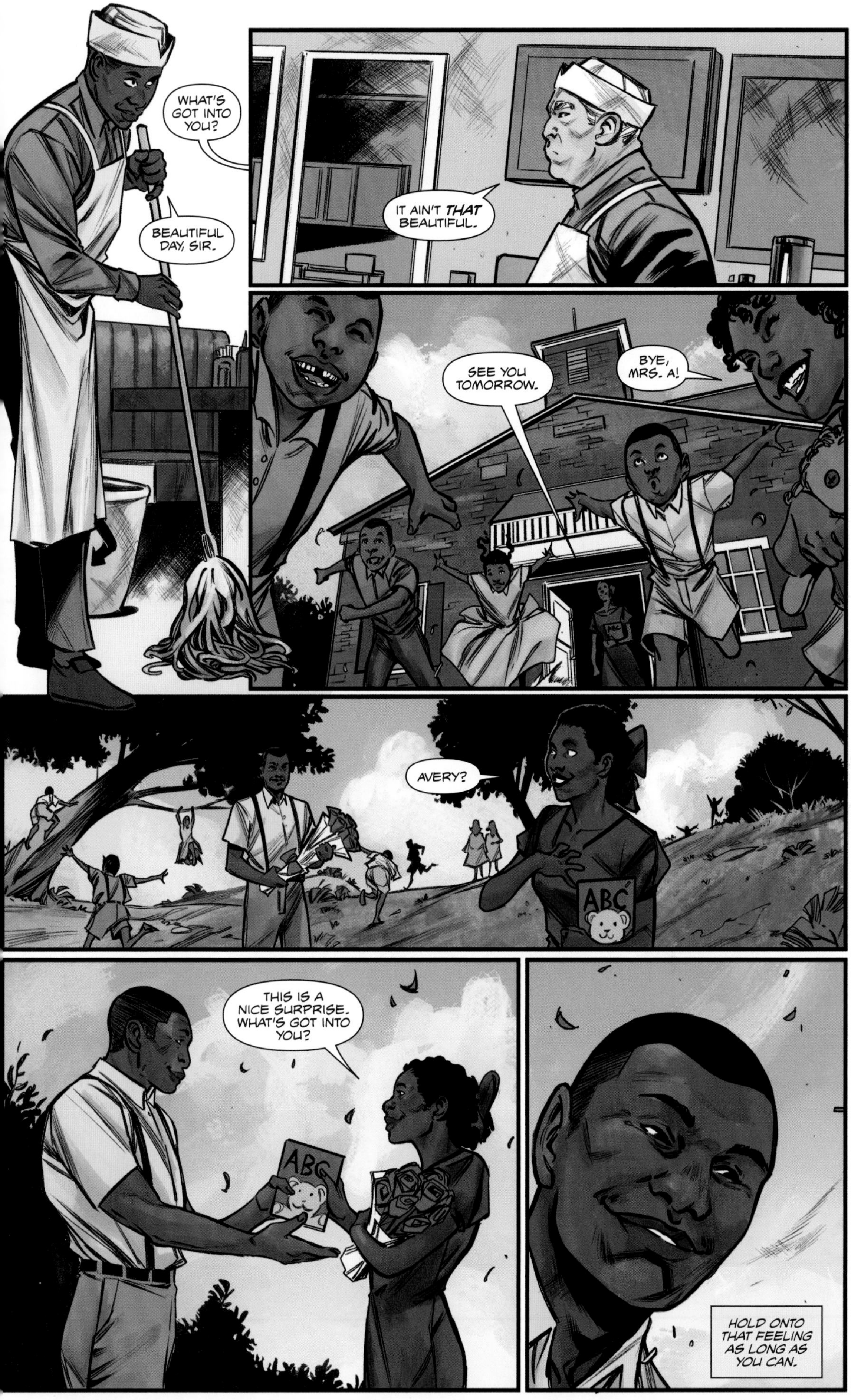

BEAUTIFUL DAY, SIR.
WHAT'S GOT INTO YOU?
IT AIN'T *THAT* BEAUTIFUL.
SEE YOU TOMORROW.
BYE, MRS. A!
AVERY?
ABC
THIS IS A NICE SURPRISE. WHAT'S GOT INTO YOU?
ABC
HOLD ONTO THAT FEELING AS LONG AS YOU CAN.

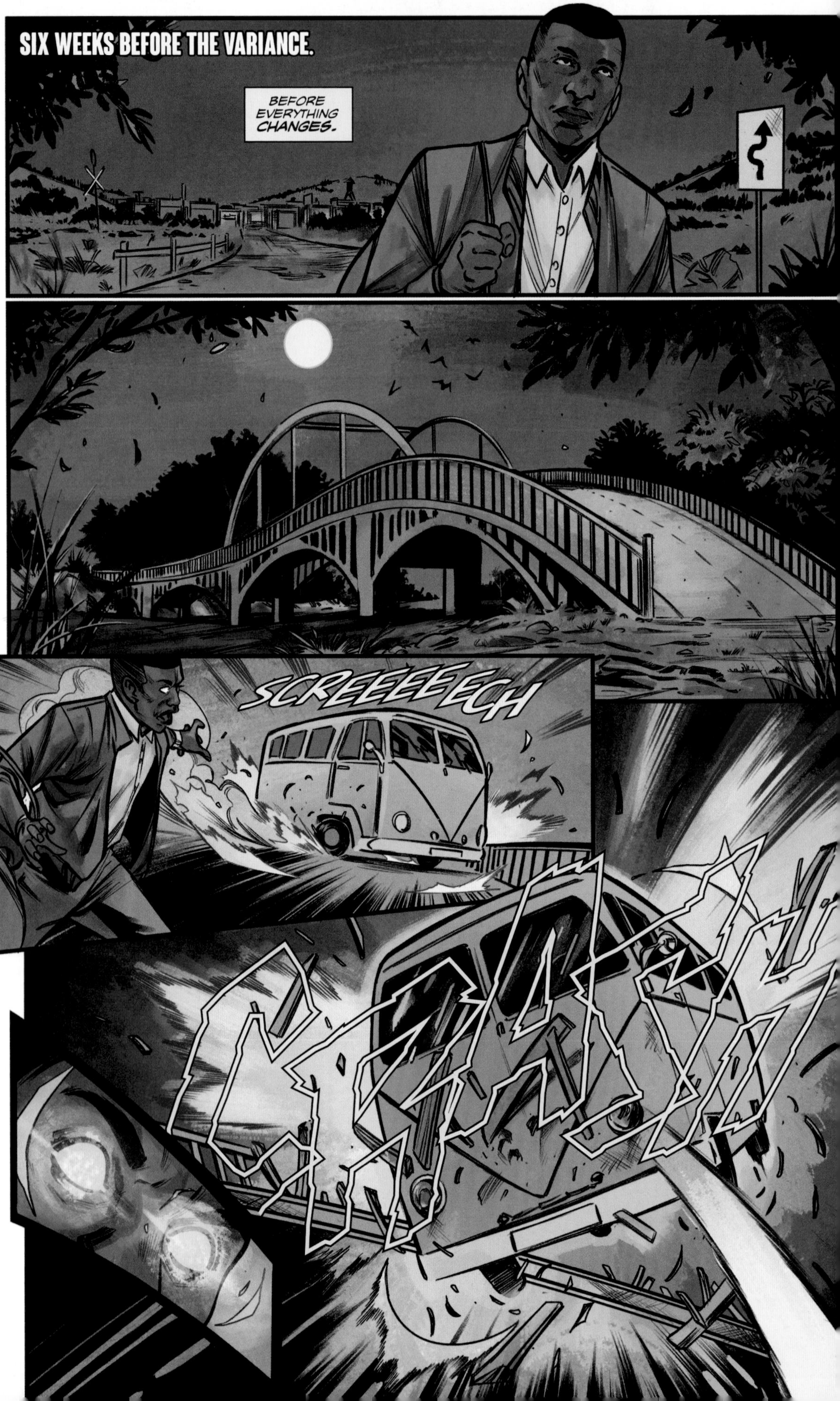
SIX WEEKS BEFORE THE VARIANCE.
BEFORE EVERYTHING CHANGES.
SCREEEEEECH

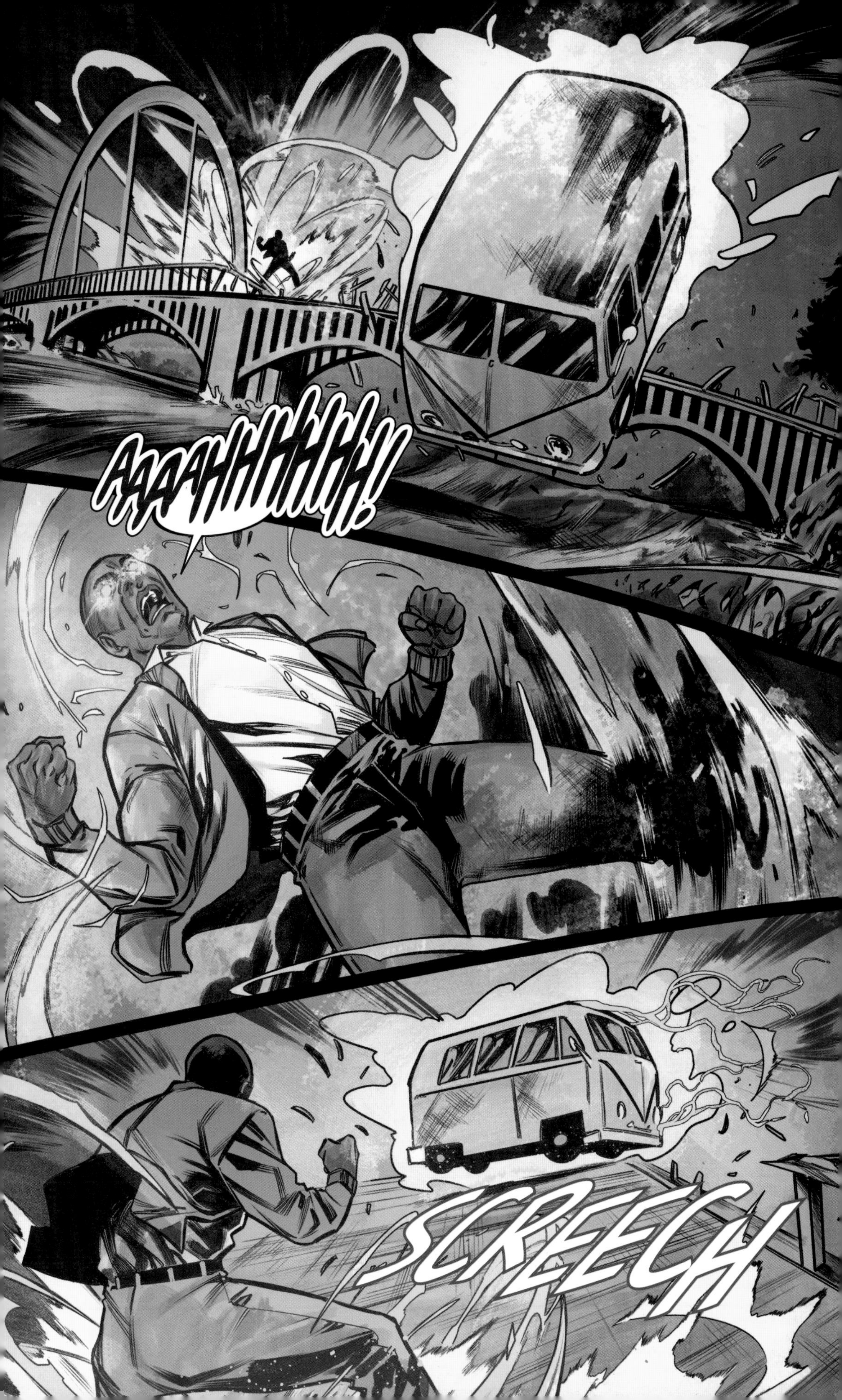
AAAAHHHHHHH!
SCREECH

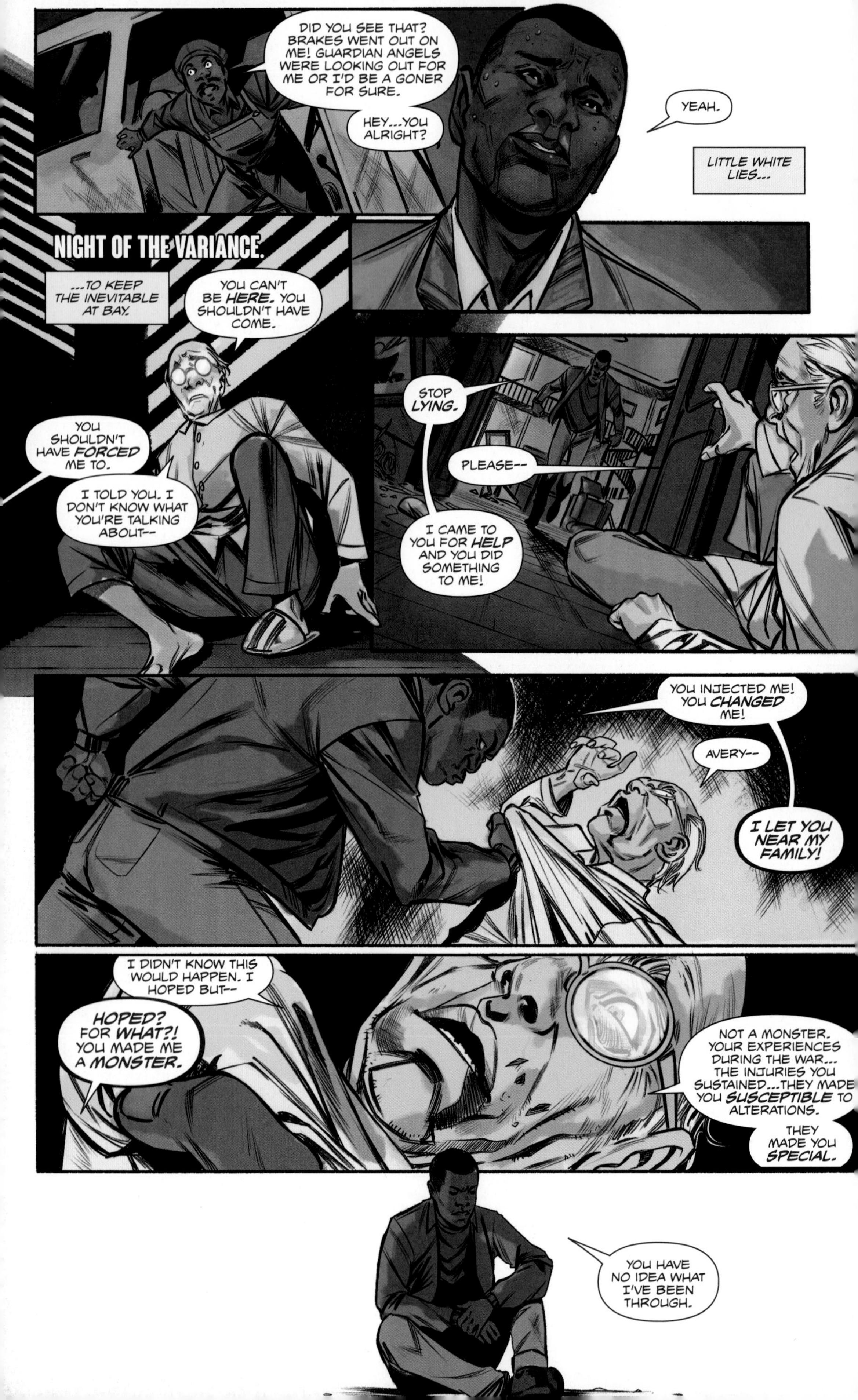

DID YOU SEE THAT? BRAKES WENT OUT ON ME! GUARDIAN ANGELS WERE LOOKING OUT FOR ME OR I'D BE A GONER FOR SURE.
HEY...YOU ALRIGHT?
YEAH.
LITTLE WHITE LIES...
NIGHT OF THE VARIANCE.
...TO KEEP THE INEVITABLE AT BAY.
YOU CAN'T BE HERE. YOU SHOULDN'T HAVE COME.
YOU SHOULDN'T HAVE FORCED ME TO.
I TOLD YOU. I DON'T KNOW WHAT YOU'RE TALKING ABOUT--
STOP LYING.
PLEASE--
I CAME TO YOU FOR HELP AND YOU DID SOMETHING TO ME!
YOU INJECTED ME! YOU CHANGED ME!
AVERY--
I LET YOU NEAR MY FAMILY!
I DIDN'T KNOW THIS WOULD HAPPEN. I HOPED BUT--
HOPED? FOR WHAT?! YOU MADE ME A MONSTER.
NOT A MONSTER. YOUR EXPERIENCES DURING THE WAR... THE INJURIES YOU SUSTAINED...THEY MADE YOU SUSCEPTIBLE TO ALTERATIONS.
THEY MADE YOU SPECIAL.
YOU HAVE NO IDEA WHAT I'VE BEEN THROUGH.

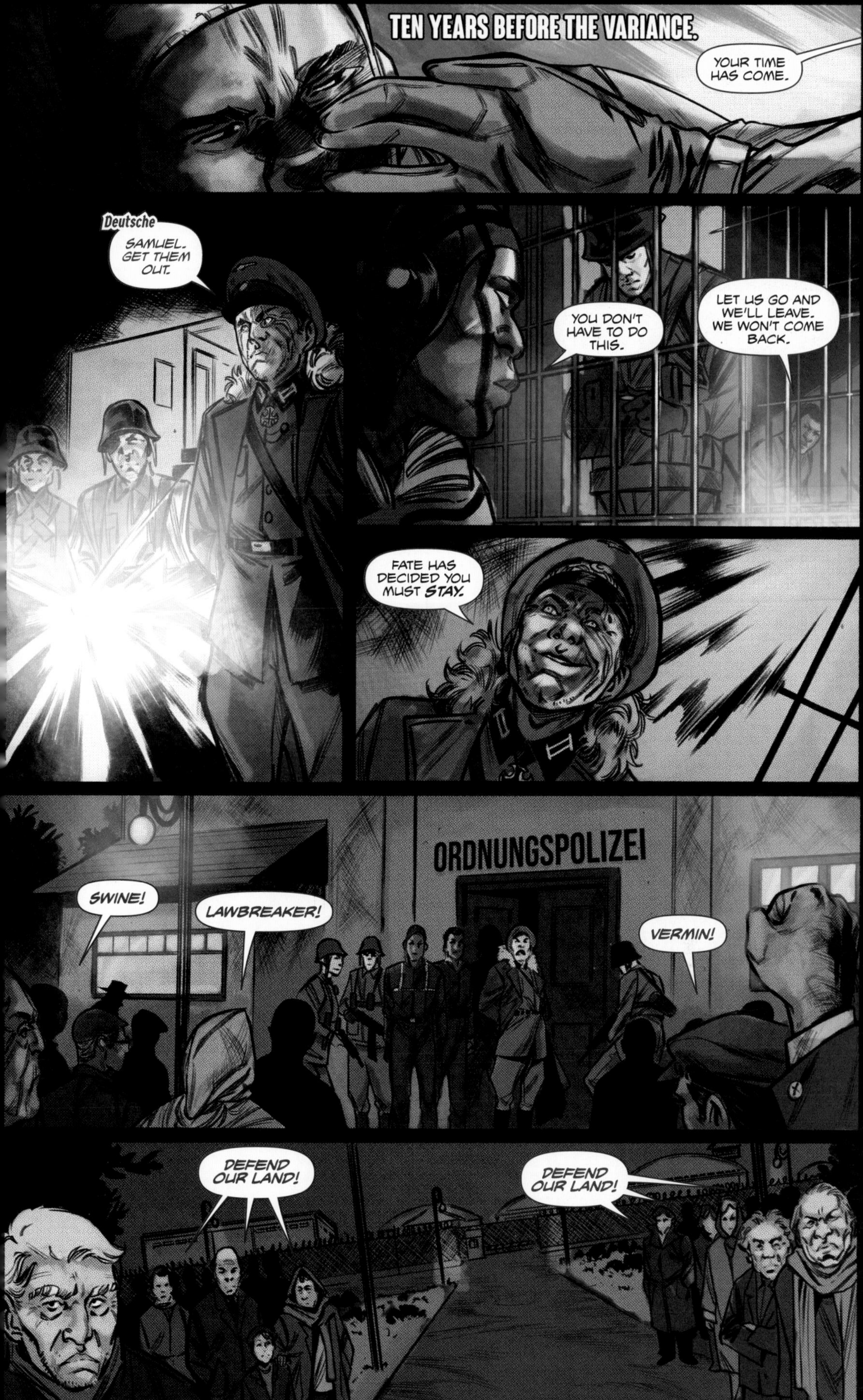
TEN YEARS BEFORE THE VARIANCE.
YOUR TIME HAS COME.
Deutsche
SAMUEL. GET THEM OUT.
YOU DON'T HAVE TO DO THIS.
LET US GO AND WE'LL LEAVE. WE WON'T COME BACK.
FATE HAS DECIDED YOU MUST STAY.
ORDNUNGSPOLIZEI
SWINE!
LAWBREAKER!
VERMIN!
DEFEND OUR LAND!
DEFEND OUR LAND!

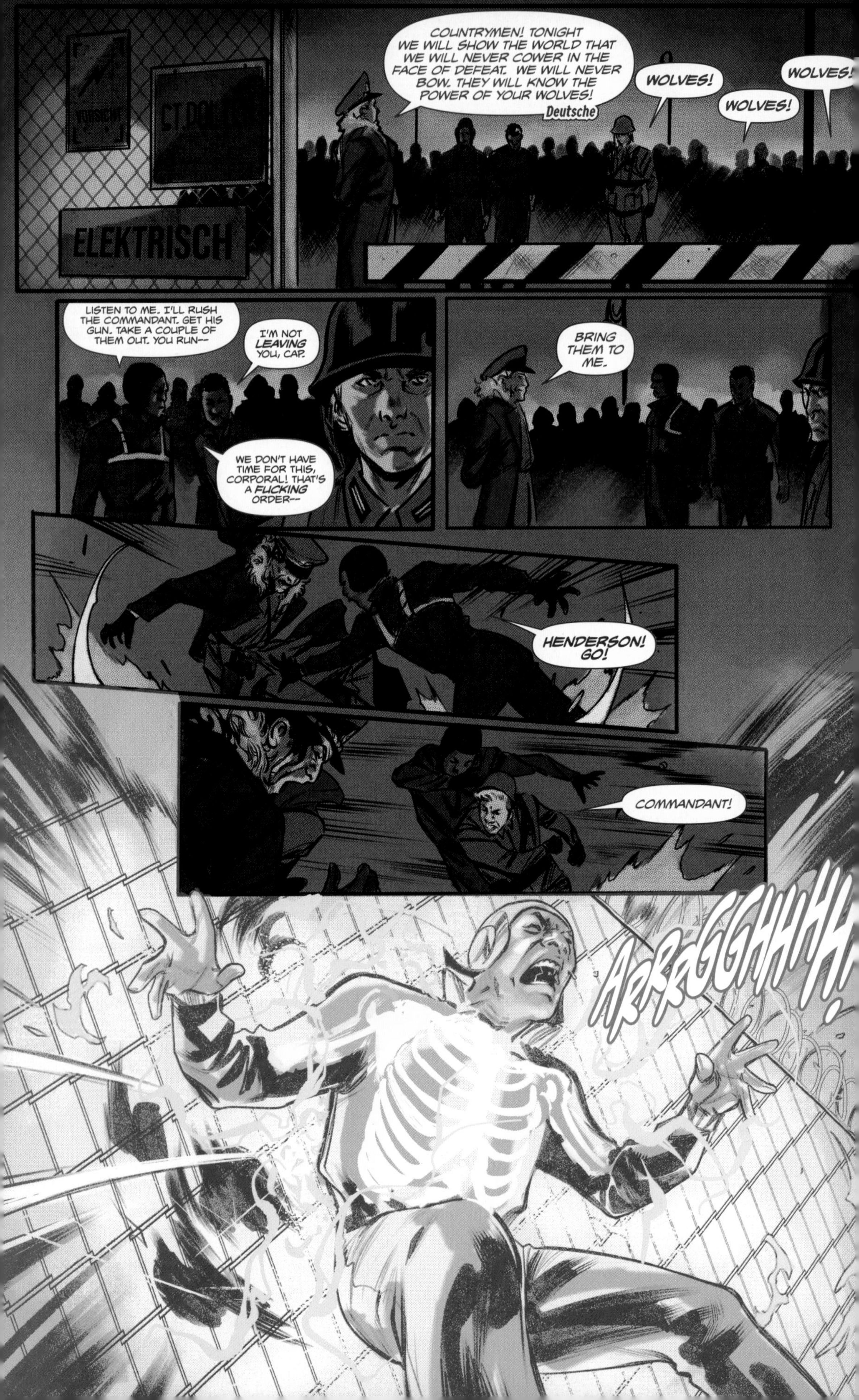
VORSICHT
ST. DOM
ELEKTRISCH
COUNTRYMEN! TONIGHT WE WILL SHOW THE WORLD THAT WE WILL NEVER COWER IN THE FACE OF DEFEAT. WE WILL NEVER BOW. THEY WILL KNOW THE POWER OF YOUR WOLVES!
Deutsche
WOLVES!
WOLVES!
WOLVES!
LISTEN TO ME. I'LL RUSH THE COMMANDANT. GET HIS GUN. TAKE A COUPLE OF THEM OUT. YOU RUN--
I'M NOT LEAVING YOU, CAP.
WE DON'T HAVE TIME FOR THIS, CORPORAL! THAT'S A FUCKING ORDER--
BRING THEM TO ME.
HENDERSON! GO!
COMMANDANT!
ARRRGGHHHH!

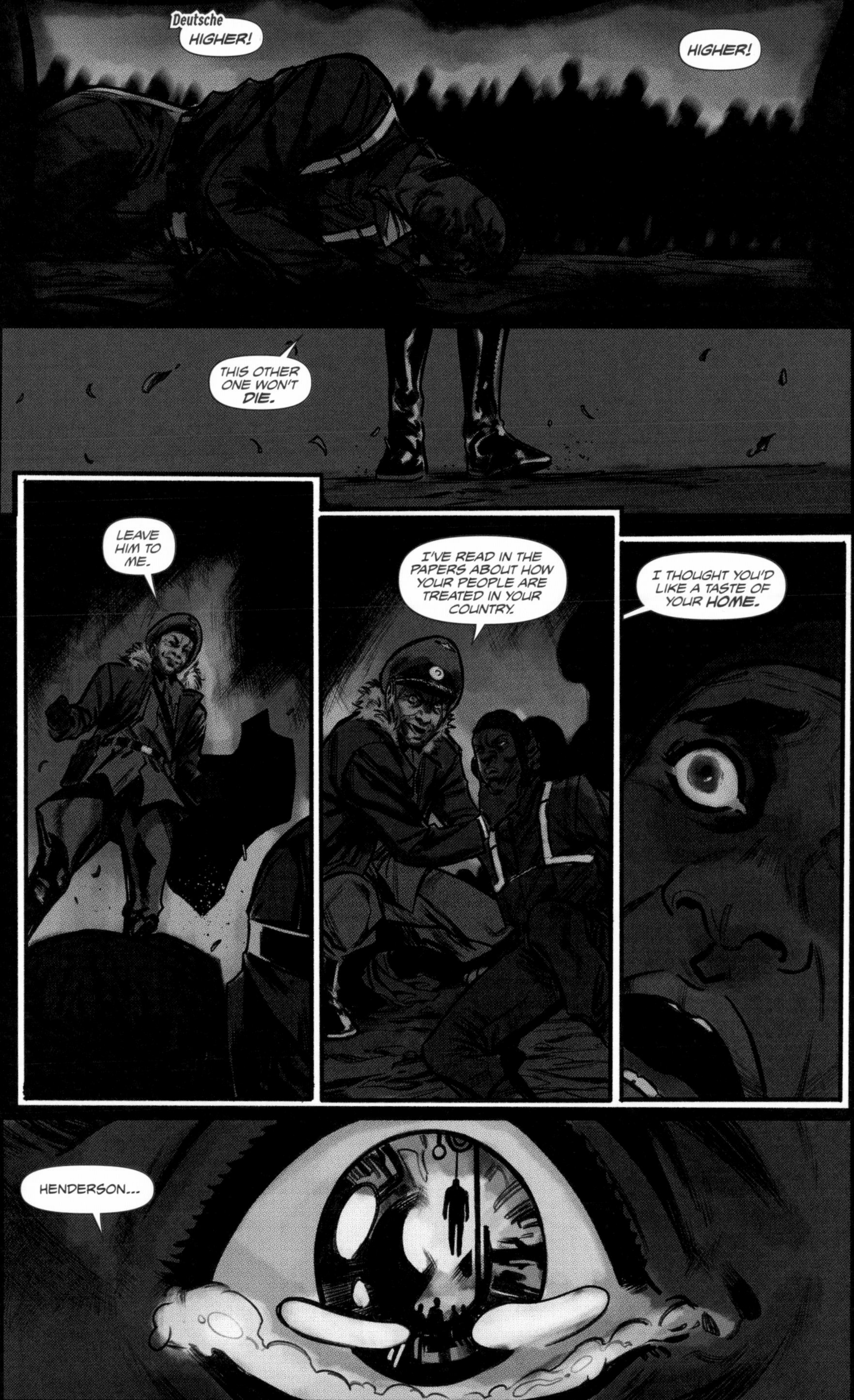
Deutsche
HIGHER!
HIGHER!
THIS OTHER ONE WON'T DIE.
LEAVE HIM TO ME.
I'VE READ IN THE PAPERS ABOUT HOW YOUR PEOPLE ARE TREATED IN YOUR COUNTRY.
I THOUGHT YOU'D LIKE A TASTE OF YOUR HOME.
HENDERSON...

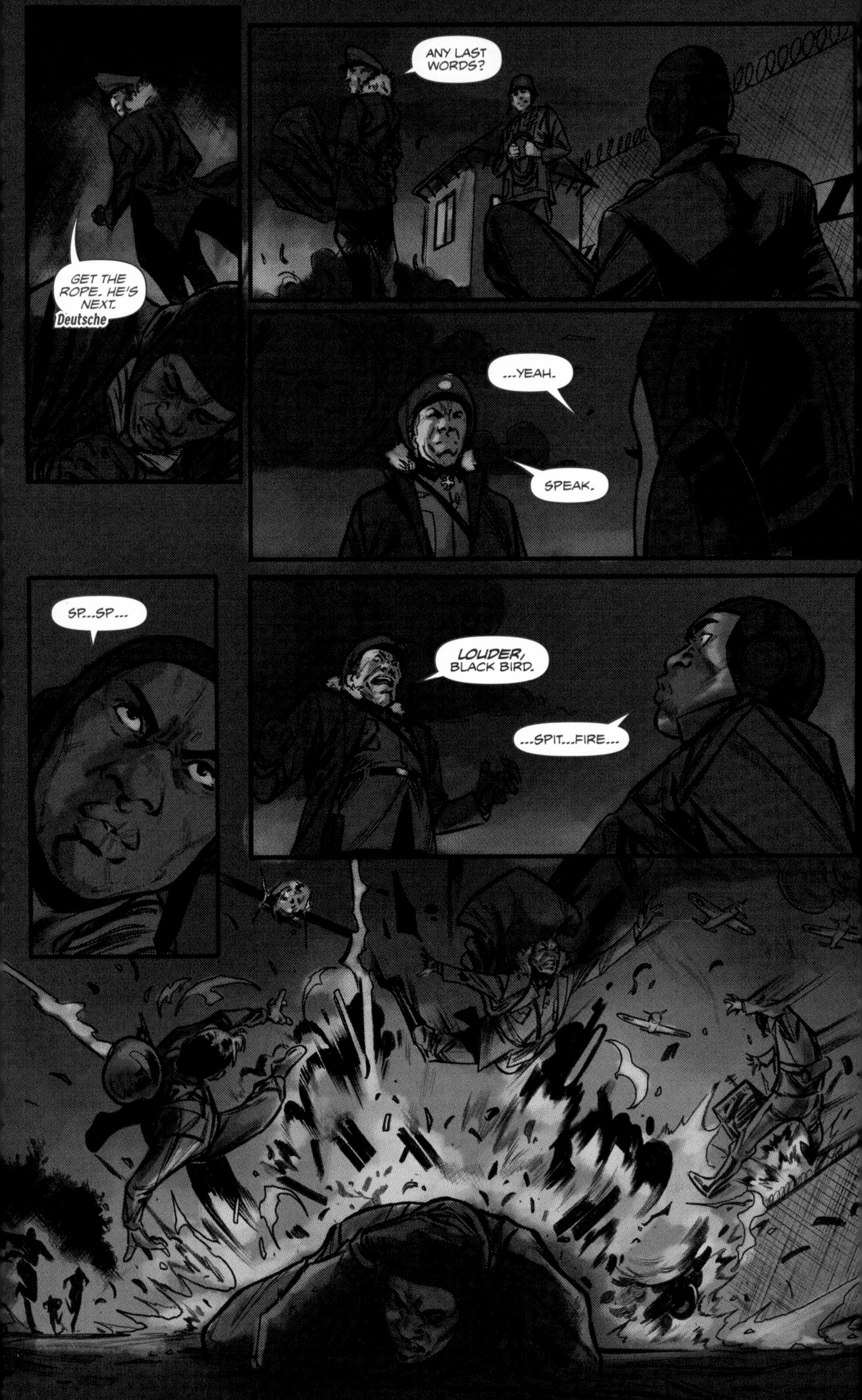
GET THE ROPE. HE'S NEXT.
Deutsche
ANY LAST WORDS?
...YEAH.
SPEAK.
SP...SP...
LOUDER, BLACK BIRD.
...SPIT...FIRE...

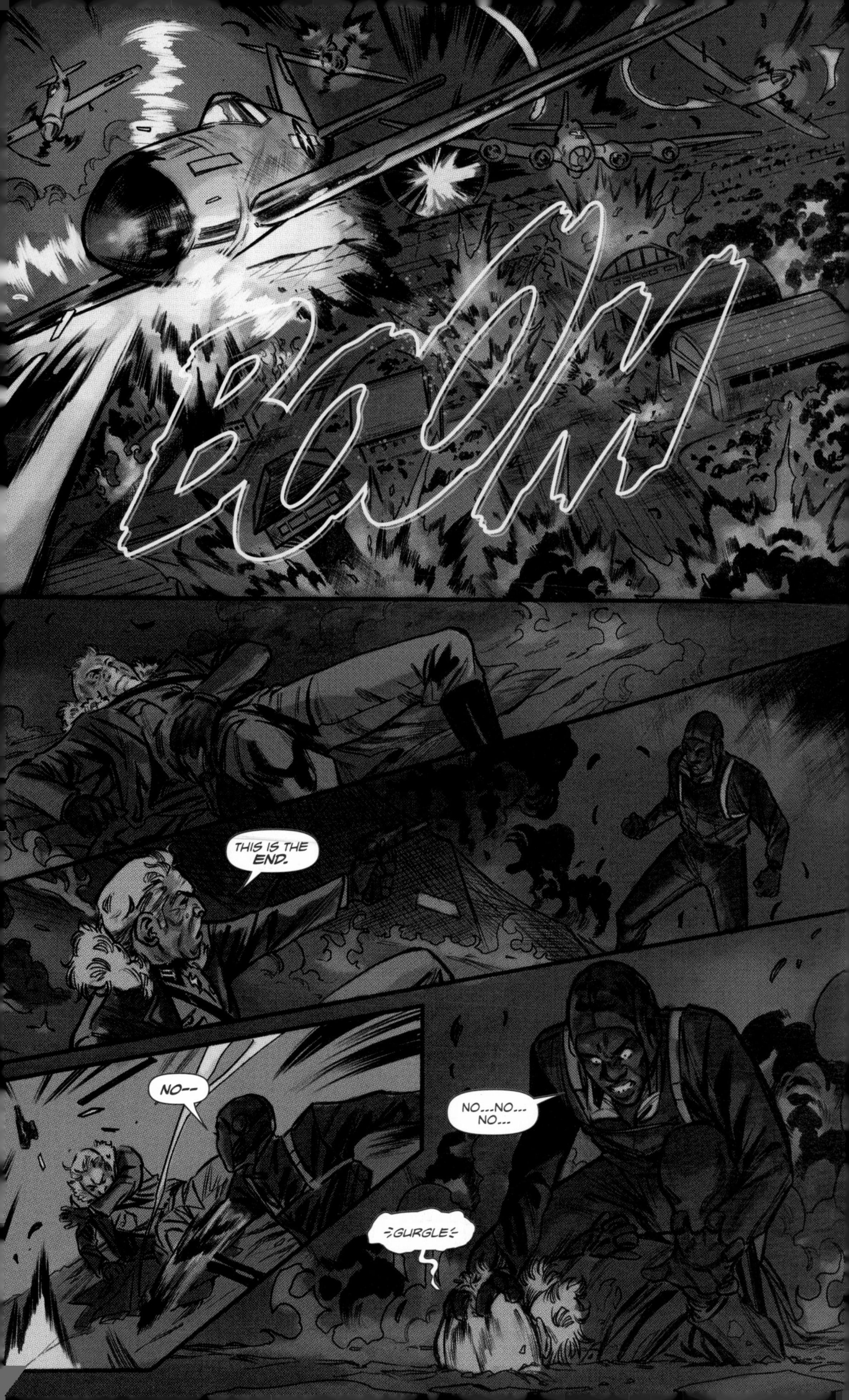
BOOM
THIS IS THE END.
NO--
NO...NO... NO...
GURGLE

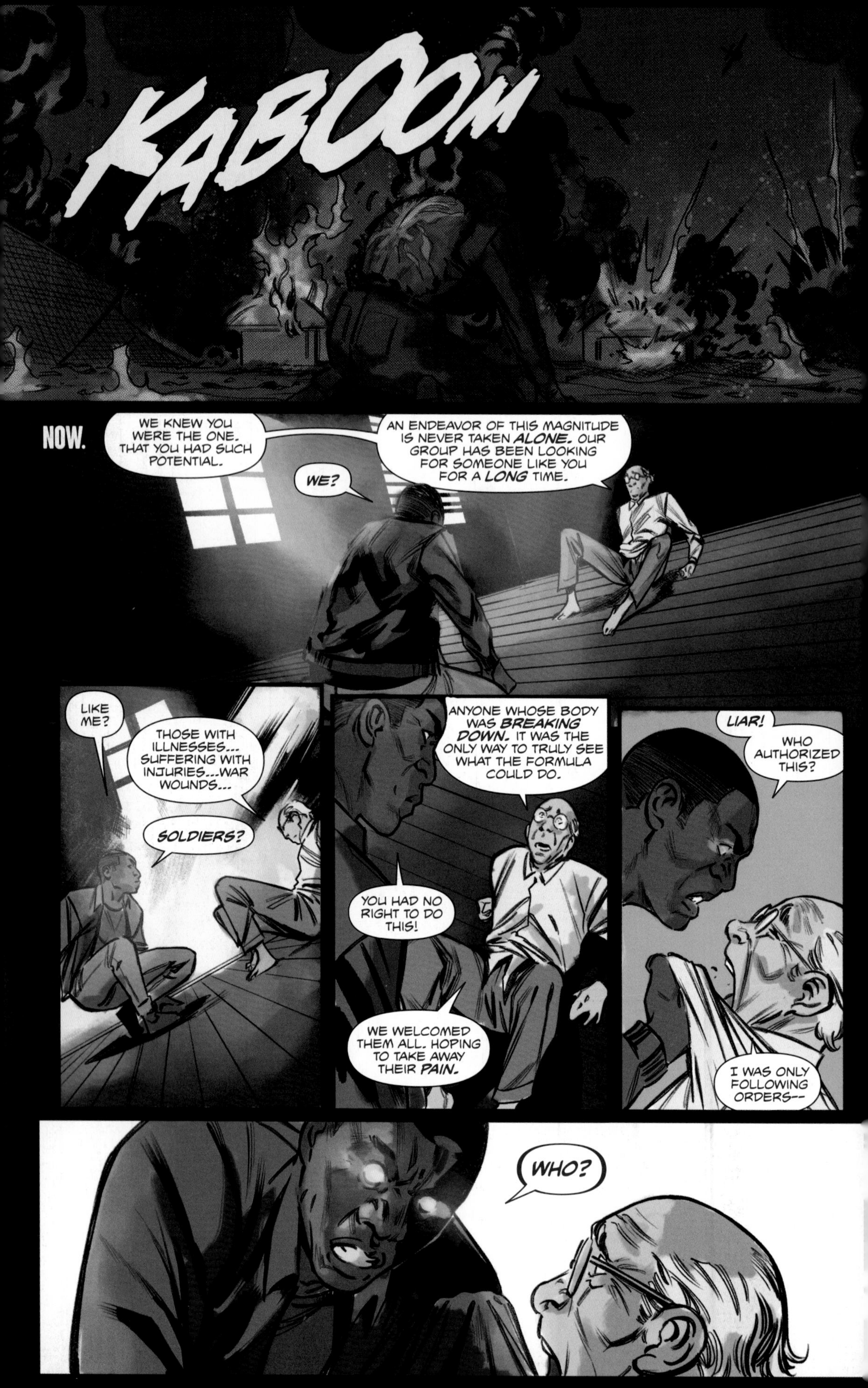
KABOOM
NOW.
WE KNEW YOU WERE THE ONE. THAT YOU HAD SUCH POTENTIAL.
WE?
AN ENDEAVOR OF THIS MAGNITUDE IS NEVER TAKEN ALONE. OUR GROUP HAS BEEN LOOKING FOR SOMEONE LIKE YOU FOR A LONG TIME.
LIKE ME?
THOSE WITH ILLNESSES... SUFFERING WITH INJURIES...WAR WOUNDS...
SOLDIERS?
ANYONE WHOSE BODY WAS BREAKING DOWN. IT WAS THE ONLY WAY TO TRULY SEE WHAT THE FORMULA COULD DO.
YOU HAD NO RIGHT TO DO THIS!
WE WELCOMED THEM ALL. HOPING TO TAKE AWAY THEIR PAIN.
LIAR!
WHO AUTHORIZED THIS?
I WAS ONLY FOLLOWING ORDERS--
WHO?

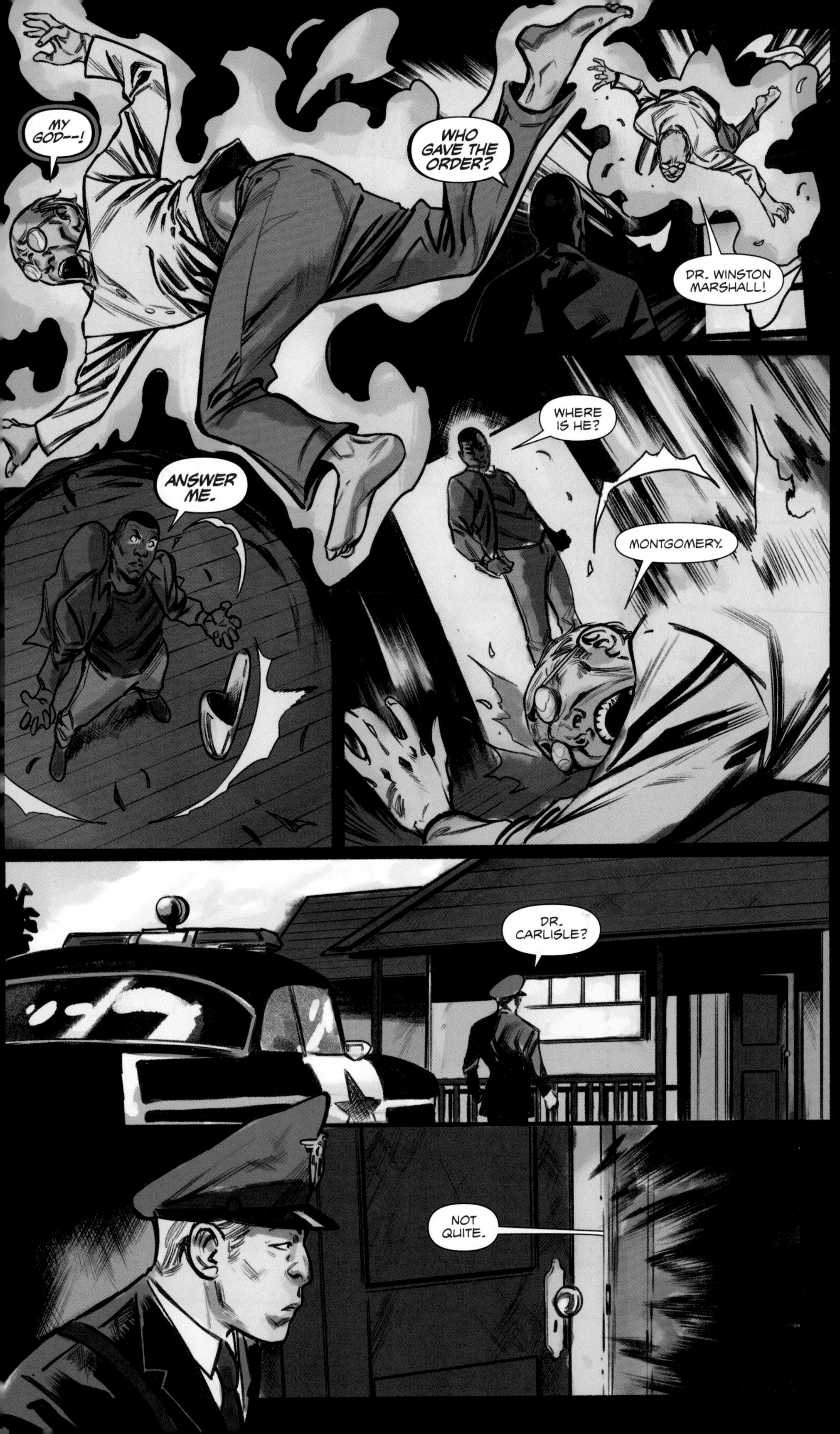
MY GOD--!
WHO GAVE THE ORDER?
DR. WINSTON MARSHALL!
ANSWER ME.
WHERE IS HE?
MONTGOMERY.
DR. CARLISLE?
NOT QUITE.

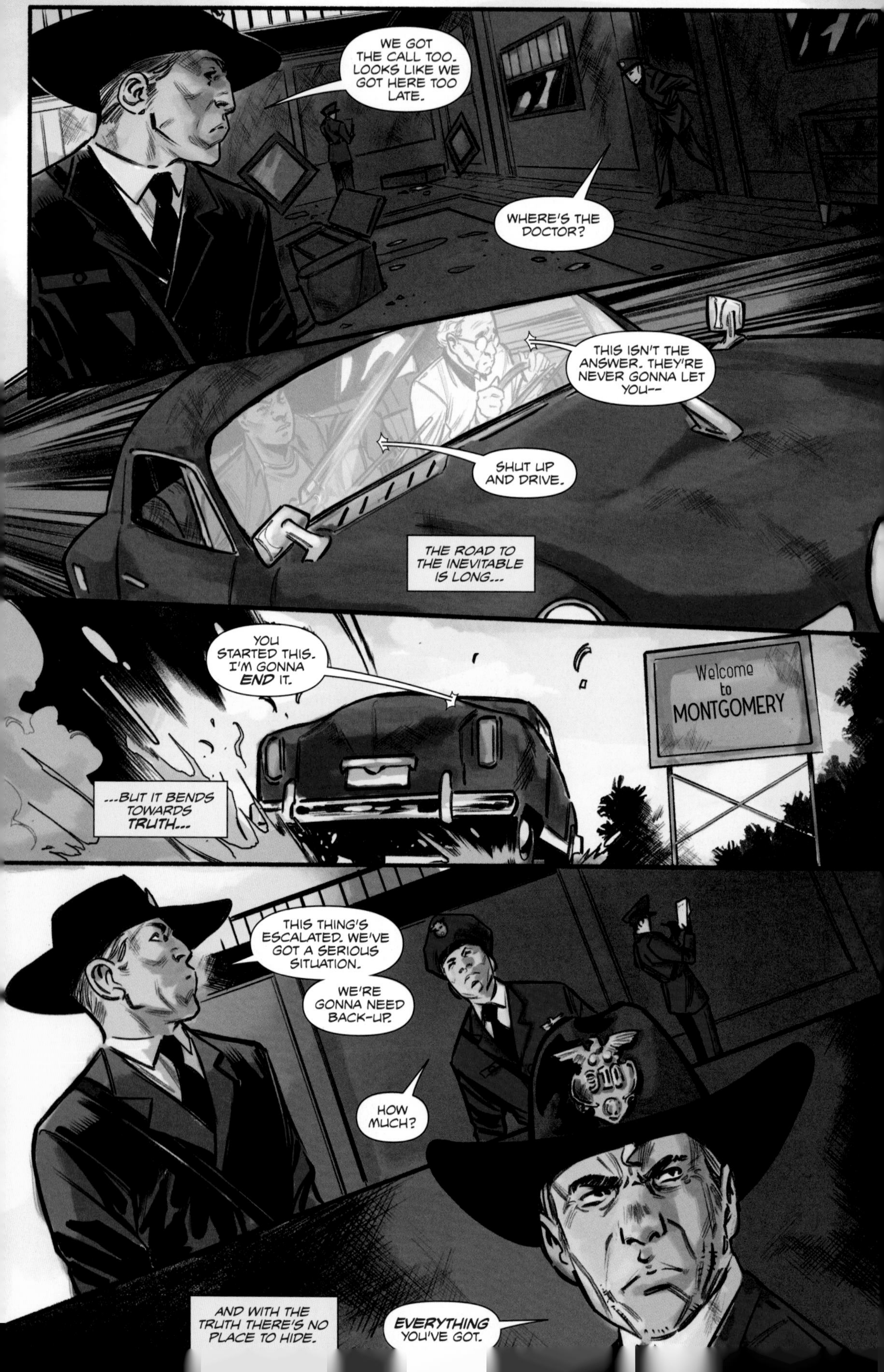
WE GOT THE CALL TOO. LOOKS LIKE WE GOT HERE TOO LATE.
WHERE'S THE DOCTOR?
THIS ISN'T THE ANSWER. THEY'RE NEVER GONNA LET YOU--
SHUT UP AND DRIVE.
THE ROAD TO THE INEVITABLE IS LONG...
YOU STARTED THIS. I'M GONNA END IT.
Welcome to MONTGOMERY
...BUT IT BENDS TOWARDS TRUTH...
THIS THING'S ESCALATED. WE'VE GOT A SERIOUS SITUATION.
WE'RE GONNA NEED BACK-UP.
HOW MUCH?
AND WITH THE TRUTH THERE'S NO PLACE TO HIDE.
EVERYTHING YOU'VE GOT.

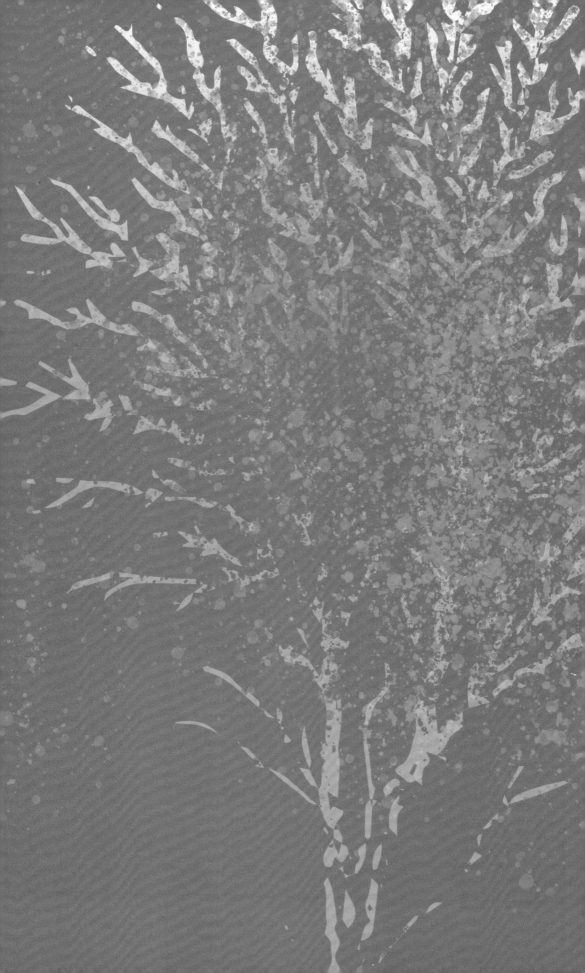

CHAPTER SIX

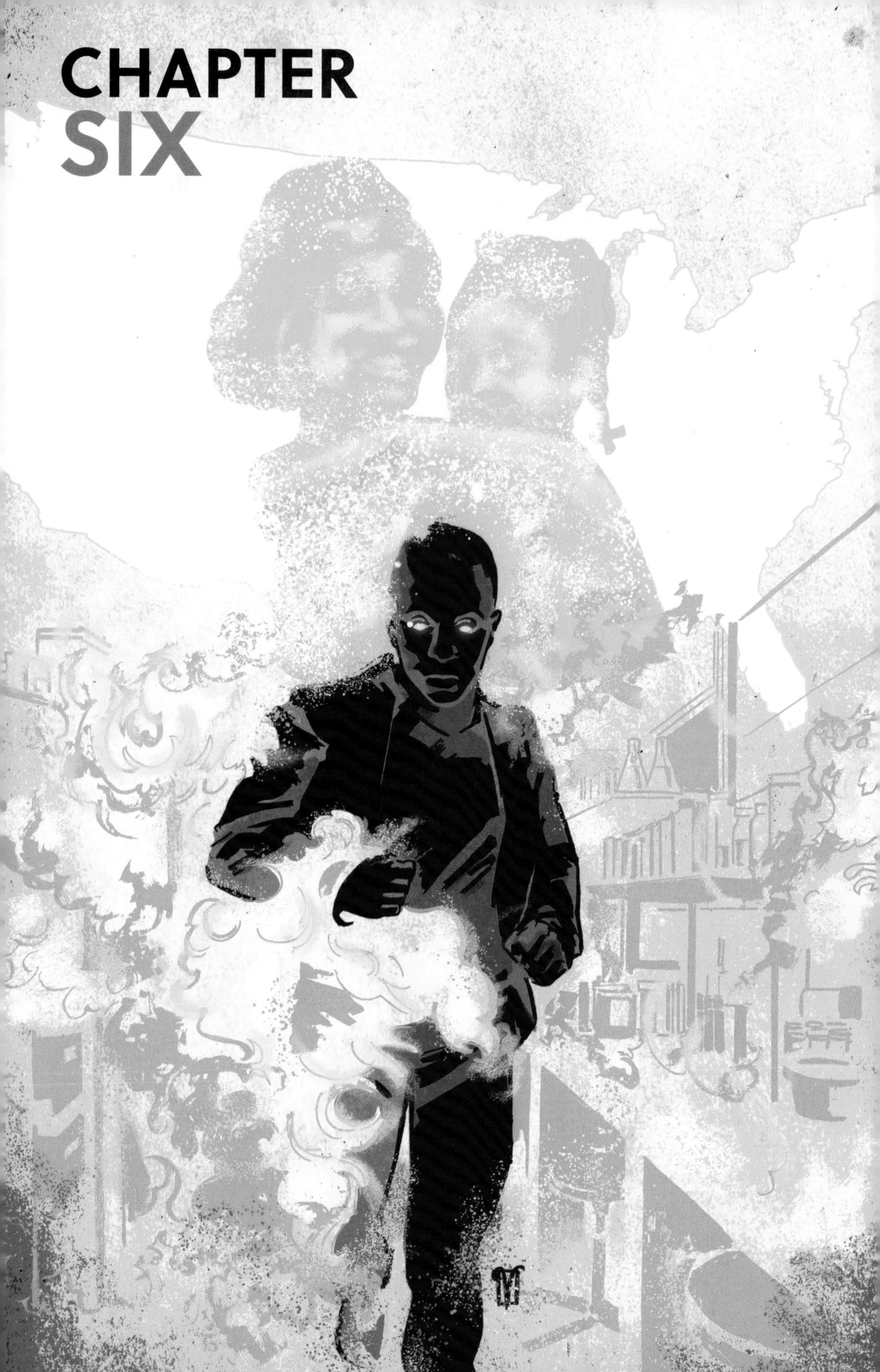

Issue #6 Cover
VALENTINE DE LANDRO

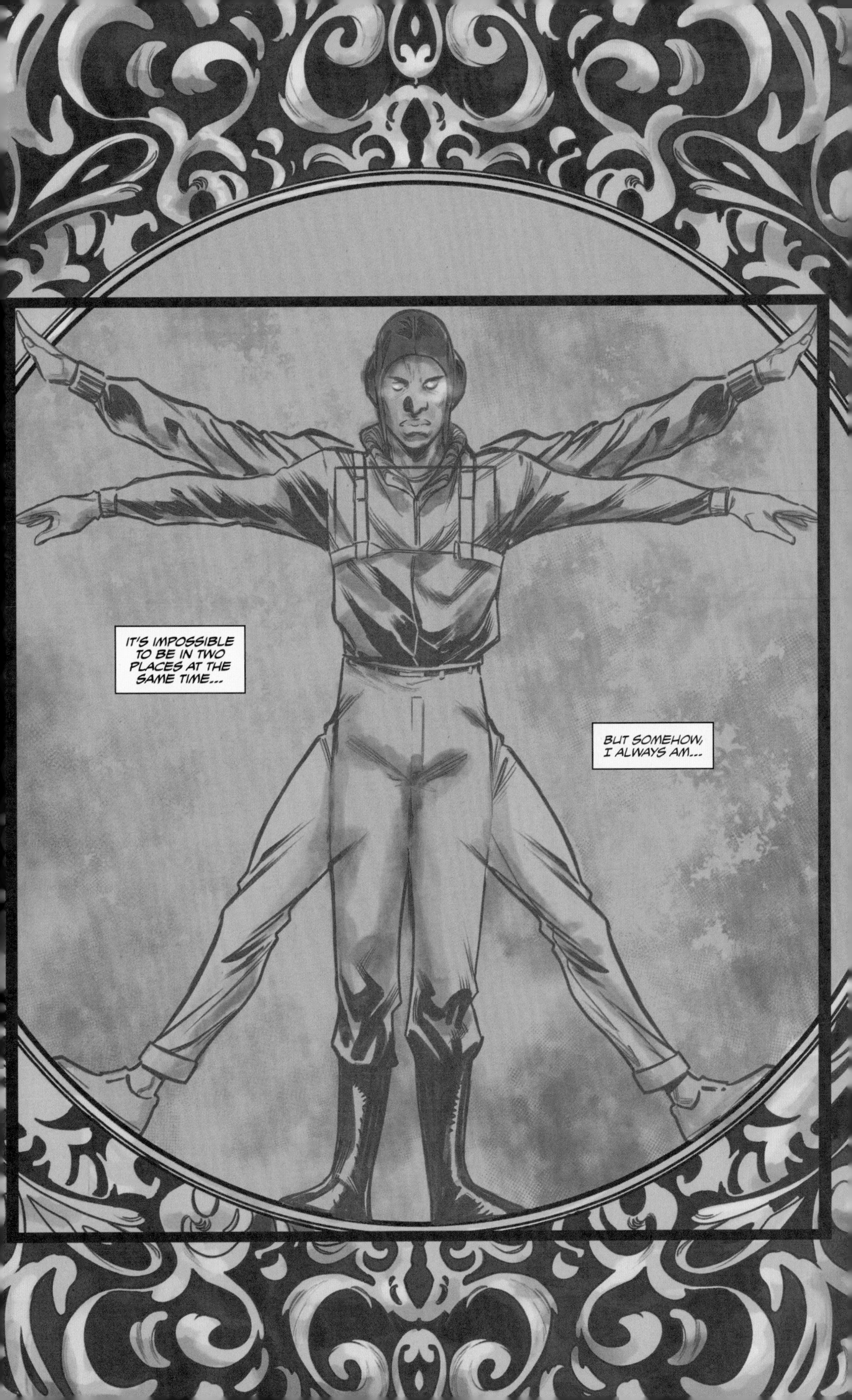
IT'S IMPOSSIBLE TO BE IN TWO PLACES AT THE SAME TIME...
BUT SOMEHOW, I ALWAYS AM...

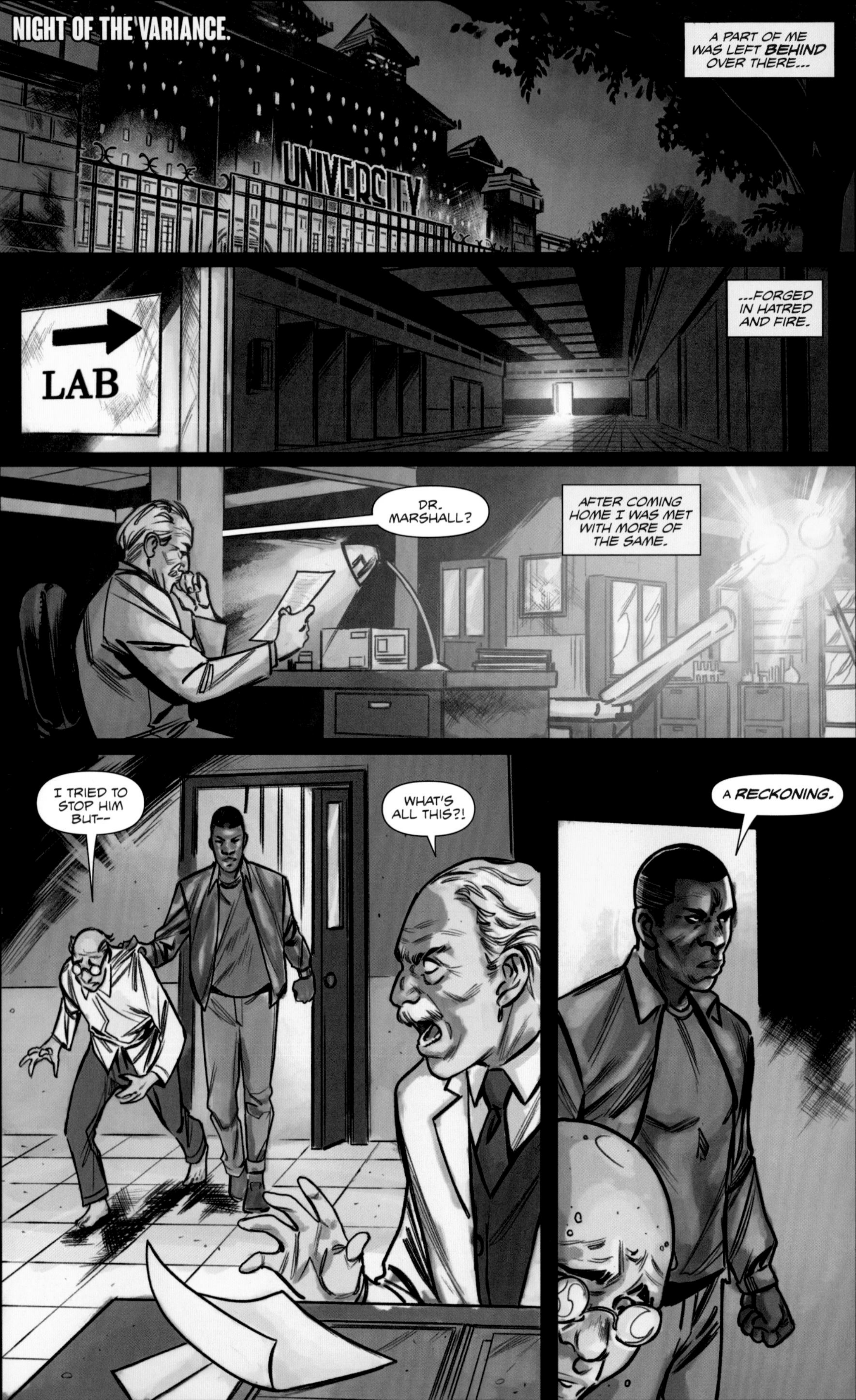
NIGHT OF THE VARIANCE.
A PART OF ME WAS LEFT BEHIND OVER THERE...
UNIVERCITY
LAB
...FORGED IN HATRED AND FIRE.
DR. MARSHALL?
AFTER COMING HOME I WAS MET WITH MORE OF THE SAME.
I TRIED TO STOP HIM BUT--
WHAT'S ALL THIS?!
A RECKONING.

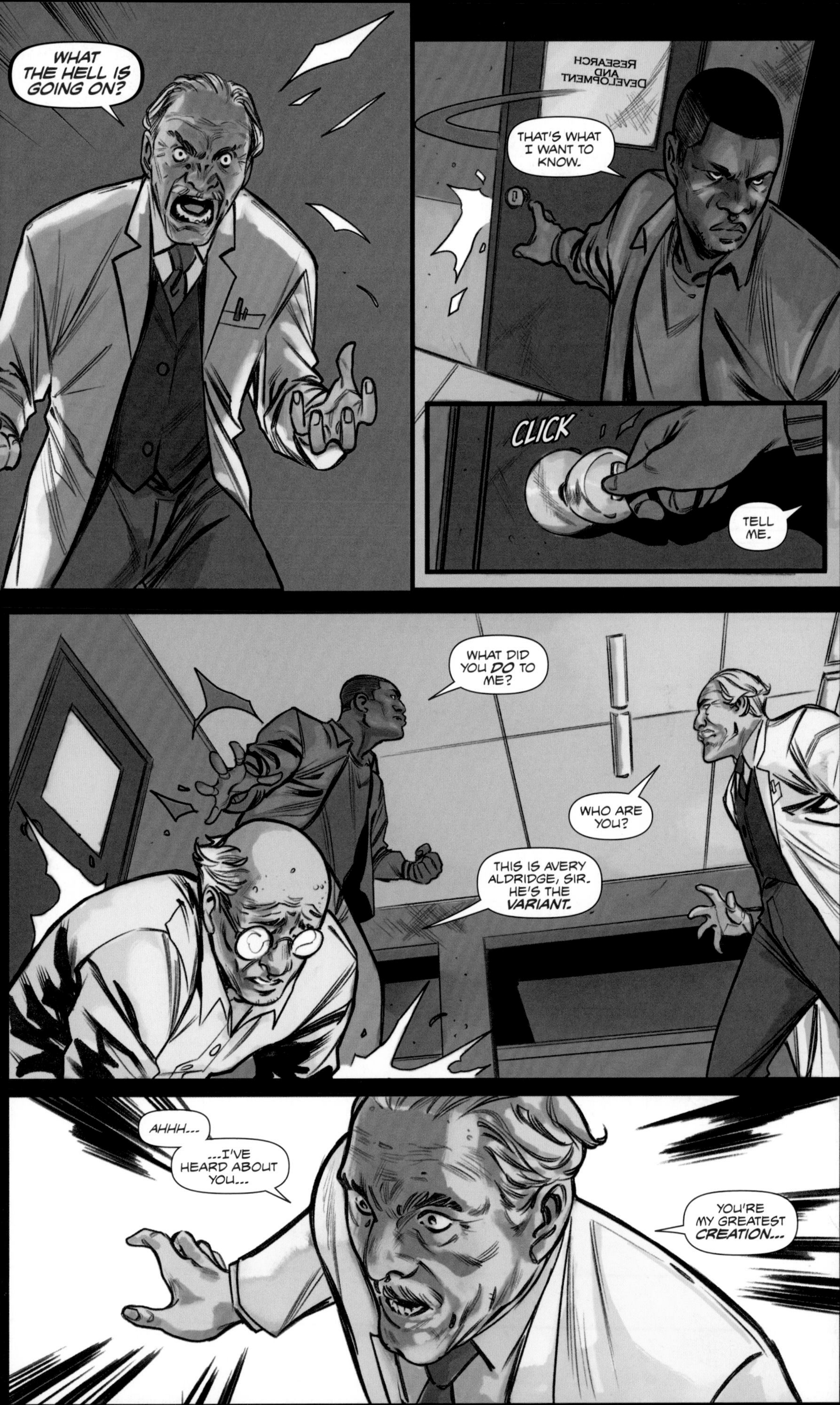
WHAT THE HELL IS GOING ON?
RESEARCH AND DEVELOPMENT
THAT'S WHAT I WANT TO KNOW.
CLICK
TELL ME.
WHAT DID YOU *DO* TO ME?
WHO ARE YOU?
THIS IS AVERY ALDRIDGE, SIR. HE'S THE *VARIANT*.
AHHH...
...I'VE HEARD ABOUT YOU...
YOU'RE MY GREATEST *CREATION*...

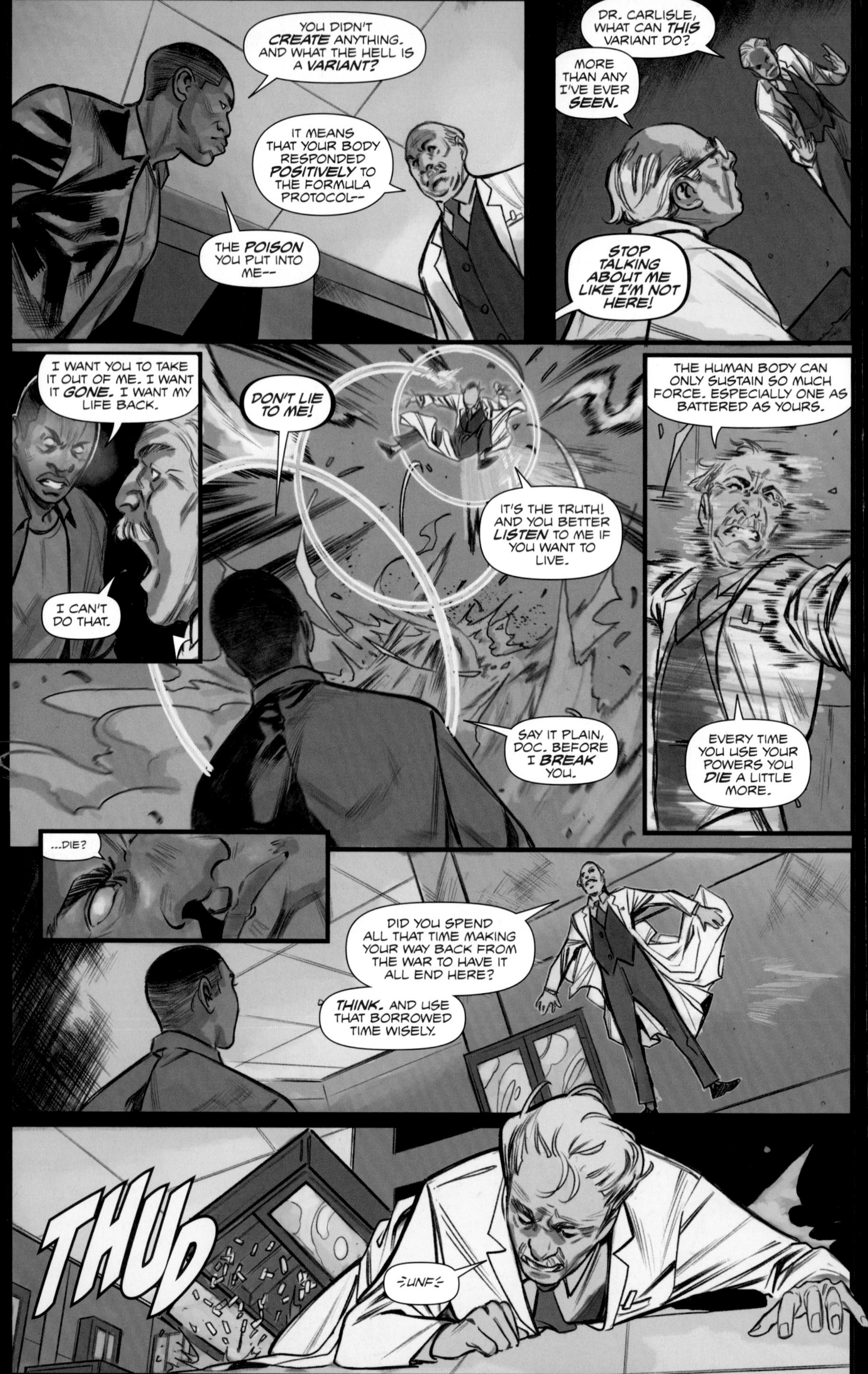
YOU DIDN'T CREATE ANYTHING. AND WHAT THE HELL IS A VARIANT?
IT MEANS THAT YOUR BODY RESPONDED POSITIVELY TO THE FORMULA PROTOCOL--
THE POISON YOU PUT INTO ME--
DR. CARLISLE, WHAT CAN THIS VARIANT DO?
MORE THAN ANY I'VE EVER SEEN.
STOP TALKING ABOUT ME LIKE I'M NOT HERE!
I WANT YOU TO TAKE IT OUT OF ME. I WANT IT GONE. I WANT MY LIFE BACK.
I CAN'T DO THAT.
DON'T LIE TO ME!
IT'S THE TRUTH! AND YOU BETTER LISTEN TO ME IF YOU WANT TO LIVE.
SAY IT PLAIN, DOC. BEFORE I BREAK YOU.
THE HUMAN BODY CAN ONLY SUSTAIN SO MUCH FORCE. ESPECIALLY ONE AS BATTERED AS YOURS.
EVERY TIME YOU USE YOUR POWERS YOU DIE A LITTLE MORE.
...DIE?
DID YOU SPEND ALL THAT TIME MAKING YOUR WAY BACK FROM THE WAR TO HAVE IT ALL END HERE?
THINK. AND USE THAT BORROWED TIME WISELY.
THUD
UNF

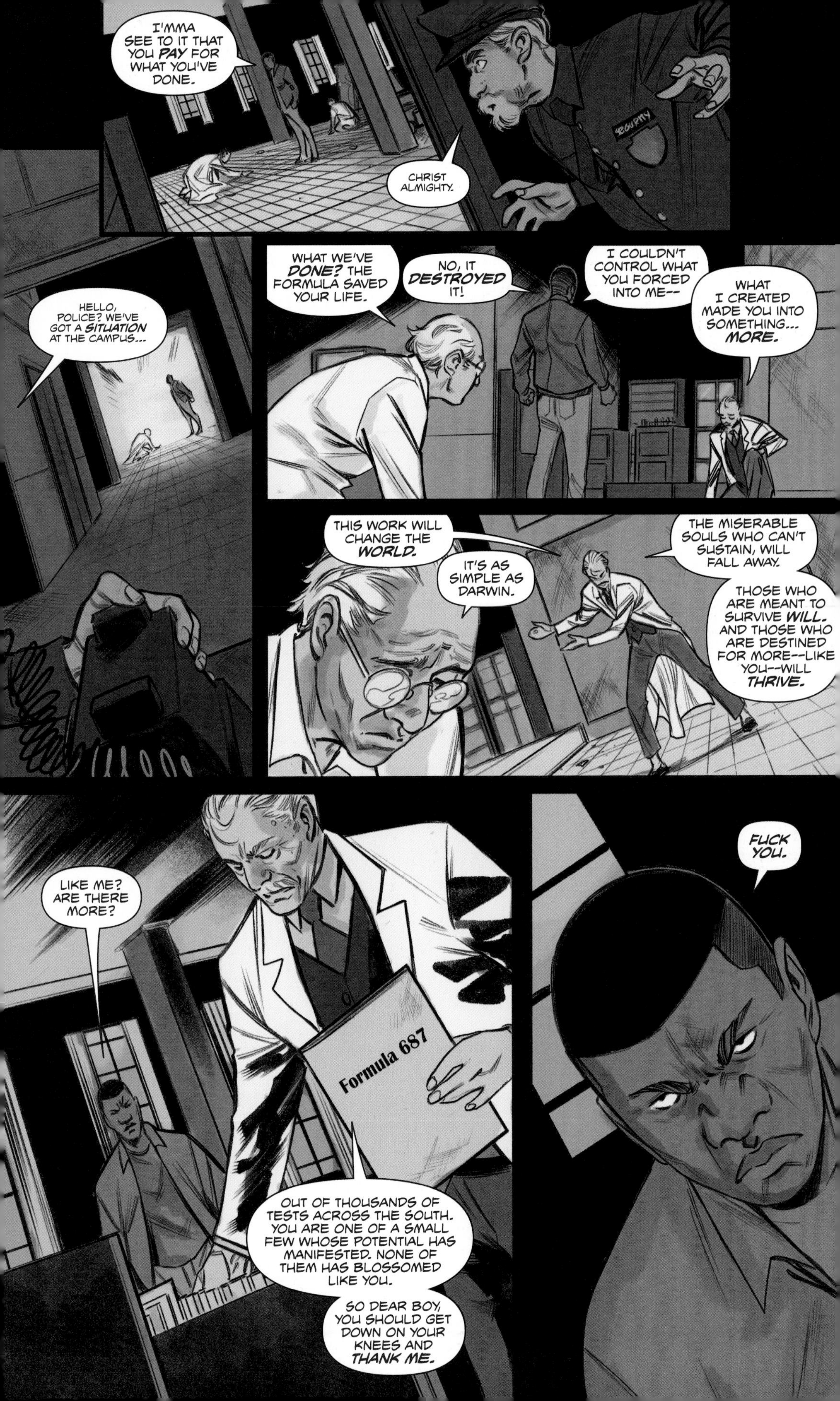
I'MMA SEE TO IT THAT YOU PAY FOR WHAT YOU'VE DONE.
SECURITY
CHRIST ALMIGHTY.
HELLO, POLICE? WE'VE GOT A SITUATION AT THE CAMPUS...
WHAT WE'VE DONE? THE FORMULA SAVED YOUR LIFE.
NO, IT DESTROYED IT!
I COULDN'T CONTROL WHAT YOU FORCED INTO ME--
WHAT I CREATED MADE YOU INTO SOMETHING... MORE.
THIS WORK WILL CHANGE THE WORLD.
IT'S AS SIMPLE AS DARWIN.
THE MISERABLE SOULS WHO CAN'T SUSTAIN, WILL FALL AWAY.
THOSE WHO ARE MEANT TO SURVIVE WILL. AND THOSE WHO ARE DESTINED FOR MORE--LIKE YOU--WILL THRIVE.
LIKE ME? ARE THERE MORE?
Formula 687
OUT OF THOUSANDS OF TESTS ACROSS THE SOUTH. YOU ARE ONE OF A SMALL FEW WHOSE POTENTIAL HAS MANIFESTED. NONE OF THEM HAS BLOSSOMED LIKE YOU.
SO DEAR BOY, YOU SHOULD GET DOWN ON YOUR KNEES AND THANK ME.
FUCK YOU.

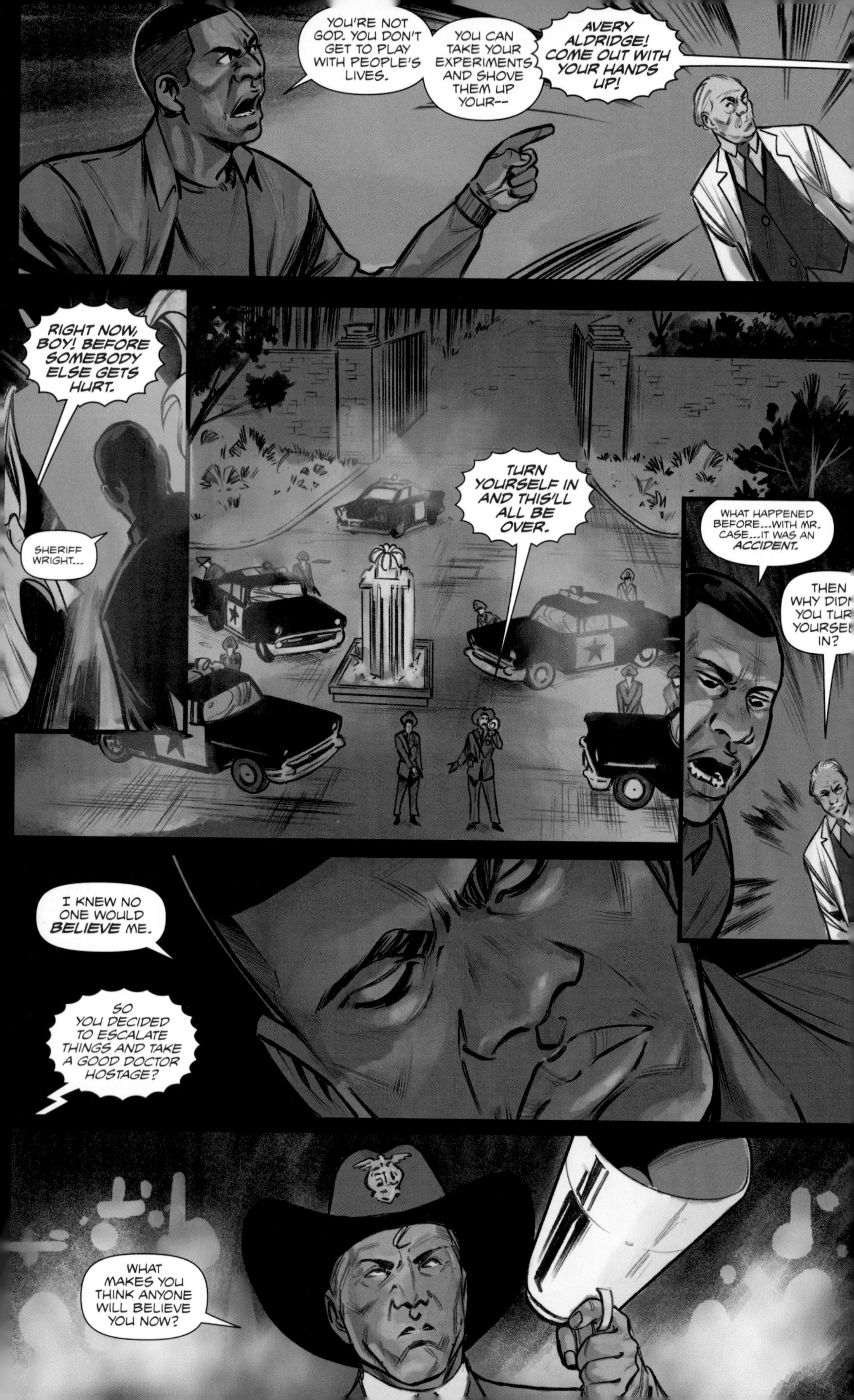
YOU'RE NOT GOD. YOU DON'T GET TO PLAY WITH PEOPLE'S LIVES.
YOU CAN TAKE YOUR EXPERIMENTS AND SHOVE THEM UP YOUR--
AVERY ALDRIDGE! COME OUT WITH YOUR HANDS UP!
RIGHT NOW, BOY! BEFORE SOMEBODY ELSE GETS HURT.
SHERIFF WRIGHT...
TURN YOURSELF IN AND THIS'LL ALL BE OVER.
WHAT HAPPENED BEFORE...WITH MR. CASE...IT WAS AN ACCIDENT.
I KNEW NO ONE WOULD BELIEVE ME.
SO YOU DECIDED TO ESCALATE THINGS AND TAKE A GOOD DOCTOR HOSTAGE?
WHAT MAKES YOU THINK ANYONE WILL BELIEVE YOU NOW?

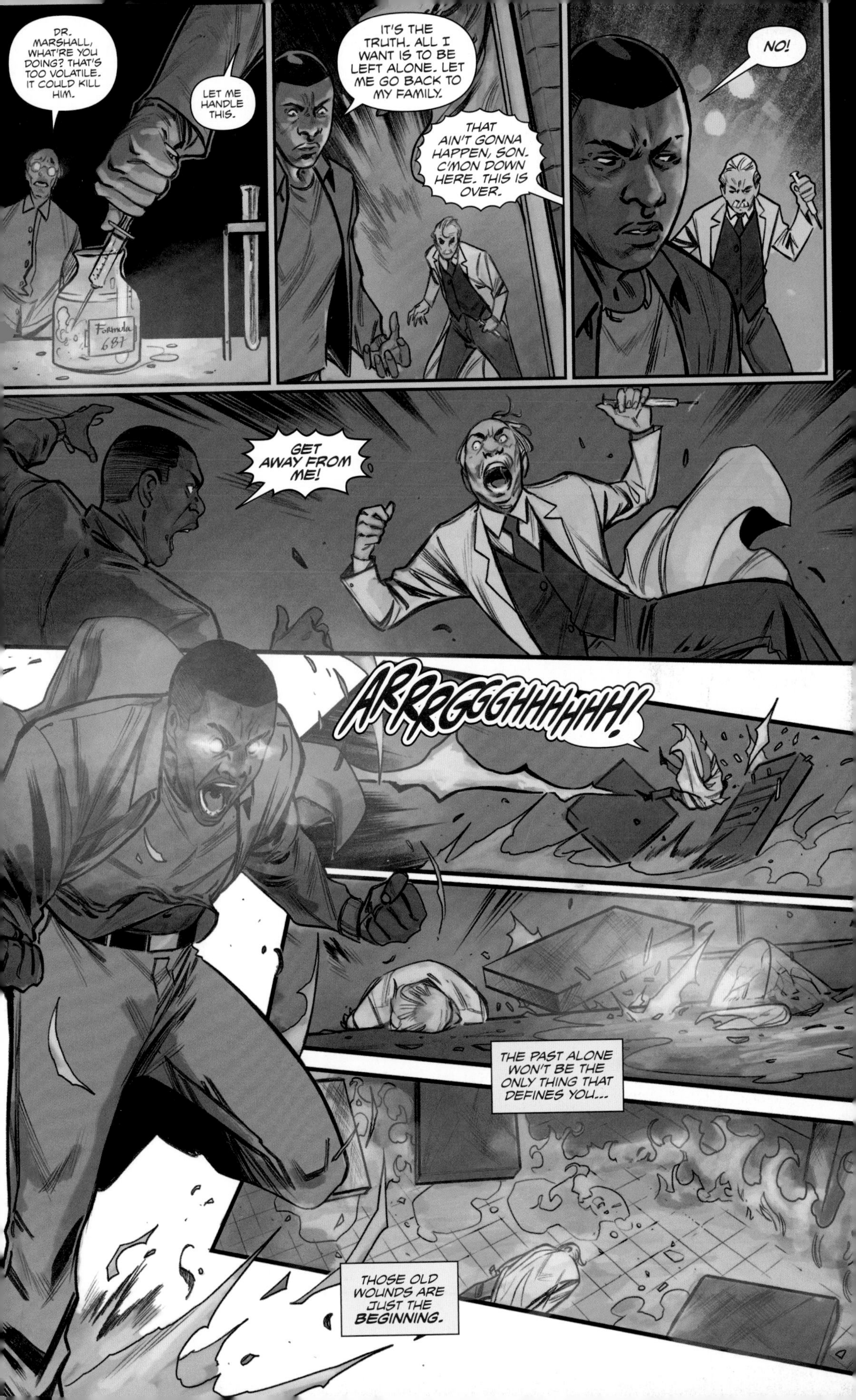
DR. MARSHALL, WHAT'RE YOU DOING? THAT'S TOO VOLATILE. IT COULD KILL HIM.
LET ME HANDLE THIS.
Formula 687
IT'S THE TRUTH. ALL I WANT IS TO BE LEFT ALONE. LET ME GO BACK TO MY FAMILY.
THAT AIN'T GONNA HAPPEN, SON. C'MON DOWN HERE. THIS IS OVER.
NO!
GET AWAY FROM ME!
ARRRGGGHHHHHH!
THE PAST ALONE WON'T BE THE ONLY THING THAT DEFINES YOU...
THOSE OLD WOUNDS ARE JUST THE BEGINNING.

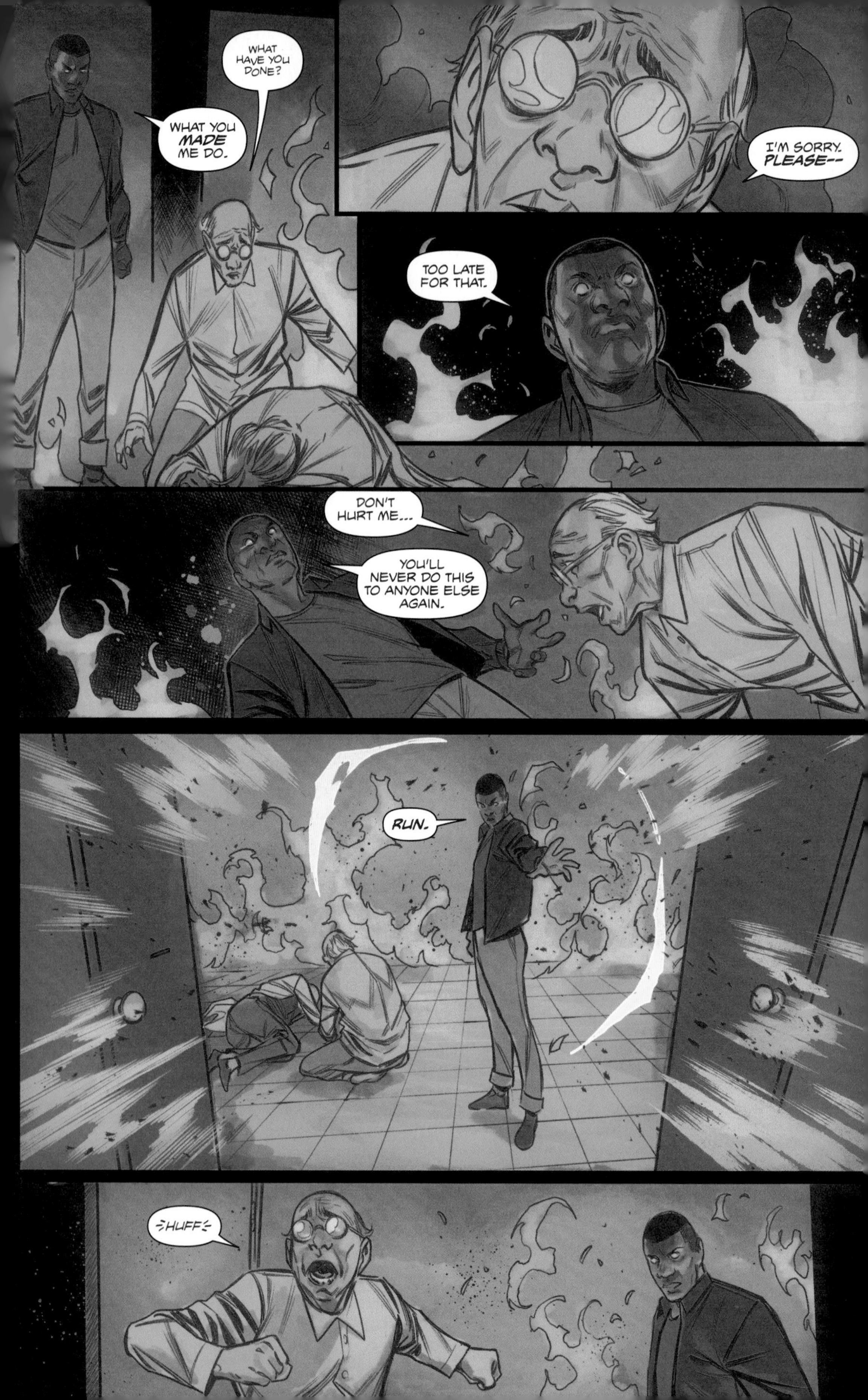
WHAT HAVE YOU DONE?
WHAT YOU MADE ME DO.
I'M SORRY. PLEASE--
TOO LATE FOR THAT.
DON'T HURT ME...
YOU'LL NEVER DO THIS TO ANYONE ELSE AGAIN.
RUN.
HUFF

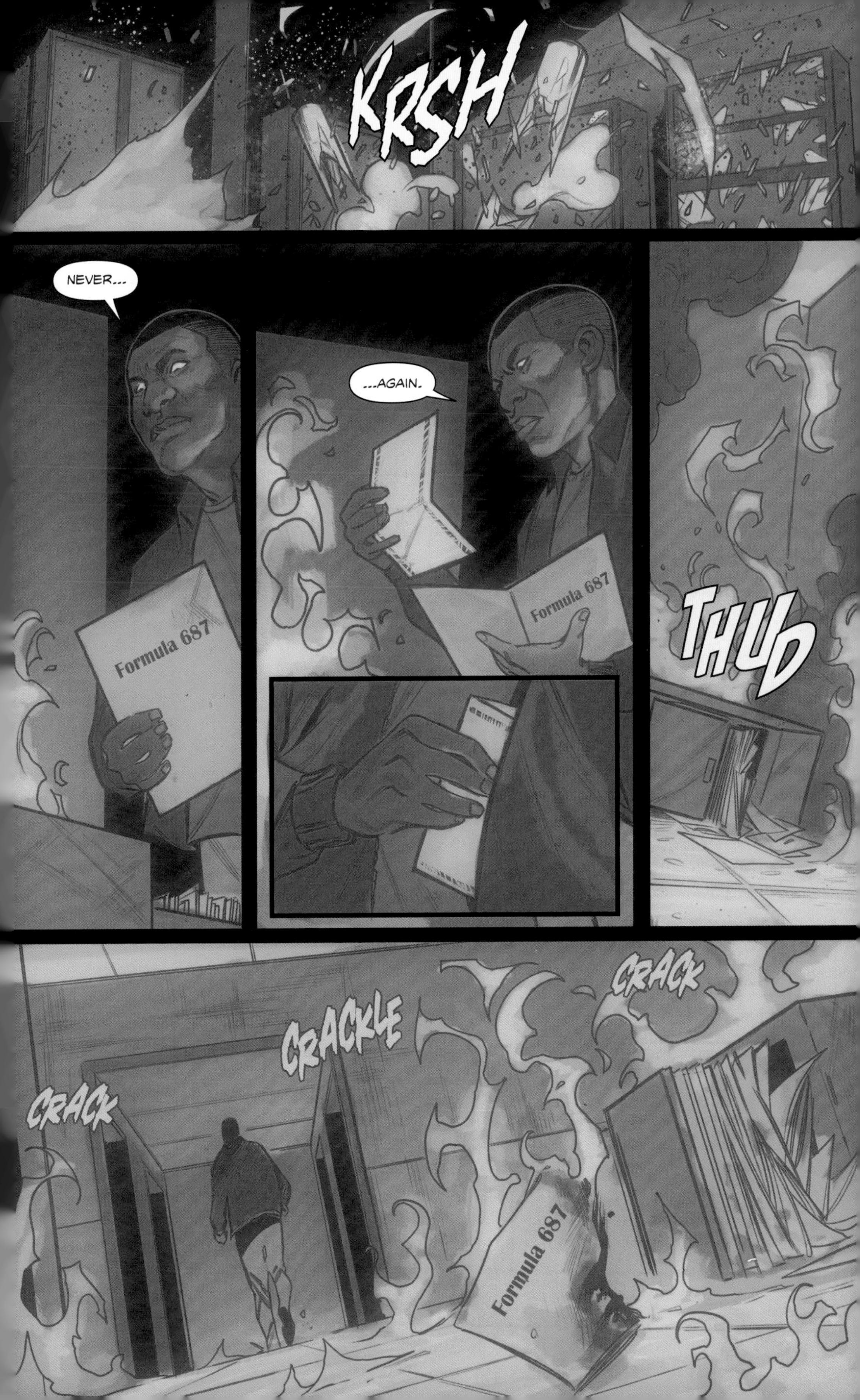
KRSH
NEVER...
...AGAIN.
Formula 687
Formula 687
THUD
CRACK
CRACKLE
CRACK
Formula 687

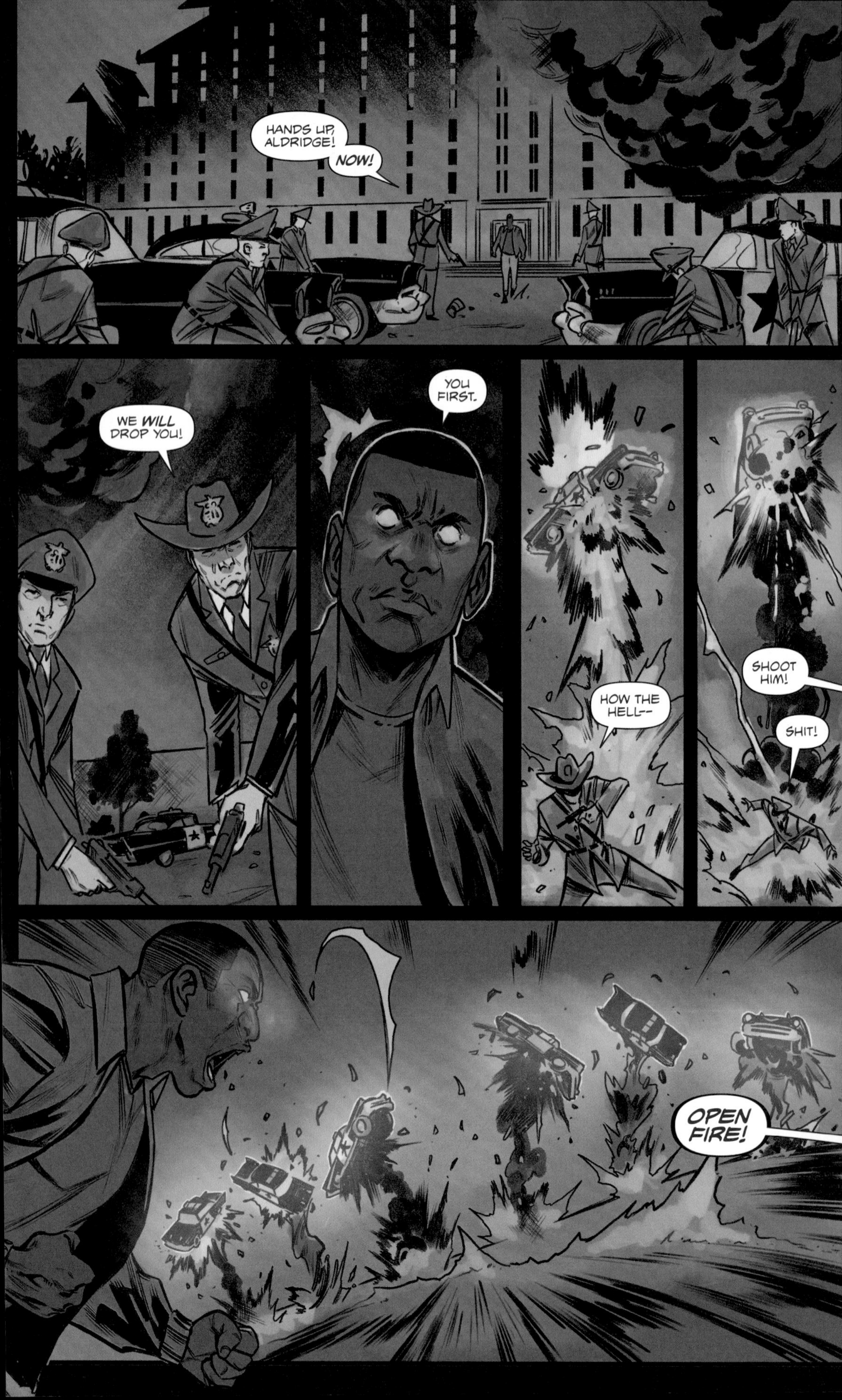
HANDS UP, ALDRIDGE!
NOW!
WE WILL DROP YOU!
YOU FIRST.
HOW THE HELL--
SHOOT HIM!
SHIT!
OPEN FIRE!

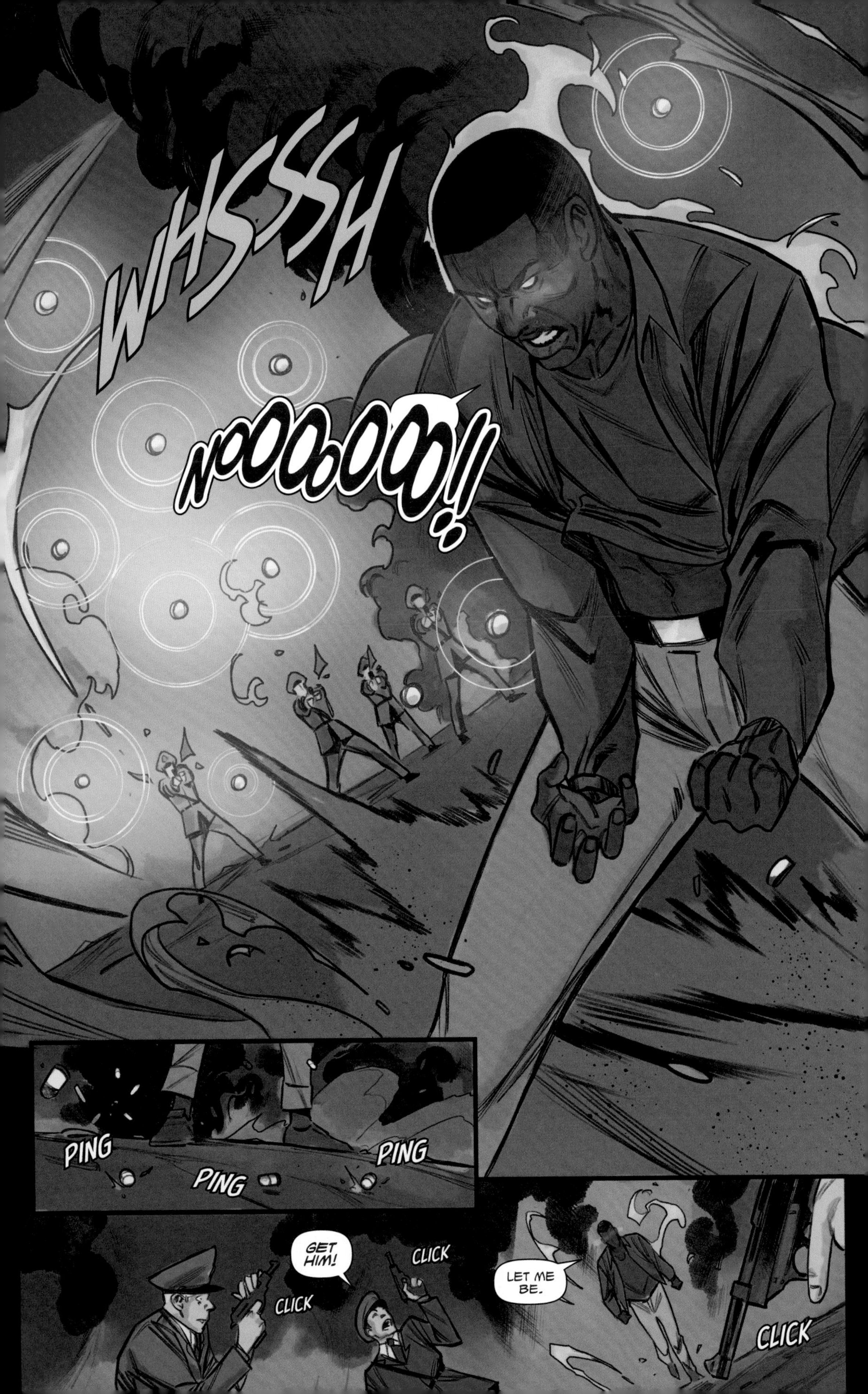

WHSSSH
NOOOOOOO!!
PING
PING
PING
GET HIM!
CLICK
CLICK
LET ME BE.
CLICK

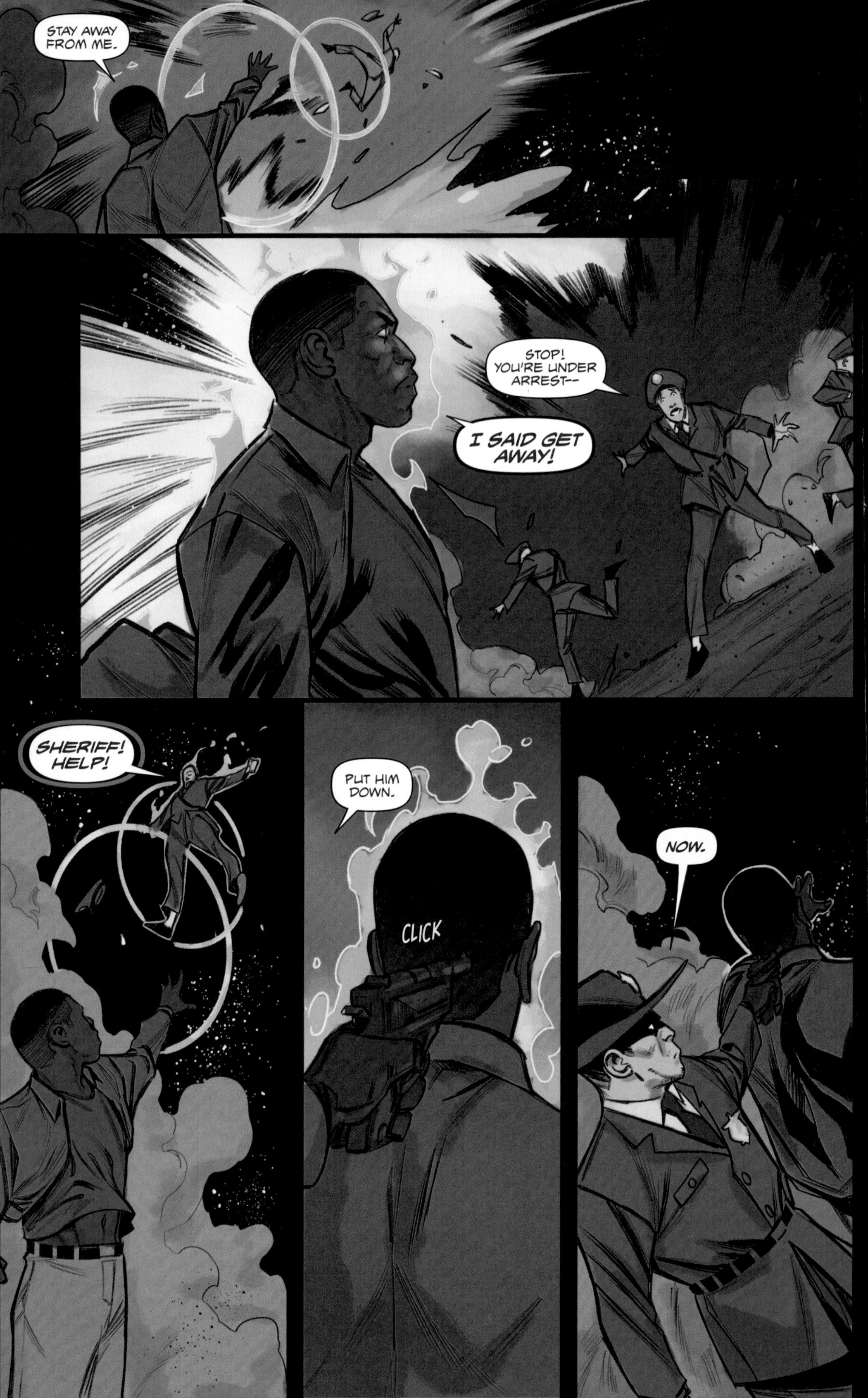
STAY AWAY FROM ME.
STOP! YOU'RE UNDER ARREST--
I SAID GET AWAY!
SHERIFF! HELP!
PUT HIM DOWN.
CLICK
NOW.

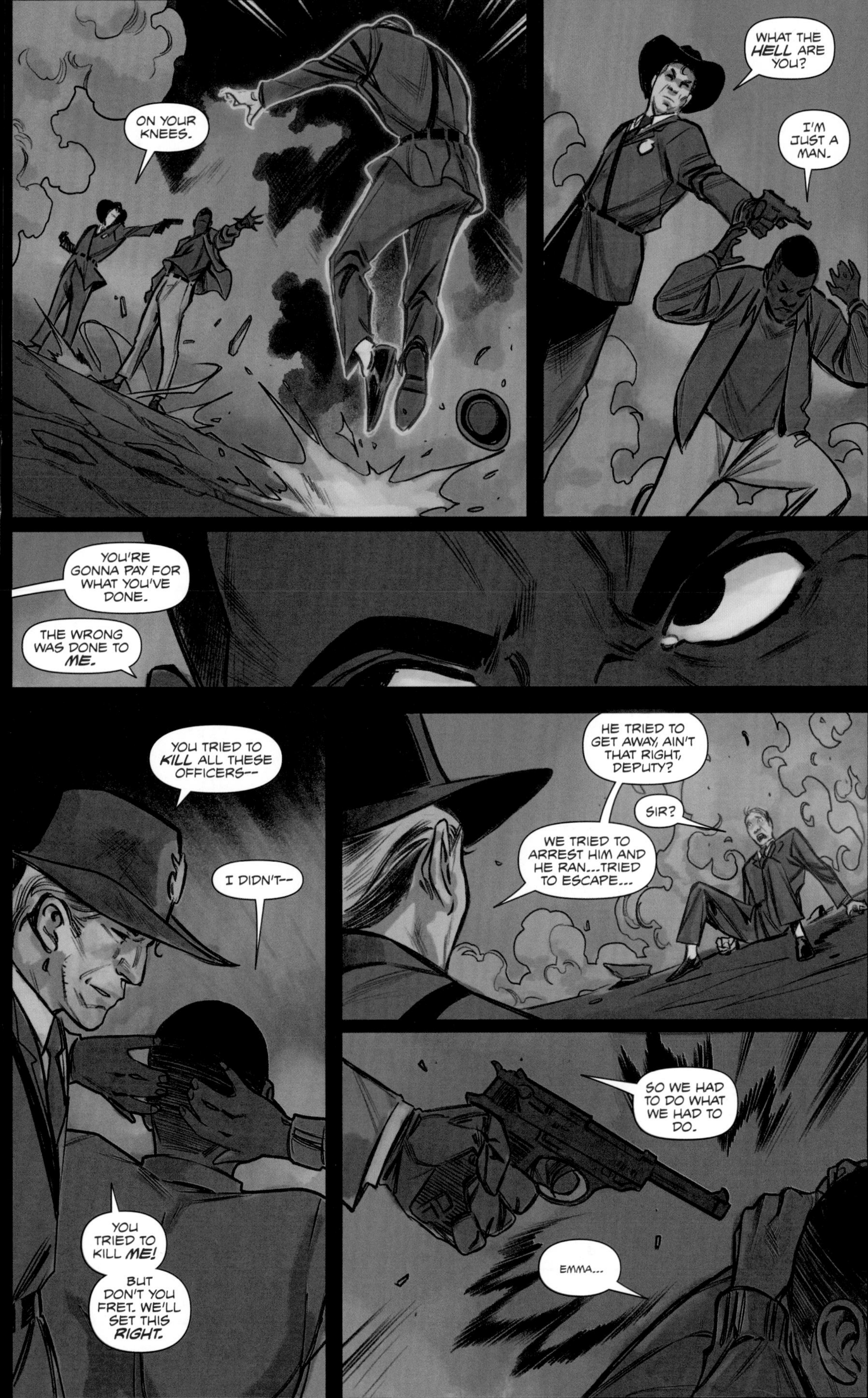
ON YOUR KNEES.
WHAT THE HELL ARE YOU?
I'M JUST A MAN.
YOU'RE GONNA PAY FOR WHAT YOU'VE DONE.
THE WRONG WAS DONE TO ME.
YOU TRIED TO KILL ALL THESE OFFICERS--
I DIDN'T--
YOU TRIED TO KILL ME!
BUT DON'T YOU FRET. WE'LL SET THIS RIGHT.
HE TRIED TO GET AWAY, AIN'T THAT RIGHT, DEPUTY?
SIR?
WE TRIED TO ARREST HIM AND HE RAN...TRIED TO ESCAPE...
SO WE HAD TO DO WHAT WE HAD TO DO.
EMMA...

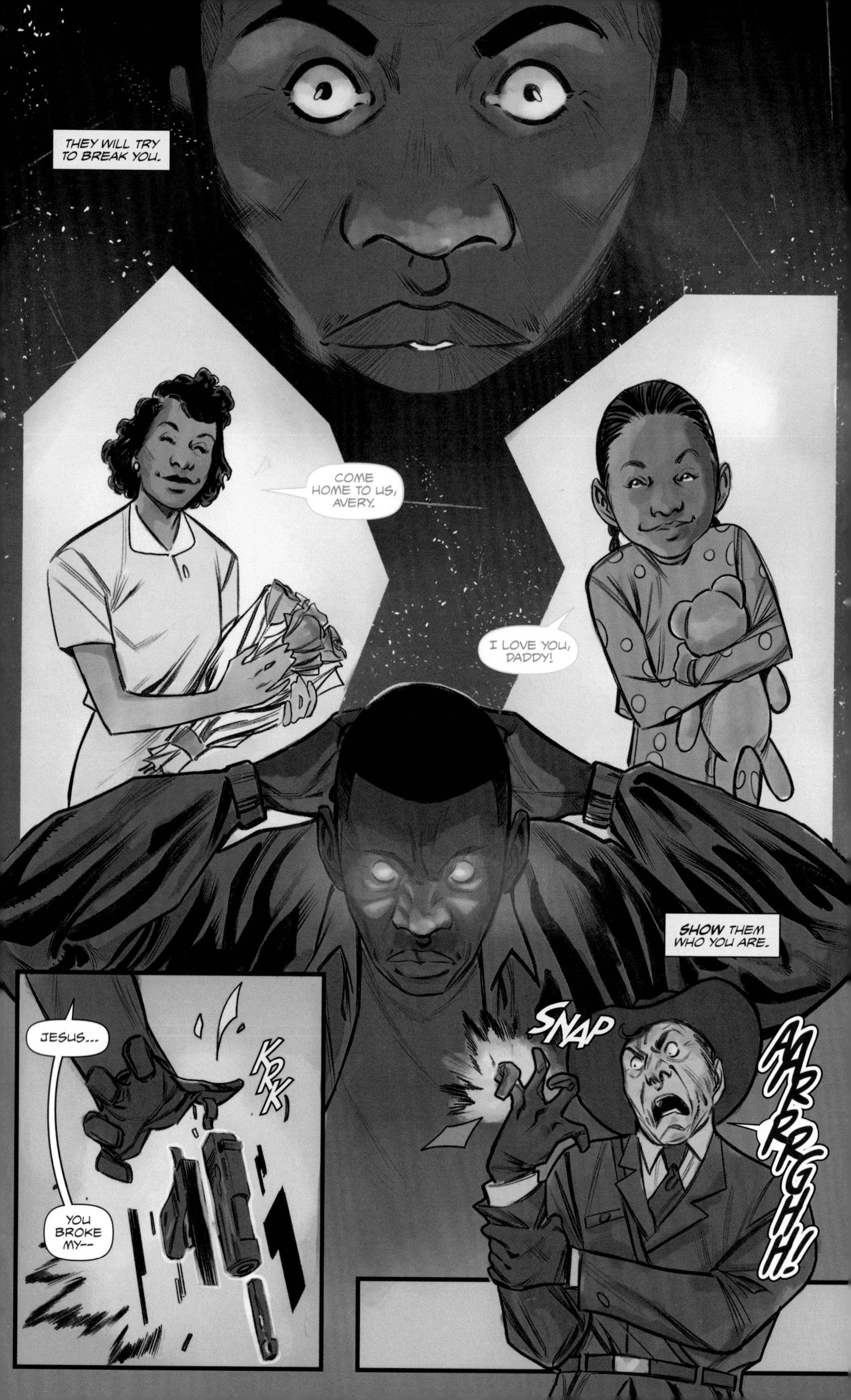
THEY WILL TRY TO BREAK YOU.
COME HOME TO US, AVERY.
I LOVE YOU, DADDY!
SHOW THEM WHO YOU ARE.
JESUS...
YOU BROKE MY--
KRK
SNAP
AARRGHHH!

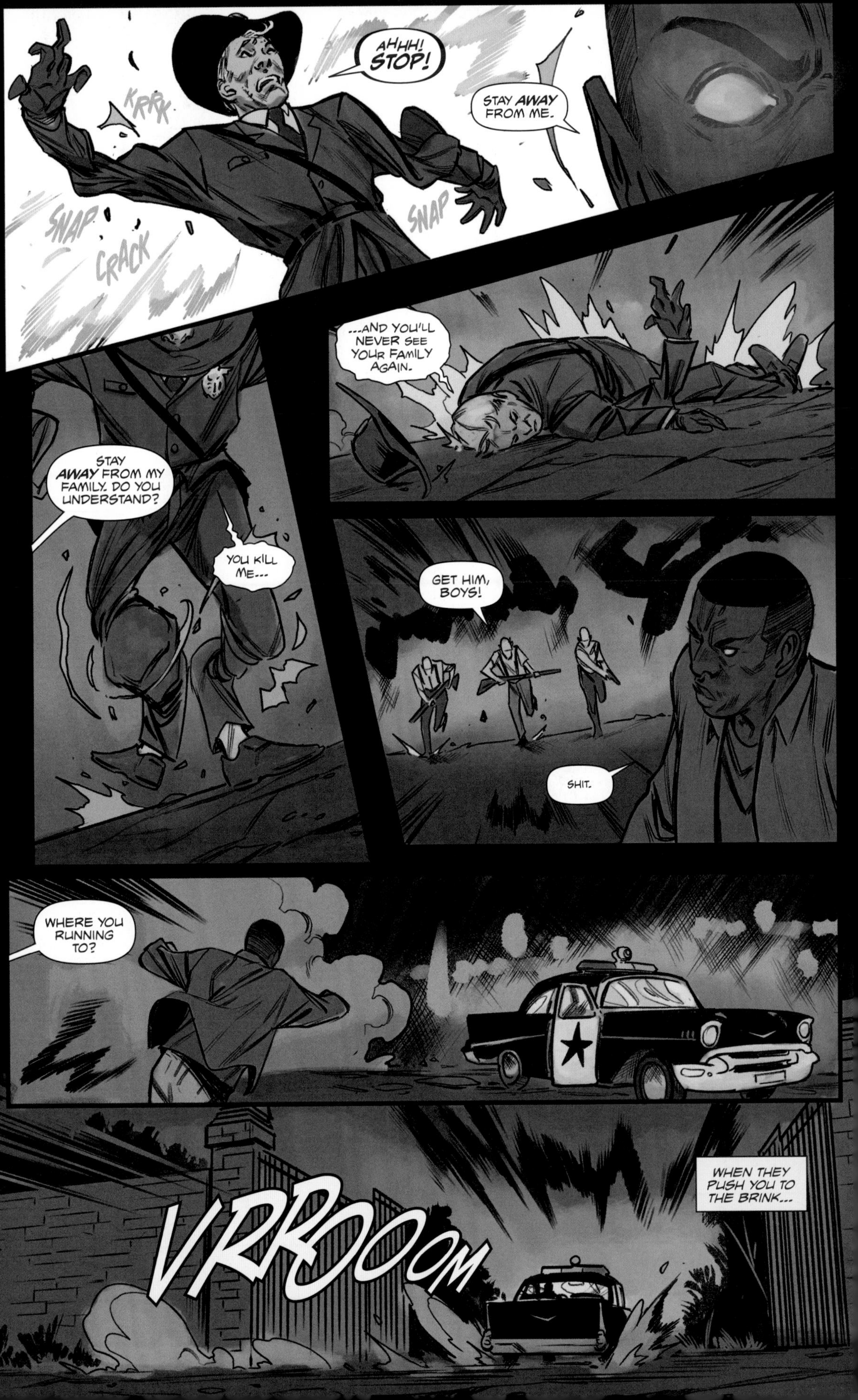
AHHH! STOP!
KRRK
STAY AWAY FROM ME.
SNAP
CRACK
SNAP
STAY AWAY FROM MY FAMILY. DO YOU UNDERSTAND?
YOU KILL ME...
...AND YOU'LL NEVER SEE YOUR FAMILY AGAIN.
GET HIM, BOYS!
SHIT.
WHERE YOU RUNNING TO?
WHEN THEY PUSH YOU TO THE BRINK...
VRROOOM

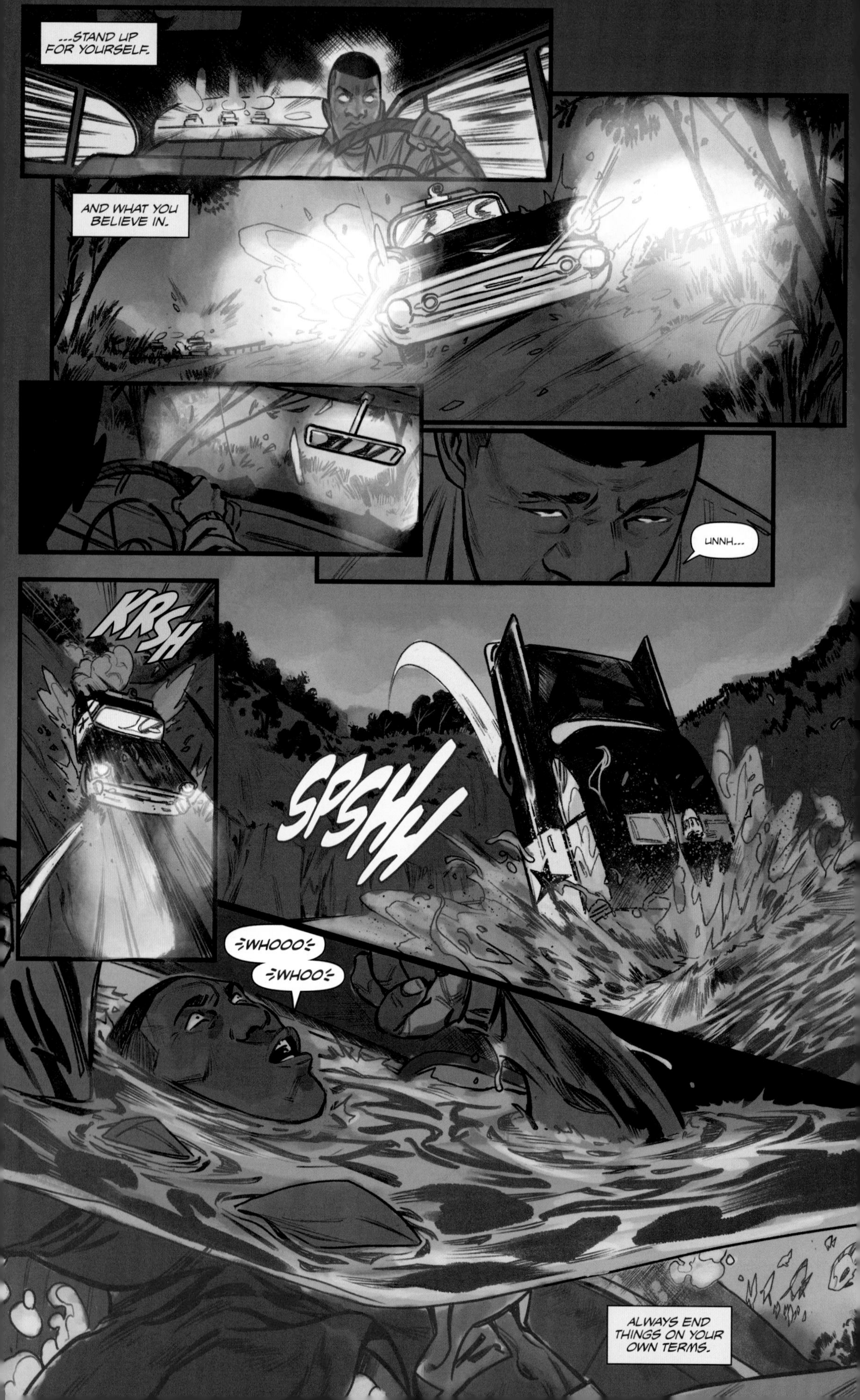
...STAND UP FOR YOURSELF.
AND WHAT YOU BELIEVE IN.
UNNH...
KRSH
SPSHH
WHOOO
WHOO
ALWAYS END THINGS ON YOUR OWN TERMS.

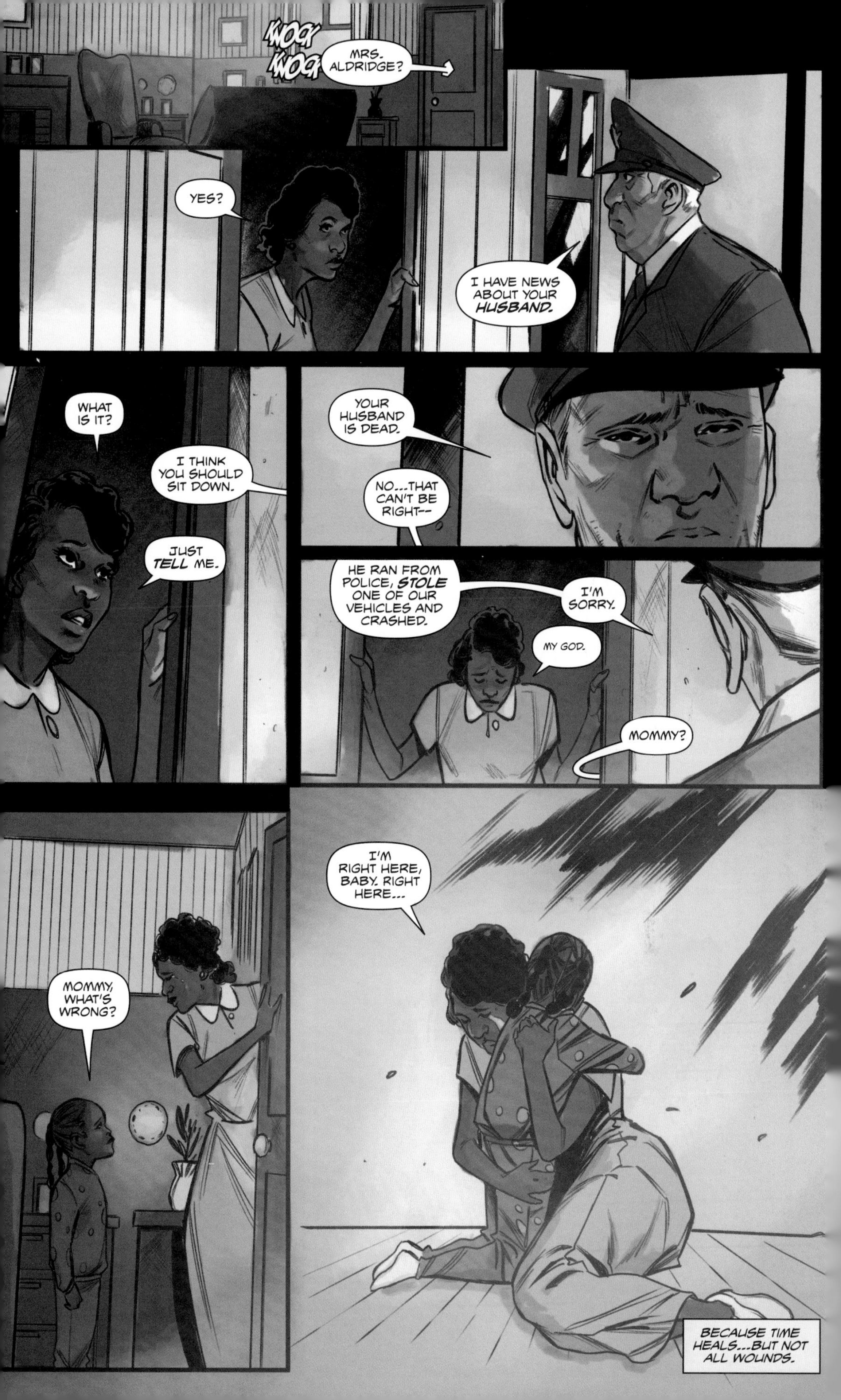
KNOCK KNOCK
MRS. ALDRIDGE?
YES?
I HAVE NEWS ABOUT YOUR HUSBAND.
WHAT IS IT?
I THINK YOU SHOULD SIT DOWN.
JUST TELL ME.
YOUR HUSBAND IS DEAD.
NO...THAT CAN'T BE RIGHT--
HE RAN FROM POLICE, STOLE ONE OF OUR VEHICLES AND CRASHED.
I'M SORRY.
MY GOD.
MOMMY?
MOMMY, WHAT'S WRONG?
I'M RIGHT HERE, BABY. RIGHT HERE...
BECAUSE TIME HEALS...BUT NOT ALL WOUNDS.

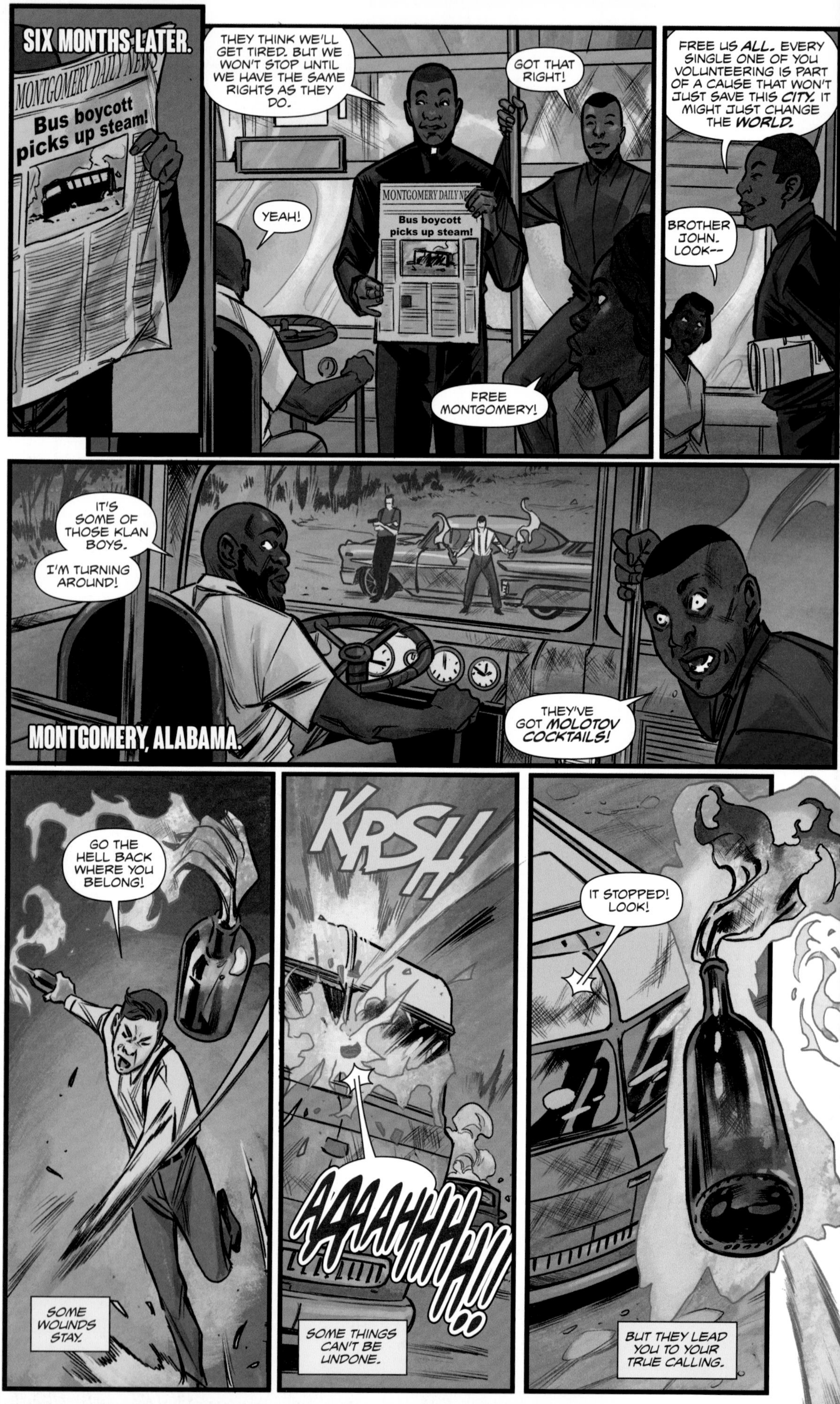

SIX MONTHS LATER.
MONTGOMERY DAILY NEWS
Bus boycott picks up steam!
THEY THINK WE'LL GET TIRED. BUT WE WON'T STOP UNTIL WE HAVE THE SAME RIGHTS AS THEY DO.
GOT THAT RIGHT!
YEAH!
MONTGOMERY DAILY NEWS
Bus boycott picks up steam!
FREE MONTGOMERY!
FREE US ALL. EVERY SINGLE ONE OF YOU VOLUNTEERING IS PART OF A CAUSE THAT WON'T JUST SAVE THIS CITY. IT MIGHT JUST CHANGE THE WORLD.
BROTHER JOHN. LOOK--
IT'S SOME OF THOSE KLAN BOYS.
I'M TURNING AROUND!
MONTGOMERY, ALABAMA.
THEY'VE GOT MOLOTOV COCKTAILS!
GO THE HELL BACK WHERE YOU BELONG!
SOME WOUNDS STAY.
KRSH
AAAAHHHH!!
SOME THINGS CAN'T BE UNDONE.
IT STOPPED! LOOK!
BUT THEY LEAD YOU TO YOUR TRUE CALLING.

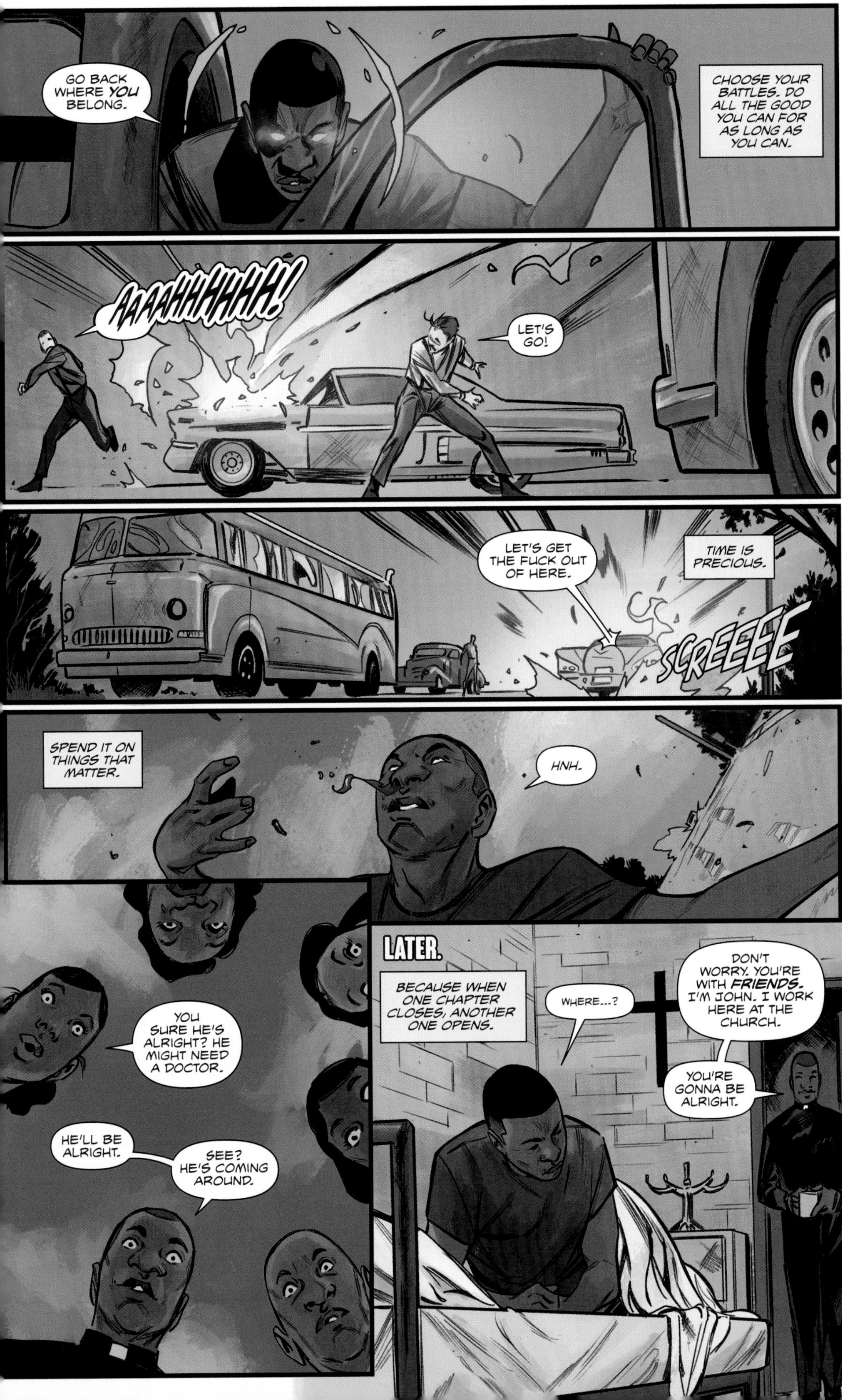
GO BACK WHERE YOU BELONG.
CHOOSE YOUR BATTLES. DO ALL THE GOOD YOU CAN FOR AS LONG AS YOU CAN.
AAAAHHHHHH!
LET'S GO!
LET'S GET THE FUCK OUT OF HERE.
TIME IS PRECIOUS.
SCREEEEE
SPEND IT ON THINGS THAT MATTER.
HNH.
YOU SURE HE'S ALRIGHT? HE MIGHT NEED A DOCTOR.
HE'LL BE ALRIGHT.
SEE? HE'S COMING AROUND.
LATER.
BECAUSE WHEN ONE CHAPTER CLOSES, ANOTHER ONE OPENS.
WHERE...?
DON'T WORRY. YOU'RE WITH FRIENDS. I'M JOHN. I WORK HERE AT THE CHURCH.
YOU'RE GONNA BE ALRIGHT.

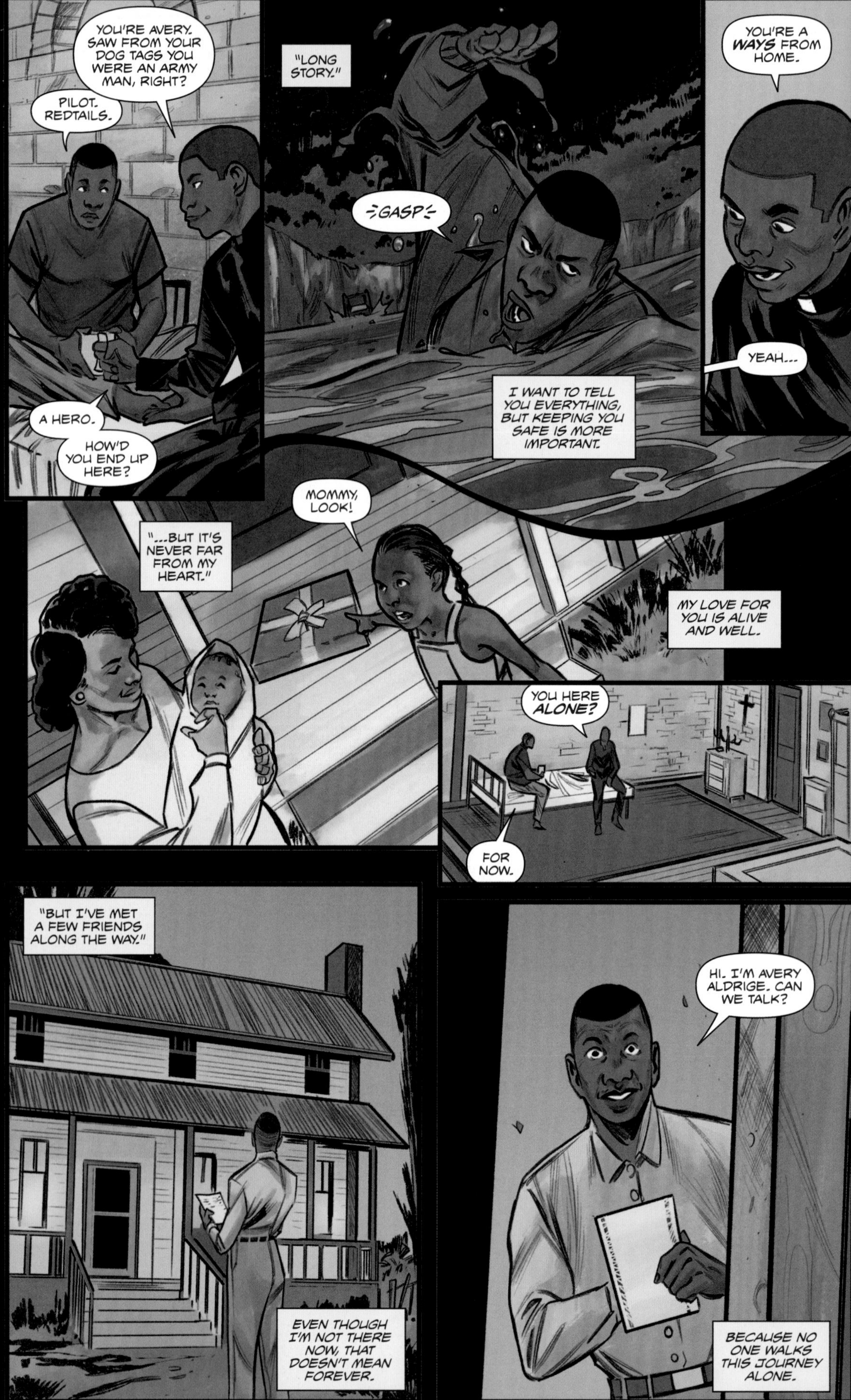
YOU'RE AVERY. SAW FROM YOUR DOG TAGS YOU WERE AN ARMY MAN, RIGHT?
PILOT. REDTAILS.
A HERO.
HOW'D YOU END UP HERE?
"LONG STORY."
=GASP=
I WANT TO TELL YOU EVERYTHING, BUT KEEPING YOU SAFE IS MORE IMPORTANT.
YOU'RE A *WAYS* FROM HOME.
YEAH...
"...BUT IT'S NEVER FAR FROM MY HEART."
MOMMY, LOOK!
MY LOVE FOR YOU IS ALIVE AND WELL.
YOU HERE *ALONE?*
FOR NOW.
"BUT I'VE MET A FEW FRIENDS ALONG THE WAY."
EVEN THOUGH I'M NOT THERE NOW, THAT DOESN'T MEAN FOREVER.
HI. I'M AVERY ALDRIGE. CAN WE TALK?
BECAUSE NO ONE WALKS THIS JOURNEY ALONE.

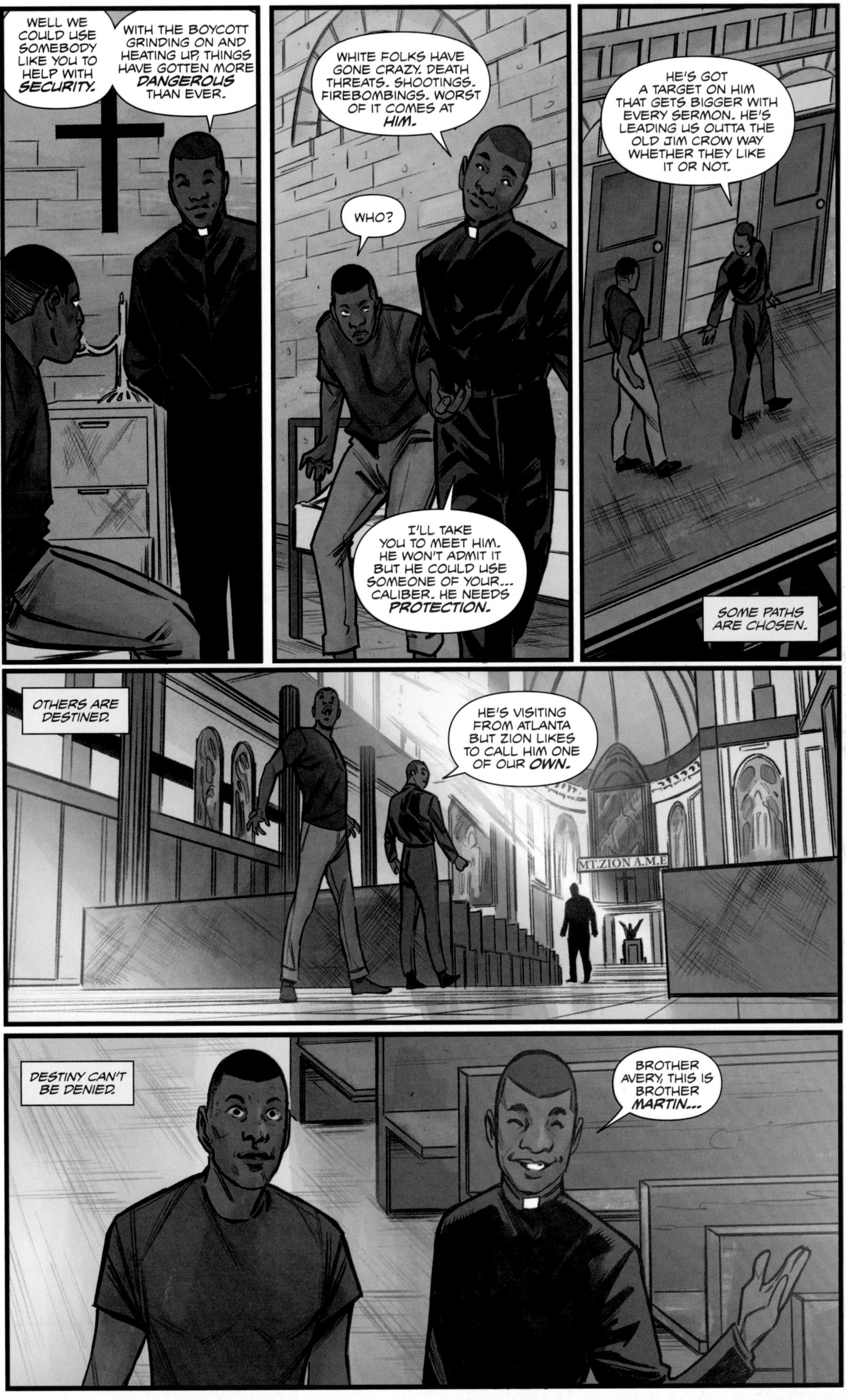
WELL WE COULD USE SOMEBODY LIKE YOU TO HELP WITH SECURITY.
WITH THE BOYCOTT GRINDING ON AND HEATING UP, THINGS HAVE GOTTEN MORE DANGEROUS THAN EVER.
WHITE FOLKS HAVE GONE CRAZY. DEATH THREATS. SHOOTINGS. FIREBOMBINGS. WORST OF IT COMES AT HIM.
WHO?
I'LL TAKE YOU TO MEET HIM. HE WON'T ADMIT IT BUT HE COULD USE SOMEONE OF YOUR... CALIBER. HE NEEDS PROTECTION.
HE'S GOT A TARGET ON HIM THAT GETS BIGGER WITH EVERY SERMON. HE'S LEADING US OUTTA THE OLD JIM CROW WAY WHETHER THEY LIKE IT OR NOT.
SOME PATHS ARE CHOSEN.
OTHERS ARE DESTINED.
HE'S VISITING FROM ATLANTA BUT ZION LIKES TO CALL HIM ONE OF OUR OWN.
MT.ZION A.M.E
DESTINY CAN'T BE DENIED.
BROTHER AVERY, THIS IS BROTHER MARTIN...

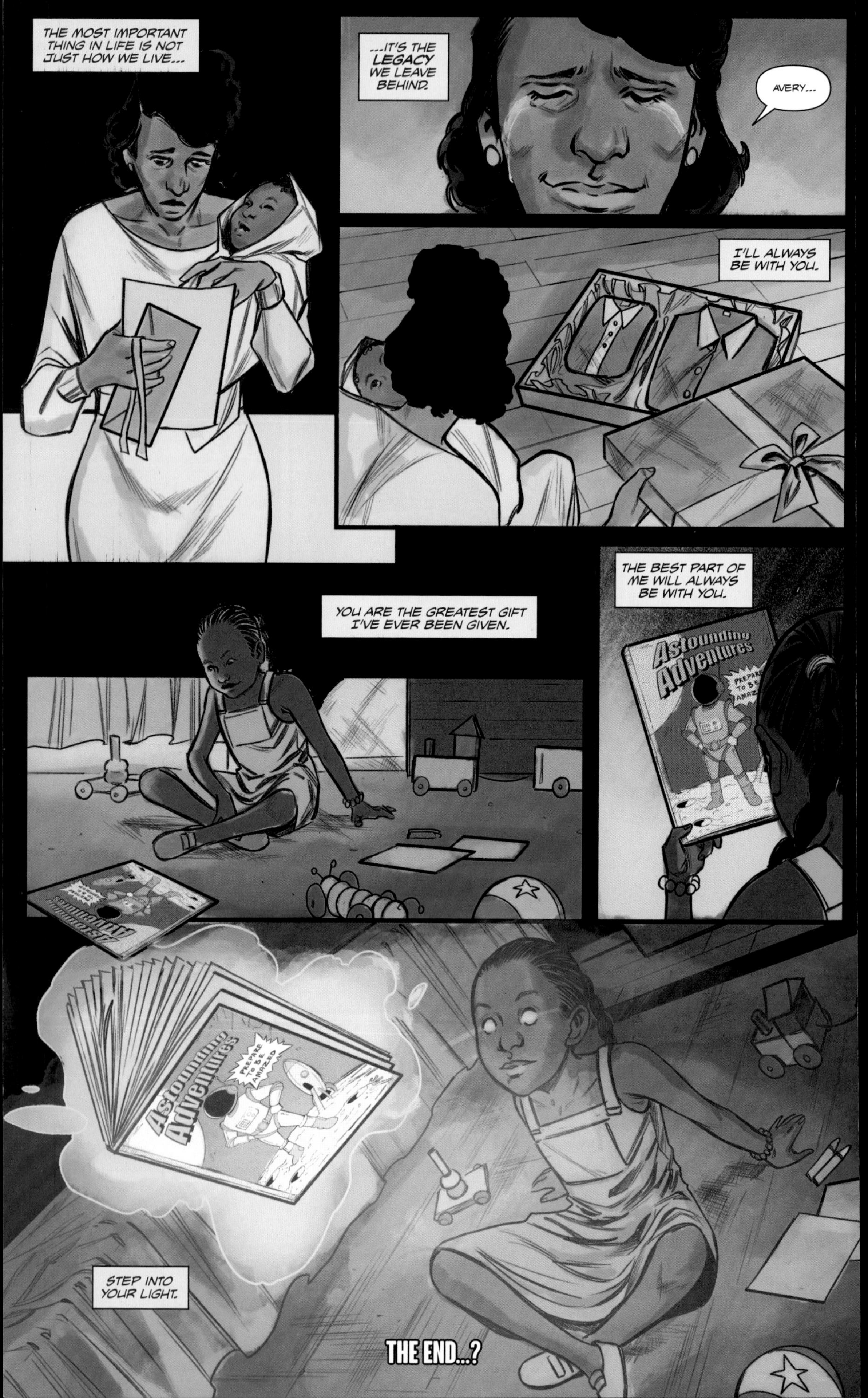
THE MOST IMPORTANT THING IN LIFE IS NOT JUST HOW WE LIVE...
...IT'S THE LEGACY WE LEAVE BEHIND.
AVERY...
I'LL ALWAYS BE WITH YOU.
YOU ARE THE GREATEST GIFT I'VE EVER BEEN GIVEN.
THE BEST PART OF ME WILL ALWAYS BE WITH YOU.
Astounding Adventures
PREPARE TO BE AMAZED
STEP INTO YOUR LIGHT.
THE END...?

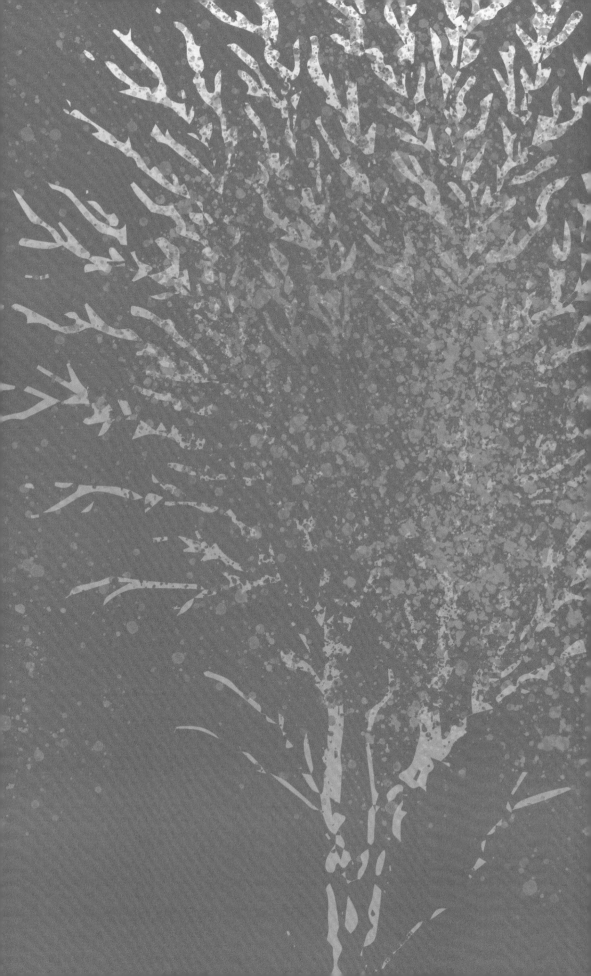

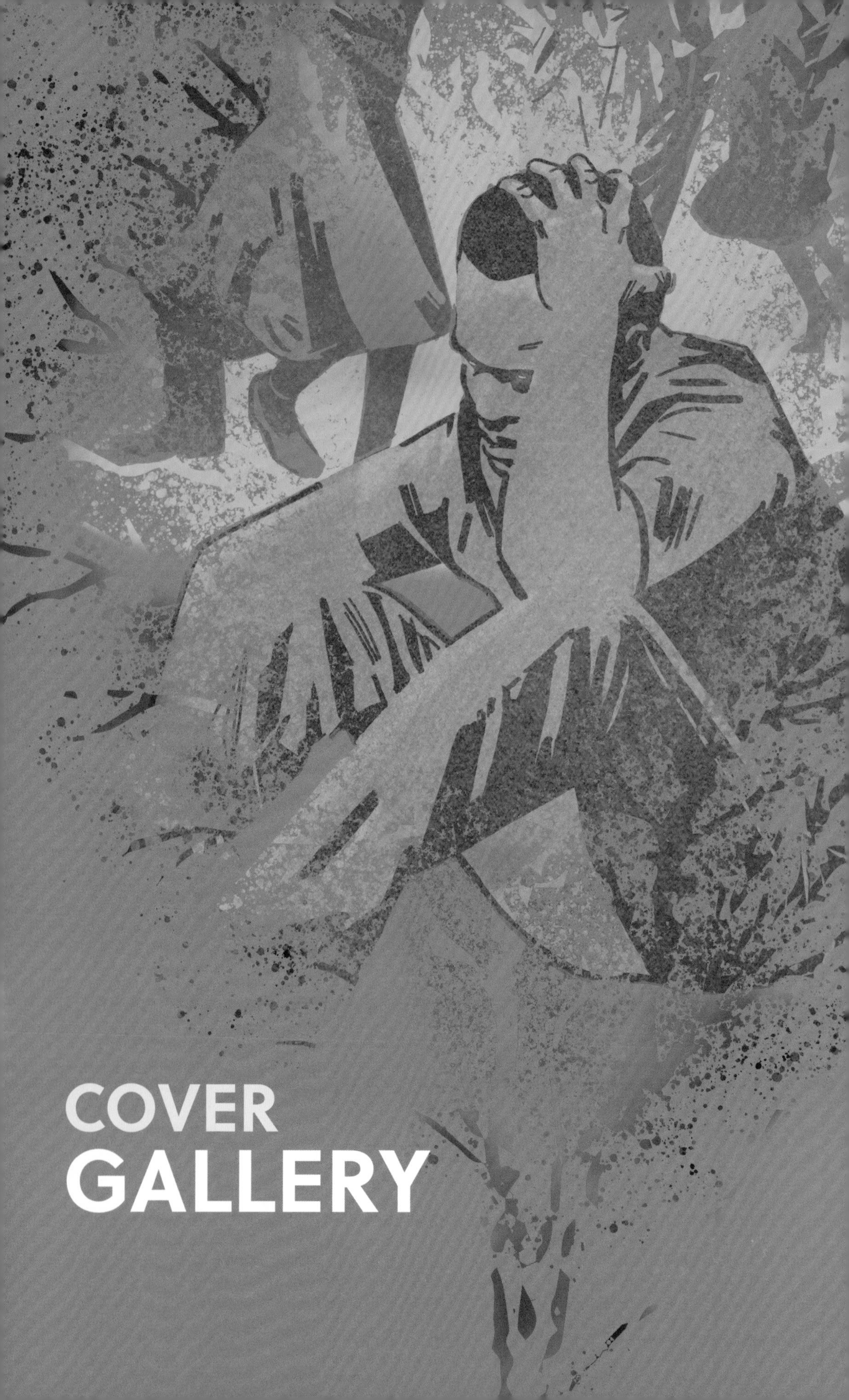

COVER GALLERY

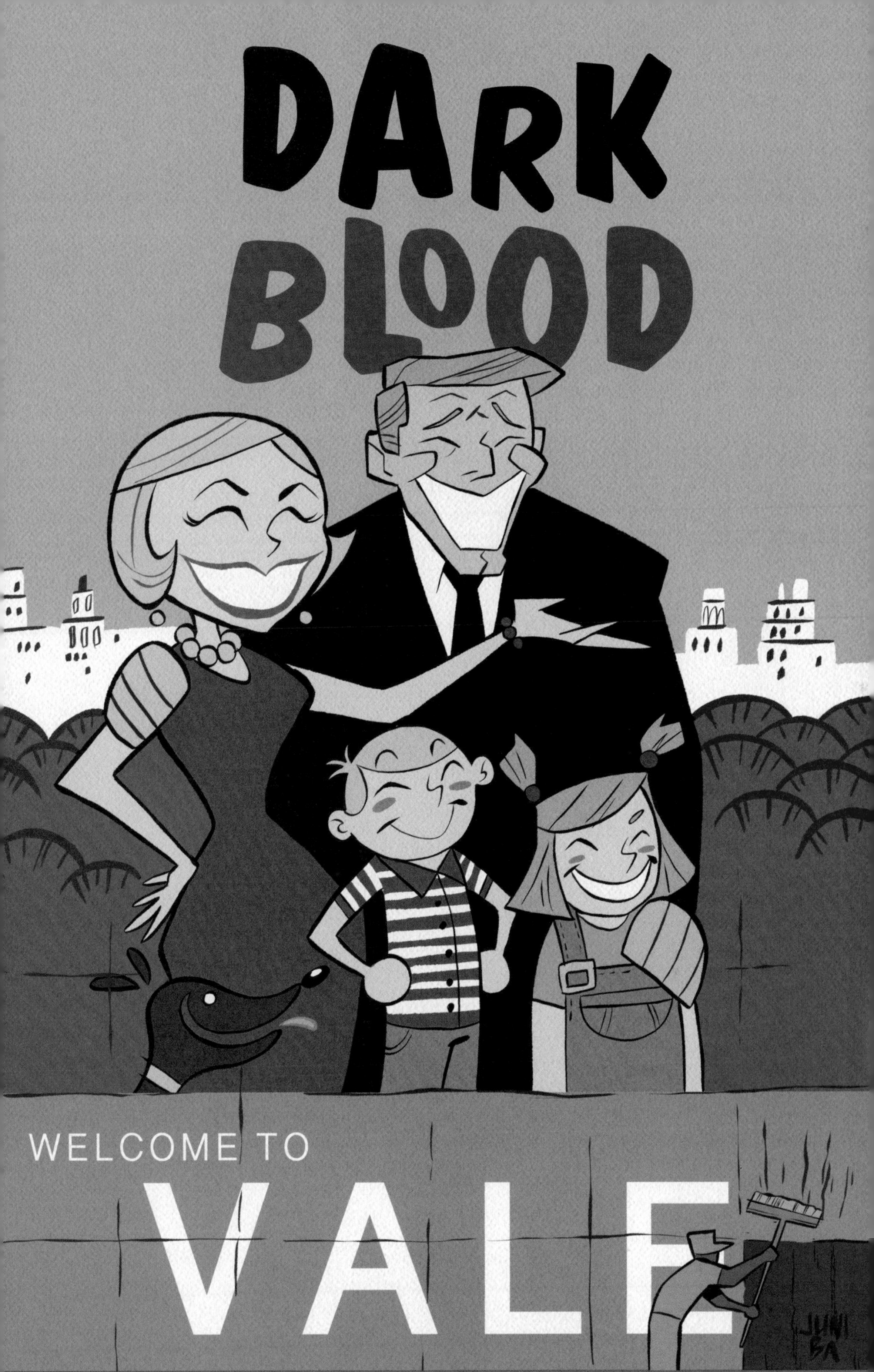
DARK
BLOOD
WELCOME TO
VALE
JUNI
BA

Issue #1 Variant Cover
JUNI BA

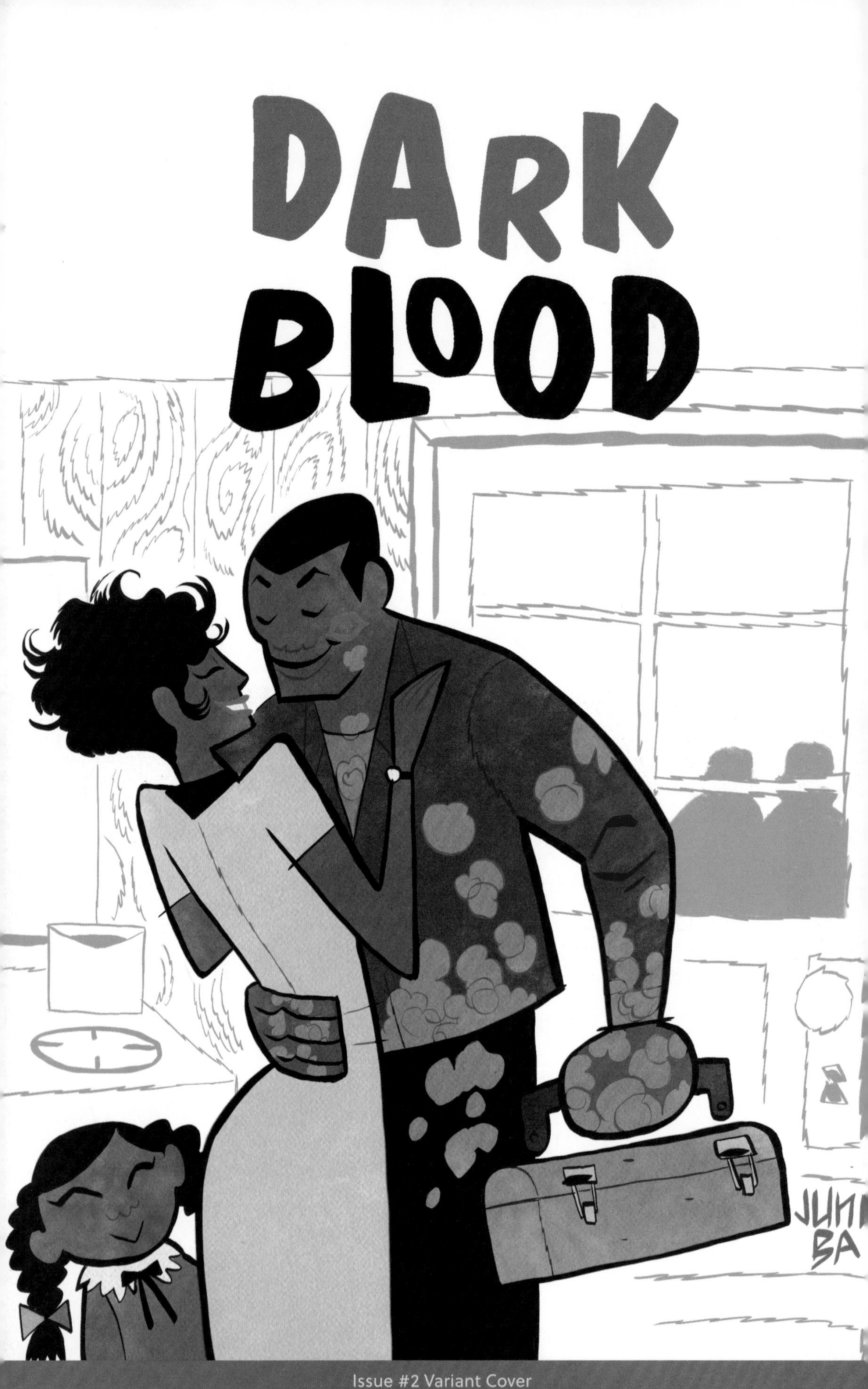
DARK
BLOOD
JUNI
BA

Issue #2 Variant Cover
JUNI BA

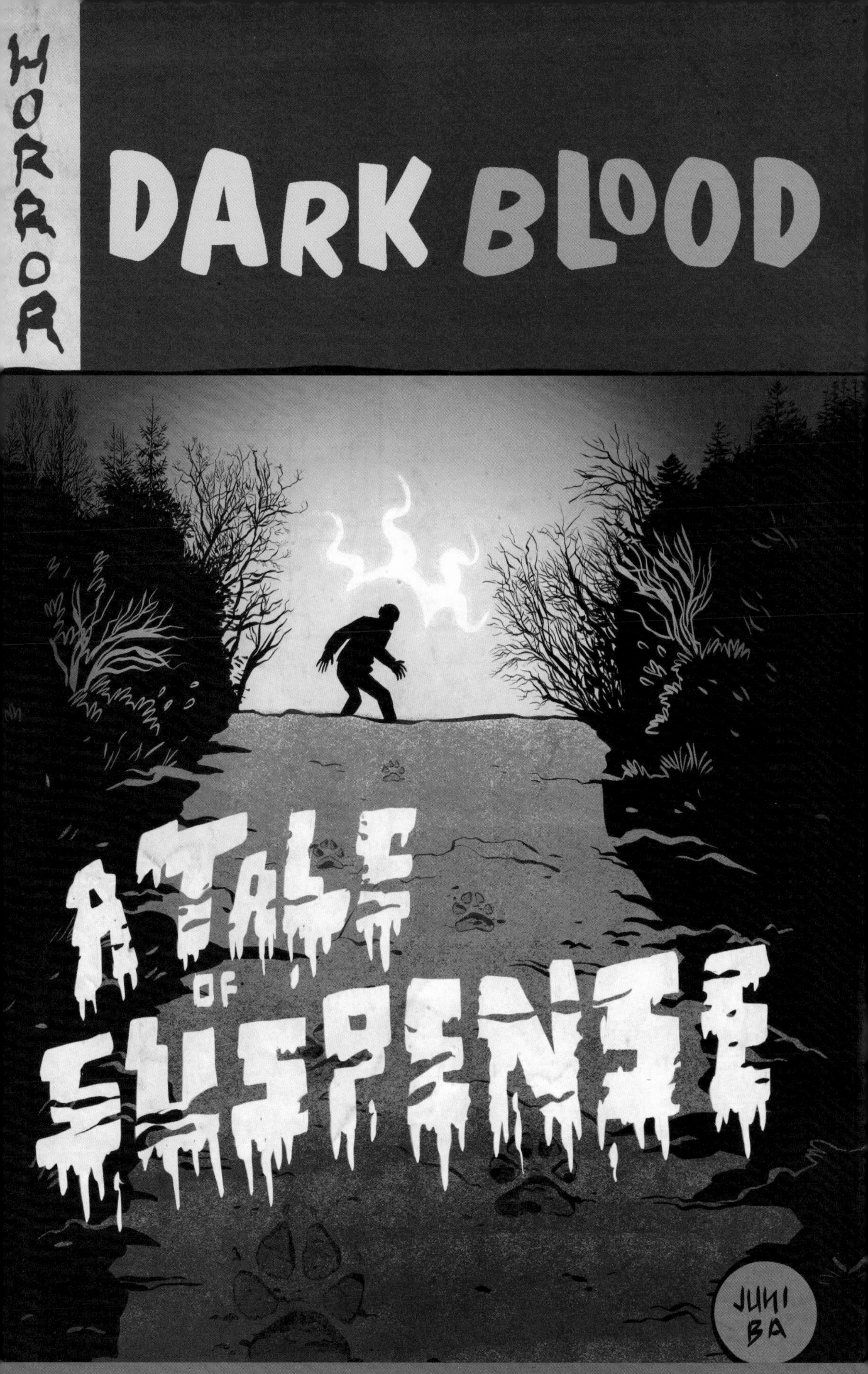
HORROR
DARK BLOOD
A TALE OF SUSPENSE
JUNI BA

Issue #3 Variant Cover
JUNI BA

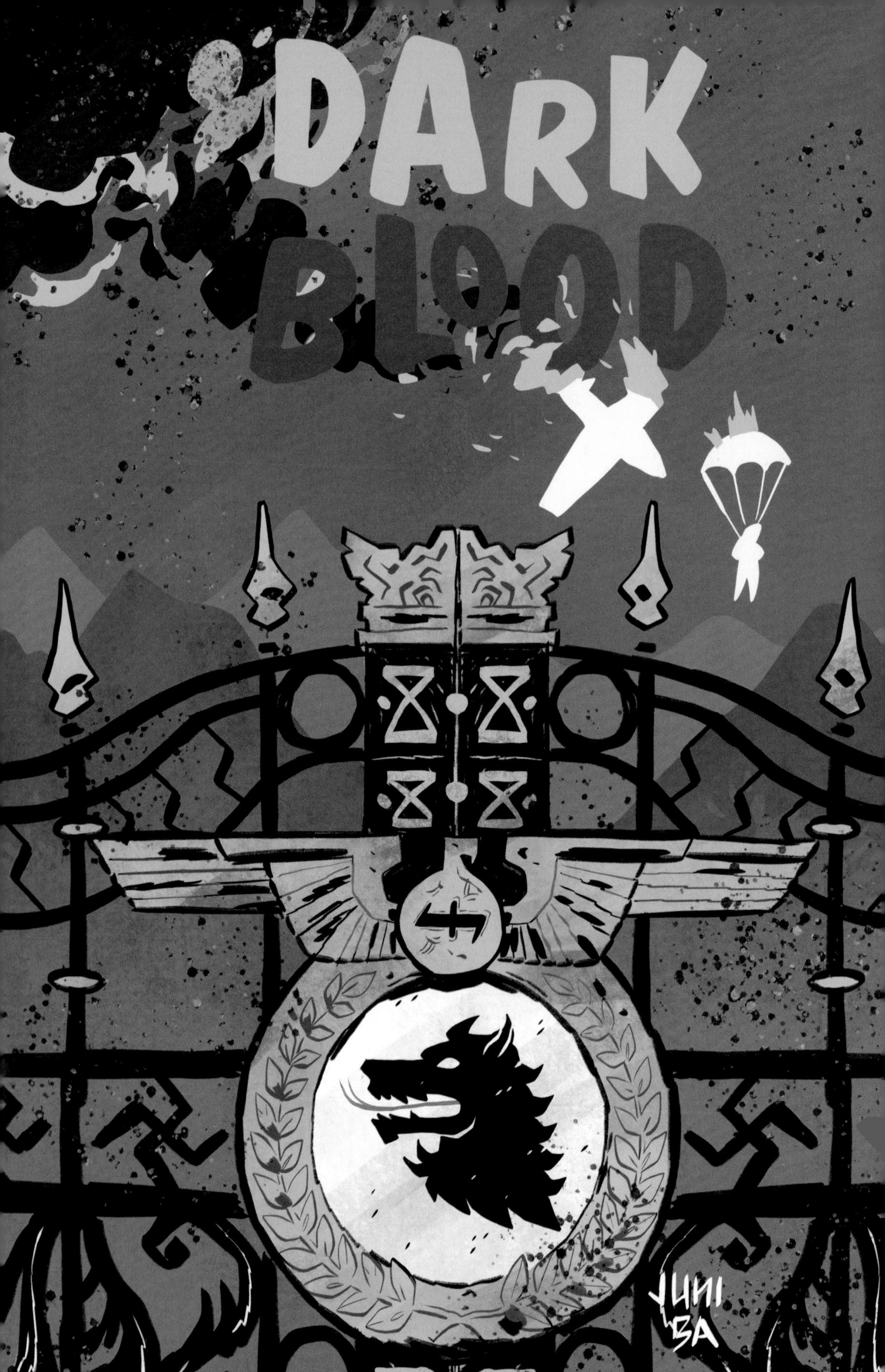
DARK
BLOOD
JUNI BA

Issue #4 Variant Cover
JUNI BA

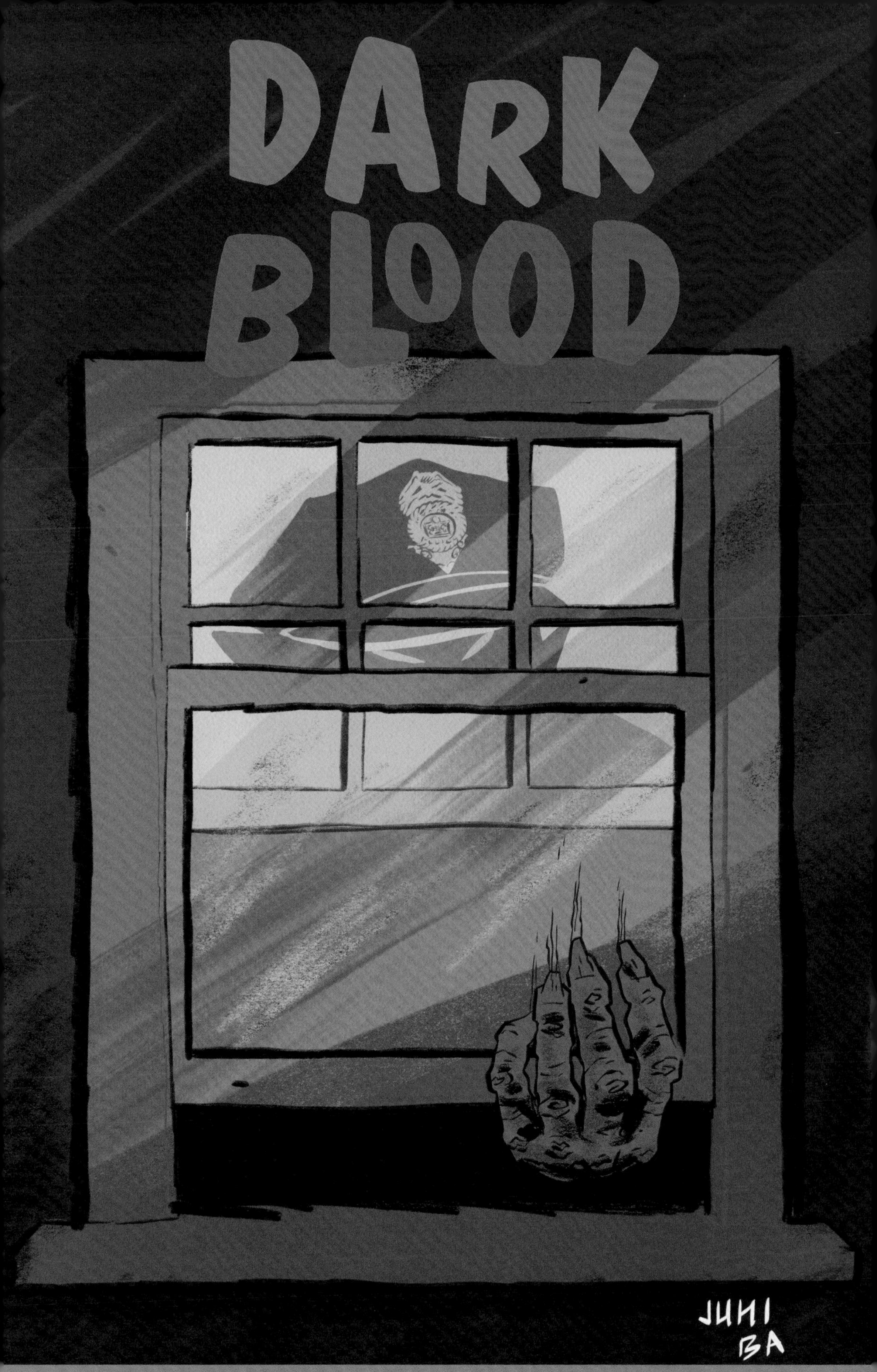
DARK
BLOOD
JUNI
BA

Issue #5 Variant Cover
JUNI BA

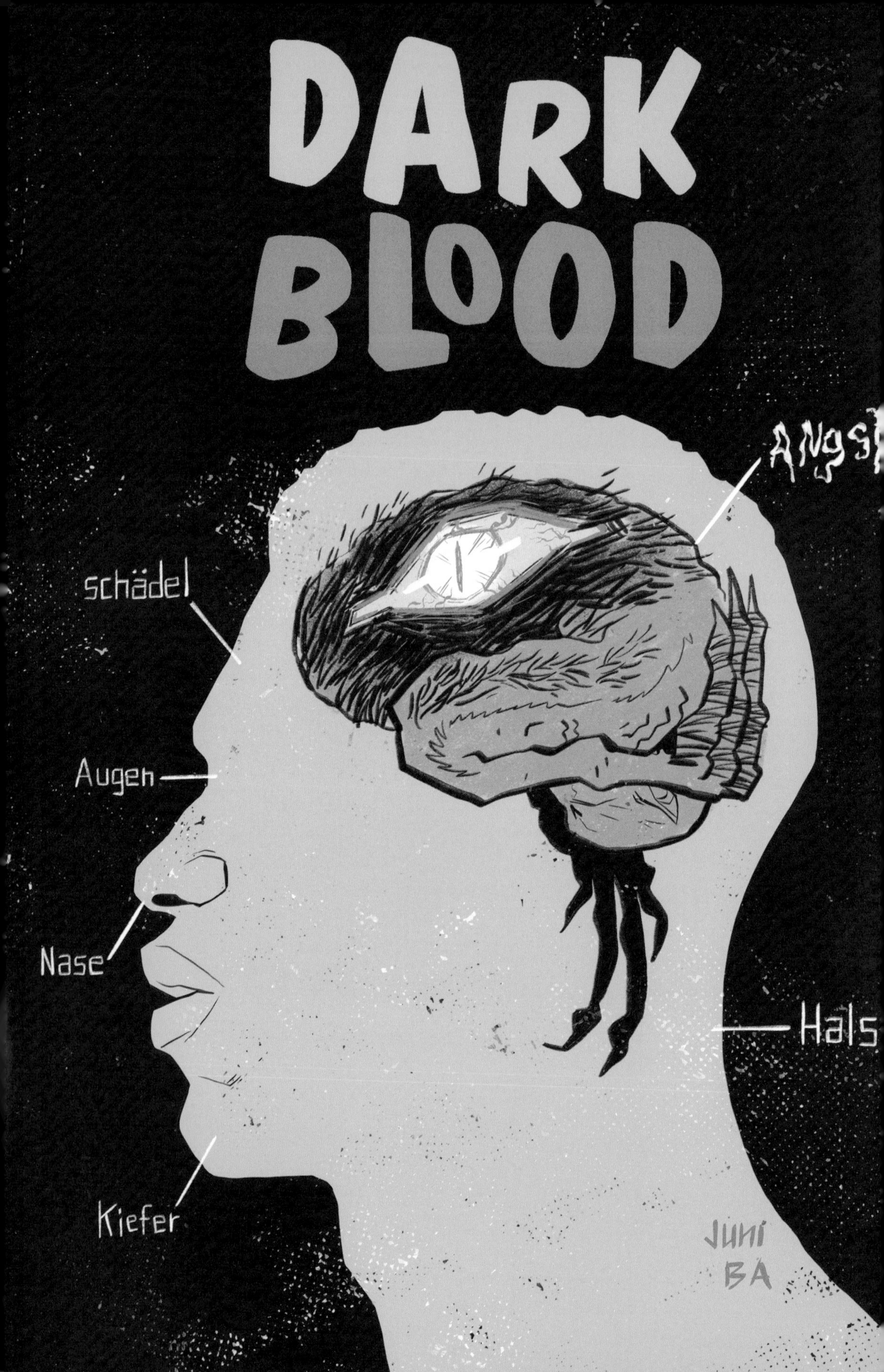

Issue #6 Variant Cover
JUNI BA

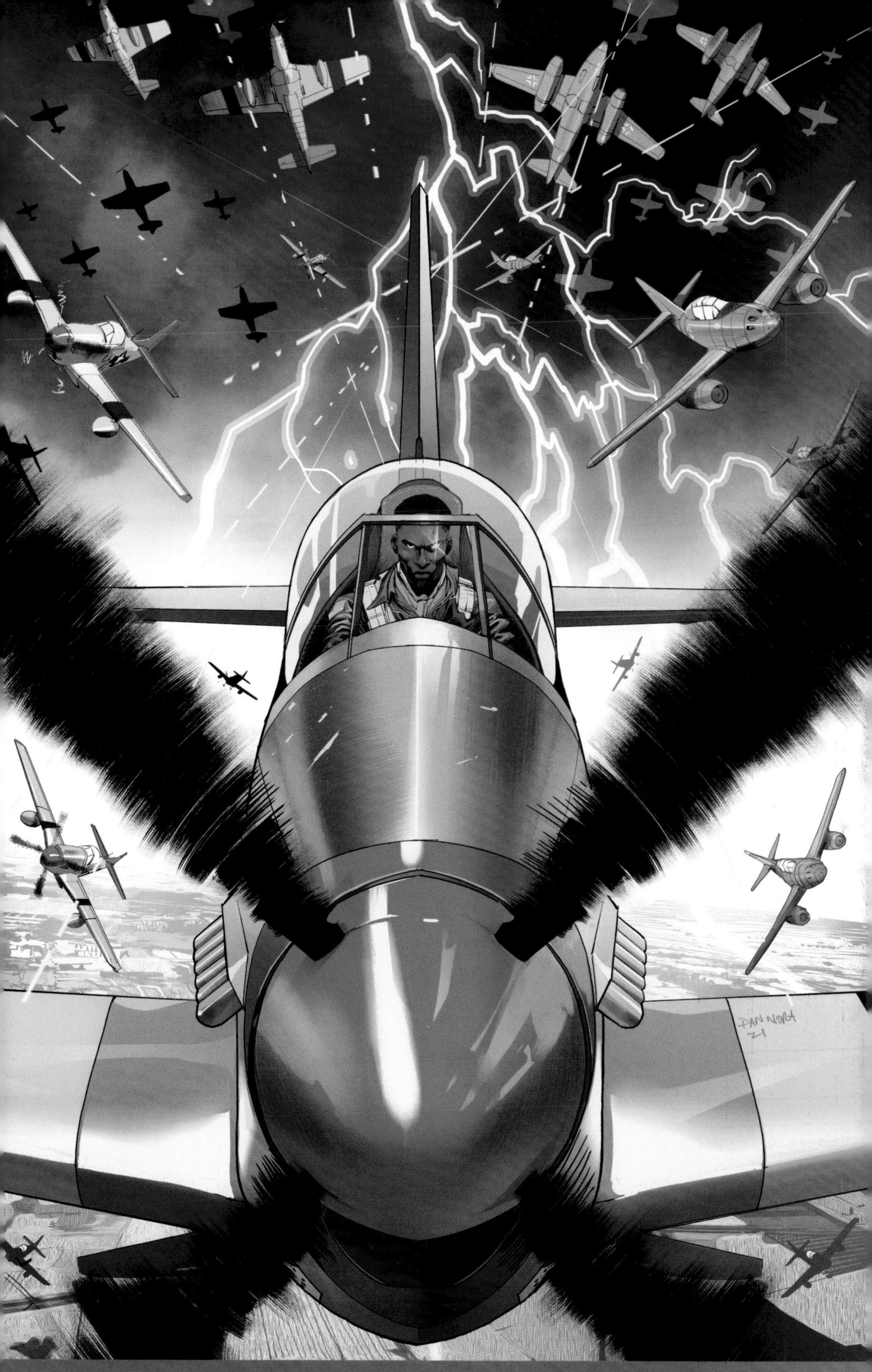
DAN MORA
21

Issue #1 Variant Cover
DAN MORA

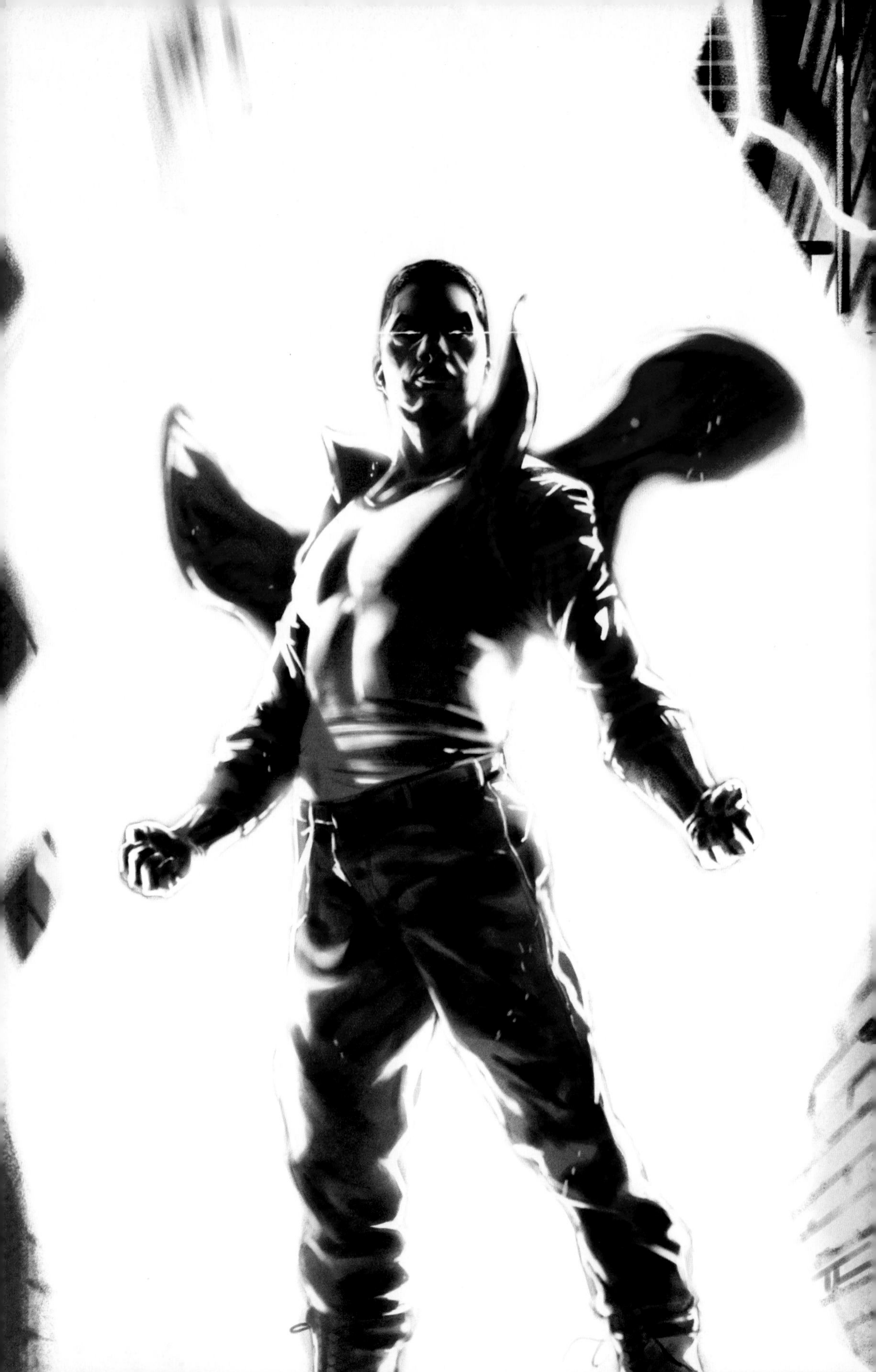

Issue #2 Variant Cover
TAURIN CLARKE

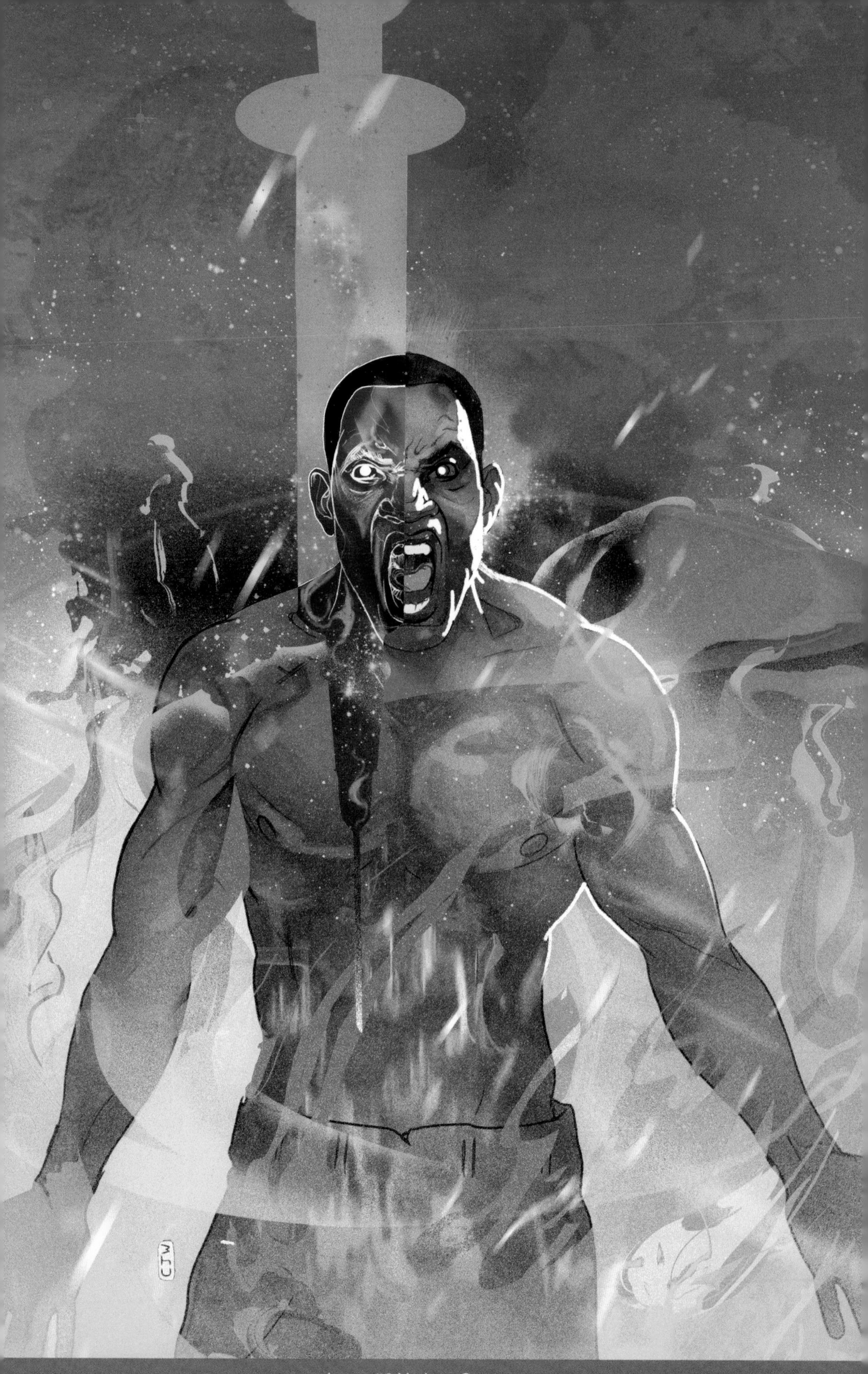
CTW

Issue #3 Variant Cover
CHRISTIAN WARD

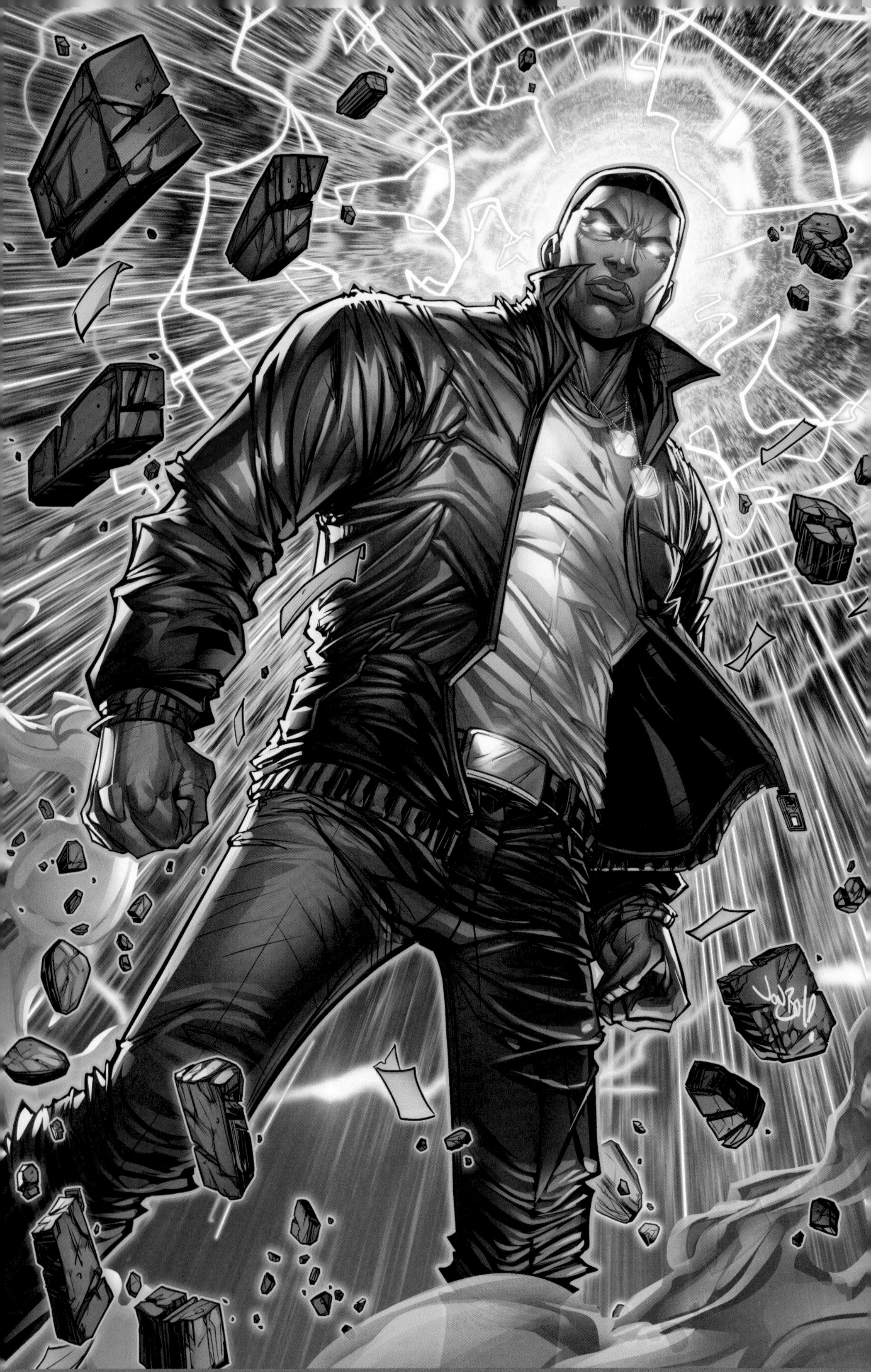

Issue #4 Variant Cover
JONBOY MEYERS

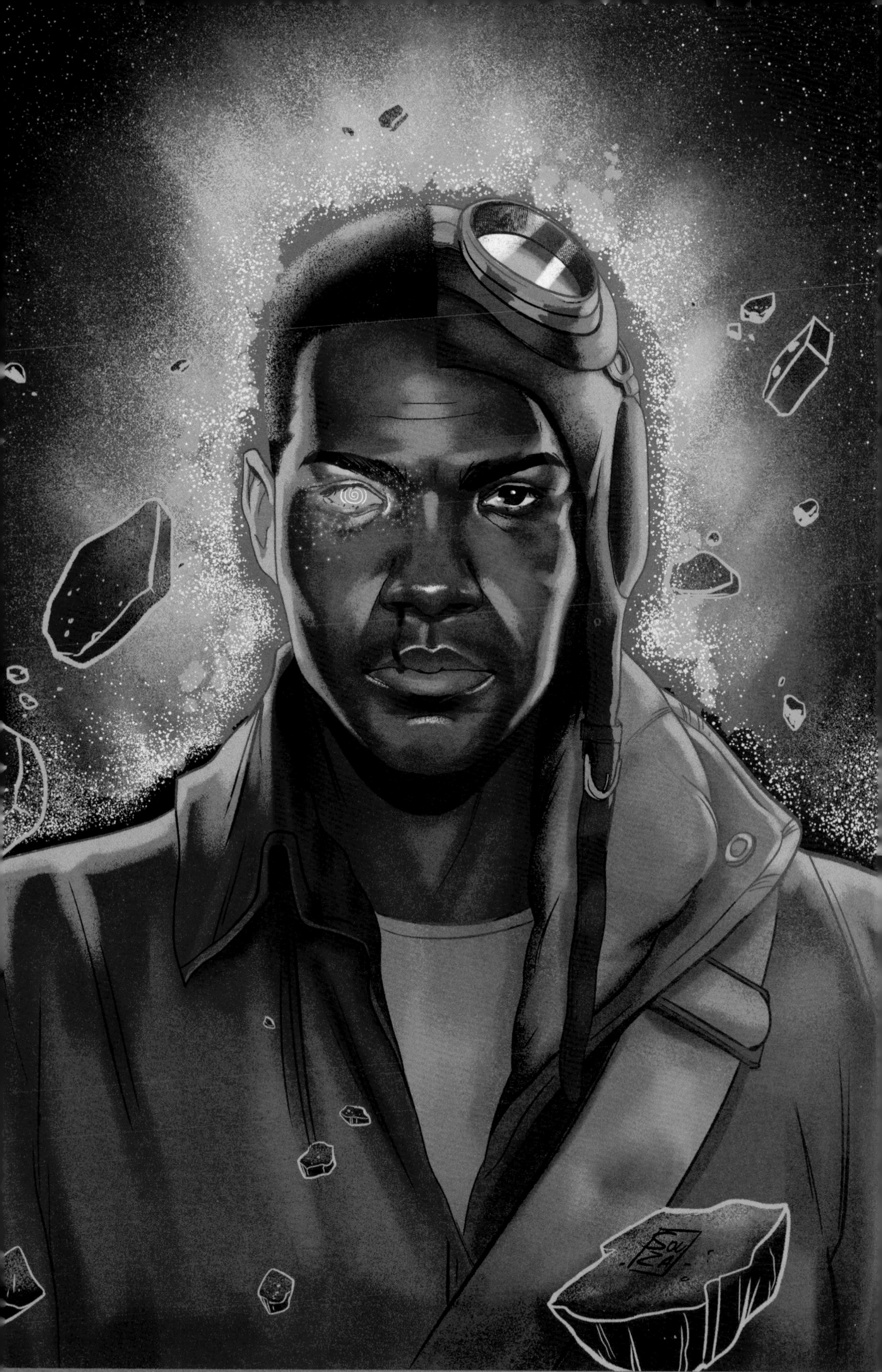

Issue #5 Variant Cover
ERNANDA SOUZA

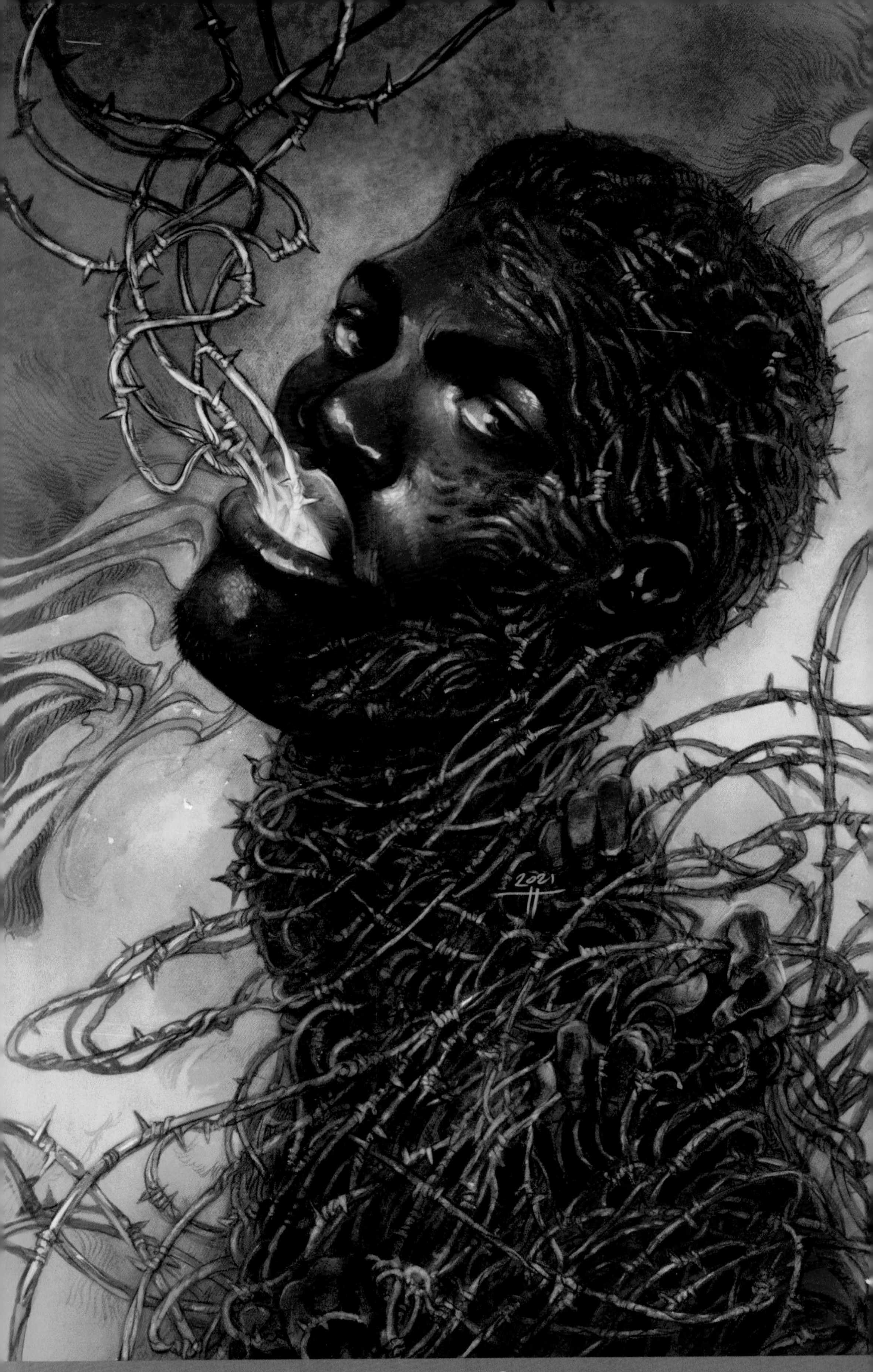
2021

Issue #6 Variant Cover
TIFFANY TURRILL